THE MYTHICAL ORIGIN OF THE EGYPTIAN TEMPLE

TO THE MEMORY
OF
MY FATHER

THE MYTHICAL ORIGIN OF THE EGYPTIAN TEMPLE

by

E.A.E.REYMOND

MANCHESTER UNIVERSITY PRESS
BARNES & NOBLE, INC., NEW YORK

MANCHESTER UNIVERSITY PRESS
316–324 Oxford Road, Manchester 13, England

U.S.A.

BARNES & NOBLE, INC.
105 Fifth Avenue, New York, N.Y. 10003

G.B. SBN 7190 0311 3

Printed in Great Britain
at the University Printing House, Cambridge
(Brooke Crutchley, University Printer)

Contents

PART V

The Doctrine of the Origin concerning the Temple

Illustrations

Preface

The greatest number of documents concerning the history of Egyptian temples that have come down to us and have been made available for further studies are, in the main, records commemorating various acts of foundation and all the good deeds which the Egyptian kings did on behalf of their gods and temples. Very little, however, is known about the essential nature and condition of the Egyptian temple. Although archaeological and textual sources abound, no coherent picture has ever been given of all the functions of the temple in the life of Ancient Egypt. What the temple as an entity meant to the Egyptians and how they came to regard their temples in the course of the history remains as a subject for future studies.

Scarcely any attention had been given to documents from Graeco-Roman times, in particular to the inscriptional treasures preserved on the walls of the temples in Upper Egypt. These documents are a rewarding source of study for they throw new light on the characteristics of the Egyptian temple and permit us to gain a fairly clear idea of what the temple was for the Egyptians, and what was its part in the history of the country. These texts, so far as we are aware, have never been translated or commented upon, and despite their outstanding interest and value for the position of the temple in the ancient world in general, they seem to have entirely escaped the notice of scholars. We think that it is necessary to remedy this neglect and to attempt to trace the way of approach to the contents of the documentary sources from Graeco-Roman times.

The history of the Egyptian temple, though not unknown in many respects, is still a fresh field, and each new step in this field throws new light on the part which the temple, as an entity, played in the life of Ancient Egypt. Our study is only a starting-point, a mere attempt to interpret Egyptian views on the beginnings of their temple. The background of this study was my Ph.D. thesis at the University of Liverpool submitted in September 1960. Between the thesis, conferment of the degree and the present book only a short period of time has elapsed. Nevertheless, the work was subject to many modifications and rearrangements, which, naturally, added to its extent. In preparing this work for publication I have retained the general form and organization into parts. I have made, of course, substantial changes in the exposition of facts, and supplemented them with more evidence which, of course, came to light after the thesis had been written. Many of the footnotes of the original version were expanded and subsequently incorporated in the main parts of the text. This necessitated some alteration in the order of chapters within the larger 'parts' of the book.

I cannot close these lines without expressing my gratitude for their patient endurance to all who, like martyrs, stood alongside the path of all the preliminary studies which led to this work, and finally to those who have assisted in the elaboration of this book. I wish to express my warmest thanks to my colleague, Dr J. Gwyn Griffiths, of University College, Swansea, for his kind assistance in the final preparations for publication. My deepest gratitude is to my parents, to my father in particular, whose endless patience and generosity permitted me to follow my academic pursuits wherever I chose. To my sorrow pitiless fate destroyed sincere wishes. This writing is only a humble tribute to him who departed from our midst.

I also owe much to Sir James Mountford, Vice-Chancellor of the University of Liverpool, and to the authorities of the University of Liverpool for all the facilities which they made available to me; to the Trustees of the Leverhulme Research Fund for their kindness in awarding me a grant which enabled me to pursue research in the history of Graeco-Roman Egypt, and also to write this book. Finally, I am grateful to the authorities of the University of Manchester for their help in arranging for the publication of this book, and to Manchester University Press for their care in publishing it.

E. A. E. Reymond

Liverpool
September 1960

Manchester
December 1961

Abbreviations

AEO	Gardiner, *Ancient Egyptian Onomastica.*
APAW	*Abhandlungen der Preussischen Akademie der Wissenschaften*, Berlin.
ASAE	*Annales du Service des Antiquités de l'Egypte*, Cairo.
AWLB	*Akademie der Wissenschaften und Literatur*, Berlin.
BIFAO	*Bulletin de l'Institut Français d'Archéologie Orientale*, Cairo.
BJRL	*Bulletin of John Rylands Library*, Manchester.
C.D.	E. Chassinat, *Le temple de Dendara.*
DAWW	*Deutsche Akademie der Wissenschaften, Denkschriften*, Vienna.
E.	E. Chassinat, *Le temple d'Edfou.*
JEA	*Journal of Egyptian Archaeology*, London.
KO	J. de Morgan, *Kom Ombo.*
M.	E. Chassinat, *Le mammisi d'Edfou.*
M.D.	Mariette, *Dendérah.*
MMAF	*Mémoires de la Mission Archéologique Française du Caire.*
Wb.	*Wörterbuch der Ägyptischen Sprache.*
ZÄS	*Zeitschrift der Ägyptischen Sprache.*

PART I

Sources

CHAPTER I

The Edfu Documents on the History of the Egyptian Temple

On the walls of Egyptian temples of the Graeco-Roman period are inscribed numerous ritual texts, among which occurs a series of texts that is found only in a very abbreviated form in certain of the Pharaonic temples. Those texts make it possible to reconstruct a reasonably complete history of the building of each temple concerned and a picture of the lay-out of its rooms and halls, and their ritual purpose and significance.[1] The latest temples all contain such texts,[2] but nowhere are they so numerous or so extensive as in the temple of Edfu, which for this reason must be regarded as our most important source.[3]

The Edfu documents include the great *Building Texts*, which are always found written in bold characters, very often in part in the characteristic decorative Ptolemaic script in broad bands on prominent architectural features, such as the exterior of the Naos, or the

[1] Little attention has been given to the history of the building and organization of the Egyptian temple. Dümichen's *Bauurkunden der Tempelanlagen von Dendera* (1865) and *Baugeschichte des Denderatempels* (1877), pp. 1–13, are the first attempts at such a work. They were followed by: Erman, *Die Religion der Ägypter*, pp. 361–77; Bonnet, *Reallexikon der ägyptischen Religionsgeschichte*, pp. 778–88; Badawi, *Les sanctuaires de Kom Ombo*; Lacau, 'Notes sur les plans des temples d'Edfou et de Kom Ombo', *ASAE*, LII, 215–28; Daumas, 'Les mammisis des temples égyptiens', *Annales de l'Université de Lyon*, XXXII; see also below, p. 4, n. 1 and pp. 316, 318, n. 1, and van de Walle, 'Le temple égyptien d'après Strabon', *Latomus*, XXVIII, 480 ff. For a very brief account of Egyptian temples, cf. Drioton–Vandier, *Égypte*, pp. 90–4, 118–24; Vandier, *Manuel d'archéologie égyptienne*, II, 555 ff.; Sauneron, *Quatre campagnes à Esna*, pp. 1–39.

[2] Cf. Brugsch, *Thesaurus Inscriptionum Aegyptiacarum*, VI (1891), 1318–1406: *Bautexte und Inschriften* are, so far, the only works codifying a good deal of records bearing on the foundation and building of temples.

[3] Except for the studies listed below, the Edfu documents have hitherto been scarcely utilized; reference can only be made to: Brugsch, 'Bau und Masse des Tempels von Edfu', *ZÄS*, VIII, 153–61; *ibid.* IX, 32–45, 137–44; *ibid.* X, 1–6; 'Eine neue Bauurkunde des Tempels von Edfu', *ZÄS*, XIII, 113–23; Chassinat, 'Le temple d'Horus Behouditi', *Rev. de l'Ég. anc.* I, 298–308; and H. W. Fairman, 'Worship and Festivals in an Egyptian Temple', *BJRL*, XXXVII, 165–203.

inner and outer faces of the Enclosure Wall.[1] These texts are primarily, though not exclusively, concerned with the history of the building of the Edfu Temple, and disclose a broad, generalized verbal picture of the temple, its rooms, and their dimensions.

In addition to these general descriptions, each room or hall in the temple has its own individual *Building Text*, also engraved in conspicuous bands or on such prominent features as door-jambs, its purpose being to give briefly the name, nature, ritual significance and sometimes even the contents of decoration of the particular room.

By conflating these greater and lesser *Building Texts*, it is possible to draw up an outline picture of the nature and significance of the temple as a whole, and, using this knowledge as a foundation, it is possible to embark on a deeper study of the life in the temple, and the significance and function of the historical temple.[2]

The series of texts mentioned is not solely concerned with an exposition of facts about the historical temple, but occasionally hints at the existence of certain mythological events.[3] The first hint of the existence of these *mythological circumstances* is to be found in the *Building Text* of the Naos,[4] where the foundation, building and bringing to life of the historical temple is described as happening in a mythical age. The historical temple is interpreted as the work of the gods themselves, and as an entity of a mythical nature. This short record seems to indicate a belief in a historical temple that was a direct continuation, projection, and reflexion of a mythical temple that came into existence at the beginning of the world.

The idea of a *mythological situation* that would seem to surround

[1] The great *Building Texts* of the temple at Edfu are to be found on the 'soubassement' (i) of the Naos, E. IV. 1,13–20,4; (ii) of the Forecourt, E. V. 1,10–10,16; (iii) of the inner face of the Enclosure Wall, E. VI. 5,5–18,15; (iv) of the outer face of the Enclosure Wall, E. VII. 1,9–27,15; (v) similar in content, but more concise, are the *Building Texts* of the main entrance of the temple and those of the Temenos doorway, cf. E. VIII. 152,12–17; 159,5–9; 160,7–11; 161, 6–12; 162,16–163,2; 164,9–12. The great *Building Texts* of the temple at Dendera trace a less precise and less rounded picture of the temple entity; cf. Dümichen, *Baugeschichte*, Pl. XII–XVI.

[2] Cf. H. W. Fairman, *BJRL*, XXXVII, 168–74, which gives an introduction to the significance of the historical temple and a summary account of the contents of the Edfu *Building Texts*.

[3] Cf. pp. 9–10.

[4] E. IV. 14, 4–10; for translation see below, pp. 308–9.

the existence of the historical temple can be supported by further evidence. I have found on many occasions that the Edfu Temple was described by names of mythical shrines and sacred places. The use of these names can hardly be incidental, since they substitute the name of the temple of Horus the Behdetite in such texts as the main *Building Texts*[1] or the *Morning Hymns* which were recited at the opening of the daily life of the temple.[2] This manner of describing the historical temple at Edfu was in my view based on even deeper reasons, and may eventually attest a belief in a relationship between the temple at Edfu and the sacred places of a mythical age.

Much decisive evidence of the same idea is disclosed by the *Building Text* of the inner face of the Enclosure Wall, where two mythological events in primaeval times are recorded in addition to the description of the actual temple. They appear to have a direct bearing on the origin of the temple of Horus the Behdetite. In the first record we read about the origin of a primaeval resting-place of the Falcon;[3] the other pictures the life in a primaeval domain of the Falcon.[4] This *Building Text* ends with a description of the events believed to have led to the foundation of the Solar Temple.[5] The importance of the mythical past in the life of the historical temple may be illustrated by a ritual episode represented in the third register of the north wall (west side) of the inner face of the Enclosure. This scene shows Thoth, who is described as

Thoth twice great, lord of Eshmunen, sweet of tongue, efficacious of speech, the august Ibis who writes (*hb*) for (?) those who are greater than him, who issues commands to him who came into being before him.[6]

He is depicted offering a sacred book to Horus the Behdetite while uttering the words:

I came unto thee, O, my father the Behdetite. I am thy child who issued from thee. I bring thee the charter (*snn*) for magnifying (*swr*)

[1] Cf. pp. 310–11.

[2] E. I. 14–18, and Blackman and Fairman, 'A Group of Texts inscribed on the Façade of the Sanctuary in the Temple of Horus at Edfu', *Miscellanea Gregoriana*, pp. 397 ff., and below, p. 294.

[3] E. VI. 14,13–15,11.

[4] E. VI. 17,4–11.

[5] E. VI. 17,12–18,11.

[6] E. VI. 180,15–181,1.

thy domain from the reign of Tanen until the present day. Thou art the Sanctified God who came into being at the First Occasion, in whose name the temples are inscribed.[1]

The same scene contains a spell which alludes to another mythological event, and seems to imply the belief that these were the words of Rēᶜ, who said: 'Behold me', and Rēᶜ proclaimed: 'Settle down beside me. And gladness is in the *pāy*-lands of Djeba. The name of our lord (*ndm*) is Horus, so said the crew.'[2]

The mention of the *snn*-book offered by Thoth to Horus the Behdetite brings to mind a sacred book the memory of which is preserved in the *Building Text* of the Enclosure of the Edfu Temple. Its title reads *bꜣw-Rᶜ n gs-prw, the Sacred Book of the Temples.*[3] It is certain that this book did not contain regulations of the temple ritual services or descriptions of the structural development of the Edfu Temple. The part of this document preserved at Edfu reveals that it included lists of names of mythical shrines and sacred places; each name listed is accompanied with a brief explanation of the mythological significance implicit in that particular name. We venture to suggest that this book might be a codification of the traditions and beliefs that surrounded sacred places of remote date. These records might have been copied and rewritten at a later date with special reference to the historical temples. This evidence would seem to witness to the idea of a continuity and relationship between the actual historical temple and far distant sacred places which the tradition regarded as being of a mythical nature.

With the aid of the clues and information provided by these inscriptions, it has been possible to isolate and identify a number of other texts which seem to be closely related to them. It has not hitherto been fully appreciated that there is at Edfu an extensive series of texts which give in considerable detail an account of the mythological origin of the temple, and throw valuable light on the way in which the Egyptians looked on the temple and its origin. It is largely an unknown and untranslated group of texts that forms the centre of this study. These texts can be found in various parts of the Edfu Temple. The most important of them are

[1] E. VI. 181,2–4. [2] E. VI. 181,1–2.

[3] E. VII. 22,6; cf. also the Satrape Stela, l. 3 = *Urk.* II, 14, 10; *bꜣw-Rᶜ n gs-prw* are mentioned together with other temple equipment.

a group of texts in the third (uppermost) register of the east and west wall of the inner face of the Enclosure Wall. These are, in fact, cosmogonical documents. They seem to be capable of being divided into five sections, each of which on the walls of the temple is associated with a ritual scene. The study of them permits us to say that there is a definite order in which these records were arranged and engraved on the wall, and which goes, alternately, from the west wall to the east wall of the temple.

It is highly probable that the first cosmogonical record[1] is on the west wall, and is connected with a scene of adoration of the *Sanctified God who came into being at the First Occasion*. This act of adoration was believed to have been performed in a primitive sacred place described as *Djeba in Wetjeset-Neter*, which is depicted on the wall of the temple together with all the divine beings who were believed to have dwelt there.[2]

The second record, again on the west wall, is associated with a scene of *Bringing an oblation to the Divine Beetle and to the gods who are in his train*.[3] In the left part of the scene we find the king presenting an offering to the protective deities; the right part is occupied by another scene of adoration of the *Sanctified God who came into being at the beginning*. He is described as the Great *sꜣ*-Falcon of the primaeval age, and is associated with Ptah.

The third record is on the east wall, and is added to a scene of *Elevating the choice pieces of meat*.[4] This scene of adoration resembles the scene linked with the second record.

The fourth record is connected with one of the episodes of the foundation ritual, the *Stretching of the Cord over the Temple*.[5] The accompanying relief and ritual text describes the *Foundation of the Great Seat of Harakhte* by the king, Thoth and Seshat. On the right of this scene is represented the procession of the Builder Gods, and seated figures of the Ogdoad.

The fifth record is incorporated in a scene of adoration the *Great Seat* and bears the title *Adorning the Festival Hall*.[6] We find in

[1] E. VI. 181,6–186,10 = XIV. Pl. DLX–DLXI.

[2] This relief is studied in all details in my article on the 'Primaeval djeba', see *JEA*, XLVIII, 81–8.

[3] E. VI. 175,13–179,4 = XIII. Pl. DXLVI–DLI.

[4] E. VI. 327,14–332,9; no photographs published.

[5] E. VI. 168,10–175,11 = XIII. Pl. DXXXIX–DXLV.

[6] E. VI. 318,15–327,3 = XIV. Pl. DCIII–DCVI.

the centre of the scene the figures of Horus the Behdetite, Hathor and Ptah seated in a kiosk and presented with the symbol *ḥts* by the king. Beyond them an assembly of gods is represented; in front of them, following the king, there is depicted a procession of thirty gods.

Two extracts from the same records are engraved on the front part of the Pronaos.[1] Nevertheless, taken together, these records appear to form a connected set of mythological narratives of which extracts and adapted versions are to be found in other parts of the Edfu Temple and are incorporated in the ritual texts to be recited at the worship of the Ancestor Gods of the Edfu Temple[2] and in the scenes of *Offering the Lotus*.[3] In addition each of the main *Building Texts* contains, apart from the lists of *mythological names*, concise or modified versions of the cosmogonical narratives preserved in the scenes described above.[4]

It seems inherently probable that this rich repertory of various documents primarily formed parts of a single book that was called *šsr ἰ꜡wt n p꜡wt tpt, Specification of the Mounds of the Early Primaeval Age*.[5] Although this book is mentioned only in the Edfu inscrip-

[1] E. III. 7,2–13 = VI. 182,11–183,5; E. III. 31,11–15 = VI. 181,14–15; 182,2–5.

[2] These scenes are to be found mainly on the outer walls of the temple; they refer to the worship of: (i) the *Shebtiw*: E. IV. 357,15–359,8; (ii) the *Ogdoad*: I. 288,15–289,11; III. 312,2–9; IV. 139,11–141,11; V. 84,12–86,14; (iii) the *Sages*: I. 295,8–296,4; III. 314,13–315,5; IV. 389,10–391,2; (iv) the *Builder Gods*: III. 317,9–17; IV. 352,2–353,15; (v) the *Seven Souls of Rēꜥ*: III. 303,17–304,5; IV. 383,15–385,4; (vi) the *14 Kas*: III. 320,6–13; IV. 295,6–297,6; V. 180,11–182,17; (vii) the *Little Ennead*: IV. 296,11–15; 265,9–267,5; (viii) the *Great Ennead*: IV. 109,9–111,2; V. 166,16–167,10; (ix) the *God of the Temple*: IV. 103, 8–13; IV. 259, 3–9. See also my study of the 'Worship of the Ancestor Gods at Edfu', *CdE*, LXXV, 49–70.

[3] These scenes are also engraved mainly on the outer parts of the temple: (i) *Pronaos*: E. III. 185,13–186,6; IV. 139,11–141,11; 392,12–393,3; (ii) *Forecourt*: V. 50,17–51,13; 84,12–86,13; 149,15–150,10; 220,13–221,6; 245,7–17; (iii) *Enclosure Wall*: VI. 247,10–248,9; 338,13–340,4; VII. 78,6–79,4; 162,6–163,2; 321,5–16.

[4] *Building Text of the Naos*: E. IV. 1,13–2,2; 10,7–11; 14,5–9; 19,14–15; 328,4–9; 330,1–7; *Building Text of the Forecourt*: V. 7,7–9,6; 9,10–10,14; *Building Text of the inner face of the Enclosure Wall*: VI. 11,1–9; 12,11–13,6; *Building Text of the outer face of the Enclosure Wall*: VII. 21,2–22,5; 22,6–23,10.

[5] Cf. E. VI. 181,11; 326,1–2; *šsr* is used as a noun, cf. *Wb.* IV, 548 (10). The content of our documents seems to require the meaning 'specification' which can be confirmed by the occurrence of the word *šsr* in the headings of detailed descriptions of the temple; cf. E. IV. 56,12; 353,14; VI. 326,5; VII. 11,9; 12,1; 18,3; M.D. I, 72*a*; II, 17*c*, 51*a*; III, 15*b*, 29*a*.

tions, there are good reasons for supposing that this book was of general application, and not a special work with restricted reference to the Edfu Temple. It can be taken as certain that this book was different from the normal type of the temple service books, for its name does not occur in the list of the 'books' kept in the library of the temple at Edfu.[1] It was most probably of another origin than these sacred scripts and did not belong to the group of temple service books described as the *Sacred Books of Atum*.[2] At Edfu the set of the cosmogonical records is described as being of divine origin. The introduction to the first Edfu cosmogonical record discloses the tradition that the contents of these records were the *words of the Sages*. We are told that this sacred book was believed to be a *Copy of writings which Thoth made according to the words of the Sages of Mehweret*.[3] The use of the word *ỉ3t*, *mound*, in the plural suggests that this book included, *inter alia*, lists of cultus-places which were believed to have been founded before historical times. It can tentatively be suggested that in this context the expression *ỉ3wt n p3wt tpt*, the *Sacred Mounds of the Early Primaeval Age*, might have been used as a general name of the prehistoric cultus-places of Egypt.[4]

It has been noticed on a close examination that the Edfu version of the sacred book combines in a continuous narrative two myths that may originally have been separate. The summarized versions of these mythological narratives incorporated in the *Building Texts* of the inner face of the Enclosure Wall[5] make it evident and show as titles of the myths the *Sacred Book* (*b3w-Rᶜ*)[6] *of the Early Primaeval*

[1] E. III. 347,11–348,1; 351,7–371,10. [2] E. III. 339,9.

[3] E. VI. 181,10–11; for Thoth as author of divine words cf. Boylan, *Thoth, the Hermes of Egypt*, pp. 92–7.

[4] It is unlikely that this expression can be read *ỉ3wt n p3wtyw tpyw*. *p3wtyw tpyw* is, in the late period, a subsidiary name of the Ogdoad, cf. Sethe, 'Amun und die Acht Urgoetter von Hermopolis', *APAW*, (1929), 46–7. On the evidence of the Edfu texts it is certain that this book was not written with special reference to the original places of worship of the Ogdoad.

The word *ỉ3t* is a common formative of topographic names, cf. Gauthier, *DG*, I, 21ff.; in historic times it is clearly the equivalent of the late Arabic *Kom* or *Tell*, cf. Gardiner, *P. Wilbour*, *Texts*, II, 33–4, and my *Djed-ḥer-le-Sauveur*, p. 88. In the terminology of the mythological records the word *ỉ3t* seems to have a specific significance which will be discussed below, p. 300ff.

[5] E. VI. 14,13.

[6] For the use of the expression *b3w-Rᶜ* as a name of ancient records and sacred

Age of Gods and the *Coming of Rēᶜ to his Mansion of Ms-nḫt*. These two titles are unknown to the main sources. It may be suggested, therefore, that the main Edfu records listed above are to be divided into two groups: nos. 1 and 2 and the end of no. 5 seem to preserve a substantial portion of the myth which may primarily have been included in the *Sacred Book of the Early Primaeval Age of Gods*, which was concerned with the origin of the sacred domains and temples of the Falcon. Nos. 3 and 4 and the greater part of no. 5 appear to yield most probably a portion of the second myth described as the *Coming of Rēᶜ to his Mansion of Ms-nḫt*, in which the origin of the Solar Temples seems to have been explained. There is no argument that these titles were of a later date or were even the Edfu tradition. Their significance, however, seems to indicate that we have here two originally independent myths which might have been included in the sacred book of the *Specification of the Sacred Mounds* at a later date.

The analysis of the surviving part of the sacred book shows that it was primarily concerned with the interpretation of the origin of sacred places of the Falcon and those of the Sun-God, to which was added an account and explanation of various mythical events believed to have led to or preceded the foundation of the sacred domains of these two gods. This book seems also to include the interpretation of the origin of the Temple of the Falcon and that of the Sun-God. It also contains descriptions of the lay-out of some primitive temples which might eventually have evolved in the places in which these two gods were first worshipped. These descriptions and interpretations are detailed so that it is possible to trace the development of these temples and to reconstruct their physical appearance.

All the cosmogonical records which are known from the Edfu tradition can hardly preserve the entire original version of the myths, and the Edfu texts may be regarded as mere summaries or epitomes of the more important parts of the complete myths. It is probable that we have preserved only a restricted number of

books of the temples, cf. Gardiner, 'Horus the Behdetite', *JEA*, xxx, 23–60, and Blackman and Fairman, 'The Myth of Horus at Edfu', *JEA*, xxix, 22–3, n. (7), giving a list of quotations in the Edfu inscriptions; my *Djed-ḥer-le-Sauveur*, p. 133, n. (7).

extracts which from the Egyptian point of view were considered as vital. We incline to the opinion that this set of the Edfu documents enables us to embark on a fresh field of study which may reasonably be described as the *mythological history* of the Egyptian sacred places and their temples.

Translations of and commentaries on the main sources of our study are not incorporated in the present work, since a proper philological study of these texts would require a volume of great proportions and of high cost. In view of the importance of these texts, however, it has been thought useful for the present to make available a detailed summary of the chief Edfu cosmogonical documents concerned.

CHAPTER 2

Myth about the Origin of the Domains and the Temple of the Falcon

This myth is the contents of the first and second cosmogonical record and of a part of the fifth record[1] which seem to have been originally included in the *Sacred Book of the Early Primaeval Age of Gods.*[2]

The Edfu myth is the unique source that discloses the Egyptian tradition concerning the origin of the sacred domains of the Falcon and the creation of his first temple. It is doubtful whether the beginning of the first Edfu record preserves the commencement of the original version of this myth. It appears that a certain number of interpretations of various mythological events, which might precede the first events recorded in the Edfu texts, were omitted. The part of this myth that survives in the Edfu inscriptions, however, seems to allude to a continued and consecutive set of mythical events, which were presented only in a somewhat abbreviated form. Each record seems to consist of a series of sections, each of which illustrates a definite period in the development of the primaeval domains of the Falcon, and which we attempt to follow in our exposition of facts.

FIRST RECORD

First section: E. VI. 181,11–16

THE PRIMAEVAL ISLAND OF TRAMPLING

The first record, which is added to a scene of the worship of the *Sanctified God who came into being at the First Occasion,*[3] sets out a picture of a primaeval island (*iw*). This island has a principal name

[1] See p. 71. [2] See pp. 9–10.

[3] *nṯr nṯri ḫpr m sp tpy* is in the Edfu tradition the Falcon Horus, cf. E. VI. 181,3.10; III. 123,13–14; similarly E. II. 36,11; III. 111,2; 121,10; VI. 179,6; VII. 31,3; in E. III. 32,13 only does his name apply to Ptah-Nefer-Ḥer. For the connexion between this ritual scene and the mythical event recorded, see my article in *JEA*, XLVIII, 81–8.

Island of Trampling (*iw titi*), and two subsidiary ones: *Island of Combat* (*iw ᶜḥ3*) and *Island of Peace* (*iw ḥtp*). *The Island of Trampling*, as the name of a region in which the creation took place, is known to us only from the first Edfu cosmogonical record.[1] None of these three names recurs in the main part of the myth.[2] This island seems to have been in darkness, surrounded by the primaeval water (*ḥbbt*)[3] called *wāᶜret* .[4]

When the light came and the primaeval water grew radiant, two divine beings seem to have emerged from the water and were led to the island. These deities were by name *Wa* and *ᶜAā*. They are also called the *Two Companions of the Divine of Heart* (*tšwi ntri-ib*),[5] and are said to be leaders of a group of divine beings called *Shebtiw*, .[6]

These two Shebtiw perceived reeds at the edge of the primaeval water, a god named *Ḥtr-ḥr*[7] being above it. They landed there, and this place seems to have been given the name *Ges-wāᶜret*[8], . Wa and ᶜAā made their first home there. The tradition regarded them as the *Lords of the Island of Trampling*.[9]

[1] E. IV. 358,13; VI. 181,12.13, below, p. 55 ff.

[2] Cf. p. 88 ff.

[3] *ḥbbt*, cf. *Wb.* III, 63 (3); in the Edfu records this word seems to be used mainly to indicate the primaeval water from which the earth emerged: E. V. 118,11–12; VI. 177,5.8.14; 181,12; 184,12.13.

[4] *wᶜrt*, cf. *Wb.* I, 288 (6). Although in E. VI. 181,12.14 *wᶜrt* seems to be used as a synonym of *ḥbbt*, in E. I. 295,17; VI. 14,15; 176,9; 181,16 it is rather the name of a land lying in the primaeval water; in E. VI. 170,5; 328,15; 330,8 it seems to describe the primaeval domain of the gods. Cf. also Gardiner, *Notes on the Story of Sinube*, p. 30; de Buck, *De Egyptische Voorstellingen betreffende den Oerheuvel*, p. 60; E. I. 223,12 and below, p. 131 ff.

[5] *tšwi* occurs only in E. VI. 181,12; the suggested interpretation is a guess. This name may be a derivative of the verb *tš*, cf. *Wb.* V, 329 (10). Another possibility of interpretation may be given by the divine name *tštš*, cf. *ibid.* 330 (11), (12); there is no authority to confirm it. For the deity *ntri-ib*, cf. below, p. 97.

[6] See my article 'The Shebtiw in the Temple at Edfu' in *ZÄS*, LXXXVII, 41–54.

[7] Cf. pp. 94–5.

[8] The name *gs-wᶜrt* occurs only in E. VI. 181,16; VI. 14,14 gives *gs ḫnty* and IV. 358,13 describes it as *st tn, this place*. An alternative interpretation can be suggested: either 'region of the *wāᶜrt*' or 'edge of the *wāᶜrt*'; cf. below, p. 108.

[9] E. IV. 358,13; *nbw iw titi*; cf. *ZÄS*, LXXXVII, 41; 46 n. (*t*).

Second section: E. VI. 181,16–182,4

FASHIONING OF THE PERCH (DJEBA)

The reed having been split in two, a slip of it was planted in the primaeval water, and thus *djeba*[1] became the name of the slip of reed which was planted in the primaeval water and assumed the function of a perch.[2] It is explained that the perch of reed in the water is the *reed that uplifts the god* (*nbỉ wṯs nṯr*),[3] and it is equated with the *relic* (*ỉḫt*)[4] of a divinity called *This One* (*Pn*),[5] *the overlord of the ḏd-pillar.*[6] Another deity, the Ka,[7] arrived on the scene and a protection rite (*nhp*)[8] was performed probably by Wa and ʿAā.

These incidents are quoted as the origin of the cultus-place named *Djeba in Wetjeset-Neter.*[9] It is said:[10]

The slip (*ḏbꜣ*) of reed is the name of the Perch in Wetjeset-Neter. Thus Djeba ⟨in⟩ Wetjeset-Neter became the name of this domain (*nỉwt*),[11]

1 The significance of the word *ḏbꜣ* is studied in my article in *JEA*, XLVIII, 83 f. The picture of the planting of *ḏbꜣ*-perch recurs in E. IV. 328,5; 358,14; VI. 15,14–15,1; 184,13–14; 224,11; 323,4; VII. 22,8–9; cf. below, p. 133 ff.

2 Cf. p. 144 ff.

3 E. VI. 182,2; for the expression *wṯs nṯr* applying to the function of the reed, see: E. IV. 328,5; 358,15; VI. 15,1; 177,8; 182,2; 183,3; 184,14; *wṯs* is replaced by *twꜣ* in E. IV. 2,2; VI. 11,7; 184,5; for the symbolic meaning of this action, cf. below, p. 118.

4 *ỉḫt*, lit. 'thing'; the context seems to require for *ỉḫt* the meaning: the thing of the god who once existed but died, thus 'relic'; the same meaning is indicated by E. I. 15,16; 205,18; 371,16; 273,16; IV. 158,10; 328,8; VI. 288,13.17; 289,1–2; VII. 22,10; *Urk.* VIII, 50, 7; and below, p. 111.

5 *Pn* is a divine name and occurs in E. I. 29,18; III. 202,16; IV. 161,1; 326,2; V. 7,1; 9,4; 85,9; 181,12; VII. 10,11; VII. 23–5; Shabaka Stone, l. 3; Temple of Khonsu, Karnak, Sanctuary, East Wall (unpublished); *Urk.* VIII, 13, 15; cf. below, pp. 94–5.

6 E. VI. 182,2; for the *ḏd*-pillar see: E. VI. 177,3; 177,5; 176,5.8; 182,2–7; 183,9; 184,13.18; and for its meaning in the creation see below, p. 96; *ḥr ḏd* is the sole instance in this text; the interpretation 'overlord' is more likely than 'on, upon', because *ḥr* shows the writing .

7 is to be taken as a name of a primaeval god, cf. pp. 131, 183.

8 *nhp* in E. VI. 182,2 appears to be the title of a description telling us about the way in which the protection of the sacred place was established. For the protection of the early sacred places, cf. p. 25.

9 Cf. p. 132 ff.

10 E. VI. 182,2–3 = III. 31,12–13.

11 *nỉwt* occurs here as a technical name as well as the determinative of the name of any sacred place which was created in the primaeval age; there is no authority to confirm that the form of the sign *nỉwt* reflects the genuine aspect of the prehistoric sacred place.

great being the waterflood ⟨in⟩ the fields[1] that surround the region of reed (*gs nbi*).[2]

The abbreviated versions[3] give us grounds for supposing that this description preserves the tradition concerning the origin of the *Seat of the First Occasion* (*st n sp tpy*) of the god. The god for whom this resting-place of reed pictured as the *djeba*-perch was created, is the Falcon, also called *Lord of Djeba.*[4]

Third section: E. VI. 182,4–8

EVENTS FOLLOWING THE CREATION OF THE FIRST SACRED PLACE

The sacred place *Djeba in Wetjeset-Neter* having been created, the *Sanctified Ruler* (*ḥḳ3 ntri*)[5] appeared. He came from the Underworld (*dw3t*) as a *protector*,[6] and is said to resemble the *Nefer-ḥer*.[7] Subsequently the sacred place received the name *Underworld of the Soul* (*dw3t n B3*).[8]

The two Shebtiw acclaimed the 'Divine Falcon' and said:

1 is surely not the determinative of *nḏ3yt*, cf. *Wb.* II, 377 (11) and E. IV. 358,16; is most probably used to denote either *ww* or *iḥw*, and indicates the plots of land which were in the surroundings of the Perch but still beneath the water; cf. below, pp. 17–18.

2 *gs nbi* in E. VI. 182,3 suggests two interpretations; *gs* means either the edge of the island in which the reeds grew, or the region, the field of the reeds. The abbreviated version in E. IV. 358,16 mentions the reed only: *ʿ3 nḏ3yt iḥ w3ḥ r-gs nbi*, *Great was the inundation in the field(s) that lie close to the reed.*

3 E. IV. 358,13; similarly VI. 17,10; 224,10–11.

4 It is noteworthy that the records show only in describing the god of the primaeval domain; two readings can be suggested, either *ntr* or *bik*; cf. my article in *JEA*, XLVIII, 82 and below, p. 169; occasionally this god is called *nb ḏb3*, cf. E. VI. 15,2; 177,8; 182,8; 185,18.

5 This name occurs only in E. VI. 182,4; VI. 185,12–14 indicates that this is a subsidiary name of the *Lord of the Wing*.

6 The expression in E. VI. 182,3 and occurring also in 182,13; 183,3.4 is a curious one. We wonder whether is not used with the meaning *s3 protection*. The suggested interpretation will fit in 183,3, cf. below, pp. 97–8; in E. VI. 182,7 this *Sanctified Ruler* seems to be present as *s3*, *protector* (?) of the *ḏd*-pillar.

7 *Nfr-ḥr*, cf. E. IV. 358,16; VI. 15,1; in *Urk.* VIII, 4, 1 he is the sanctified Falcon. Although it is one of the names of Ptah (cf. Sandman, *The God Ptah*, pp. 108–11; E. III. 32,13), here it seems to indicate another deity, cf. below, p. 95.

8 This name occurs in E. III. 31,14; V. 67,6; 253,6; 291,5; 396,7; VI. 207,2; cf. below, p. 110.

Who comes from the Underworld? so said the Shebtiw. The Underworld of the Soul is this place, so said the Falcon. Thus Underworld of the Soul became the name of this domain (*niwt*).[1]

Thereafter great joy was in the island which, on this occasion, is described as the *Great Foundation Ground of the Ruler of the Wing*.[2]

Then the *Lord of the Wing* (*ndm ndb*)[3] arrived in the island and his blessed offerings (*iḫt nfr*)[4] were presented to the *Lord of the Perch* (*nb ḏbꜣ*).

The same event is described in the abbreviated version differently and also in a more explicit way. We read that it was believed that 'the Ka arrived in the capacity of the Flying Ba',[5] 'with face like unto Nefer-ḥer'. An act of acclamation was completed by the two Shebtiw; then the narrative proceeds:

He came close and gave offerings (*iḫt*) from his mouth to the Lord of Djeba so that he may unite with the sky of Him-whose-command-is-unknown. He gave thanks for the *ḏrty*-falcon upon the willow. Though his voice was heard, no men had seen him.[6]

The consorting of the primaeval Falcon with the Soul, the *Flying Ba*, is regarded as the first event that came to pass in the primaeval Djeba after this was given the name *Underworld of the Soul*.[7]

Fourth section: E. VI. 182,9–10

THE PLACE-OF-UNITING-OF-THE-COMPANY

Allusion to another mythical event seems to follow. Probably the text preserves only the heading of a record describing what had happened in the *bw-smꜣ-ḏꜣjsw*, the *Place-of-Uniting-of-the-Company*.

[1] E. VI. 182,5–6 = E. III. 31,13–14.

[2] The sole evidence of this name is in E. VI. 182,6–7; the reading *snṯt* is based on the example in E. IV. 390,6.

[3] *ndm ndb* is a divine name; see E. III. 199,12–13; IV. 169,15–16; VI. 182,8; 185,14; the word *ndm* is known from the Edfu texts only. Its etymology is obscure. The suggested interpretation is conjectural and can be supported by the parallel use with *ḥḳꜣ ndm* in E. VI. 182,7.10; 185,14; while used absolutely, *ndm* seems to substitute for *nb* = lord, cf. E. VI. 176,12; 181,2; 185,1; 328,18.

[4] *iḫt* only in E. VI. 182,8 and 15,2 seems to indicate some divine substances; certainly *iḫt* does not mean here the 'relic'; cf. p. 14, n. 4.

[5] For the identity of the *ndm ndb* with the Flying Ba, cf. p. 116.

[6] E. VI. 15,2–3, and below, p. 127.

[7] Cf. pp. 114, 118.

The meaning of the name is not clear.[1] The word *ḏ3jsw*, which we translate, very tentatively, as 'company', might refer to a group of divine beings who had died.[2] There is no relevant text to clarify the significance of this name.

The Falcon is then described as wandering[3] through the *bw*-Place.[4] It is not clear whether there is an allusion to the foundation of a definite settlement in that place or whether this *bw*-place refers to the original *Wetjeset-Neter*. This *bw*-place may well be another place in the *Island of Trampling*. Speculation is vain. This section ends with a spell which is obviously an interpretation of a later date, and most probably an Edfu tradition. It is said that

Horus the Behdetite is the Lord of Djeba, the Djeba is the Behdet, and the Ruler of the Wing, the Flying Ba, is the name of the Behdetite.[5]

Fifth section: E. VI. 182,10–15

CREATION OF THE FIRST PĀY-LAND AND THE ORIGIN OF THE GREAT PRIMAEVAL MOUND

The revelation of the *Sanctified Ruler* and the *Lord of the Wing* seems to have marked a definite period in the development of the first primaeval sacred place.[6] The next stage is pictured as an act of creation. Reference is made to the appearance of the first *pāy*-land[7] upon the *Foundation ground of the Ruler of the Wing*. Probably this *pāy*-land is one of the  *iḥw*-fields which are said at the beginning of this record to be beneath the water.[8] The creation of this *pāy*-land seems to be connected with an act of uttering of names, which, most probably, was performed by Wa and ʿAā. As a result of this action, it is said that a new domain (*niwt*) came into existence, the name of which was the *Blessed Island* and *Hareoty*. The Falcon was

[1] The only instance is in E. VI. 182,8–9.

[2] *sni* to be taken with the meaning *to pass away* = *to perish*, cf. *Wb.* III, 455 (2); for *ḏ3jsw*, cf. *Wb.* V, 521 (8) (*a*) and below, p. 109.

[3]  for 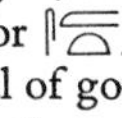, cf. *Wb.* IV, 146 (6) and E. VI. 329,1, where *smd* describes the arrival of gods in a place in which a new settlement was to be founded.

[4] *bw*, in these records, describes any place which should be made as a foundation ground of a sacred place; cf. E. IV. 357,17; VI. 169,3; 176,4; 177,12–13.14; 184,3.13.

[5] E. VI. 182,9–10.

[6] Cf. pp. 114–18.

[7] For the *pāy*-land, cf. pp. 137–9, 171–3; *dj-ʿ ḥr.s* seems to be the heading of the presumed original version; *dj-ʿ* (cf. *Wb.* V, 419 (10)) seems to be used as the synonym of *bs*, cf. E. VI. 184,12; cf. below, pp. 26–7; *-.s* seems to refer to the *sntt*-foundation ground.

[8] Cf. p. 15, and p. 153 ff.

then greeted as their lord.[1] The occurrence of the verb *ḫpr* and *dj-ʿ* suggests that this mythological event might illustrate the Egyptian idea about the creation of the ground of a sacred domain.[2] The spells uttered (*nis*) are described as *ḏ3jsw*, *learned spells*.[3] What follows may be taken as a ceremony of giving names to the *ḏd*-pillar.[4] Then the Shebtiw again are described as uttering sacred names, such as *Khenem-aten* and *Tep-tôwi*. These names might have been believed to produce the emerging of other *pāy*-lands. It is not clearly stated in the narrative whether these names refer to the *pāy*-lands or whether they describe sacred places on the *pāy*-land previously created. The narrative ends in an exclamation in which the Falcon is invited to arrive (*s3ḥ*) in that place.[5]

The subsequent stage of the creation was the origin of the *Great Primaeval Mound* ( *ḫʿy-wr*).[6] The emergence of the mound seems to be connected also with uttering of names.[7] These names are: *Place-in-which-the-enemies-were-annihilated*, *Territory of the Ancestor*, and *Land-of-him-who-is-great-of-arm*. These three names appear as names either of one or of several sacred places which were created on the *Great Primaeval Mound*. It may be surmised on the other hand that they indicate the mythological events which were believed to have come to pass there.[8] We think that the Shebtiw were responsible for this act of creation though the text does not say it;[9] at any rate, they were the only creators in that place. With this episode of creation seems to end a definite stage in the development of the earliest sacred world of the gods.[10]

[1] Probably here is an allusion to the recognition of the rulership, cf. pp. 138–9.

[2] Cf. pp. 178–9.

[3] *nis ḏ3jsw*; we suspect that in E. VI. 182,11 = III. 7,2, we have the same expression as in E. VI. 184,11; *ḏ3jsw* appears to be used as the name of the magical spells the Shebtiw were believed to utter during the creation of the earth, cf. below, p. 139.

[4] E. VI. 182,12, reading *in k3 ḏd* (?), *to recite the name of the ḏd-pillar* (?). The sentence is somewhat enigmatic and our suggestion is a guess.

[5] E. VI. 182,13; *mj s3ḥ r bw pn*, *come to this place*; therefore only one sacred place was created in this action; cf. below, pp. 138, 146.

[6] *ḫʿy-wr*, cf. E. III. 7,4; IV. 4,6; 165,7; 390,6; VI. 15,8; 183,18; VII. 2,3; 23,9; de Buck, *Oerheuvel*, pp. 63–71; *Urk*. VIII, 92, 22; *ASAE*, XLIV, 135; *Pétosiris*, 61, 14.

[7] E. VI. 182,13; *iy m s3*, *To be uttered as* (?) *protection* (?), cf. p. 15, n. 6.

[8] Cf. pp. 139–40.

[9] E. IV. 358,16–17, on the other hand, indicates that the mound was the work of Hedjeti; in E. V. 188,10–11 the *ḫʿy*-mound is said to have been led forth from the primaeval water before the *s3t3w*-ground existed.

[10] Cf. p. 141 ff.

Sixth section: E. VI. 182,15–17

ASSUMING THE KINGSHIP OF THE KA

The enemy came over afterwards in the form of the snake (*rꜣ*).[1] We suspect that a period of time came to pass between the emergence of the *Great Primaeval Mound* and the appearance of the enemy, but the events which might have occurred within the original domain of *Wetjeset-Neter* are not described in this version. It can reasonably be expected that in this primaeval Djeba a sacred act came to pass in which the Falcon assumed the 'Kingship of the Ka'. Much is enigmatic in this description, and the hypothesis concerning the 'Kingship of the Ka' is based on the expression *ẖnm ḥpt* only.[2] As far as we can reconstruct the picture, it seems that the Ka revealed sacred things to the Falcon, but what these sacred things were is not clear from the main source.[3] The abbreviated version, however, furnishes a clue, for it relates that the Falcon told his crew about the *praises of Rēʿ which the Ka ordered* (wḏ) *for him in the Djeba.*[4]

Seventh section: E. VI. 182,17–183,1

REVELATION OF THE PROTECTOR GOD AND THE GOD-OF-THE-TEMPLE

When the enemy-snake appeared, the Shebtiw seem to have recited sacred spells again. As a result of this action a protective deity appeared. This deity is named *ntr-ḥn, Protector God,*[5] and is described as the *Likeness of the Radiant One with face like unto the Ḥeter-ḥer*. A supplementary description of this deity is to be found in the abbreviated version and reads:

[1] The snake *rꜣ*, cf. *Wb.* II, 393 (7), is in this myth described as the first enemy of the god; cf. E. VI. 182,16; 184,17; 176,5.13; 329,1.2.3; 330,7.8; 328,9.10.16.

[2] E. VI. 182,16 = III. 7,6 is the only evidence in our sources; for *ẖnm ḥpt*, cf. *Wb.* III, 69 (16).

[3] E. VI. 182,17 = III. 7,6 reads: *ḥfḥf Kꜣ*; *ḥfḥf* is known with the meaning 'to listen'; cf. *Wb.* III, 75 (2); however, it is difficult to agree on this meaning here.

[4] E. VI. 17,11.

[5] ; the reading *ntr-ḥn* is theoretically suggested; as a divine name it is known from the Edfu texts only: E. III. 7,6; VI. 15,7; 182,17, and below, p. 140.

Men say that the Protector God came forth thereupon in this place (*st* = *Djeba*) to protect (*ḥn*) the god (*ntr*) within the Wetjeset-Neter in the capacity of the Segemeḥ.[1]

In the tradition of a later date Ptah replaces this Protector.[2]

Thereafter another deity appeared on the scene. He is the *God-of-the-Temple* (),[3] who is also described as the *Likeness of the Radiant One with the face like unto the Ḥeter-ḥer*,[4] and whose true name seems to be 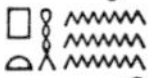 *Ptḥ-nwyt, He-who-created-the-primaeval-water*.[5] The next stage of this history, again, seems to be an act of creation. The *ptḥ-nwyt*-water was created by the agency of the Creator (*ptḥ*)[6] and this water contained the power of protecting.[7] This act of creation occurred after the enemy-snake was overthrown.

Eighth section: E. VI. 183,1–2

SETTING OUT THE SBḪT-ENCLOSURE

The following event seems to be the consequence of the attack by the enemy on the sacred area. This part of the narrative seems to describe what had been created and fashioned within the original domain of the island. Allusion is made to the setting out of a *sbḫt*-enclosure and to the digging out of a channel[8] which contained

[1] E. VI. 15,7–8.

[2] E. IV. 358,17.

[3] This deity is known from the Edfu texts only; cf. E. III. 7,8; IV. 103,8; 259,4; 182,18; 183,5.8.10; 186,3; below, pp. 141–2.

[4] E. VI. 186,4–5.

[5] E. III. 7,8; 132,5; 182,18; 186,5; it is certainly a divine name here, unlike E. VI. 186,6, where *ptḥ-nwyt* seems to be the name of the canal, 'the Water of Ptah (creator ?)'.

[6] E. VI. 183,1; *ptḥ* can hardly mean the historical Ptah; we would prefer the interpretation 'Creator'; thus here *ḫpr...m-dj ptḥ, came into being...by agency of the Creator*; *ptḥ*, unlike *Wb.* I, 565 (11), seems to be connected in this myth with the creation of the water (*mw*) only, cf. VI. 183,2; cf. *Wb.* I, 565 (15); the discussion by Sandman, *The God Ptah*, pp. 8–11, about the meaning of the word *ptḥ* has little relevance.

[7] E. VI. 186,5 specifies: *the Sanctified Water that protects.*

[8] E. VI. 183,1 = III. 7,9: *ỉr ḫ3ʿ sbḫt p3y ẖnw*; for *ḫ3ʿ* cf. *Wb.* III, 227 (16). The reading *sbḫt* is suggested by E. VI. 324,1–2; the reading *p3y ẖnw* would be plausible regarding the second instance in E. VI. 183,1 and that in 186,6; cf. *Wb.* III, 373 (5); *JEA*, XXX, 16, n. 36.

water of a special sort, and which was sanctified against the snake (*rꜣ*).[1] This moment was the origin of the *mw*-water by the agency of the *Divine of Heart*.[2]

Ninth section: E. VI. 183,2–3

REVELATION OF TANEN

The *Lord of the Creation* (*nb ptḥ*)[3] is mentioned thereafter. This part of the record is of importance, and no parallel can be quoted. The lord of the creation (*ptḥ*) is said to be Tanen.[4] It appears that after the water (*mw*) was in existence, it was possible for Tanen to emerge. His emergence seems to be also the result of a 'saying'. We are told that

Tanen was led forth (*bs*) as a protection (*sꜣ*)[5] (?) when the Shebtiw said: He is Tanen, the Revered One.[6]

Probably after the Shebtiw had pronounced this spell, Tanen was brought out of the water.

Tenth section: E. VI. 183,3–5

ARRIVING AT THE FIELD OF THE ANCESTORS

The next stage in the history of this primaeval domain is described as *sꜣḥ* ⟨*r*⟩ *nbi Wṯst-Nṯr twꜣ tpyw-ꜥ*, *Arriving at the* (*field of*) *Wetjeset-Neter which restores the Ancestors*.[7] We suspect that this sentence

[1] Reading (*s*)*nṯri*, cf. *Wb*. IV, 180 (6).

[2] For the sentence in E. VI. 183,2 *ỉr Nṯri-ib ptḥ mw* we suggest, very tentatively, the interpretation: *the Divine of Heart created the mw-water*. *ptḥ* is used here as a verb with the meaning suggested on p. 20, n. 6. Cf. the first mention of this deity in E. VI. 181,12 and below, pp. 119, 165.

[3] This is the sole occurrence of this name in our narrative.

[4] E. VI. 183,2 = E. III. 7,10–11. The way in which this narrative is written seems to point to a rather unusual equation between Tanen and the *Nṯri-ib*. This passage would indicate a new function of Tanen in the creation; cf. E. VI. 15,3: *ptḥ Ṯni m nwyt r ḥn nṯr*, *Tanen created the water to protect the god*. Perhaps Tanen is the true form in which the *Nṯri-ib* emerged.

[5] *m sꜣ*; *s* can hardly be a pronoun; reference to the quotation in E. VI. 15,3 makes the interpretation *as a protection* plausible, cf. above, p. 15, n. 6.

[6] In *in šbtjw*, *in* must be used as a verb.

[7] E. VI. 183,3 = E. III. 7,11; *sꜣḥ r nbi* can also be used as a participle epithet referring to Tanen. If this be so, it would mean that the whole sentence was only a part of the speech of the Shebtiw. In the light of E. VI. 182,3, *sꜣḥ* can also

might have originally been the heading of a record describing what happened in the original domain of *Wetjeset-Neter* subsequently to the revelation of Tanen and to the creation of the water that protects. It seems as if this passage reveals an additional meaning attached to the *Wetjeset-Neter*. It is interpreted as *twꜣ-restoring*[1] *the Ancestors*. Who these Ancestors are is not stated.[2]

This field seems to have been a place of protection. Allusion is made to a shelter (*nht*) laid out as a protection[3] of the Creator, who is represented by  *ḏt-wṯt*, the *Member of Progenitor*.[4] The dimensions of this shelter are said to be 5 by 15 cubits.[5] The following description is only a summary of events which were believed to have taken place in that same field after the symbol of creation was given a shelter.

The next event appears to have been the building of *what had been planned*.[6] Reference is made to a mansion (*ḥwt*), named the *Mansion of Isden*,[7] but only the title of this section is preserved. If this inference be correct, it follows that the house of another god was erected on the same field and close to the shelter of the Creator. The statement *Entering by the God-of-the-Temple into what was in decay* suggests that this mansion might have been found destroyed.[8]

be an imperative, supposing that the Shebtiw invited Tanen to come close to the field of reeds.

1 *twꜣ, id.* E. VI. 177,3, lit. *to uplift*, is used with somewhat modified meaning—to uplift in order to bring to a new life, cf. below, p. 164 ff.

2 Cf. p. 149.

3 Reading *nht sk rdj m sꜣ* (?); no parallel can be quoted.

4 E. VI. 183,4 = E. III. 7,11 is the only occurrence of this expression in our text; possibly it means the symbol of the first creating power, below, p. 148.

5 *nht* used as a name of a very primitive shelter of the gods occurs in E. VI. 177,4.5; 184,5; 329,9; 330,6; III. 7,11; VI. 183,10.

6 *wdꜥ*, lit. *to delimit* (cf. *Wb.* I, 404), seems to be used with a modified meaning: delimit with a view to laying out, similarly E. III. 7,12; IV. 295,9; 299,7; VI. 177,11; 177,14; 323,7; 329,4.

7 Also mentioned in E. VI. 177,4.

8 E. VI. 183,4 = III. 7,12; *ẖn* is used as an infinitive, *to enter*, cf. *Wb.* III, 373 (15), in parallel to *sꜣḥ* in 183,3; *m šꜣš*, cf. *Wb.* IV, 413; *ỉn* is the agent, 'by'.

Eleventh section: E. VI. 183,5–10

THE FALCON INVESTED AS SUCCESSOR OF THE EARTH-MAKER

The domain of the *Wetjeset-Neter* is now attacked by the enemy-snake, and *Ḥeter-ḥer*, who is represented defenceless, is hard pressed. As a result Tanen created (*sw*)[1] two divinities, the *Segemeḥ* and *Sekhem-Ḥer*, who were symbolized as two staffs (*ṯbw*) which had the duty of repelling danger from the island. This passage is important in indicating the origin of the spear of the historic time. It was believed to have primarily been a staff upon which Tanen conferred the power of protecting.

The following scene shows the presentation of the mace 'the Great-White' (*ḥḏ-wr*) of the Earth-Maker to his son, the Falcon. This is the sole evidence, according to our present knowledge, which shows that this mace was believed primarily to have been connected with the Earth-Maker, and might have been the symbol of his sovereignty.[2] Here is the only allusion to the Earth-Maker, who, in this drama of creation, is never said to act.[3]

Then Tanen brought two other symbols, the *ḏd*-pillar and the *Similitude of the Front of the God*, while another symbol was placed before the God-of-the-Temple, whom we suppose to reside in the shelter (*nht*). If we agree that this shelter is the same as that mentioned above, it would mean that the ceremony of presenting the mace of the Earth-Maker and the other symbols to the Falcon took place in the shelter of the Creator in the presence of the God-of-the-Temple. This shelter would appear to be the most sacred spot of the domain.[4]

[1] For the meaning of *sw*, cf. my article 'The Shebtiw in the Temple at Edfu', *ZÄS*, LXXXVII, 43–5, n. (*f*).

[2] In E. VI. 184,6, however, the *ḥḏ-wr* seems to be a deity who was capable of acting; cf. *JEA*, 50, 134–5.

[3] Cf. pp. 193–4.

[4] Cf. pp. 149–50.

Twelfth section: E. VI. 183,10–12

VISITING THE PLACE FOR CONSTRUCTING

Following the ceremony in the *shelter* there is an allusion to *ḥḥ bw-ẖnm.*[1] The expression is not clear. Although there is no authority for this view, the interpretation *to visit the Place-for-construction* may tentatively be suggested. It is possible that the text alludes to a place in the island other than those already described. The Shebtiw Wa and ᶜAā had been summoned by the God-of-the-Temple. What follows seems to be a command given by the God-of-the-Temple to the Shebtiw by virtue of which he conferred upon them the power of fashioning (*nḥp*) and advised them to visit the *Place-for-constructing*. However, much is enigmatic in this statement. As a result of this, it seems that the Shebtiw were *specifying by naming* (*dm*) some substances which are described only by the word *iḫt.*[2] The Shebtiw are also said to utter an invocation of the *Arm.*[3] Probably there is an allusion to the worship of the Creator which preceded a new action of creation of the lands. The spells which were uttered on that occasion are described as *ḥsi Rᶜ*, *Praise of Rēᶜ.*[4]

Thirteenth section: E. VI. 183,12–184,2

CREATION OF THE PĀY-LANDS

The next stage in the history of this domain is, in the main, occupied by the Shebtiw, whose function is described as *dm iḫt to name* (= create) *the things*. Probably this action diffused from the

[1] The expression *ḥḥ bw-ẖnm* occurs in E. VI. 177,11; 183,10; 184,2. There is nothing relevant in these records to confirm that *ẖnm* can either describe an act of creation or that it can be an alternative name for the *bw-sw-iḫt-tꜣ-im.f*, cf. below, p. 155 ff.

[2] Cf. my article 'The Shebtiw in the Temple of Edfu', *ZÄS*, LXXXVII, 45.

[3] 𓂝, for which we suggest very tentatively the interpretation ᶜ, *the Arm*, cf. *ASAE*, XLIII, 223; E. VI. 176,7; 177,3; 183,7.9.12; 184,4.9.16. The context suggests that this might have been another symbol of the Creator, cf. below, pp. 148, 158.

[4] *ḥsi Rᶜ* occurs in E. VI. 117,11; 183,12.18; in the terminology of this myth it seems to indicate sacred spells which were recited before a new phase of creation started. There is no confirmative evidence that *ḥsi Rᶜ* were merely another name for the *ḏꜣjsw, learned spell*, above, p. 18, n. 3, though a parallel use can be quoted in the text, cf. E. VI. 184,11.

bw-ẖnm. What in particular they were creating were the 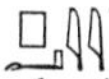 *pāy*-lands[1] and other sacred places, and these are now listed: (1) the Mound of the Radiant One, (2) the Island of Rēʿ, (3) the *ḏd*-Pillar of the Earth, (4) the High Hill, (5) the Oil-tree, (6) He-who-is-rich-in-Kas, (7) Mesen, (8) He-who-makes-prosperous-places, (9) Behdet, which seems to have a subsidiary name such as the *First of the Mounds* (*ỉꜣwt*)[2] which is said to be in the presence (*ḫr*) of the Primaeval Deities (*pꜣwtyw*); (10) the last *pāy*-land seems to bear the name *the Place* (*bw*) *of the Ghosts*.[3] As a result of this act of creation, the Sages (*ḏꜣjsw*) were believed to (*s*)*wr ỉḫt*, *magnify the things*,[4] probably for the sacred places to be created in these domains. We suspect that there is an allusion to the making of the *magical protection* of the newly created *pāy*-lands and their sacred places.[5]

When this episode came to an end, a new act of creation of the *pāy*-lands followed. These are: (1) the Great Seat in which the enemies were annihilated, (2) the Throne (*nst*), and (3) at the time of the 'praise of Rēʿ' the second 'Great Primaeval Mound' (*ḫʿy-wr*) emerged; its names apparently were 'the Territory of the Circuit' and the 'Great Place (*bw-wr*)'. Subsequently, the meadow grew radiant.

Fourteenth section: E. VI. 184,2–10

VISITING THE BW-ẖNM

After the creation of the *pāy*-lands there followed again what is called *ḥḥ bw-ẖnm*. The meaning of this expression, as stated, is obscure. However, it is possible that here the name meant a place in which a sacred settlement was made. Tanen summoned the Shebtiw. They reached a place called the *Place* (*bw*) *of Wa*[6] which gave origin to the later *bw ḥmr*, *Place of the Throne*. Rites were performed in front of a willow when offerings were brought in.[7]

[1] *pʿy* in E. VI. 183,12 is used in the plural differently from 182,10, cf. below, p. 153 ff.

[2] E. V. 396,6; VII. 23,3–4; p. 18 and below, pp. 154–5.

[3] E. VI. 183,16 = 11,4 and below, p. 184.

[4] E. VI. 8,15; 203,4; 320,10; VII. 25,9, alternatively *swr mdw* in E. IV. 14,8; 175,2 and *swr snṯt* in VII. 49,7–9; cf. below, p. 204.

[5] Cf. p. 169 ff.

[6] The sole evidence is in E. VI. 184,3; cf. below, p. 158.

[7] For *ṯrt* cf. Keimer, *BIFAO*, XXXI, 177–234; Ricke, 'Eine Inventartafel aus Heliopolis im Turiner Museum', *ZÄS*, LXXI, 120. The *ṯrt*-willow takes the place of the reed in E. III. 10,15; 187,4; IV. 358,16; VI. 15,3; and below, p. 160.

The text reads:

Appearing in speed. Coming close to the willow. Bringing the offerings in the presence of the Arm.[1]

Then an enclosure (*sbty*)[2] seems to have been erected around this place. The Builder Gods appeared on the scene;[3] following episodes of acclamation and offerings the sacred lance was lifted up. A special ritual of protection was performed.

Then the Falcon was uplifted by the willow[4] and other protective rites were performed. It appears that there is an allusion to the creation of sacred symbols which were believed to protect the Falcon in his seat upon the willow. The gods seem to have created them when they gave names to certain objects which are not described. Probably through these rites the 'Place-of-the-Throne' enshrining the willow became protected.[5] All this section is enigmatic.

Fifteenth section: E. VI. 184,10–15

CREATION OF THE PĀY-LAND OF WETJESET-NETER

This section starts with mention of the Ghosts, Builder Gods and Shebtiw. The name of the first company suggests alternative interpretations; either 'Ghosts' or 'Pillars' which we may imagine standing on a definite part of the island.[6] Their presence might have been connected with the phase of creation which was about to start.

The Shebtiw continued the work of creation by reciting more names and spells.[7] They are said to have been put in a place of

[1] Possibly there is allusion to the same symbol *Arm* and to the same *i͗ẖt*-substance already known from E. VI. 183,12; cf. below, p. 158 ff.

[2] The suggested reading *sbty* for is conjectural.

[3] *sꜣḥ* in the terminology of this myth appears to describe the arrival of a new and not yet known company of gods to a land not yet occupied, cf. E. III. 7,3; IV. 356,13–14; 358,14; V. 64,11; VI. 15,2; 17,7; 18,9; 136,3; 172,5; 177,5; 177,7; 181,15; 181,16; 182,13; 184,13; 184,12.18; 320,7; 320,13; 329,2.

[4] Cf. p. 25; also E. VI. 15,3, where the Falcon is said to have dwelt on the willow instead of on the Perch; similarly E. IV. 358,16 the willow is said to be within the field of reeds of *Wetjeset-Neter*.

[5] For the protection of the primitive places, cf. p. 14.

[6] Cf. my article 'Worship of the Ancestor Gods at Edfu', *CdE*, LXXV, 57–8, and below, p. 198 ff.

[7] E. VI. 184,11, *i͗n ḏꜣjsw*, cf. above, pp. 18, 24–5.

special significance which is described as *bw-sw-iḫt-tȝ-im*, the *Place-in-which-the-things-of-the-Earth-were-filled-with-power.*[1] As a result of the uttering of sacred spells the primaeval water (*ḥbbt*) receded and a *pāy*-land emerged.[2]

Then this company of gods, joined by the crew of the Falcon, approached the *bw-ḥbbt*, *Place-of-the-primaeval-water*, at which also the *Ḥeter-ḥer* arrived. We suspect that this *bw-ḥbbt* might have been a place at the margin of this *pāy*-land, and equal, in its nature, to the field of reeds of the original island.[3] It is stated that this *bw*-place was the *bw*-place of the *ḏd*-pillar, and it is again a *ḏbȝ*-perch of reed which seems to be the substitute for the *ḏd*-pillar.[4]

Afterwards the Falcon arrived and was uplifted by the Perch. Thus the *pāy*-land was given its name. It was the *snbt*-place[5] that ensured the protection of the god. With this act the creation seems to have come to an end and the divine beings are said to have entered in the place in which the *ḏd*-pillar of reed was enshrined.[6]

Sixteenth section: E. VI. 184,15–185,2

SETTLING DOWN ON THE PĀY-LAND

The following text is rather enigmatic and damaged in parts. We conjecture that there might be an allusion to the settling down on the *pāy*-land of *Wetjeset-Neter*. The crew of the Falcon having arrived, the Shebtiw seem to have sailed away. The crew seems to exercise protection over this land. They are described as *nḏ iḫt*, *protecting the things*. The meaning of the word *iḫt*, however, is not clear in this context.[7]

The abbreviated version reveals that the crew having arrived greeted the Ka (the Ka of the *pāy*-land?) since they saw him in the *pāy*-land. Then the Falcon welcomed the crew and invited them to

[1] E. VI. 177,14; 184,11–12; and below, p. 161.

[2] E. VI. 184,12 reads: *ʿḥm in ḥbbt bs pʿy, Receding by the primaeval water. Bringing out the pāy-land*; cf. below, p. 160; this is the only evidence showing the realistic side of this rite of creation.

[3] Cf. pp. 75–112.

[4] Cf. p. 14, 14, n. 1.

[5] *snbt*, cf. *Wb*. IV, 161 (7).

[6] *ḫn bw ḏd nbi im, entering into the place in which the ḏd-pillar was*; no parallel can be quoted to clarify the significance of the sentence.

[7] *iḫt* with presumably the same meaning occurs in E. VI. 17,9; 17,10; 177,1; 177,2.6-7; 177,12.13; 184,4; 184,18.

settle down beside him. They then took care of the *iḫt* of the *pāy*-land which was the home of the Falcon (*ḥr.f*). The Falcon spoke to them about these *iḫt* which were in the *pāy*-land and also about the way in which the *djeba*-perch was made by the Shebtiw in the *Wetjeset-Neter.*[1]

In this land the Falcon is said to have ruled as the *Child of the Ḥeter-ḥer* upon the *ḏd*-pillar of reed,[2] and as such he was acclaimed as the *lord* (*ndm*) by the crew. The place of the *djeba*-perch was declared to have been properly constructed, for it was the place which the Ka had bequeathed to the Falcon.[3]

Seventeenth section: E. VI. 326,1–327,3

FOUNDATION OF THE TEMPLE OF WETJESET-NETER

We suppose that the following section of the myth dealt with the foundation of a mansion of the god within the *pāy*-land of *Wetjeset-Neter*, which in the Edfu version of this myth is found described at the end of the fifth record. The *Wetjeset-Neter* referred to as having existed in the *reign of Tanen*[4] might well have been the *pāy*-land the origin of which is interpreted in the first record.

The description of the ground plan of this mansion was included in the same sacred book as that in which is recorded the creation of the sacred domains of the Falcon. The title of this record reads:

Laying out the foundation ground which was made in (*ìr m*) the Temple of *Wetjeset-Neter* in the reign of Tanen, in the presence of Rēʿ according to that which is in the book (*šfdw*), the Specification of the Sacred Mounds of the Early Primaeval Age as it is called.

The foundation was assisted by twenty-four gods who are: the Ogdoad, Seshat, the Seven Builder Gods, Thoth and the Seven Sages.[5] The manner in which this title is written suggests that we might have here an allusion to the existence of two primitive temples, the first of which was founded and constructed during

[1] E. VI. 17,9–11.
[2] E. VI. 176,13; 184,18; and below, pp. 164, 180ff.
[3] The context seems to require for *wḏ* a derivative meaning: *to order by will for the heir = to bequeath*; similarly E. VI. 16,4; 17,11; 176,5; 177,11.
[4] E. VI. 326,1, and below, p. 213ff.
[5] E. VI. 327,4–12 = XIV. Pl. 603.

the mythical reign of Tanen; this type of construction seems to have been used later on in the building of another primitive temple.[1]

It is said that the temple stood in a vast enclosure (*inb*) surrounding another inner enclosure which was the real temple. The temple consisted most probably of two units, of which the back part appears to be more important and possibly was of earlier date.

Its chief sanctuary, named *ḥwt-ḳni*, was apparently placed on the main axis at the rear of the temple. Its dimensions were 30 cubits from west to east, and 20 cubits from south to north. The following text is damaged, but it may be supposed that there was a large courtyard in the front of this sanctuary, and perhaps some smaller sanctuaries along the two inner sides of this courtyard.

The front section of the mansion, so far as the much damaged text permits one to make any reconstruction, consisted primarily of two halls. The inner hall, 50 by 45 cubits, had two side chapels, each 30 by 30 cubits. In front of the inner hall was another, smaller, pillared hall, 30 by 15 cubits. This hall may also have had side rooms, but the rest of the description is lost.[2]

SECOND RECORD

Eighteenth section: E. VI. 176,12–177,3

EVENTS IN THE PĀY-LAND OF DJEBA

The second record is concerned with the events which were believed to have happened in the *pāy*-land of Djeba. We suspect that this *pāy*-land of Djeba might have been one of the *pāy*-lands which surrounded the *Island of Trampling*.[3] But the narrative does not indicate the exact connexion between the *pāy*-land and the island. The description of the origin of this *pāy*-land does not survive in the Edfu records, and this would be a good reason for supposing that its origin was interpreted in the same way as that of the *pāy*-land of *Wetjeset-Neter*.[4]

The beginning of this record reveals that the Falcon was acclaimed as the lord (*ndm*) by the crew. The *pāy*-land is described as his own territory (*ww*). He seems to have ruled there also in the

[1] Cf. p. 232.
[2] Cf. p. 225 ff. for further discussion.
[3] Cf. p. 163.
[4] Cf. pp. 26–7.

capacity of the *Child of the Ḥeter-ḥer.*[1] It is interesting that this name of the Falcon occurs only in connexion with the *pāȳ*-lands.

The following part of the narrative is written in a very enigmatic manner. The Falcon spoke to his crew and seems to have revealed to them the divine words of the Ka.[2] A series of ritual episodes followed. The *ỉḫt, sacred substances,* and the reed which restores (*twꜣ*) the place of the *ḏd*-pillar[3] were adored. Thereafter the narrative alludes to an event which appears as the destruction of a shelter (*nht*).

Nineteenth section: E. VI. 177,4–11

FASHIONING OF THE PERCH

The episode of the adoration of the *ỉḫt* having been performed, the following event is described as *sꜣḥ r nbỉ nht wṯst, Arriving at the reed which shelters the throne (perch?).*[4] Then the Shebtiw seem to have entered into a place in which they restored the *ḏd*-pillar; as a consequence the primaeval water receded and the *ḏd*-pillar of the Ka[5] was adored. The Ka seems to have given the instructions for fashioning of the *djeba*-perch. The presumed words of the Ka read:

> To be cut off the top (*wpt*) of the reed. A half therefrom is what was divided from (?) it (and) which is the side to be uplifted from the cutting.[6]

Thereafter, the primaeval water became calm, the *ỉḫt*[7] were recalled, and the two Shebtiw approached the edge, the reed floating by. They divided the reed, and a cutting from it was planted.

1 Cf. p. 164.

2 This passage may tentatively be linked with the later version in E. VI. 17,9–11.

3 Cf. pp. 162–3.

4 This interpretation is rather conjectural; we suspect that there might have been again the heading of another record similar to that quoted in E. VI. 183,3; to be taken as the noun *wṯst.*

5 Cf. p. 166.

6 E. VI. 177,5–6; the suggested interpretation is very conjectural for the lack of a more explicit parallel; *wpt nbỉ* occurs only once in our text; we suspect that from this *wpt*, top part of the reed stalk, the Perch (*ḏbꜣ*) was made; cf. E. VI. 181,16; *tš* used with the same meaning as in E. VI. 181,16 and *Wb.* V, 329 (20).

7 It is evident that these *ỉḫt* were in the *pāȳ*-land before the creation of the divine seat. We suspect that here *ỉḫt* has the same meaning as in E. VI. 183,12; 184,18.

Thus the Perch (*ḏbꜣ*) became the name of what was in the water. Then the Falcon was uplifted as the *lord of the Djeba*, and thus the *Wetjeset-Neter* came into existence after the Perch was created (*ỉr*).[1] A scene of worship and a silent rite followed. The next event was possibly the performance of a protective rite. Reference is also made to a 'Blessed command' and to developing what was planned. However, much is obscure in this narrative.

Twentieth section: E. VI. 177,11–14; 176,3–5

PLANNING THE SITE OF THE TEMPLE

The Shebtiw are described acting in a search of the *bw-ḫnm* and removing some protective symbols which are described as the *Likeness of the ꜣw-ỉb*, then the symbol of the *Sekhem-ḥer* and that of the *Divine Arm*.[2] After a ceremony of praise in which all the companies of the creative deities were assembled, the place (*bw*) was declared to be the god's property. However, the divine authority who might assign this place to the god is not named in the text. It appears that the deities working on the foundation of the domain had made this declaration. Allusion is also made to an invocation of the *ỉḫt* which are said to be in view. Thereafter the Shebtiw were again placed in the *Place-in-which-the-things-of-all-the-earth-were-filled-with-power*. As a result of all these actions it is said that the primaeval water receded. The outcome of it was that a *place* (*bw*) was planned (*wḏꜥ*), probably by the Shebtiw.[3]

The Sages, the Builder Gods, Seshat and Tekh, then the crew also, approached the lord and a ceremony of acclamation followed. The place (*bw*) was declared to be fashioned (*nḥp*), because the Ka ruled therein (*ḫrp*), the sovereign, his blessed command and the *ḏd*-pillar are enshrined in it.[4] As a consequence of this action the enemy-snake was delivered.

[1] Cf. p. 14.
[2] Cf. E. VI. 183,9 and below, p. 181.
[3] Cf. p. 184.
[4] Cf. pp. 186–7.

Twenty-first section: E. VI. 176,5–9

PLANNING THE MANSION

The protection of the site was then made by Tanen, who seems also to have conducted the lord-god to his final *bw*-place.[1] All this text is very obscure. We suspect that it may contain sacred spells which were believed to provide the 'magic protection' for the site of the mansion before the foundation was laid out.[2]

The next action is the bringing in of a ritual book. It is not certain, however, whether it concerns the rites of protection or the foundation of the temple.

The laying out of the foundation ground of the temple in the *pāy*-land of Djeba, as well as the description of the probable physical appearance of that temple, does not survive in the Edfu records. One can only guess that this presumed mythical temple might have resembled *the Mansion of Wetjeset-Neter*.

[1] Cf. p. 216. [2] Cf. p. 219.

CHAPTER 3

Myth about the Origin of the Temples of the Sun-God

The 3rd, 4th and 5th Edfu cosmogonical records preserve a part of the myth described as the *Coming of Rēᶜ to his Mansion of Ms-nḫt.*[1] This myth concerns another period of the mythical age when the lands of the sacred domains were already in existence, and when the primaeval houses of gods were founded in places other than the original domains of the Falcon. It acquaints us with an entirely different order of ideas and a different conception of the origin of sacred domains from what is known from the first myth.

SECOND RECORD

First section: E. VI. 176,9–11; VI. 328,17–329,2

HINTERLAND OF THE WĀᶜRET

The first scene recorded is placed in the *pḥww wᶜrt*, the *Hinterland of the Wāᶜret*,[2] in which several sacred places or *pāy*-lands were created. These are listed: (1) Island of Fury, (2) Mansion of Shooting, (3) Har-maa, (4) Nebwet, (5) Mansion of Mystery, (6) House of Combat, (7) Tanen-ḥotep, (8) Seat of the Two Gods.[3] A company of gods[4] including the Falcon, Thoth, the Maker-of-Substances, and the Divine of Heart,[5] is said to have wandered through the *Hinterland*. They arrived in a *bw*-place in which they seem to have created their dwelling-place.[6] No description of this

[1] Cf. pp. 10, 245.

[2] *pḥwỉ wᶜrt*; the sole occurrence is in E. VI. 176,9; in this context the meaning is not entirely clear, cf. *Wb.* I, 538; Gardiner, *AEO*, II, 154–5; below, pp. 188–92.

[3] These names are divided between this and the third record in E. VI. 328,17–18. For Har-maa and Tanen-ḥotep, cf. below, p. 192.

[4] 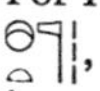, used with the meaning 'company of divine beings'; in our texts this name is used with reference to gods other than the Heliopolitan Ennead and occurs in: E. III. 355,11; IV. 109,10.14; 140,2; V. 167,1; VI. 174,12.14; according to E. VI. 322,2, *psḏt* refers to a company of 30 gods who attended the 'Festival of Entering'.

[5] Cf. pp. 165, 177.

[6] E. VI. 329,2 gives *sꜣḥ r bw* only; for *sꜣḥ* cf. above, p. 26, n. 3.

bw-place in the Hinterland survives in the Edfu text. We do not know whether this *bw*-place means one of the sacred domains listed in the beginning of the narrative or whether it describes another place in that region. Moreover, no allusion is made to the life in this *bw*-place and to the resting-place of the gods which might eventually have been erected there. The text tells us only that after the gods settled down the enemy-snake appeared.

THIRD RECORD

Second section: E. VI. 329,2–330,9

CREATION OF THE MAGIC PROTECTION

When the enemy, the snake *rꜣ*, appeared at the landing stage of that domain, a *bw-tỉtỉ, Place-for-Crushing,*[1] was planned and protective guards of the god were formed. The *Ancestor* (*mꜣ*)[2] settled down there.[3] Thoth and Seshat were present and sanctified[4] the members of the company of the god's guard. An interpretation of a later date tells us that this protecting company were regarded as the *Soldiers* (*mšꜥw*) *of Tanen* whom Tanen called up and sent in the *bw-tỉtỉ, Place-for-Crushing,* because this domain was created at the command of the Earth-Maker.[5]

This company ( *ṯt*)[6] consisted of sixty divine beings divided into four groups (*sꜣ*).[7] Each group was of a different nature and had its own chief. The chief of the first group was a hawk, called *Lord of the Spear.*[8] He was followed by fourteen hawks. The chief of the second group was a lion. He was called *Lord of the Knife*[9] and had fourteen lions in his train. The chief of the third group was a snake, named *Greatly Feared,*[10] and had fourteen snakes

[1] *bw-tỉtỉ* occurs in E. III. 9,9; 33,15; VI. 17,3; 18,2; 329,4.9; 330,6; also below, p. 195.

[2] For *mꜣ*-Ancestor, cf. pp. 235, 254.

[3] *snḏm*, cf. *Wb.* IV, 187 (23); in our text this verb seems to indicate that the god definitely took hold of a primaeval area, cf. below, pp. 196, 254.

[4] 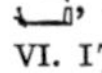, for which we suggest the reading *ḥw*, *to sanctify*, occurs in E. IV. 353,6; VI. 17,14; cf. *Wb.* III, 47.

[5] E. VI. 17,12–13.

[6] *ṯt*, cf. *Wb.* V, 338, but here it applies to the company of Tanen's soldiers, cf. E. III. 33,15; VI. 17,2; 18,9; 329,3.6.9.10.13; 332,1; 332,5.

[7] Further references to this protecting company are to be found in E. III. 8,12–9,16; 32,17–34,4; VI. 14,7; 17,14–18,2; 177,15–179,12; 329,6–330,7; 330,10–332,7.

[8] VI. 14,6; 17,5; 179,1–2; 190,16; 329,11.

[9] E. VI. 14,6; 17,5; 327,12; 331,14; 333,6; 340,9–10.

[10] E. VI. 14,6–7; 17,5; 329,8; 329,16; 331,16.

as his companions. The chief of the fourth group was a bull whose name was *Great Roarer*,[1] and whose group contained fourteen bulls.

The whole company, having been sanctified by Thoth and Seshat, became the protective powers in the *bw-tỉtỉ*.[2] Each group took up a position on one of the sides of the place. The *Place-for-Crushing* resembled a *ỉfdw* of the divine shelter (*nht*) within that domain.[3] The Hawk is said to have taken his position on the south side, the Lion on the north side; on the east was the Snake, and the Bull stood on the west. All of them had their fellows in their train.

When the enemy-snake arrived at the landing stage of the *Wāᶜret*,[4] the *Arm* was worshipped.[5] Then the ritual book of protection of Tanen[6] was given to Horus and a decree[7] against him who is rebellious against his lord was proclaimed by the Falcon, who bears here the title of *the Pre-eminent in the Mansion of Victory*.[8]

Third section: E. VI. 328,7–16

FIGHT AGAINST THE SNAKE

The fight against the snake was led by the Falcon. The text of this part of the record is very obscure, and much damaged. However, it seems that there is an allusion to a fight on the earth in front of the shelter. Another fight took place at the same time in the sky, in which the Falcon was believed to fight against the snake named *sbty*.[9] In both the Falcon while fighting was protected by the *four groups of protectors*.

1 E. VI. 14,8; 17,15; 179,3; 327,12; 329,8; 330,2.

2 E. VI. 330,6 = VI. 18,2; 179,11; 332,2; 6–7.

3 E. VI. 330,6 *nḥr ỉfdw ntr* (?); we wonder if there would be any real construction within the *bw-tỉtỉ* such as a later *ỉfdw*, cf. below, pp. 195, 199; but *ỉfdw* might describe the position the soldiers took while protecting the god and preparing for the fight; similarly E. III. 32,10; VI. 14,7; 17,1; 18,2; 332,1–2.

4 E. VI. 330,8 reads: *rꜣ sꜣḥ ᶜšꜣt wᶜrt. wāᶜret* shows the determinative ⊗, therefore the name must be taken as a name of a primaeval region, in which all the events were believed to have happened; cf. above, p. 13, n. 3.

5 *ᶜ snỉ*; it appears that in this region the same symbol of Creator, as known from the story of the *Wetjeset-Neter*, was present, cf. pp. 24, 24, n. 3.

6 *mḏꜣt* (or *ḥbt* ?) *Ṯnỉ* occurs E. VI. 330,9 and 176,9; the *ntᶜw*, *ritual* of Tanen is mentioned in VI. 14,11; 325,4; cf. below, p. 202 ff., for the tradition concerning protective rites.

7 *wsṯn Ḥr*, cf. E. VI. 330,8 = 18,2–3.

8 For Horus pre-eminent in *ḥwt-ḳnỉ*, cf. pp. 220, 241.

9 Further evidence of this fight is in E. VI. 18,2–5 and VII. 21,12–22,3.

The snake was overthrown and the fighting company settled down beside the snake.[1] The battlefield was purified (*twr*) for Rēᶜ,[2] and he became the lord of that place (*bw*).

This narrative indicates that the site selected by the gods for the foundation of the mansion was the former battlefield. It appears in this myth to be equivalent to the spot given in bequest by the Ka to the Falcon.[3]

FOURTH RECORD

Fourth section: E. VI. 169,8–170,5

SETTLING DOWN IN THE BW-TỈTỈ

The battlefield was purified and Rēᶜ with his company, the Falcon, Tanen, and the creator gods of the temple settled down in the *bw-tỉtỉ*, the *Place-for-Crushing*, together with the *Ancestor* (*mꜣ*).[4] Then the ceremony of laying out the foundation of the outer enclosure (*ỉnb*) of Rēᶜ was made in the presence of the *Eldest of Wetjeset-Neter* (*wr Wṯst-nṯr*),[5] Tanen, the Ogdoad, Rēᶜ and the Shebtiw. The Builder Gods erected the walls of the *ỉfdw*.[6] The text seems to indicate that, before the temple itself was built, the enclosure was constructed from reeds, and this enclosure (*ỉnb*) was 300 by 400 cubits. The interior of it was planned by Thoth and Seshat. The first unit constructed in this enclosure was a sanctuary described as *sḥ*[7] which measured 90 by 20 cubits, and was divided into three rooms. It is strange that in the description of the interior of the enclosure the word *ḥwt-nṯr* was not used.[8]

Subsequently a new ceremony of foundation, the *Stretching of*

[1] *nḏm gs rꜣ*, E. VI. 328,15–16, seems to reveal an important custom of the early ages; the settling down beside the overthrown enemy appears to be the sign of victory and implies a decision to make a permanent settlement.

[2] Cf. E. VI. 169,8 and below, pp. 195, 206 ff.

[3] Cf. pp. 201–4.

[4] We wonder whether the group  in E. VI. 169,10 should not be interpreted as *mꜣ* ⟨*ḥnᶜ* ?⟩ *Ṯnỉ*, because Tanen is generally described as *ḏfn*, cf. below, pp. 40, 235, 297.

[5] Cf. p. 236.

[6] *ỉfdw* occurs only in the descriptions of the Solar Temple, cf. E. VI. 170,2.5.6; 18,8 the *ỉfdw* of Mesen and IV. 353,7 the *ỉfdw* of the Great Seat; similarly VI. 322,16; 325,2; this term is not known from the myth about the Temple of the Falcon. For the various meanings of *ỉfdw*, cf. *JEA*, XXXII, 77–9.

[7] *sḥ* is used in this tradition as the name of the first elementary structure made within an enclosure of reed; cf. E. VI. 170,4; 171,1.4; 172,2.3; 326,5.8; and below, p. 240.

[8] Cf. p. 242.

the Cord, was performed. A large court was planned in front of the *sḥ*-sanctuary. The Builder Gods are said to have erected the *ifdw*, *four sides of the enclosure*. It seems that this building was 90 by 90 cubits, and that probably another wall was constructed around this courtyard at a distance of 10 cubits on both west and east. Thoth designed two sanctuaries (*sḥ*), again measuring 90 by 20 cubits, which stood along the west and east side.[1]

We suspect that this description preserves the picture of a very early sacred enclosure which the tradition regarded as being the place of worship in which the Sun-God was adored first. Nowhere is there definite evidence that this was the first Solar Temple, and nowhere is there any allusion to the *Seat of the First Occasion* of the Sun-God, such as the *Lotus*, or the *Mound*,[2] which would eventually be contained within the enclosure.

Fifth section: E. VI. 170,5–173,3

DESCRIPTION OF THE PRESUMED FIRST SOLAR TEMPLE

The first structure which was made within the outer enclosure was a chapel (*sḥ*) measuring 90 by 20 cubits; it consisted of three rooms. At its front there was erected a large forecourt of 90 by 90 cubits, which was surrounded by an outer wall extending 10 cubits to the west and to the east. Two *sḥ*-sanctuaries were erected along the east and the west side, both measuring 20 by 90 cubits. Then a hypostyle hall of 50 by 30 cubits was constructed at the front of the central room of the first unit, then another hall of 20 by 30 cubits and two consecutive halls, each 45 by 20 cubits, were added at the front of the first hypostyle hall.

Our source seems to discern in the organization of this enclosure, a *sḥ tpy*, *first sanctuary*, of four rooms, which presumably comprised three rooms and a hypostyle hall in front of them. It therefore follows that, in the development of the temple sketched above, there must have been three stages: (*a*) the creation of the *sḥ tpy*; (*b*) the erection of the large forecourt at the front of it with two side *sḥ*-sanctuaries; (*c*) the addition of the other cultus rooms and halls on the axis of the central room of the first *sḥ*. The overall dimensions of this temple were then 90 by 110 cubits.[3]

[1] Cf. p. 240. [2] Cf. p. 207 ff. [3] Cf. p. 243.

After the completion of this initial temple, a second was built at the front of this complex but contiguous to it. There seems to have been constructed at first a hypostyle hall of 30 by 50 cubits at the front of the former complex. Then again a large forecourt was erected measuring 90 by 110 cubits. In this court there seems to have been a row of smaller sanctuaries along the west and east side; finally an outer wall was made extending 15 cubits to the west and to the east of the walls of the forecourt.

These two temples, now described by the term *ḥwt-nṯr*,[1] were surrounded by a wall which formed an enclosure of 110 cubits from east to west and 240 cubits from south to north, and simultaneously created an ambulatory. Since the record also speaks of an original and large enclosure of 400 by 300 cubits, it is evident that the sacred area of the Sun-God was conceived as consisting of two enclosures, one within the other, one of 400 by 300 cubits, and the other of 110 by 240 cubits. Within the smaller, inner enclosure there were constructed the two temples. The following section of the record shows that the description given above is that of a temple in which the Sun-God and Tanen were worshipped jointly.

FIFTH RECORD

Sixth section: E. VI. 320,6–321,5

CONSECRATION OF THE TEMPLE OF THE SUN-GOD

When the construction of this sacred enclosure was completed Rēᶜ and Tanen were told of it by Thoth and Seshat. They arrived[2] with their company of gods. These were the protecting deities, then the Sages, the Builder Gods, the Ogdoad and the Shebtiw. They came near the Enclosure,[3] and Rēᶜ gave a name to it: *Speedy of construction (sỉn nḥp)*.[4]

Afterwards they proceeded to the temple which was constructed in the place where the snake was pierced.[5] Another ceremony of

[1] E. VI. 172,6.

[2] Here again the expression *sȝḥ* ⟨*r*⟩ *bw* (cf. above, p. 33, n. 6) describes the arrival of the gods.

[3] In E. VI. 320,12 as well as in E. VI. 173,1 the outer enclosure is described by *ṯsm-wr*, cf. below, p. 242.

[4] The same name occurs in E. IV. 353,7; there is no authority to explain the meaning of the names given to various parts of the mythical temple.

[5] E. VI. 320,13: *sȝḥ* ⟨*r*⟩ *bw ḥwt-nṯr m st wnp rȝ ỉm*; cf. below, p. 243.

Bestowing names upon the Temple was performed by Tanen,[1] and the name of this joint temple was: *the House-of-Appearance-of-the-Mansion-of-the-Throne.*[2] The same narrative hints also at a connexion between the creation of the temple and a divine being called *the Ka-of-the-Earth.*[3]

This description discloses the essential features of the history of the Solar Temple. It seems that, after the temple was given names by Tanen, there was completed an act resembling the episode of adoration of the temple as an entity. Rēᶜ-Harakhte is described as adoring the temple, the *Great Seat,* and uttering the spell:

O thou place in which Apopis was pierced. As the Ka-of-the-Earth lives for me, I have constructed thee as my House-of-Appearance-in-the-Mansion-of-the-God. I have hidden myself in thee and I have made thee as my Great Seat in the First Sanctuary.[4]

Seventh section: E. VI. 321,6–323,5

FESTIVAL OF ENTERING THE TEMPLE

Unlike the myth about the origin of the Temple of the Falcon, this narrative gives a description of the ceremony which started the life of the temple. It pictures the arrival of the gods in the newly created temple.

The Edfu inscriptions preserve a scene representing a procession of gods which might trace the way of approach to the *Festival of Entering the Temple* as it might have been performed in the early temples.[5] Allusion is made to an episode in which the Earth-Maker was conducted into the presence of Rēᶜ.[6] When the god reached the sanctuary, Ptah-Tanen was believed to utter: 'O, Rēᶜ, enter thy sanctuary. I enter in thy train';[7] the Ogdoad recited spells of adoration and hymns, the ritual of the *Festival of Entering the House of the God.* A procession performed by all the deities who were engaged in the creation of the temple, such as the Shebtiw, the Seven Sages with Thoth and the Seven Builder Gods with Seshat, ended this festival.

[1] E. VI. 321,5 and below, p. 252.
[2] E. VI. 321,1 = 319,4 in E. VI. 319,5 substitutes for *bḥdw* in 319,6; 321,1.2.
[3] E. VI. 321,6 and below, pp. 296–7.
[4] E. VI. 319,4–5 and below, p. 297 ff.
[5] Cf. p. 296 ff.
[6] E. VI. 321,14.
[7] E. VI. 321,16.

Eighth section: E. VI. 323,6–325,5

THE SECOND SOLAR TEMPLE—THE MANSION OF MS-NḪT

The text then proceeds to describe yet another Temple of Rēʿ. In many respects this second Solar Temple is almost identical with the third unit of the first Solar Temple; its overall dimensions, for instance, are the same: 110 by 90 cubits.[1] It differs, however, in the arrangement of its front part, where there was a hall of 15 by 45 cubits, and a second hall, called *sbḫt-mʿrt*,[2] of 45 by 50 cubits.

This temple was given the name *Great Seat* (*st wrt*) by Thoth. Tanen, on the other hand, conferred the name *Mansion of Ms-nḫt*[3] on its chief sanctuary, but the same part of the temple is also referred to as the *Seat-of-the-Two-Gods*.[4] This temple housed Rēʿ and his *Ancestor* (*ḏnf*),[5] who is said to be Tanen, and their *Company of gods* (*psḏt*). The record discloses the belief that Rēʿ himself invited the deities to settle in this mansion, saying:

May the gods settle therein, so said Rēʿ.[6] And the gods settled in the Domain-of-the-Gods.[7]

This account also refers to the *Festival of Entering the Temple*, which, in the main, is identical with that already described. There is one important difference in that the second *Festival of Entering the Temple* is described as including a procession around the temple[8] performed by all the gods before they entered and assumed their rightful places in it. It is evident that, apart from

[1] Cf. p. 37.

[2] *sbḫt-mʿrt* seems to indicate an early primitive solar temple, cf. E. VI. 10,8; 13,13.

[3] *ḥwt-ms-nḫt*, cf. E. IV. 2,1; VI. 8,6; 14,14; IV. 169,13–14; III. 199,10–11; VI. 322,11–12; 324,4–5 and below, p. 245, seems to be the name of the *ḥwyt*, the inner sanctuary. In P. Leiden T 32, II, l. 6, this name describes a place of a funerary nature.

[4] Cf. E. IV. 1,14: 'The Throne-of-gods of the gods of the Early Primaeval Age of the gods' and the 'Seat of the Two Gods of Rēʿ and his Ancestor Tanen'.

[5] Tanen as the *ḏfn*-Ancestor of the temple, cf. pp. 297–9.

[6] E. VI. 324,5: *mj snḏm ntrw im in Rʿ*.

[7] The writing 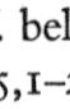 seems to indicate the spelling *nwte* for the classical *ntr*, cf. Coptic **ⲚⲞⲨⲦⲈ**; for the interpretation *niwt* ⟨*n*⟩ *ntrw* can be suggested, cf. below, pp. 246–7.

[8] Cf. E. VI. 325,1–2: *sḳdi Rʿ psḏt.f m-ḫt.f ḥr-m ifdw*.

the lord of the temple, the Sun-God, and the Ancestor God, the Solar Temple was regarded as a real home of all the gods who took part in the origin of the temple and sacred lands.

ADDITIONAL RECORDS: (1) E. VI. 174,11–175,4

ORIGIN OF THE TEMPLE OF MESEN

At the end of the fourth record there is an additional text which refers to the foundation of the *Temple in Mesen*. Here, it may be suggested, is a reference to a mythical temple other than the temples already described. This temple, we are told, was founded in the place where the Falcon dwelt. The Falcon in his primaeval seat, *the Great Seat* (*st-wrt*),[1] was assailed by his enemies, but Rēᶜ, his *Ancestor* Tanen and the Ogdoad came to protect him.[2] After his enemies had been overthrown, these ten gods ordered the *ḥwt-ntr*, the *mansion of the god*, to be built.[3]

Rēᶜ thus summoned Thoth and Seshat, who laid out the foundation. The actual work of building was accomplished by the Builder Gods, and the magical protection (*swr mdw*)[4] of that site was made by the Sages.

(2) E. VI. 173,7–9

Foundation of the Great Seat of Rēᶜ from the Primaeval Time

The Builder Gods, they sped to the Great Seat of Rēᶜ-from-the-Primaeval-Time,[5] his eye expectant at their coming. They constructed the Mesen[6] in a blessed operation (and) by the work of their skilful fingers, on the great foundation ground which *Sefekh-ᶜabwi* planned and which Isden drew up by his (own) fingers according to the command of Rēᶜ and Tanen. The Early Primaeval Deities, being assembled in their train, praised the Sun-God who created the Ka[7] on the First Occasion to the limits of Eternity.

[1] For *st-wrt* as a name of the primaeval seat of the god, cf. Sethe, *Dram. Texte*, p. 47; Lefebvre, *ASAE*, XXIII, 65–7.

[2] E. VI. 174,15: *iy.sn r Msn ḥr ir s3 n k3.f.*

[3] Cf. pp. 250–1.

[4] Cf. p. 290.

[5] The whole expression is to be taken as a name of a primaeval temple, cf. E. I. 70,16; 90,14; II. 33,10; III. 102,14; 107,14; IV. 353,10; 168,10; VI. 241,16; 173,7; VIII. 5,4.

[6] *msn* means here the sanctuary, cf. *Wb.* II, 145.

[7] The Ka of the temple, cf. pp. 296–7.

(3) E. IV. 353,4–8

Arriving in the Great Seat in the presence of their father Tanen and his grandson Horus, the son of their brethren who ordered Their Majesties to construct the mansion of the god in order to alight therein, they placed the cubit of Tekh upon their arms, Seshat (and) the Sages being together with them all. Stretching the cord by Seshat; *Rekh-sw* was sanctifying. These Builder Gods established the *ỉfdw*—four sides—of their enclosure (*ỉnb*) (namely) the enclosure (*ỉnb*) of 300 cubits by 400 cubits, 'Speedy of construction' men call it by name. The sanctuary is within it, 'Great Seat' by name, and all its chapels are according to the norm.

CHAPTER 4

Brief Survey of the Egyptian Sources bearing on the Origin of the Temple

The attempt to interpret the Edfu cosmogonical texts is beset with great difficulties, and in spite of all efforts it is quite evident that much more will have to be done before we can claim to understand the whole narrative and its allusions. Nevertheless, the events sketched in the two preceding chapters reproduce, in all probability, the essential features of the Edfu cosmogonical records.

It seems not unreasonable to claim that these texts confront us with facts and situations that are entirely new. Certain allusions to the origin of the Egyptian temple and to the fact that the Egyptians placed it in primaeval times are already known. The Egyptian temple is frequently equated with the god's *Seat of the First Occasion* (*st n sp tpy*).[1] This *Seat of the First Occasion* was conceived as a place in which the god revealed himself for the first time, and was generally pictured as a mound, sometimes named *ḳꜣy*, sometimes *ḫꜥy*.[2] It would consequently seem that the Egyptians believed that the mound of the primaeval age was the original place of the temple. The records here studied seem to show a very different theory.

Equally familiar is the oft-quoted evidence from the texts of the temple at Philae,[3] in which the temple is described as an entity that existed before everything else.[4] But nowhere are there texts that, in their length and richness, can compare with the Edfu records, which hitherto have been unknown and have not consequently been utilized in previous studies.

The essential significance of the Edfu records is that a historical fact such as the foundation of a temple and its building is projected into a mythological plane.[5] We do not think that this idea

1 Cf. de Buck, *Oerheuvel*, p. 72, and below, p. 82 ff.

2 Cf. *ibid.* p. 35, and below, pp. 59, 126–7, 139.

3 Cf. Junker, *Das Götterdekret über das Abaton*, pp. 32–6.

4 Similarly the Theban Creation Myth, cf. *ASAE*, XLIV, 132.

5 Cf. p. 308, the record concerning the foundation of the Edfu Temple which justifies this statement.

was derived from the doctrine of the Edfu priests. The cosmogonical records would hardly be extracts from sacred books which were special to the temple of Horus at Edfu or were exclusively writings of the Upper Egyptian priests according to local traditions. Doubtless, the title of the sacred book which forms the centre of this study[1] gave a fairly clear idea of the general significance of the Edfu records, and their contents seem to be of such importance as to support our hypothesis. It is most probable that these records in their full version formed part, and only part, of a much wider and more general theory concerning the origin of sacred domains and their temples.

The part of the general theory that survives on the walls of the temple at Edfu makes us familiar with the history of the temples of two gods, the Falcon and the Sun-God. Our exposition showed that the Edfu version of the sacred book consists of a series of short accounts concerned on the one hand with the history of two temples of the Falcon described as the *Temple in Wetjeset-Neter* and the *Temple in Djeba*, and on the other hand with the history of two temples of the Sun-God, which are the *Temple in the Place-for-Piercing* and the *Mansion of Ms-nḫt*. No shred of archaeological evidence for the existence of such temples has come down to us.[2] At Edfu these temples are pictured as the houses of gods in the primaeval age. The descriptions are detailed and their richness permits us to sketch out a coherent picture of the 'primaeval world of gods' which the Egyptians believed to have existed before the physical world of men and from which the temples were derived.

The Edfu records give us all the phases of the growth of these temples. They describe the way in which the land on which the temples were founded was believed to have been created. They explain the subsequent stages in the formation of the sacred places. They give an account of the various stages in the development of these temples from the primitive state of a humble place of worship to the developed *ḥwt-ntr*, *Mansion of the God*. Each of the subsequent phases in the development of these primaeval temples is accompanied with descriptions of mythical events which, from the Egyptian point of view, might have been decisive moments in

[1] Cf. pp. 8–10. [2] Cf. pp. 213 ff., 232 ff.

the course of the primaeval age and which were believed to determine the growth of the temple.

These temples, though they are described as the work of the gods themselves, appear to be conceived as actual, physical entities. The descriptions are so precise and detailed that it is reasonable to suspect that they embody an attempt to describe the history of the growth of such early temples, which are now lost. These records can well be taken not only as a source-book of the history of the Egyptian temple but also as that of the mythological situation which surrounded the origin and proceeded step by step with the growth of the temple. It would, therefore, be of interest to attempt to reconstruct the history of their development, for very little is known about the early sacred places in Egypt in general, and no record is preserved to tell us of the original cultus-places of the Falcon[1] and those of the Sun-God.[2]

The accounts of the development of the domains and temples of the Falcon and those of the Sun-God present several points of similarity, since both the temples appear to be the result of a long period of development, and the place of worship at the beginning of the world does not seem to be of the same type as the temples at the dawn of historical times. On the other hand, however, individual events are not always described in the same way. The ideas that lay behind the story of the origin of the temple of the Falcon appear to have been of an entirely different order from the tradition concerning the creation of the temples of the Sun-God. The biggest difference is that the myth about the origin of the temple of the Falcon gives an explicit picture of the primaeval world in which the temple originated. It seems to emphasize the events which were believed to lead to the foundation of the first temple at the beginning of the world. The second myth, on the contrary, seems to be more concerned with the circumstances surrounding the actual foundation of the temple, and with the description of its gradual development. It is evident that there were two distinct myths about the origin of the temple.[3]

[1] For the cultus-place of Horus, cf. Gardiner, *JEA*, xxx, 23 ff., Junker, *ZÄS*, lxxv, 72 and *Die politische Lehre von Memphis*, p. 70.

[2] In the background of this tradition there are certainly ideas other than the Heliopolitan dogmas, cf. pp. 236–8.

[3] Cf. pp. 28, 31–2, 36–8, 248 ff.

The differences which we have briefly outlined seem to accord with the significance of the titles of the myths to which we have referred in the Introduction. It will be noticed that the name of Horus or the Falcon does not occur in the title of the myth about the origin of the Temple of the Falcon,[1] and yet the origin and the development of the earliest domain of the Falcon is obviously linked with a time-period of the mythical age described in our document as the *time of the Early Primaeval Ones*,[2] and is brought into a close connexion with the domain of the Creator of the Earth.[3] The first Edfu myth would seem, therefore, to preserve, on the one hand, a picture of the *Homeland of the Early Primaeval Ones*[4] which, in its essential nature, was the place of creation; on the other hand, it describes the origin of the cult of the Falcon and the places with their mansions in which the Falcon was worshipped first. This myth is a valuable document which has every appearance of being a history of an Egyptian cult and temple. There is every reason for assuming that this narrative reflects a genuine tradition of a remote date. This circumstance seems to indicate that, according to the theory implicit in our records, the primaeval domains of the Falcon and his temple were regarded as being the original sacred places of Egypt.[5]

It has been seen on several occasions in the study of the Edfu texts how closely the creation, particularly the creation of the Earth, is associated with the interpretation of the origin of the sacred domains of the Falcon. This fact would seem to hint at the existence of an aetiological myth concerning the origin of the Earth as a pre-requisite for the foundation of the sacred domains and their temples. This myth would, accordingly, have been modified and adapted to suit the local traditions. Therefore, it is suggested that the history of the origin of the primaeval domains of the Falcon discloses, in part at least, what was once the contents of the *Sacred Book of the Early Primaeval Age of Gods* (*bȝw-Rᶜ n pȝwtyw tpyw*).[6]

The second Edfu myth bears the title *The Coming of Rēᶜ to his*

[1] Cf. p. 10.

[2] *pȝwt tpt* might have been used as a technical term for the period in which the actual land for the sacred domains was believed to have been created.

[3] Cf. p. 214.

[4] Cf. p. 75 ff.

[5] Cf. p. 258.

[6] Cf. p. 134 ff.

Mansion of Ms-nḫt.[1] The idea of the 'coming' of the god to his house is stressed and is one of the characteristics of this myth. It describes, in all probability, a later stage in the development of the temple. It has been noticed that the description of the early part of the history of the solar domains does not occur in the narrative at all. There is no allusion and no claim to explain how the primaeval domain of the Sun-God was created, nor do we find in the main sources any reference to the primaeval pool of the Sun-God from which he and his domain would emerge. This myth would seem, therefore, to record the third period in the history of the 'mythical' temples in general, when other gods began to appear in the lands of the sacred domains originally occupied by the Falcon and his companions, and temples were founded for them.

There appears to be a clear distinction between the interpretation of the origin of the sacred domains and that of the temples. There seem to have been two theories of the origin of sacred domains, and consequently two theories of the origin of the temples that were later erected on them. The 'mythical' temples seem to have been conceived as a later creation, and sometimes at least as having been created on lands originally associated with different gods. From all the evidence available one important fact seems to emerge: the origin of the sacred domain was conceived as a definite act of creation of the Earth which resulted in the origin of the temple.

There are good reasons, therefore, for assuming that the *Sacred Book of the Early Primaeval Age of the Gods* was the original writing concerned with the interpretation of the creation of sacred places. We imagine that this book enshrined the genuine expression of Egyptian knowledge on the origin of sacred places in general, a theory which included the explanation of how the first temple came into being. The trends of thought and traditions included in this book might have been the starting-point in writing much expanded books about the origin of sacred domains at a somewhat later date; each new myth which was added brought to it new traditions and pictures of a somewhat later and more advanced stage in the development of the sacred places and their temples. We can refer here to another sacred book concerned with the

[1] Cf. p. 40.

history of the Egyptian temples, the existence of which is also revealed by the Edfu inscriptions, i.e. the *bꜣw-Rꜥ n gs-prw, the Sacred Book of the Temples.*[1]

This brief survey of ideas enshrined in the main documents of our study shows that in Egypt the explanation of the origin of the sacred places in which the gods were first worshipped, as well as the subsequent development of such places, was a subject not only of vivid interest but also of deep speculation. There is certainly, in the Edfu texts, much more than mere myth. Considering the manner in which the two Edfu myths were recorded, we incline to the opinion that these records embody a history of sacred places and temples that shows a conceptual and philosophical aspect. This brings to mind the belief in the 'words' of the Sages. This belief is new and valuable, but unknown to the major part of Egyptian cosmogony, for from the Edfu sources only can we learn that the Sages of the mythical age were believed to be the only divine beings who knew how the temples and sacred places were created.

In addition to the cosmogonical records of the temple at Edfu, there are a number of other mythological texts which are concerned with the origin of the sacred places and temples. They are written in a very concise form, being sometimes reduced to mere epithets, and in all probability are derived from records of much earlier date. This would confirm our hypothesis that the manner of writing the mythological history of the temple was not limited to the temple of Edfu, but was rather a general one; doubtless, the Edfu Temple presents us with the most extensive documents of this kind.

The earliest evidence known of such a record is to be found in the text of a stela discovered at Hermopolis, dating from the reign of Nectanebo II.[2] The Hermopolitan temple is there equated with the primaeval dwelling-place of the Ogdoad, and the actual temple is interpreted as its renewal.[3]

Several allusions to the original site of a temple occur in the inscriptions of the Tomb of Petosiris. The temple of Rēꜥ was

[1] Cf. p. 6.

[2] See Roeder, 'Zwei hieroglyphische Inschriften aus Hermopolis', *ASAE*, LII, 384 ff.

[3] See *ibid.* p. 403, ll. 22–4; p. 409, l. 28; p. 413, l. 32.

believed to have been founded in a pool in which Rēꜥ was born, and which was the place of creation in general.[1]

Other references to the creation of sacred domains are to be found in the inscriptions of the Temple of Khonsu at Karnak. These inscriptions are not continuous narratives like the Edfu texts. They seem to be only extracts from cosmogonical records kept in that temple. These extracts, however, make it possible to adumbrate the Karnak theory on the origin of the temple. Mention is made of a land which emerged from Nun before the 'High Hill', and which was the birth-place of the Earth-Maker. The 'High Hill' was created before the *pāy*-land emerged,[2] and before sky, earth and underworld had come into existence. Another passage refers to the creation of the *ḫꜥy*-mound which existed earlier than the *sꜣ ṯꜣw*-ground upon which the domains (*nỉwt*) of the gods were founded.[3]

A rather more continuous and connected narrative is to be found on the jamb of the main door in the second pylon at Karnak.[4] It is obviously an abbreviated version of a myth of creation interpreting the origin of Thebes. The sacred land of Thebes is described as the god's *Primaeval Domain* (*st-ḏr-ꜥ*) which emerged from Nun and on which further actions of creation took place. The *ḫꜥy*-mound was created, then the *sꜣ ṯꜣw*-ground, finally the god's domain (*nỉwt*).[5] In the second part of this record the primaeval site of the Theban Temple is described by a series of epithets. On the whole they show ideas and hint at some mythological events similar to those contained in the Edfu cosmogonical records.

Much shorter evidence of a myth of creation is to be found in the inscriptions of the temple of Opet.[6] The relationship of the temple with the primaeval mythical time is expressed in a form of

[1] See Lefebvre, *Le tombeau de Pétosiris*, no. 61, ll. 14, 18, 19–20; no. 62, ll. 4–5; no. 81, ll. 47–8; no. 82, ll. 96–7; no. 126, ll. 3–4.

[2] Cf. p. 139.

[3] *Urk.* VIII, 34, 2–6; 89, 5–8; 92, 11–22; 93, 1–7; 94, 1–18.

[4] *Urk.* VIII, 114, 14–116, 19 = Drioton, '*Les dédicaces* de Ptolémée Évergète II sur le deuxième pylône de Karnak', *ASAE*, XLIV, 111 ff.

[5] Cf. Sethe, *Amun*, Pl. II, l. 17, *tꜣ ḳꜣy*, 'elevated land in Nun is the domain (*nỉwt*) of the god'.

[6] de Wit, *Les inscriptions du temple d'Opet à Karnak*, *Bibliotheca Aegyptiaca*, XI, 125.

epithets according to which the temple is the Seat of the Earth-Maker, the place from which the sky was uplifted, the place of the All Creator, the Sky of the Soul, the Underworld of the Mummy, the place in which everything was created at the Beginning, the Palace of the Primaeval Ones, the *hyn*-Homeland of the Ogdoad, the Great Primaeval Mound of the King of the Gods who created that which exists. From this description of the nature of the temple it is obvious that this series of epithets also must have been based on a prototype similar to the Edfu texts.

The sources cited prove that there are solid grounds for considering that the Edfu records embody a theory on the origin of the temple which was, in part at least, of general application.

In the temple of Denderah, on the contrary, very few details about the mythical past of the temple can be gleaned. In one of the *Building Texts* it is said that the site of the temple was the place in which the god issued from the lotus, that it is the province of him who created Rēᶜ.[1] The historical temple was believed to have been built on the foundation ground of the primaeval age in which the god was born.[2] In the main, however, we find repeatedly the common idea that the historical temple was the work of Ptah, the Builder Gods, and was constructed according to the regulations given by Thoth.[3]

Reference should also be made to the creation myth preserved in the temple at Esnah[4] and in that at El-Hibeh.[5] Both of them show a much modified conception of the drama of creation from which the temple resulted, and an order of ideas different from that of the Edfu cosmogonical records. The origin of the sacred places is not described in such detail as it is in our main Edfu sources.

On the other hand, there can be quoted instances of a basically different theory on the origin of the sacred places. There are a number of texts in which the idea of creation which prevails in the Edfu records and in the texts mentioned above, does not occur at all, but instead, the place on which the divine abode originated is

1 C.D. I, 90, 9. 2 C.D. II, 108, 5.

3 C.D. I, 31, 7–8; II, 4, 5; III, 9, 1–2. 8. 9; IV, 8, 11; 9, 11.

4 Daressy, 'Hymne à Khnoum du Temple d'Esneh', *RT*, XXVII, 83–93, 187–93; Sauneron, *Quatre campagnes à Esna*, p. 55.

5 Brugsch, *Thesaurus*, pp. 633–5.

said to have been a mound (*iꜣt*). This mound is described as the place in which the god found refuge during his fight against his enemies and which later developed into a constructed place of worship. This view is predominant in the *Myth of Horus*,[1] and is also expressed in the *Legend about the fight of Horus against Seth*.[2] We find the same idea in the text dealing with the origin of the temple at Kom Ombo.[3]

It is significant that in all these narratives the chief deity is Rēʿ. We suspect that this theory on the origin of sacred places is closely connected with the solar cult, and therefore reflects Heliopolitan views on the origin of the sacred domains. It should also be pointed out that these narratives do not describe all the phases of the development as found in the Edfu cosmogonical records. There is no allusion to the way in which these mounds (*iꜣwt*) were fashioned. The myths start at the moment when the gods already lived within these mounds. These are not, then, original descriptions of the creation of the sacred places, but secondary interpretations.[4] Except for the *Myth of Horus*, which refers to the arrival of Rēʿ at *Wetjeset-Hor* and to a battle with the enemies after which the Djeba was founded,[5] there is no identity between the places which evolved within the mounds (*iꜣwt*) and the sacred places named in the Edfu cosmogonical records.

We may add the evidence gathered in the inscriptions of the temple at Medamud. This temple is said to be the 'mound' (*iꜣt*) which is the place (*bw*) at which Rēʿ arrived.[6] The explanation follows that Rēʿ came to that place while invoking the Ancestors, and thus renewed the place in which they created him.[7]

There are obvious affinities between the texts at Karnak and in the Tomb of Petosiris and the Edfu records, all of which stress the connexion with the creation. None of them, however, is a continuous narrative, nor do they present a complete myth concerning the origin of sacred places and the temples, in which divine

1 E. VI. 113,2; 114,8; 115,1.8; 118,3.7; 199,8; 120,2–3.5; 121,4.8.10.12; 124,6.
2 E. VI. 134,4; 135,5.
3 *KO*, I, 148, no. 194; p. 332, no. 449; II, 67, no. 613.
4 Cf. p. 232 ff.
5 E. VI. 111,8–9; 112,5–6.
6 *Médamoud*, Rapp. Prélim. III, Inscr. 1926, p. 16, no. 14.
7 *Ibid.* p. 44, no. 98.

beings acted as creators of this world, of the sacred places, and finally of the temple itself. Only at Edfu do we find a reasonably complete and logical account. It would not be unjustified, therefore, to claim that the fact attests the originality of the cosmogonical records of the temple at Edfu and that it also confirms their general significance. Hence the Edfu records can be confidently taken as the main source for an attempt to reconstruct the Egyptian theory of how a temple came to be. This attempt takes us back to the dawn of time when the world was still in darkness.

PART II

The Primaeval World of the Gods

CHAPTER 5

The Island of Creation

The Edfu cosmogonical records begin with a picture of the primaeval island where the gods were believed to have lived first. The way in which this world is described in the Edfu texts is, at present, unique and no other similar series of texts is known. Some account of the aspect of this island has already been given in our *summaries*.[1] It is, however, essential to repeat here the main features of the description preserved in our Edfu texts.

The primaeval world of the gods is represented by an *iw*, *island*, which, in part, was covered with reeds and stood in darkness in the midst of the primaeval water (*ḥbbt*) which in this tradition bears the name *wāᶜret*.[2] Although none of the names of the island, such as *Island of Trampling*, *Island of Combat* and *Island of Peace*, shows any connexion with the idea of 'creation', it is certain that this island was the piece of land where the creation of the world began, and the earliest mansions of the gods were founded.[3]

The origin of this island, however, is not described in our principal sources. The beginning of the first cosmogonical record seems to allude to a period of the primaeval age in which the island was in existence, and was occupied by some divine beings.[4] There is nowhere in the main Edfu cosmogonical records any statement or allusion which would permit us to say how the Egyptians imagined that the Earth or the actual land of the island was created. The creative activity which had undoubtedly a prominent part in the period of creation with which the Edfu texts are concerned is described as *sw iḫt tꜣ*, *to endue with power the substances of the Earth*.[5] This does not seem to deal with the initial creation of the Earth, or specifically with the origin of the island; but as has been explained

[1] E. VI. 181,11–16, cf. above, pp. 12–13; also below, pp. 108–9.

[2] E. VI. 181,11–12; for the *wāᶜret*, cf. above, p. 13, n. 4, and below, p. 188; for the reeds cf. E. VI. 181,14.16; E. VI. 141,14 suggests that *wāᶜret* was the name of this region, and that the events our myth is concerned with came to pass in its *gs ḫnty*, *the front marginal land*; cf. also the Hymn to Sobek (*Kêmi*, I, 149), where allusion is made to the *wāᶜret* of the Sacred Mound (*iꜣt*).

[3] Cf. p. 89 ff.	[4] Cf. p. 94 ff.	[5] Cf. p. 161 ff.

in a separate study,[1] this creative activity appears to be concerned only with the origin of lands of special nature and significance. These lands then seem to represent the second period in the development of the primaeval world of gods, as will be explained in greater detail below.[2]

To describe the Egyptian theory concerning the origin of the Earth (*tꜣ*), and the earliest configuration of the Earth, is a task which meets with difficulties. The question of the origin of the island mentioned in our sources, however, seems to be so important as to attempt to outline the Egyptian views on the beginnings of the terrestrial world.

Naturally, there are frequent allusions to the creation of the world in the Egyptian religious texts, but these are all rather stereotyped, and yield only marginal thoughts of the Egyptian cosmogony.[3] Another difficulty is the state of the sources. The general state of the extant sources of Egyptian cosmogony can rightly be described as *disiecta membra* of what might once have been a complete cosmogonical doctrine. Scarcely do we come across texts which give a connected account of the successive phases of creation or such texts as make it possible to reconstruct a rounded picture of the initial period in the existence of this world. Many of the cosmogonical documents are compositions written in a rather literary form either on some deliberately chosen doctrinal themes or on some favourite mythological events. These, then, seem to aim at boasting the merits which the local god was believed to have had in the creation of the world. In this respect reference can be made to the three texts surviving from the Memphite doctrine of creation, such as the text preserved in the Stone of Shabaka,[4] the hymn to Ptah in P. Berlin 3048[5] or a frag-

[1] Cf. my article in *ZÄS*, LXXXVII, 43–4, specially comm. n. (*f*).

[2] Cf. p. 169.

[3] A selected number of Egyptian cosmogonical texts are to be found in *Sources orientales*, I, *La naissance du monde*, pp. 45–78; cf. also Morenz, *Die ägyptische Religion*, pp. 167–91, giving an interesting survey of various doctrinal views on the origin of the world; cf. also Müller, *Egyptian Mythology*, p. 69 ff., and Roeder, *Urkunden der ägyptischen Religion*.

[4] Cf. Sethe, 'Denkmäler der memphitischen Theologie', *Untersuchungen*, X, 46 ff.; Junker, 'Die Götterlehre von Memphis', *APAW* (1939); Sandman, *The God Ptah*, pp. 19–22; Morenz, *Religion*, pp. 168–9.

[5] Cf. Wolf, 'Der Berliner Ptah-Hymnus', *ZÄS*, LXIV, 17 ff.

ment of the 'Memphite philosophy' known from P. dem. Berlin 13603.[1] These three documents present a somewhat generalized verbal picture of the creation of the world. But they are merely arbitrary compilations of traditions claiming a prominent role for Ptah in the creation of the world. The text of the Shabaka Stone gives a survey of Egyptian thoughts on the creation, but does not present an adequate picture of the elementary creation.[2] Although emphasis is laid on the idea that the Creator was an Earth-God from whom the world and all existing beings evolved,[3] the process of creation interpreted does not, in fact, involve the creation of the Earth (*tȝ*) itself, nor is there any allusion to what was believed to have been the elementary form of the Earth. The text tells us only that after the Creator had brought the world into existence in general by virtue of his 'thought and word', he then created the sacred domains and placed the gods in them.[4]

The same order of ideas is reflected in P. Berlin 3048. Ptah, the Earth-God, is the eldest of the primaeval deities. He is the *Mesenty*, the lord of begetting who created that which exists.[5]

P. dem. Berlin 13603 also shows signs of being a dogmatic composition. Although the existence of the world is interpreted as the work of Ptah, who is the *ȝgrty*-Earth-God,[6] the document deliberately combines Heliopolitan and Hermopolitan views on the creation of the world. It is stated that the Earth and its divine inhabitants were created before Phrē was born,[7] but it is obvious that Heliopolis was regarded as the centre of the creation. The primordial aspect of Heliopolis is not described; however, there is a clear allusion to the theory according to which Heliopolis existed before the Earth (*tȝ*) was created. From the primaeval Heliopolis, so it is explained in our text, the Earth-God created the Earth (*tȝ*), which received the name *Mn-nfr*, *Memphis*; thereafter he proceeded to create living beings, in the first place the gods.[8] This

[1] Cf. Erichsen and Schott, 'Fragmente memphitischer Theologie in demotischer Schrift'.

[2] Junker, 'Die Götterglaube', *APAW* (1939), p. 59.

[3] Cf. *ibid.* pp. 63, 75; Gardiner, *PSBA*, XXXVIII, 43 ff.; Sandman, *The God Ptah*, pp. 56–63; P. Berlin 13603, II, 2–21.

[4] Junker, op. cit. p. 65.

[5] P. Berlin 3048, III, 2, cf. *ZÄS*, LXIV, 18; for *Mesenty* see below, p. 76.

[6] P. Berlin 13603, II, 8.

[7] P. Berlin 13603, II, 19.

[8] P. Berlin 13603, I, 21; II, 27.

document does not permit us to gain any fair idea of how the Earth-God was believed to proceed in the creation of the Earth itself, nor is there any allusion to the appearance of the earliest terrestrial world in which the gods were believed to have first lived.

On the other hand, an account of creation which is incorporated in P. Bremner-Rhind[1] explains that when the creator came into being as Khopri on the First Occasion, the existent things came into being. Then he made the 'Primaeval time' and the 'Primaeval Ones'. This document seems to be concerned in particular with the origin of *ḫpr*, *being* and *coming into existence*, which was the work of the Sole Unique God. Here again, however, nothing is said of the creation of the terrestrial world. On the contrary, P. Berlin 3047[2] tells us that the Creator, after he had revealed himself, created in the first place the *sꜣṯꜣw*, *ground*, to settle upon it on the *First Occasion of his coming into being*. The Earth (*tꜣ*) was then created and everything was brought into existence. Combining the view contained in P. Bremner-Rhind with that of P. Berlin 3047, we may suggest that the Egyptians believed that after *being* (*ḫpr*) in general was brought into existence, the creator fashioned for himself a dwelling-place in the midst of Nun, which in this tradition is described as *sꜣṯꜣw*, and that from such a ground he created the world. The same idea occurs in the creation myth which is preserved in the texts covering the second pylon of the temple at Karnak.[3] This myth refers to the *original place* (*st-ḏr-ꜥ*) of the creator which is said to have emerged from Nun, and on which the creator settled in order to create the world.[4]

None of the texts mentioned, however, alludes to the process of the creation itself; none describes the fashioning of the *sꜣṯꜣw*, *ground*, and its physical appearance. It looks as though the Egyptians were interested to record only the results of the creation; the interpretation of the causes of the creation does not seem to have been the real interest of their cosmological speculation.

It may, very tentatively, be suggested that the elementary aspect

[1] P. Bremner-Rhind 28, ll. 20–1 = Faulkner, 'The Papyrus Bremner-Rhind', *Bibl. Aeg.* III, 69–70 = *JEA*, XXIV, 41 ff.

[2] P. Berlin 3047, II, 7 = *Hieratische Papyri Berlin* II = de Buck, *Oerheuvel*, p. 11.

[3] *Urk.* VIII, 114, 14–116, 19 = Drioton, *ASAE*, XLIV, 111–55.

[4] Cf. *ibid.* pp. 112–20.

of this primaeval *ground* for the creation of the world might, perhaps, have been conceived as a *mound* which emerged from the primaeval waters, and assumed the function of the resting-place of the creator of the world.[1] This view can be supported by the Heliopolitan version of the myth of creation which was formulated probably about the time of the Vth dynasty, and which can, in part, be reconstructed from the Pyramid texts. The Earth in its earliest shape was pictured as a mound which emerged from the primaeval water.[2] This mound itself was then considered as a divine being,[3] and as the original terrestrial configuration on which the creator, Atum, dwelt, and from which he created the Four Elements represented as tangible divine beings.[4] Closely related ideas are also reflected in the Hermopolitan doctrine of creation, in which the elementary terrestrial world is described as a mound upon which the Sun-God revealed himself.[5] From all this evidence we can conclude that the *primaeval mound*, sometimes named *ḳ3y*, sometimes *ḫʿy*,[6] was indeed regarded as the original nucleus of the world of the gods in the primaeval age, from which this world was created.[7] The way, however, in which the mound was fashioned, is never stated in the sources. It would consequently seem that, as has already been pointed out,[8] the Egyptians conceived the origin of the Earth as a mere emerging of the land from the primaeval water, and that they believed that the appearance of the Earth was caused by the revelation of the Creator. The Egyptian cosmogony, then, as far as it can be judged from evidence that is Heliopolitan or partly Hermopolitan in origin, would seem to contain neither an interpretation of the causes, a description of the natural forces concurring in the creation of the Earth, nor any adequate account

[1] Cf. de Buck, *Oerheuvel*, p. 16; Grapow, *BD*, ch. 19, pp. 37–8.

[2] Pyr. 627, 640, 645, 648, 1587, 1652; de Buck, *Oerheuvel*, pp. 23–34; Kees, *Götterglaube*, pp. 215–18.

[3] Pyr. 1587, 1652.

[4] Pyr. 1521*a*, 1546*a*; Kees, *Götterglaube*, pp. 215 ff.; Morenz, *Religion*, pp. 170–2.

[5] Cf. de Buck, *Oerheuvel*, pp. 35–42; Kees, *Götterglaube*, pp. 305 ff.; Morenz, *Religion*, pp. 186–9.

[6] de Buck, *Oerheuvel*, pp. 35, 43–8, 63.

[7] Cf. p. 69; here once more reference can be made to the Karnak Myth of Creation, cf. Sethe, *Amun*, Pl. II, l. 2, in which the first terrestrial configuration is described as the *t3 ḳ3y*, the *High Earth* in Nun.

[8] Cf. de Buck, *Oerheuvel*, pp. 10–22, mainly p. 13, and below, pp. 160–1.

of the appearance of the primaeval world in which the gods were believed to have first lived.

The analysis of the main Edfu cosmogonical records, however, seems to show ideas of the creation and of the primaeval age which are unlike the generally known theory, a fact also suggested by the mythological situation described at the beginning of the first Edfu cosmogonical record. It is, therefore, important to mention here certain allusions to mythical events which we can glean from Edfu inscriptions other than the main sources of our study. They seem to throw more light on the initial period of the primaeval world of gods, and on the mythological circumstances with which our creation story begins.

We know from the Edfu texts that the Egyptians believed that the Earth-Maker (*ỉr-tꜣ*) created the grounds for the domains of the gods (*nỉwt*), but exactly how he did so is never stated. In the summary of the *Myth about the origin of the Temple of the Sun-God*, we come across a statement to the effect that the God's domain (*nỉwt*) was created by virtue of *the word of the Earth-Maker*.[1] Since this view, however, is not contained in the main sources, and the Earth-Maker, though mentioned there,[2] takes part neither in the process of the creation of the Earth, nor in the origin of the grounds for the divine domains,[3] it would, consequently, appear to be a derivative conception of a later date.

A somewhat similar view on the origin of the earth occurs in the text of a scene of *Presenting libation and incense*, to be found among the inscriptions on the walls of the Forecourt of the Edfu Temple.[4] The god-beneficiary is, of course, Horus the Behdetite. He is equated with Tanen, and is described as the god

who created that which exists, father of the fathers, who created gods and men, the unique one without peer.[5]

He is said to be the

ꜥḥꜥ-snake who created the Primaeval Ones, the august sakhem[. . .]who uplifted the sky, even the *ḥt*-sky, for its disk, who created the Earth (*tꜣ*)

[1] E. VI. 17,13: *ỉr nỉwt nbwỉ m ḏdw.n 'Ir-tꜣ*; similarly E. V. 68,7; 253,6; the Earth-Maker is said to have uplifted the sky and founded (*smn*) the earth (*tꜣ*); in the second instance he is also called *Mesenty*, cf. below, pp. 62, 76–7, and above, p. 57.

[2] E. VI. 183,9; cf. above, pp. 22–3.

[3] Cf. p. 147 ff.

[4] E. V. 156,8–157,4.

[5] Similarly E. IV. 21,11–12; 14–15.

for him who issued from him, who first came into being when no existing being had yet come into being.

This quotation seems to reveal a tradition according to which the first creative power, represented eventually as a snake, was believed to be the Earth-God.[1] But surprisingly the origin of the Earth comes last in this order of creation. The text indicates the reason for which the Earth was created: the Earth-God created it for his intimate offspring, his successor in the rulership over the mythical world.[2] But here again, nothing is said of the process through which the Earth, as a substance, was believed to have been brought into existence, and nothing is mentioned about the primal shape of the Earth upon which the successor of the Earth-God was to dwell.

In connexion with this tradition, it is appropriate to mention here that in the Edfu inscriptions a deity called the *First Primaeval One* (*pꜣwty tpy*) is twice equated with the *Great Lotus* (*nḫb wr*) and is said to have been

he who caused the Earth to be when he had come into existence in the past, the Sole Unique One without peer, who was first to fashion the Earth upon his (potter's) wheel, who created men, gave birth to the gods, Lord of the Universe, Ruler of the Primaeval Ones, the First Primaeval One who came into being before the Primaeval Ones.[3]

The idea of fashioning the Earth on the potter's wheel is foreign to the ideological background of the main Edfu records.[4] The creators of the Earth acting in our creation story[5] are never said to be the *pꜣwtyw tpyw*, *Primaeval Ones*, and there is no allusion to the fact that they were believed to participate in the creation of gods and other animate beings; it is likely that these statements also belong to the speculative theory of a later date. But one cannot deny that such views on creation as are known from the theory of the late period might be useful in tracing the development of the

[1] Cf. pp. 57, 63–5; the first creative power, there, was the creator of substance.

[2] For this tradition cf. p. 179.

[3] E. III. 42,14 = III. 116,5–6; for the idea of the unique Creator called *pꜣwty tpy*, cf. Sethe, *Amun*, p. 82–4.

[4] Cf. pp. 137, 161.

[5] Cf. p. 119.

ideas of the original creative powers who fashioned the elementary shape of the world of gods.

We have seen that there is nowhere preserved a doctrinal document either of an earlier or later date which gives a full account of how the Earth-Maker (*ỉr-tꜣ*) was believed to have proceeded in bringing the Earth into existence. All the evidence known from the temple inscriptions is short texts telling us that the Earth-Maker was the divine being who existed before the world and all other gods,[1] and that he was the initiator of the existence of the world. The name *ỉr-tꜣ*, however, appears to be somewhat arbitrary. We may hazard a guess that the Egyptians might have believed that the Earth, as a substance, was created by a nameless and undefined power. This power then, in the course of historical times, might have been imagined as a tangible deity. It may be surmised that, perhaps, the Heliopolitan doctrine concerning Atum was based on such an idea, and that, on the other hand, in a tradition which originated in another place, the same power was simply called *ỉr-tꜣ*, because the Earth was regarded as the essential outcome of his creative capacity.

Nevertheless, the mention of the *First Primaeval One* in the text cited above is a clear allusion to the belief in an unspecified power that created the Earth. It brings to mind yet another view of the creation of the Earth which is contained in the formula that accompanies a scene of *Offering the Lotus*, engraved on the outer wall of the Naos of the Edfu Temple.[2] This ritual scene concerns the adoration of the primaeval deities (*pꜣwtyw*) who are said to be the

> gods who first came into being at the beginning, and all the beings came into existence after they had come into being.[3]

The text accompanying this ritual scene appears to preserve an aspect of Egyptian cosmogonical thought that is of interest and

[1] For the *'Ir-tꜣ*, the *Earth-Maker*, cf. Sethe, *Amun*, pp. 26–7, 57–9; Junker, 'Götterglaube', p. 38; E. II. 37,8; IV. 21,15; V. 68,17; 321,1; VI. 174,13; 183,9; 321,15; *KO*, I, 89, no. 108; *Médamoud*, 1925, no. 117, 1.2; no. 257, 1.11; *Opet*, pp. 122, 189, 196; *Urk.* VIII, 11, 7–8; 54, 7–8; 92, 19; *ZÄS*, LXII, 94; LXVII, 54; Sobek is equated with the Ka of the *wr*-god and his great image is the Earth-Maker who created Nun as his creation. He is the Great God who issues from the Mound every day. In *BD*, ch. 17, the Primaeval Power is the Great God who is the Water.

[2] E. IV. 139,11–141,11 = X, Pl. LXXXV.

[3] E. IV. 140,2–3; 226,1; 296,1.

importance, but for which, at present, no parallel can be quoted. The words of invocation to these creative powers read:

Take to yourselves the lotus (*nḫb*) which came into being at the beginning and which drives away the storm cloud even though it knows it not. You placed your seed into the *bnnt* which you fertilized with your phallus (*wbꜣ iwꜥw*), which you have plunged in Nun, being united as one. May your heir shine in the capacity of the Stripling.[1]

This text seems to imply a belief in the existence of a group of nameless deities who existed before the origin of the world, and who were believed to act as a single creating power. Here, and in some other Edfu texts, these powers are described as *pꜣwtyw*, the *Primaeval Ones*.[2] The general definition of their nature as having existed before everything else shows close affinities with the descriptions of the Earth-God, the *ir-tꜣ*, who is frequently, in the Edfu texts, and in some other late sources, equated with Tanen.[3] If we agree that in these definitions there is rendered the Egyptian thought of how they conceived the nature of the creator (or creators) who produced the first and fundamental substance for the existence of the world—the Earth—it would mean that the text accompanying the scene of *Offering the Lotus*, translated above, introduces us to the creators of the Earth, and reveals the original Egyptian conception of the nature of such a power.[4] Since these deities were believed to act as a single creative power, it is not surprising that on the basis of such a belief the theory of the sole unique Creator was elaborated in course of time. This sole Creator might have then received varying names as might have been dictated by local traditions and beliefs. This secondary theory might in fact have prevailed, and thus we may venture to say that in the speculation of the historic period the *ir-tꜣ*, the *Maker of the Earth*, replaced the original creative powers (the *pꜣwtyw*). If this deduc-

[1] E. IV. 139,11–15.

[2] Cf. Sethe, *Amun*, pp. 46, 82–6; E. III. 42,15; 312,2–9; IV. 109,14; 140,2; 266,6–7; V. 85,2–3; VI. 173,9; 174,11.12.14; 175,8; 179,8; 183,15; 186,8; 320,4; 325,3; 339,2; *Urk.* VIII, 75, 15.

[3] For Tanen cf. p. 290 ff; E. I. 85,5; II. 37,9–10; 57,4; III. 7,11; 8,6; 231,10–11; 312,6; IV. 353,4; 390,15; V. 8,10–9,1; 68,15–17; VI. 14,12; 15,3; 173,7; 181,3; 183,3.8.9; 184,2.5; 319,9; 324,5; C.D. V, 44, 11; P. Berlin 3048, 4.7; Sethe, *Dram. Texte*, pp. 33–4; Junker, *Die politische Lehre von Memphis*, p. 21 ff.

[4] Cf. pp. 64, 273 ff.

tion be accepted, we may say, with all due reserve, that the Edfu text translated above shows that the first supernatural power to open the drama of creation was conceived in the Egyptian cosmogony as a multitude of nameless divine beings.

A further deduction that can be made from this Edfu text is that the first act of creation which the original powers were believed to have completed would seem to be the fertilization of the *bnnt*. It is nowhere stated what exactly this *bnnt* was, and evidence is scanty. We can add from the Edfu inscriptions that it was believed that everything was brought out from the *bnnt* by agency of the *seed of Nun* (*mtwt n Nwn*), which, in this tradition, is pictured as the lotus (*nḫb*).[1] Another allusion to the *bnnt* occurs in the Theban Myth of Creation preserved in the Temple of Khonsu at Karnak. It is said of the *bnnt*:

It is the place in the Nun that (? in which? was) fashioned the *bnnt* on the First Occasion.[2]

The word *bnnt*, therefore, would seem to have been used in the Egyptian cosmogony to describe a definite place within Nun in which a specific substance was formed by a process of creation which is not interpreted. This substance may also be called *bnnt* after the place in which it became solid matter. The *bnnt* seems to describe the place in which the mystic union between the *Primaeval Ones* (*pꜣwtyw*) and Nun occurred, as well as the specific matter which filled that place but which was inert. The latter, after having been fertilized, assumed creative powers and was capable of producing other substances. Since *swḥt*, *egg*,[3] in the Edfu text, is not employed in connexion with the process of the creation

[1] E. VI. 16,5–6; the text reads: 'When the bud of the lotus grew verdant, even the seed of Nun that uplifted everything from the *bnnt*.'

[2] Cf. Sethe, *Amun*, Pl. II, l. 5 and pp. 118–19; *Wb.* I, 460(5) does not define the meaning of *bnnt*. The meaning of this text is not entirely clear; it is possible that this definition refers to Amon equated with the *Soul* of the *Kmꜣt.f*; then an alternative reading may be suggested: 'He is the *bnnt* in Nun who fashioned the *bnnt* on the First Occasion.'

[3] As far as our instances go, *swḥt* seems to describe the embryo of the animate beings; cf. E. IV. 140,2.11; V. 85,11; VI. 154,1; 173,5; *Urk.* VIII, 34, 5; 36, 2; 36, 16–17; 94, 7.15; 107, 5; *Médamoud*, 1925, no. 201, p. 95; P. Leiden I, 350; II, l. 26 (= *ZÄS*, XLII, 25); Brugsch, *Oase El Kargeh*, Pl. 26, 1.24; Sethe, *Amun*, Pl. II, ll. 1.2.6–7.12; pp. 122, 131, 157, 159, 160; *Pétosiris*, no. 62, 15, no. 81, 68; Lefebvre, *ASAE*, XXIII, 65–7.

described, and since, on the other hand, the original creating powers are at Edfu interpreted as being equal to the Earth-God, the *ỉr-tꜣ*, the *Earth-Maker*, it is tempting to speculate on the significance of the action of creation described in the Edfu text. The *bnnt* appears here to be the essential matter in the creation of the Elements; it is, therefore, suggested that from this *bnnt* the most elemental terrestrial substances were believed to have evolved.[1] In spite of the lack of other relevant sources, we incline to the opinion that the short Edfu text discussed in the course of our study may disclose not only a genuine view of the nature of the original creators, but also a true conception of the origin of the Earth (*tꜣ*). It would follow that this *bnnt* was regarded in the Egyptian cosmogony as the embryo of the Earth (*tꜣ*), and that the Egyptians viewed the origin of the Earth as the result of the union of an undefined male creating power with Nun, who would seem to play the role of the *Mother of the Earth*.[2] The result of this union and the subsequent fertilization of the *bnnt*-embryo would seem to be the appearance of a piece of solid matter which was thought to be the primary shape of the Earth. The new-born Earth might have been imagined as an island (*ỉw*) which emerged from the primaeval waters. This hypothesis seems to receive some support from the fact that the text of the scene of *Offering the Lotus* which we discussed, refers, indeed, to an island (*ỉw*)[3] which appears to be the original nucleus of the world.

The names of this island confirm the concept of the Earth having been an island when it was first created. They appear to summarize doctrinal thoughts and traditions which the Egyptians may have connected with the original island of the primaeval age.

This island is described in our Edfu sources as *this Pool which came into existence at the Beginning*,[4] and it is also called the *Province*

[1] Cf. Sethe, op. cit., Pl. II, l. 2, who briefly stated that Ptah created the Earth (*tꜣ*) in Nun.

[2] No other evidence of the same thought is known; generally Nun is regarded as the father of the forthcoming existence of the world; cf. Sethe, op. cit., pp. 120, 145; Junker, *Götterglaube*, pp. 21–5. That the original powers were only male in nature can be confirmed by another statement in the Edfu text, cf. E. IV. 267,5; cf. *ZÄS*, LXVII, 54, the Earth-Maker is said to have created Nun.

[3] E. IV. 140,2.

[4] E. IV. 392,16.

of the Beginning,[1] of which an alternative name is *the Island of the Egg*.[2] Hints of a theory according to which the Earth in its primordial form was imagined as an island floating in Nun, are already known.[3] Nowhere, however, is anything said about how the Egyptians imagined that the Earth came to be, what were then the essential functions of the primaeval island in the creation of the world, and what was the part this island played in the mythical sphere of the gods. From the analysis of the Edfu texts it would appear as though the Egyptians believed that in order to effect the creation of the world it was necessary to constitute a small piece of ground in the midst of the primaeval water from which the natural forces would operate in the creation of the world. It appears as though the Edfu texts propound the theory that the primaeval island bearing the name *Island of the Egg* acted as a real 'foundation ground' existing before the world. This seems to be indicated also in a statement which we come across in the texts that accompany another scene of adoration of the original creative powers at the Edfu Temple. These are the *ḏ3jsw*, *Sages*.[4] They are said to have created a *snṯt*, *foundation ground*, which preceded the origin of any terrestrial configuration, even that of the primaeval mound (*ḫʿy*).[5] This view, finally, finds support in the main Edfu cosmogonical records, as will be explained below.[6]

The ideas concerning the creation of the *foundation ground* existing before the world, pictured as an island (*iw*), may well have been derived from a hitherto unknown myth of creation. There is clear evidence for assuming that, at Edfu, extracts from a myth of creation, the main concern of which was precisely the interpretation of the origin of the Earth (*t3*) and the explanation of the initial phase of the existence of this world, were used for the redaction of the spells accompanying the scenes of the *Offering the Lotus*.[7]

[1] Cf. Sethe, op. cit., p. 49; E. v. 84,15; VII. 162,9.

[2] E. IV. 140,2; 392,16; VI. 339,9; M. 23,7.

[3] Kees, *Götterglaube*, p. 218; *Totenglaube*, p. 89; Schaeffer, *Weltgebäude der alten Aegypter*, pp. 87 and 118; Clère, *MDIK*, XVI, 30ff.; Grapow, 'Die Welt der Schöpfung', *ZÄS*, LXVII, 34 ff.

[4] E. IV. 390,3–15.

[5] E. IV. 390,6; similarly E. IV. 358,10; cf. Junker, *Götterglaube*, p. 46; the same idea occurs in the Karnak Creation Myth, cf. Sethe, op. cit., pp. 103–4.

[6] Cf. p. 138.

[7] Cf. p. 8, n. 3 for the list of the Edfu instances.

The study of these scenes enabled us to identify a good deal of the various extracts. They accord with and develop the ideas which we have discerned in the text already analysed above[1] and permit us to follow the Egyptian theory concerning the development of the *Island of the Egg* in the initial period of its existence.

In this respect special reference should be made to a scene of *Offering the Lotus* which is to be found in the Forecourt of the Edfu Temple.[2] This is again the text to be recited at the performance of the rite of offering the lotus, but apparently it is another extract from the supposed cosmogonical document. Its content is of outstanding interest because it illustrates what followed after the *Island of the Egg* had emerged from Nun. We learn from this text that the first event to happen in the island was the creation of the *ḏt, form.*[3] The process of the creation of this physical form is not described in the text. Apparently the *Primaeval Ones* were believed to have created their physical appearance themselves, since they were regarded as self-created divine beings *who begat themselves without father to fashion them* (*when*) *there was no vulva to bring them into form.*[4] They are said to be the seed of their own creation.[5] This belief seems to indicate that the *Primaeval Ones* were thought to have acted first in a somewhat insubstantial form while creating the island. After the 'substance' in general was brought into existence by the fertilization of the *bnnt*-matter[6] and had its manifestation in the emergence of the island, then it was possible for the primaeval powers to undergo a metamorphosis and assume a physical form.

The narrative does not explain how the Egyptians imagined the primaeval *ḏt*, the primal physical embodiment of the first divine generation, but we are told that this *ḏt* played an important part in the subsequent stage of the creation.

The following act of the creation occurring in the island is interpreted as the immediate result of the existence of this *ḏt*, the

[1] Cf. pp. 60–4. [2] E. v. 84,12–86,14.

[3] For the primaeval *ḏt* see: E. II. 37,5; IV. 110,4; 266,1; 296,1; V. 84,13; *Urk.* VIII, 17, 9–10; 54, 7; 64, 1; 65, 15.18.

[4] E. IV. 140,13. [5] E. VI. 174,12.

[6] Cf. p. 64; Karnak Myth, cf. Sethe, op. cit., Pl. II, l. 5: the effective creators conceived as the Soul (*Bꜣ*) of the *Kmꜣt.f*, therefore an insubstantial divine being.

bodily form of the Primaeval Ones. And this event is described in the text of the scene of *Offering the Lotus* in the following terms:

Take for yourselves that God who resides in his pool. He was led (*bs*) from your embodiment (*ḏt*), even the Great Lotus that issued from the pool in the Island of the Two Flames, the Province of the Beginning, which initiated light ever since the First Occasion in the High Hill at the beginning of Coming into Existence.[1]

A closely related view of creation occurs in the text of another scene of *Offering the Lotus* to be found on the outer face of the Enclosure Wall. This text reads:

Receive for thyself that God who resides in his pool, who initiated the radiance at the First Occasion, (even) the Great Lotus that emerged from the pool in the Island of the Two Flames, the Province of the Beginning.[2]

It follows that the *Island of the Egg* was believed to have been the place in which the natural forces, the *Primaeval Ones* in our sources, lived and, after they had shaped their bodily appearance, performed other actions of the creation which caused the world to be. The second extract from the supposed myth of creation makes it clear that the *Primaeval Ones* were believed to have been responsible for all the initial actions of the creation. Strictly speaking they were the initiators of the Elements, in particular the Earth and Radiance; the latter is said to have issued from their physical form. These beliefs are further illustrated by one of the spells in which these creating powers were addressed during their worship in the Edfu Temple:

the Senior Ones (*wrw*) who gave adoration to Rēʿ, who brought into being everything which had not yet come forth upon the edges (*nprt*) of the High Hill.[3]

The *Island of the Egg* was conceived, then, as the actual spot of land in which the Elements were created; after the Radiance, the *swḥt*, *egg*, is said to have been created. The narrative does not say more about its nature. We venture to suggest that this *swḥt* might have been the embryo of the subsequent generation of gods and of the other animate beings.[4] We have no doubt that all the spells cited

[1] E. V. 84,12–16.
[2] E. VII. 162,6–8; M. 33,16–17.
[3] E. IV. 140,2.8; VI. 247,12.
[4] E. IV. 140,11–13; V. 85,11–13.

from the ritual text of *Offering the Lotus* preserve, in part at least, the aspect of a hitherto unknown cosmogonical document. They are valuable as the sole texts which make us familiar with the Egyptian conception of the earliest terrestrial world.

The first existent world of the gods started on what appeared to the Egyptians as a *snṯt, foundation ground*, and which they were wont to describe as the *Island of the Egg*. The prominent feature of this island was a *pool* (*š*). No tradition seems to be connected with its origin. On the other hand, however, the island seems to have been extended by the creation of a mound. Both of the texts translated mention the *ḳꜣy ḳꜣ*, *High Hill*, but they do not explain its origin. Nevertheless, since the island and the hill appear to be closely connected in this drama of creation we may hazard a guess that perhaps the hill might have been created in the same manner, and that this hill might have resulted from the creative activities of the same powers who created the island. It represented the second terrestrial configuration in the creation of the primaeval world. This hypothesis agrees with the account of the creation completed by the Sages,[1] telling us that the primaeval mound was a secondary creation subsequent to the origin of the *foundation* (*snṯt*), and that it was the work of the same creating powers as those who fashioned the island.

The Egyptians seem to have believed that both the island and the hill were of an earlier origin than the *sꜣṯꜣw*, *ground*. Another Edfu inscription referring to the Creator reads:

Thou hast led forth the *ḫꜥy*-mound when the *sꜣṯꜣw*-ground had not yet existed, the *ḥbbt*-primaeval water still lying around.[2]

It appears that, after the *sꜣṯꜣw*-ground was brought into existence, the creation of the primaeval world was completed, and that in these 'grounds', probably, the gods were believed to have founded their first sacred abodes.[3] At this stage ends the Edfu account of the order of creation in which the first terrestrial world, that of the gods, was believed to have been brought into existence.

Surprisingly, none of these extracts alludes to the creation of the

[1] Cf. p. 66; Sethe, op. cit., pp. 50, 96, points to the difference between the island and the mound; however, on pp. 117–18, 250–1, he argues for the mound as the earliest shape of the terrestrial world.

[2] E. v. 118,12 = vii. 23,9.

[3] Cf. pp. 75 ff.

sky, though the radiance is mentioned. Nowhere is there any mention of the astral creation. The lotus is said to have emitted the radiance, but the lotus issued from the body of the Creators of the Earth and remained within the pool of the island. It looks as though the Egyptians believed that during the first period of the island the nucleus of the radiance remained on the ground, and that from the island the radiance illumined the primaeval waters.

There appear, on the whole, affinities between the doctrine of creation in the Edfu texts and the Hermopolitan theory of creation. The Hermopolitan doctrine was based on the myth concerning an 'egg' which was believed to be the essential matter in the creation.[1] The Hermopolitan doctrine also propounded the idea that the world in its primal form was an island that contained a pool within which Rēᶜ was born, and this island was named *The Island of the Two Flames.*[2] The view of the commencement of the world which we have been outlining on the basis of the Edfu texts, might therefore have been essentially Hermopolitan in origin, or, at least, a theory adapted by and later propounded from Hermopolis. This suggestion can be supported by the Edfu records, since the primaeval powers, the *pꜣwtyw*, are in two instances identified with the Ogdoad.[3] The ritual text describes the *pꜣwtyw*, but the deities represented are the Ogdoad. Moreover, the original island of the creation is described in three instances as the *pool of Hermopolis.*[4] From this point of view the relationship with Hermopolitan ideas can in no way be denied, and the Hermopolitan version of the myth of creation might well have been used at Edfu for the redaction of texts accompanying the episodes of *Offering the Lotus.* We must admit, on the other hand, that nowhere in the Hermopolitan texts is the original island referred to as the *Island of the Egg*; it is described by the name *Island of the Two Flames.*[5] Since the Edfu texts, however, show an alternative use of these two names[6] while referring to the same

[1] Recently Morenz, *FS-Schubart*, 1959, pp. 74–83, and *Religion*, pp. 187–8.

[2] Cf. Sethe, op. cit., p. 49; E. v. 51,6; 84,14; vi. 16,9; 247,11; 339,1; vii. 162,8; M. 23,10–11; 81,7; *Pétosiris*, no. 61, 18–28; no. 62, 4; no. 81, 51; no. 82, 96.

[3] E. iv. 140–1; v. 85–6.

[4] E. iii. 185,13–15; vi. 247,11; 338,14; M. 81,7.

[5] Cf. Sethe, op. cit., pp. 49–50; Pyr. 265*b*; 397*c*; T.T. 145*b* in particular.

[6] Cf. p. 68.

land, it is possible that the name *Island of the Two Flames* was properly a Hermopolitan tradition, and that this name was given to the original island in connexion with the belief that Rēᶜ was born in it and emitted the radiance from his two flaming eyes.[1] Sethe in his valuable account of the Egyptian cosmogony emphasized the Heliopolitan doctrine and described it as the oldest one, deriving it from prehistoric times.[2] The Heliopolitan idea was that Nun existed before everything else, and that from this primaeval water the Sun-God rose to create the world. Sethe admits that the Hermopolitan system was also of prehistoric origin and that this system sets the Ogdoad in contrast to the monotheistic conception of the original creative power. They, after having taken origin in Nun, emerged to create the light and the primaeval hill. But in these two doctrines no explanation is given of the manner in which Atum or the Ogdoad created the primaeval world. Equally important is the fact that none of the main Egyptian doctrines describes all the functions which the island of creation was believed to have had in the constitution of the primaeval world of gods. In contrast, our Edfu texts explain the causes of the creation. When we compare in detail what is known of the Hermopolitan theory from the texts in Theban Tombs and from the inscriptions of Petosiris[3] with the Edfu sources, differences appear. The latter disclose at some length a myth of creation which is of much earlier date. In our opinion, there may well have been a single myth about the origin of the island of creation which, though of unknown origin, might have been earlier in date than the time when the Hermopolitan and Heliopolitan doctrines were elaborated. We venture to suggest that there are, in the Edfu sources, concealed ideas that were used at a later date in the writing of myths of creation in various religious centres of historic Egypt. Two characteristic features of the Edfu myth are not prevalent in the Hermopolitan and Heliopolitan theories. Neither of them seems to have as its main concern the interpretation of

[1] E. vi. 16,2–9; *Pétosiris*, nos. 61, 62, 82; Kees, *Götterglaube*, p. 309; de Buck, *Oerheuvel*, p. 40; Sethe, op. cit., p. 49.

[2] *Ibid.* pp. 122–3.

[3] Cf. Lefebvre, *Le tombeau de Pétosiris*, inscriptions quoted on p. 70. n. 2, extracts from the inscriptions in the Theban Tombs; cf. too Sethe, op. cit.; Junker, *Götterglaube*, pp. 307–9.

the origin of the primary matter and the description of all the activities of the natural forces, represented as a group of nameless divine powers.

It is evident that our Edfu sources agree with the common Egyptian idea that Nun existed before everything else and that from Nun emerged the first creative power.[1] The Edfu accounts attest a theory essentially naturalistic in conception[2] which sees the primary matter represented by two elements, Water and Earth, a belief which was certainly familiar to several primitive cultus-places of the Thinite period.[3] The Edfu evidence asserts this view, but we are still uncertain of where the belief in natural forces was first made into a myth and then elaborated as a doctrine.[4] As against the predominance of the Heliopolitan conception of the creation, our Edfu texts show that there was a theory that emphasized the creation of the *substances*. This idea is definitely foreign to the Heliopolitan and Hermopolitan doctrines. We see in the Edfu texts decisive evidence for concluding that the main concern of the Edfu theory was the origin of the Earth. The essential features of this theory are, therefore, that there was *at the Beginning* a nameless creative power in a dark and empty space and the *bnnt*-embryo in the primaeval water. This embryo (*bnnt*) was regarded as the real and factual nucleus of the *ḫpr*, *coming into being*, of the substances. After having been fertilized by the nameless creating powers, this *bnnt*-embryo produced the primal terrestrial substances which formed the nucleus from which the world gradually developed. This foundation-ground was pictured in the Egyptian cosmogony as an island (*ỉw*) and was given names such as *ỉw swḥt*, the *Island of the Egg*, or *spt ḥ3t*, the *Province of the Beginning*.[5]

The emergence of the island, therefore, represented the first period of the primal creation. During its second phase the *ḏt*, the primary physical form, took origin. This form was believed to be of divine nature, and to represent the bodily shape of the first generation of the gods, the *p3wtyw*, the *Primaeval Ones*. No accurate picture of their original appearance has been preserved.

[1] Cf. p. 63.

[2] Cf. Morenz, *Religion*, pp. 8–9, 167 ff.

[3] Cf. Morenz, *Der Gott auf der Blume*, p. 74.

[4] Neither Sethe nor Kees refers to the time when the Egyptians adored natural forces only.

[5] Cf. pp. 65–6.

From the existence of this *ḏt* was derived the subsequent stage of creation. After the primaeval mound came into existence, the lotus was created in which the radiance originated. The origin of the radiance is interpreted in our sources as that of the radiance-element.[1] From all the statements which we can glean in the Edfu texts, the fact emerges that the original 'substance' had its manifestation in three physical forms: the island, the *ḏt*-embodiment of divine nature, and the lotus that emitted the radiance.

Another striking feature of this cosmogonical theory is the organic aspect of the creation. The origin of the elemental shape of the Earth was conceived as the outcome of an organic and physical process. It derived from the competition of natural forces which are represented by Nun and the nameless powers (*sḫmw*). These Powers (*sakhemw*) were imagined to be of a rather undefined appearance at the beginning of the creation.[2] By way of contrast, this account does not include the explanation of how the astral corpus in general was created.[3] It is true that this theory embraces the explanation of the origin of some existing beings, but only such as might have been believed to be the direct outcome of the existence of the island of creation or of the same process of creation through which the spot of creation was brought into existence. Therefore, the origin of the radiance is included in this theory because it was believed that the radiance issued from a substance which was created by the same natural forces as brought the island into existence.

As a whole, the Edfu documents show a mode of approach to the phases of the primary creation which is in many respects unlike the Hermopolitan, Heliopolitan and also the Memphite systems.[4] None of the three main Egyptian doctrines is concerned with the initial phase in the beginning of the world, nor do they give a detailed picture of the natural forces concurring in the drama of creation, as it can be discerned in the Edfu sources.

[1] Cf. pp. 69–70 and Morenz, *Der Gott auf der Blume*, pp. 73–8.

[2] E. IV. 296,1, these powers are said to be 'the ones who were produced in their physical form though their shape had not yet been fashioned'.

[3] See for the differences between this theory and other cosmogonical doctrines the Dramatic Text at Abydos in Frankfort and de Buck, *The Cenotaph of Seti I at Abydos*, Pls. 84–5, Piankoff, *La création du disque solaire*, and P. dem. Carlsberg I.

[4] Cf. p. 273 ff.

Neither the Heliopolitan nor the Memphite doctrine differentiates the creation of the Earth and Radiance from the period in which the rest of the world was created. And this is, undoubtedly, one of the essential ideas that can be deduced from the Edfu cosmogonical records. In the Heliopolitan and in the Memphite theory, too, the creative powers and the Elements appear as tangible and physical deities who bear specific names, whereas our Edfu texts stress the idea of nameless powers (*sḫmw*). This evidence is of value and is important for the probable date of this myth; it seems to indicate that the myth of creation that can be reconstructed from the Edfu evidence is based on beliefs from the time when the Egyptians adored only nameless natural forces.[1] The fact that the deities acting in our drama of creation are not conceived as physical divine personalities, and do not bear specific names, is, in our opinion, evidence for assuming that at Edfu, in the texts accompanying the episodes of *Offering the Lotus*, there are enshrined fragments of the oldest conception of the origin of the Earth.

The order of creation as described appears logical, and renders it likely that from this hitherto unknown myth of creation were derived the formative ideas of the main Egyptian cosmogonical doctrines. In spite of the lack of other relevant documents, we are inclined to conclude that the Edfu accounts of the origin of the primaeval island, and of its function in the creation of the physical world of gods and men, disclose genuine thoughts and beliefs of a remote date.

[1] Cf. p. 89 ff.

CHAPTER 6

The Homeland of the Primaeval Ones

The attempt to investigate the Egyptian theory concerning the origin of the primaeval island (*iw*) mentioned at the beginning of the first Edfu record[1] led us far from the main purpose of our study. This was, however, necessary in order to clarify the background of the various traditions which the Egyptians seem to have connected with the beginnings of the Earth. As will be seen below, these traditions are important in the 'mythological history' of the Egyptian temple.[2] This study enabled us to identify a number of short texts which, on close examination, appeared to be extracts from a rather extensive cosmogonical work which once might have been a complete myth about the island of creation referred to as the *Island of the Egg*. What can be deduced from the Edfu texts has every appearance of a single theory which introduces us to a period which the Egyptians regarded as the *pꜣwt tpt*, the *Early Primaeval Age*. This brings to mind the *Sacred book of the Early Primaeval Age of Gods* (*bꜣw-Rꜥ n pꜣwtyw tpyw*) mentioned in the Edfu inscriptions.[3] The myth about the origin and functions of the *Island of the Egg* might well have been the contents of this sacred book. Probably this myth, in its complete form, constituted one of the biggest portions of the original version of the sacred book. The main contribution of the short cosmogonical records at Edfu is that they acquaint us with a primaeval island which seems to have played an important part in the constitution of the sacred domains.[4] Using all the textual evidence which we have translated and discussed in part in the course of our study, we may attempt to reconstruct the mythological situation in the *Island of the Egg*. The

[1] Cf. pp. 12–13.

[2] Cf. p. 273 ff.

[3] The myth about the Temple of the Falcon was probably included in this sacred book, see p. 12 ff. If our deduction be correct, the shorter Edfu cosmogonical records make it quite evident that originally the aforesaid book was solely concerned with the origin of the Earth, a theory which might have been used at a somewhat later date for the interpretation of the origin of sacred domains. For further arguments for this view see p. 137 ff.

[4] Cf. pp. 131–5.

idea inherent in our myth is that a muddy island, that emerged from the primaeval water by virtue of the activities of the nameless creative power, constituted the foundation ground for their own domain. They seem to have created the actual land for their realm. In the first period of its existence the *Island of the Egg* was closely associated with the divine generation of the Primaeval Ones. These nameless Creators of the Earth seem to have been regarded as its original inhabitants, who lived in it at first in a somewhat insubstantial form. The Edfu texts, in addition to the accounts concerning the origin of the island, give a fairly clear idea of how the Egyptians conceived the characteristics of the original creative powers. We suspect that the texts which were used at Edfu to define the nature of the gods of historical times were originally parts of an extensive doctrinal document of an early date. We incline to the opinion that the *Sacred Book of the Early Primaeval Age of Gods*[1] might have included also the descriptions of the divine beings who were believed to be the first to live in the island before light and radiance were created. These shapeless creative powers were regarded as a generation of gods who were older than the *ntrw*-gods.[2] They are described as the *wrw n wrw*, the *Most Aged Ones*,[3] and are said to be the *First Generation* (*ẖt tpt*) *of Mesenty*.[4] Who this *Mesenty* is, is not certain, for we know him mainly from the Edfu texts; there is no authority to explain the nature of this god. It is only a guess to say that he might have been an Earth-God.[5] In these instances we have probably a view deriving from the speculative theory of a later date, because, on the other hand, it is known that these *pꜣwtyw* were believed to be self-engendered who *begat themselves without father and mother*[6] and were the seed of their own creation.[7]

The text of another ritual scene referring to their cult at Edfu[8] speaks of them as of

[1] For the use of the name *pꜣwtyw* in the Edfu texts cf. p. 9, n. 4.

[2] E. I. 289,1; in VI. 174,11 they are said to have *ḫpr m ḥꜣt ntrw*, *came into being before the gods*.

[3] E. IV. 267,5; 296,4.

[4] E. VI. 174,11; similarly in P. Berlin 3048, III, 2, cf. above, pp. 56–8.

[5] The main evidence for this theory would be in E. V. 252,17–18 and 253,6; in E. V. 85,8 the Mesenty appears on a par with Tanen.

[6] E. IV. 140,13.

[7] E. VI. 174,12.

[8] For the cult of the Creators at Edfu, cf. *CdE*, LXXV, 55 ff.

the Fathers who fertilized, the Mothers who gave birth, the ones who were first to beget and to create the egg (*swḥt*); the bulls who impregnated, the cows who conceived, the Builder Gods who fashioned in the primaeval time (*ḏr-ʿ*); the lords of the light, the makers of the radiance and sunlight, who were first to illumine and to give the light, who begat themselves without father to give shape to them when there was no vulva to bring them into existence; the Children of Tanen[1] who created Rēʿ and the Generation of the Great Shining One.[2]

A closely related account of the nature of the primaeval powers is to be found in a text engraved on the wall of the Forecourt[3] and reads:

The Powers (*sḫmw*) who created everything, the progeny of Tanen, the Children of Mesenty; the august Kas who created the *Pn*-God (?) at the commencement, the fathers of the fathers, the creators of the Radiant (god);
The Ghosts, the Ancestors whom the Nun created, who raised the seed for gods and men;
the male gods who created sexual pleasure, the females who bore forth the egg that fertilized them; the bulls who impregnated, the cows who conceived, the Kas, the Senior Ones who came into being at the beginning, who illumined this land when they came forth unitedly, who created the radiance by the work of their hands.

They are also described as

the Great Ennead who brought into being the forms, who caused the gods to be, who gave birth to the Primaeval Ones, the self-engendered ones who equipped the Two Lands in their names (and) by every form they wished.[4]
The Fathers of the fathers who came into being at the Beginning, the Mothers of the mothers who were born since the primaeval time (*ḏr-ʿ*), whose bodily forms (*ḏt*) were divinized in the Mounds (*iȝwt*) of the lands.[5]
The beneficent gods who first came into being at the dawn of time; they came into being before any existing being came into existence, they created themselves, (and ?) issued from themselves (?); the Progenitors who begat themselves.[6]
The Builder gods, the Senior Ones who fashioned in the Beginning

[1] *msw Tni* replaces *msw Msnty* in E. v. 85,8.
[2] E. IV. 140,11–14.
[3] E. v. 85,8–12.
[4] E. IV. 110,1–2.
[5] E. IV. 110,3–4.
[6] E. IV. 266,1–2.

and who created all things; the sanctified Ghosts beyond compare, whose Kas are the Primaeval Ones.[1]

The Ghosts, the Sanctified Ones who came into being on the First Occasion; the ones who created their own bodily form for themselves, who fashioned themselves as their (own) work.[2]

The Ones who created their embodiments, who were begotten at the beginning, who came into being before the existing beings had come into being, who were produced in their bodily form though their nature had not yet been shaped, the Most Powerful of the Powers who created the Builder Gods.[3]

The Most Aged Ones, the progenitor(s) and Mother of the mothers who gave birth. There are no gods like unto them.[4]

They are the Senior Ones (*wrw*) of the gods (*ntrw*), the males without female among them, who came into being at the beginning, who were born at the commencement, the Most Aged Ones of the primaeval time.[5]

It may be noticed that in this long series of quotations the deities who were believed to have opened the drama of creation are never referred to as single individual divine beings, and that they are not described as physically real deities. In all these instances they are addressed as a group of divine beings. If we decide for the theory that these spells of invocation were made in accordance with a document of earlier date, it will follow that in the Egyptian cosmogony the Creator of the Earth and Radiance was not conceived as a sole, unique god. On the contrary, the Egyptians seem to have believed that the 'primary matter' was created by a group of nameless and insubstantial divine powers. A further deduction that can be made from these texts is that the primaeval *ḏt*, *embodiment*, was not regarded as having a definite and specific appearance.

At one point, however, we notice a difference between the descriptions of the *Primaeval Ones*. In the texts interpreting the origin of the island of creation[6] the primaeval creative powers are said to be a single male power;[7] but on several occasions the descriptions refer to different sexes. It has been pointed out that there are definite hints that in the beginning these primaeval powers lived in the island in a somewhat insubstantial form,[8] and this view can

1 E. IV. 266,6–7.
2 E. V. 181,10–11.
3 E. IV. 296,1–2.
4 E. IV. 296,4–5.
5 E. IV. 267,4–5.
6 Cf. p. 63.
7 This view accords with E. IV. 267,4–5.
8 Cf. p. 76.

be developed by the statements that they existed before any other being and were produced in their physical form when their nature had not yet been shaped. This, however, neither explains nor agrees with the idea that their primary appearance (*ḏt*) was that of bulls and cows. The allusion to bulls and cows, indeed, does not fit in with the idea of the origin of the Radiance. Yet the clear implication of the text is that the first physical form of the original divine beings, the *ḏt*,[1] was self-created and was imagined as being that of a bull and cow; consequently this was the primary form in which the original creators emerged from Nun.

There is no authority to confirm the idea that the form of the bulls and cows was conceived to be the original appearance of the primaeval *ḏt*, the *physical body*,[2] of the Primaeval Ones. It may, very tentatively, be suggested that this view might have been a secondary one and derived from the fact that these primaeval powers were believed to have initiated procreation and fertility in general.

We incline to the opinion that the descriptions of the characteristics of the *pꜣwtyw*, the *Primaeval Ones*, such as are preserved at Edfu, combine views on the nature of two distinct generations of gods. Since we can quote in these texts the use of names such as the *Most Aged Ones* and the *pꜣwtyw tpyw*, the *Early Primaeval Ones*,[3] and descriptions such as *ḏdw*, *Ghosts*, the *Ancestors* whom Nun created,[4] it is possible that the Egyptians believed that in the beginning of the world there were two generations of Creators distinct in their physical appearance and nature. Evidence in support of this explanation is found in the theory preserved in P. Berlin 13603.[5] There it is stated that in the first place there was the Earth-God who created the four couples of bulls and cows. This text is undoubtedly a deliberate compilation of doctrinal views and certainly made at a later date, but seems to allude to the same trends of thought of which the Edfu texts might reveal a somewhat earlier expression. In our opinion the Edfu texts reveal the

[1] Cf. p. 77.

[2] E. IV. 296,1 seems to suggest that the *ḏt*, *embodiment* or *bodily form*, might primarily be an amorphous existing being.

[3] E. III. 42,14; 312,2; VI. 173,9; 174,11; 175,8; 179,8. [4] Cf. *CdE*, LXXV, 57–9.

[5] P. Berlin 13603, II, 4–9, and Erichsen and Schott, *Fragmente memphitischer Theologie*, VII, 14–15.

ideological background on which was based the theory prevailing in all the main cosmogonical doctrines of Ancient Egypt.[1]

There are also in our sources hints of a theory according to which there was a long period between the emergence of this island and the creation of the rest of the world, a period during which life was believed to have developed within the island. The Egyptians imagined that, after the phases of the primary creation were completed,[2] these *Primaeval Ones* lived in it in the vicinity of the pool (*š*) containing the lotus,[3] and continued their creative task. The nameless creative powers seem to have founded their home on the island. Their resting-place, however, is portrayed as of the most primitive appearance: the bare edges of the pool. The Egyptians regarded this *Home of the Creators* as a sacred domain and believed that its existence represented a definite stage in the 'mythological history' of the Egyptian sacred places. The time-span of this *Home of the Primaeval Ones*, we may anticipate, appears to be limited, and ended in the darkness.

The first event that was believed to have occurred in this *Home* seems to have been the bringing into existence of the *form*. We suspect that this statement alludes to the origin of the subsequent generation of gods,[4] who are in our sources described as the *Kas* of the Primaeval Ones[5] or the *Generation of the Great Shining One*.[6] The Egyptian idea evidently was that the *Island of the Egg* housed two generations of creators during the first period of its existence. The latter were born in the island only after the first phases of the creation in general were fulfilled.

In accepting this view we may suggest that the *Island of the Egg*, the original domain of the *Most Aged Ones*, was the birth-place of the succeeding generation of creators. It was their *ḥn, homeland*.[7] This interpretation can be supported by textual evidence in which

1 Cf. p. 56, n. 3.

2 Cf. pp. 66–7.

3 Cf. above, p. 69, and E. II. 232,8; III. 186,4; IV. 141,11; V. 84,14; 150,4; VI. 247,11; 338,14; VII. 162,8; M. 80,19; 204,19.

4 E. V. 85,10 contains an allusion to the creation of the seed for *ntrw*-gods. See also E. IV. 296,2: the Most Aged Ones are said *sḫpr ẖnmw, to create the Builder Gods*.

5 E. IV. 266,6–7.

6 E. IV. 140,14.

7 *ḥn*, cf. *Wb.* II, 484, gives only the meaning 'district' and 'dwelling-place'; from our instances it is clear that *ḥn* indicates a part of a primaeval region; cf. E. I. 295,17; IV. 2,1; *the blessed ḥn of the company of gods*; VI. 186,8; *Opet Temple*, p. 125; *ASAE*, LII, 394; *RT*, XVIII, 183.

the word *hìn* applies to the *wāᶜret*,[1] probably to a part of this *wāᶜret*. One of the Edfu texts discloses the view that the new generation of creators were born in the water of this *wāᶜret*, from where they came to the land.[2] Since at that stage of the primaeval age the only solid land was the island, we suspect that the mention of the *tȝ*-land refers to the actual island of the creation. In another tradition the word *hìn*, *homeland*, seems to describe that part of the island in which was the pool (*š*)[3] from which the new divine generation emerged after the creation of the Radiance. The tradition regarded this *hìn*, the birth-place of the Creators, as the most sacred part in the first primaeval domain of the gods.

The primary appearance of the second generation of the Creators is described as that of *Kas*. Which real form this name denotes cannot be defined. Our sources seem to indicate, however, that these *Kas* might have been equated with the bulls and cows at a very early date. It is doubtful, on the other hand, whether this conception was general. It may be suggested that the original form of the *Kas* might have been conceived differently in the various local traditions and beliefs. These modifications could have resulted from the conception of the nature of the creative task which they were believed to complete, and might have been affected by the equation of these original *Kas* with local deities. In the Hermopolitan doctrine we find the Ogdoad linked with these primaeval *Kas* frequently described as the *pȝwtyw*.[4] At Memphis, on the other hand, the Shebtiw and the Sages seem to have the same rank. They are said to be the *msw Ṯnì*, *Children of Tanen*[5] and the *Progeny of the Creator*.[6]

There are also reasonable grounds for assuming that these Kas replaced the shapeless Creators of the Earth and the Radiance. These latter seem to have continued the work of creation primarily by extending the original island and creating the rest of the world. It was perhaps believed that the creative capacity of the *Most Aged Ones* had ceased when the new generation of the Creators appeared on the scene. The original natural forces,

[1] Cf. p. 13, n. 4.

[2] E. I. 295,17: the Sages *were born of the Nbt-cow on the wāᶜret of Nun in her homeland* (*hìn*) *by the Southern Sykomore. They came to land from the water.*

[3] Cf. p. 68.

[4] Cf. p. 9, n. 4.

[5] Cf. p. 77.

[6] E. IV. 358,12.

though present in the *Island of the Egg*, do not seem to be longer active.[1]

According to the Hermopolitan version of the doctrine of creation the era of the second generation of creators begins with the birth of the Sun-God,[2] who is said to have been created in the pool of the primaeval island. One of the Edfu texts[3] reveals that they were the fathers and the mothers of the 'August Stripling' and that they created him to complete their number as the tenth god. Since, however, the Radiance was already in existence, two interpretations of this event are possible: either the Primaeval Ones were believed to give to the 'Radiance-element' the form of a god, or we here come across evidence of a modified version of the original myth. It is possible that the view according to which the origin of the Radiance was interpreted as the birth of the Sun-God was properly the Hermopolitan tradition. As far as one can judge this event from the Edfu evidence, it is certain that the birth of the Sun-God replaces the origin of the Radiance only in texts in which the original pool is equated with the sacred pool of Hermopolis, and the primaeval powers are identified with the Ogdoad.[4] In these texts also the original Island is named *the Island of the Two Flames*.[5] As has already been pointed out above, the difference of the names which the island was given renders it probable that the Hermopolitan myth about the birth of the Sun-God was based on an earlier tradition.

We find in several Edfu texts that the origin of the Radiance was interpreted as the birth of the Sun-God within the lotus. We read in the invocation formula of one of the Edfu scenes of *Offering the Lotus*:

This august god who came into being in the Great Pool and was led forth from Nun within the lotus.[6]

In the Hermopolitan tradition the Sun-God, after having emerged from Nun, assumed the power of creating this world and the gods and the mankind. It was believed that

[1] Cf. p. 106ff.
[2] E. IV. 141,11; V. 86,14; VI. 174,13; 339,1–3.
[3] E. VI. 174,13–15.
[4] Cf. pp. 72–4.
[5] Cf. p. 70.
[6] E. III. 186,4; cf. Morenz, *Der Gott auf der Blume*, pp. 42–50.

When he (the Sun-God) opened his eyes, he had illumined the Two Lands, he divided the night from the day. The gods issued from his mouth and men from his eyes. Everything attains being in him.[1]

In an inscription engraved on the inner face of the Enclosure Wall another extract from a similar doctrinal writing is incorporated, and illustrates this view in the following words:

When the *št3*-egg was created they (= the two protecting deities) opened its interior within the lotus (and) Rēʿ as stripling was between the Two Mistresses. His embodiment is Khopri, (even ?) Ptah who initiated his creation. The slumber shall pass away when the light comes forth from him, even the Child. He burnt everything in its surroundings by his two flaming eyes from the Island of the Two Flames.[2]

The same text propounds the idea that the Sun-God succeeded to the *Throne of the Eldest Ones* (*nst wrw*), and his father handed to him the decree to create mankind, the gods and all animate beings.[3] When we recall the tradition concerning the *hin*, *Homeland*, this *nst wrw*, the *Throne of the Eldest Ones*, of the Hermopolitan tradition appears to be very like it. It follows that we have here another allusion to the belief that creative powers were transferred from one generation of creators to another, and that here also the birth-place of the new generation of creators, in the Hermopolitan doctrine the birth-place of the Sun-God, was regarded as the centre from which all the acts of creation were believed to have started. It is interesting that the terrestrial world is said to have been created last in the order of creation.[4] Here again no description is given of the process of the creation of the Earth-substance, but the brief account refers only to the appearance of the Earth from the primaeval waters. This text is one of the rare pieces of evidence in the present state of our knowledge which tells us how the Egyptians imagined the way in which the Earth was caused to emerge from Nun: by virtue of the radiance of the Sun-God who was believed to dry up the water around his primaeval seat. It would follow that in the Hermopolitan doctrine the creation of the terrestrial world was conceived as a mere emergence of the

[1] E. v. 85,4–5; similarly IV. 140,5–6.
[2] E. VI. 16,6–9.
[3] E. VI. 16,4.
[4] Cf. pp. 60–1.

Earth,[1] and that this process was the result of the activities of the solar energy.[2]

It is important, on the other hand, that the Sun-God was believed to operate from his birth-place, which was also the place of origin of the *Kas*, his creators. This short text, therefore, furnishes an additional argument to support our hypothesis concerning the *foundation ground* as a pre-requisite for the creation of the world.[3] It confirms, too, that this *hin*, *homeland*, in essence the pool with the lotus, the very spot of the creation within the island, was conceived as being the most sacred part of the primaeval domain of gods. This *hin*, *homeland*, has every appearance of being the private domain of the Sun-God since it is described as his *nst*, *throne*.

It may be that the theory concerning the primaeval 'throne' of the god was the distinctively Hermopolitan tradition, because this view is known only from that part of the myth about the primaeval island which reveals stronger Hermopolitan influence. We can add that the Ogdoad themselves were described as the *Rulers of the Throne of the Primaeval Ones*.[4] Another text tells us that this primaeval *nst*, *throne*, was, indeed, imagined as the lotus in which the Sun-God was believed to rest.[5]

It follows that it was believed that in the *pꜣwt tpt*, *the Early Primaeval Age*, the first sacred domain of gods came into existence in the *Island of the Egg*, and that the Creator of the world and all animate beings, the Sun-God in our myth, shared the primaeval sacred domain with other and earlier creating powers. In its essential nature this primaeval sacred domain was the very place from which the Radiance issued first, in which the Primaeval Ones were initiated, in which also their successor was born and

[1] None of the other fragments of the Hermopolitan doctrine goes as far as to describe in detail the creation of the terrestrial world, cf. p. 63 ff.

[2] For another view cf. p. 137 ff.

[3] Cf. pp. 58, 66, 93.

[4] E. VI. 174,13; similarly *Urk.* VIII. 31,5; E. IV. 1,14: *the Throne-of-the-gods of the gods of the Primaeval Age.*

[5] C.D. II, 177, 7; this view will fit in E. VI. 16,4; cf. also Morenz, *Der Gott auf der Blume*, pp. 14–22; Morenz deals with the aspects of the tradition that the lotus was the first seat of the god, and states that the belief in Nefertum on the lotus was a Memphite tradition and that this is the historical aspect of that belief; see also *ibid.* pp. 22–72. The theory implicit in the Edfu records seems to lead to somewhat different conclusions.

assumed the power to create the rest of the world. Since this place is found described by the word *nst*, *throne*, it is highly probable that the Egyptians imagined it as a real, though primitive, sacred place.[1] The Egyptians probably imagined that in the centre of this domain or 'homeland' there was the lotus as the first seat (*nst*) of the Creator of this world; assembled around this spot there were the two earlier generations of the creators: the nameless powers with their *Kas*.

It is quite evident that the Egyptians did not imagine the place in which the creation was effected as a place in which an omnipotent Creator would reign alone. On the contrary, he was brought out of Nun by a pre-existing creative power and lived in the island with other divine beings who performed the actual work of creation, probably at his command. The evidence quoted in the texts of the scenes of *Offering the Lotus* and in some connected inscriptions seems to preserve quite a coherent picture of the *Homeland* of the primaeval deities in the island of creation. This conception of the appearance of the primaeval *hìn*, *homeland*, might have had a realistic background. It seems to reflect the appearance of a very primitive sacred place as it might once have existed in the dim past of prehistoric Egypt.

The remarkable fact which emerges from the Edfu accounts is, therefore, the association of a primitive cultus-place with the conception of the initial spot of earth in which this world began to exist. In this creation story we can follow a connected line of acts of creation which are described as mythical events, and which at a definite moment of the primaeval age resulted in the creation of the sacred domain of the Creator.

In deciding in favour of the theory concerning the cultus-place of the Creator, it may be suggested that the belief in the existence of the Creator's sacred place may well have been familiar to several sacred domains that existed in the early stages of Egyptian history; this belief might have been common to sacred places of protodynastic Egypt; each of them would claim for itself the honour of being the original island in which the first sacred realm had been

[1] Cf. p. 48; according to the Hermopolitan doctrine the temple was to be founded in the place in which Rēʿ was born; the same trends of thought are known from an inscription at Medamud, cf. p. 51.

created, in which the world of men took its origin, but each would introduce such modifications as might have been dictated by local legends and beliefs. We can refer to other texts acquainting us with interpretations of the original world of the gods, and which were certainly formulated in places other than Hermopolis. It is true that none of them contains as detailed a description of the origin and aspect of the initial island as can be found in our Edfu sources. The major thought in all of them, however, is the same: there was at the beginning of the world an island in which the first sacred domain was constituted.

This thought is apparent in the Heracleopolitan version of the myth of creation. Heracleopolis claimed for itself to have been the original place where the Creator first came to land. Heracleopolis was the primaeval land in which the Creator made his dwelling-place from which he created the world thereafter.[1]

The same mythological situation can be found described in the Theban version of a creation myth to which we have only briefly referred above.[2] The narrative preserved in the Theban Temple does not speak of a *iw*, *island*, but of a *st ḏr-ʿ*, *original place* (or *the place of the primaeval time*), which emerged from Nun and became the centre of the creation of the world. We are told that in this primaeval land the Creator revealed himself, and from his resting-place he then created other lands to settle the gods there. And thus the world of the gods came into existence. Thereafter the Creator proceeded to create other animate beings. We have no doubt that in the background of these explanations concerning the origin and the functions of the primaeval realm of the gods, as they are known from the Hermopolitan, Heracleopolitan and Theban texts, there were the same trends of thought.[3] The *st ḏr-ʿ*, the

[1] Cf. Brugsch, *Thesaurus*, pp. 633 ff.; Kees, *ZÄS*, LXII, 73; LXV, 71; *RT*, XXXII, 63; *Götterglaube*, pp. 322–3; Newberry, *Beni Hasan*, I, Pl. 7; Jéquier, *Mon. fun. Pepi II*, t. II, Pl. 39.

[2] Cf. p. 58.

[3] Cf. the Fayyum myth, col. II, which gives a long list of sacred places, among which many are described as *ỉ3t* and are said to have originated beside a *š*-pool; Pl. III, l. 8 explains that there were 66 *ỉ3wt*, *sacred mounds*, in the nomes of Upper Egypt and 42 in Lower Egypt. Botti in *Glorificazione di Sobek*, p. 39 does not explain the significance of these lists.

The sacred area of Hermonthis seems to have had its own myth of creation. Allusions to this myth are known from which we can deduce that Hermonthis,

original place, is only another name of the primaeval island in our tradition.

Thus it may be suggested that the island (*iw*), mentioned at the beginning of the first Edfu cosmogonical record, was really equivalent with the original *Island of the Egg* (*iw swḥt*), though, in fact, it bore a different name and is never equated with it. This island, so far as the Edfu tradition is concerned, is named *iw titi*, *Island of Trampling*, and was believed to have been occupied also by some divine beings before the process of creation of the lands, as far as this myth is concerned, began. In view of all these affinities there was, in all probability, a belief in the existence of one sole primaeval island, which was regarded as the centre of creation, and which received varying names according to the local traditions. These names might have been derived from or affected by other myths and traditions connected with the original island in various places in the course of time. Although the early time-span of the *Island of Trampling* is not included in the part of the myth that survives on the walls of the Temple at Edfu, it is tempting to speculate and to suggest that this island was believed to have been brought into existence by the same primaeval powers and by the same process of creation as the *Island of the Egg*. The analysis of the first Edfu record shows that the *Island of the Egg* and the Island at Edfu are very similar in their physical appearance and their nature.

too, claimed to be the *spt-ḥ3t*, the *Province of Commencement*, the Place of the Ogdoad, the Birth-Place of the Sun-God and the primaeval mound; cf. Otto, *Topograph. Theb. Gaues*, p. 87.

CHAPTER 7

The Island of Trampling

The Edfu account gives us convincing evidence that the Island of Trampling was essentially the primaeval piece of land on which the drama of creation commenced. When we examine the physical appearance of the island, we notice that both islands contained an area of still water which was regarded as the place where creation occurred. In the *Island of the Egg* it was the *pool* (*š*) which contained the lotus carrying the Sun-God,[1] and to which a tradition was attached later on that the Sun-God created it for himself.[2] Although we do not know anything about the origin of the pool in the second island, the picture of it is very detailed. It was undoubtedly a reed pool standing on the marginal land of the island; the Edfu evidence describes it only as a *gs-nbỉ*, *area* (or *the edge*?) *of reeds*.[3] This pool is said to bear the name *wṯst-nṯr*, the *elevated seat of the god*, which, however, seems to have originated in the circumstances and events connected with this pool during the second period of existence of the island.[4] In the midst of this field of reeds there seems to have been the seat of a divine being who is not the Sun-God, as will be stated below. His resting-place is pictured as the *ḏd*-pillar,[5] and it is stated that it was made from reeds.[6] The *ḏd*-pillar appears to have the same function as the lotus, to carry the god (*wṯs nṯr*),[7] and it could apparently be replaced by another sacred symbol, a slip of reed which had a special name: *ḏbꜣ*-perch.[8] The god who was believed to rest on this *ḏd*-pillar is not described in the surviving part of the myth. We know only that the Egyptians called him *Pn*, *This One*, and that only his *Ba* and his *Ka* acted in the drama of creation when a new period of the existence of the island dawned.[9]

[1] Cf. p. 82.
[2] E. v. 85,2.
[3] E. vi. 183,3 and above, pp. 21–2.
[4] Cf. pp. 14, 23; lit. *wṯst-nṯr* means the 'carrier, uplifter of the god'; this indicates that the primary function of the reed was identical with that of the lotus: to carry the god.
[5] E. vi. 182,2 and below, pp. 115, 123 ff.
[6] E. vi. 184,18.
[7] Cf. pp. 117–18.
[8] Cf. p. 133 ff.
[9] Cf. p. 136 ff.

Our hypothesis that this reed pool in the *Island of Trampling* represented the actual spot of creation receives some support from a number of facts described in the second part of the first cosmogonical record. We are convinced that the narrative preserves an original tradition concerning the nucleus of creation for which no parallel can be quoted at present.

The part of the record concerned bears the title *Arriving at the (field) of reed, (even) the Wetjeset-Neter that restores the Ancestors.*[1] Several interpretations of this episode are possible,[2] but here we draw attention to what is said to have been found *in situ* at the time when a new generation of gods arrived in that place. The narrative refers to two symbols pictured as a *ḏt wṯt* and *tỉtᶜ*.[3] Both expressions are unknown elsewhere and we may, tentatively only, suggest the interpretation *member of the Progenitor* and *image of the Arm.* These sacred objects may have been symbols of the creating powers, though the text does not state who were the powers embodied in these symbols. But the creators who were eventually represented by these symbols could hardly have been conceived as living deities. One is tempted to speculate on this matter. In our opinion it seems logical to infer that these two symbols might represent the natural nameless forces which created the island. We are acquainted with the belief in two generations of creators who lived in the initial island. We know also that the original nameless powers who created the first terrestrial substance, and who brought the island into existence by fertilizing the *bnnt*-matter, the 'embryo of the Earth',[4] were believed to have been at first insubstantial, and have acted as such at the beginning of the creation.[5] After they had fulfilled their creative task they assumed a specific and concrete form, but do not seem to have acted at the time when the new generation of creators appeared on the scene. It follows that their activities were believed to have been limited to a definite period of time, and that when the second generation began to create, the original powers, though remaining in the island and being enshrined in their concrete form, were inert. Since it is nowhere stated that these deities would live in the island in a form

[1] E. VI. 183,3 and above, p. 21.
[2] Cf. p. 133.
[3] E. VI. 183,4.7 and above, p. 22.
[4] Cf. pp. 64, 72.
[5] Cf. p. 78 ff.

which would be like that of the Kas or like that of the later *nṯrw*-gods, the first generation of creators may have been regarded as having assumed the form of members which were believed to have acted in the initial phase of the creation in general: that is, in the origin of the island. It would follow that the concrete shape of the original creators may have been believed to have been concealed in the Earth, in the actual land of the island which they created first. We learn from our sources that the Egyptians believed in the divinization of the physical form (*ḏt*) of the original creators, and that their *ḏt*-embodiment became divine in the *iꜣwt n tꜣw*, the *Sacred Mounds of the Earth.*[1] This belief is nowhere explained in detail, and perhaps the original creators were believed to undergo a metamorphosis in the island, and this, possibly, gave them what is described in our text as the *ḏt*-embodiment. An act of consecration of their final physical form presumably followed, and this is what is probably described in the tradition of a later date as the episode (*s*)*nṯr*, *to make divine* in the *Sacred Mounds of the Earth.* We suspect that the expression *iꜣwt n tꜣw* replaced the name of the original island. There are, indeed, in the Edfu texts, instances which make this surmise possible and show an alternative use of the word *iw*, *island* and *iꜣt*, *mound*, while referring to the same piece of land in the primaeval age.[2] Although no relevant texts can be cited, we incline to the opinion that our text alludes to the end of the life-span of the original creators and acquaints us with the Egyptian view on their fate. The fact that the nameless creators were believed to survive in the island in the form of an image in which they might reside in their mysterious life seems to indicate that this theory might have been derived from the belief in the 'entering into a body' by a divine power.

As far as the *Island of Trampling* is concerned it seems that in the form of the two symbols, the *Member of the Progenitor* and the *Image of the Arm*, the original creative powers remained in the very place where the creation of the world started. These two symbols might have represented the most sacred objects in the *Homeland of the Primaeval Ones*. If this suggestion be accepted it will emphasize

[1] E. IV. 110,4: *nṯr ḏt.sn m iꜣwt n tꜣw*; *tꜣ* is used in the plural here; *nṯr* can be an adjective here, but can also be used instead of the causative *snṯr*.

[2] Cf. pp. 8–9.

the theory concerning the cultus-place of the Creator.[1] These symbols might have had yet another function in the island. Their presence *in situ* might have made it possible for the creation of the world to be carried out. It is certain from the ensuing narrative that the *Image of the Arm* was invoked before the start of a new act of creation of the Earth.[2] Thus there would seem to have been a connexion between the creation of the substances and the symbol itself. Another hint to support this view is that these symbols are said to have been found in the place where the Creator of the Earth, the Earth-Maker (*'Ir-tꜣ*),[3] dwelt. The connexion with the creation of the Earth cannot be denied. The Edfu text may disclose the Egyptian view of how they conceived the final appearance of the original creators. Unique as it is, this picture is of importance. The fact that in a field of reeds in the primaeval island there were found two symbols representing unspecified creative powers can be taken as decisive evidence that the *Island of Trampling* was the primaeval island of creation in which the world took origin, in which the nameless powers lived and were enshrined in its land after their life-span had come to an end.

The interpretation suggested seems to accord with the chief act of creation that was performed in the *Island of Trampling*: the making of the Earth. It is, therefore, evident that this activity might require the symbols representing the original creative powers; from this point of view the scene in which the *Image of the Arm* was invoked before the new period of creation of the Earth started, becomes clear. Further confirmation can be seen in the nature of the new phase of the creation. As has already been said above,[4] this process of creation is described in our texts by the expression *sw iḫt tꜣ*, and appears in its essential nature to be unlike the properly organic mode of creation from which the island had resulted.[5] We attempted to explain in one of our previous studies the significance of the action described as *sw iḫt tꜣ*, *to endue with power the substances of the Earth*.[6] It appeared as though this *sw iḫt tꜣ* action had the aspect of a symbolic and magical rite of creation. The main part of that rite consisted of uttering sacred spells by the

[1] Cf. p. 84ff.
[2] E. VI. 183,12 and above, p. 24 and below, p. 152.
[3] Cf. pp. 21–2.
[4] Cf. p. 24.
[5] Cf. p. 63.
[6] Cf. *ZÄS*, LXXXVII, 43–5.

creators over certain *iḫt-tꜣ* which, we may say, might have been believed to symbolize the Earth to be created. We suspect that by virtue of this rite it was believed that the symbols (*iḫt*) of the Earth were filled with special power. This power then caused the Earth to emerge in the form of specific plots of earth[1] along and around the edges of the island. This process of creation of the Earth by the word of the creators has no equivalent. Such a manner of creation can be compared with the Hermopolitan conception of the creation of the world; according to the latter, the Earth was believed to have been created by drying up the primaeval waters that surrounded the island.[2] Both of these ways of creating, the magical process as well as the procedure by the solar radiance, had the same result, they seem to have made manifest what was created previously by the nameless powers, but was hidden beneath the primaeval waters. The Edfu accounts set out clearly that according to the Egyptians the Earth was not believed to have been created in a single action. On the contrary, there seem to have been two distinct periods of creation; at first, the substance was created by a properly organic and physical act; then, in the second period, the already existing substance was brought by a further action to the surface of the primaeval waters; the nature of the creative activity completed during the second period seems to vary according to the places in which the myth of creation was either elaborated, or adopted and adapted. Description of the creation of the Earth, as completed in the second period, may explain why in the majority of the Egyptian cosmogonical texts the origin of the Earth is described only as an emergence of the Earth from the water.[3]

The creation of the Earth performed in the *Island of Trampling* was, therefore, interpreted as being essentially symbolical in nature. This fact might help to explain the idea that the earlier creating powers were believed to be present as symbols only. Since the creation of the primary matter was completed, their presence appears to have been required only with a view to effecting the second phase of the creation of the Earth. Moreover, the process of creation executed in this island seems to apply to the origin of lands of a special nature. As will be seen below,[4] the lands

[1] Cf. p. 137ff. [2] Cf. p. 82ff. [3] Cf p. 56ff. [4] Cf. p. 138.

created from the *Island of Trampling* were sites needed for the foundation of sacred places which came to be the earliest sacred domains of the god, in which enclosures of the gods were set up, and in which temples were built later on. It thus appears as though in the speculative theory implicit in our Edfu texts we have much explicit evidence of the idea of the *foundation ground* existing before the origin of the world. We can conclude that the part played by the *Island of Trampling* in the drama of creation was that of a veritable foundation. This may explain why the subsidiary name of the island was that of the *Foundation Ground* (*snṯt*) *of the Ruler of the Wing.*[1] This proves that the *Island of the Egg* and the *Island of Trampling* were equal in respect of their primary function in the creation.

The close affinities between these two islands can also be proved by the essential features of their configuration. They show a striking resemblance, so that it can justly be claimed that the description of these two islands, as they are known to us from the Edfu texts, was inspired by the same doctrinal ideas. The second myth, however, shows slightly modified views, such as might have resulted from the traditions of the place in which this second myth was written down first.

Another point of similarity with the *Island of the Egg* can be found in the mention of the primaeval mound. We know from the myth about the *Island of the Egg* that there was created, in a secondary act, a mound, the *ḳ3y ḳ3*, *High Hill*,[2] where the subsidiary phases of creation took place. The Edfu island has also a primaeval mound called *ḫ'y wr*.[3] Our creation story makes it clear that in its origin this mound was a secondary terrestrial configuration and that it was also created by virtue of the 'word'.

The *Island of Trampling*, too, seems to have been the homeland of the primaeval deities. There is clear evidence of a belief that the island was occupied by some divine beings prior to the time of the creation of lands with which our cosmogonical theory is concerned. The divine beings of the *Island of Trampling*, however, seem to be deities of a nature entirely different from the divine inhabitants of the *Island of the Egg*. In place of the Kas we find allusion here to a

[1] E. VI. 182,6 and above, p. 84.

[2] Cf. p. 69.

[3] Cf. p. 139.

rather obscure company of divine beings described as *ḏꜣjsw*.[1] The text does not preserve a description of their nature, and we do not even know to whom the word *Company* might refer. *ḏꜣjsw* may have been the name of some divine beings who eventually formed the company of the nameless god described as *Pn*, *This One*. This deity, to whom we have already referred, is another divine being peculiar to the myth.[2] The text neither interprets his origin nor describes his appearance. His epithet *the overlord of the ḏd-pillar* indicates that he might well have been the ruler of the *Island of Trampling*, or, at least, have governed the field of reed. We imagine this god, therefore, as resting on the *ḏd*-pillar of reed in the midst of the pool. Perhaps around his seat were assembled the other obscure deities mentioned on a single occasion in our narrative.

The name *Pn* as a divine name is known to us only from our main documents and from some additional inscriptions at Edfu, from which we can deduce that this *Pn*-God was imagined as resembling the *ḏrty*-falcon[3] and that he was regarded indeed as the Creator.[4] If our interpretation of the *Island of the Egg* be correct, this *Pn*-God resting on the *ḏd*-pillar of reed would appear on a par with the Sun-God on the lotus. In an inscription of the temple at Karnak we find that a god represented residing in the lotus is described as the *Pn*-God.[5] Unlike the myth about the *Island of the Egg*, in this myth the *Pn*-God is never said to have acted; but the text acquaints us with his *Ba* and *Ka*, who appeared on the scene when the new period of creation started and then played a prominent part.[6] Furthermore, apart from the obscure company of divine beings this *Pn*-God seems to have had yet two other fellows. We read in the narrative about a deity described as the *Ḥtr-ḥr*, and yet another falcon named *Nfr-ḥr* who bears two subsidiary names as the *Sanctified Ruler* and the *Ruler of the Wing*.[7]

The name *Ḥtr-ḥr* is known, in the main, as the name of the sacred spear of Horus,[8] but this can hardly be so in our myth. In

[1] Cf. p. 17, and E. VI. 182,9. [2] Cf. p. 131 ff.
[3] E. III. 202,16; IV. 326,2; V. 7,1; 181,12; VII. 10,11; 23,5.
[4] E. V. 9,4; in 181,12 he is said to be the overlord of the gods.
[5] Unpublished; Temple of Khons, Sanctuary, east wall.
[6] Cf. p. 136. [7] Cf. p. 115 ff.
[8] Cf. *Wb.* III, 202 (4).

the account of the situation in the *Island of Trampling* this *Ḥtr-ḥr* is described as a divine being who also dwelt on a *ḏd*-pillar of reed.[1] This suggests that he might have been in the same place as the *Pn*-God, and that he, eventually, might have ruled in the primaeval island. This hypothesis is admissible because in the tradition of a somewhat later date the *Island of Trampling* is described as the *Great Mound* (*iꜣt wrt*) of the *Ḥeter-ḥer*.[2] It is possible that in the island the *Ḥeter-ḥer* functioned as the protector; so much is suggested by the account of the creation of a new sacred domain. And this idea can be confirmed by the tradition of a later date. The *Ḥeter-ḥer* is interpreted as a deity who repulses the evil-doer from the Mansion of the God.[3] The significance of the name *Ḥtr-ḥr*, however, remains unsolved, and very little is known of his physical appearance; the text tells us only that he was conceived to be an armless deity.[4]

The name of the second fellow of the *Pn*-God, the *Nfr-ḥr*, is not unfamiliar as a divine name. It occurs frequently as a subsidiary name of Ptah.[5] It is certain, however, that in our mythological story this name does not apply to Ptah himself but to another deity who is said to be the *Ruler of the Wing*, who revealed himself in the island as the *protection* (*sꜣ*) *of the ḏd-pillar*,[6] and on whom the tradition of a later date looked as on the *Great God* (*ntr ꜥꜣ*).[7] These facts seem to hint at a tradition which connected the very spot of creation, in this myth the field of reeds, with the realm of the falcons, which was believed to have existed in the primaeval age. That the Egyptians believed that deities resembling falcons took part in the drama of creation is already known from the text that accompanies the scene of adoration of the Sages at the Edfu Temple, and which we have discussed above.[8] We also pointed to the tradition concerning the *wāꜥret*, the primaeval region in which the Sages were believed to have been born,[9] and to which allusion is

[1] E. VI. 184,18.
[2] E. VI. 11,5.
[3] E. III. 201,8 and III. 204,17.
[4] E. VI. 183,6 and below, p. 140 ff., for his role in the creation of the sacred domain.
[5] Cf. Sandman, *The God Ptah*, pp. 108–11.
[6] E. VI. 182,7 and above, p. 15.
[7] E. IV. 358,15–16.
[8] Cf. p. 8. That the Sages were not a peculiarly Edfu tradition can be confirmed by evidence in the inscription of the Karnak Temple (unpublished).
[9] Cf. pp. 66, 81.

made by another ritual scene to be found among the inscriptions of the Chapel of Rēᶜ at Edfu. The text tells us that in the *wāᶜret* the Sages assumed the form of falcons, and from their native *wāᶜret* they foretold the creation of the world.[1]

There is much that is similar in these accounts. Both furnish us with a clear allusion that some divine beings resembling the falcons were believed to be the creators of the Earth and lived in the island of creation. We suspect that the pool of reeds in our main record and the *wāᶜret* in the second tradition may be the same primaeval region.[2] If this suggestion be accepted, the main source will permit us to gain a fairly clear idea of this primaeval *wāᶜret* in which the sacred falcons were believed to live at first. It would follow that this *wāᶜret* was imagined as a field of reeds which enshrined a small group of supports. These supports were made, in all probability, from the stalks of reed which were tied up together to form the resting-place of the bird; the tradition regarded it as the earliest form of the *ḏd*-pillar.[3] It may, very tentatively, be suggested that the beginning of the first cosmogonical record preserves the memory of one of the earliest Egyptian places of worship that were constituted in an open field. The description of the *wāᶜret* gives a clear idea of a primitive enclosure in which the falcons were reared in the dim past of prehistoric Egypt,[4] and which had for its centre the *ḏd*-pillar of reed.

The high date of the domain of the *ḏd*-pillar might have resulted in the realm of the falcons being associated with the idea of the dwelling-place of the Creator. Here, therefore, in an entirely different context, we have unambiguous evidence that the birth-place of some divine beings was conceived as the first sacred place in

[1] E. I. 296,1–2; this belief accords with what the title of the Edfu set of cosmogonical records tells us; see also E. IV. 103,11, where allusion is made to the age of the *ḏrty*-falcons in a close connexion with the Earth-God.

[2] E. VI. 14,14 the primaeval region in which the Shebtiw created is described as a *wāᶜret*, and this is precisely the pool of reeds.

[3] Cf. *ASAE*, XXV, Pl. 5; XXVII, Pl. 2; *Meir*, I, 2, and II, 38; Schäfer, *Stud. Griffith*, pp. 424–31; unlike the statements of Schäfer the Edfu account makes it clear that the tradition concerning the *ḏd*-pillar is a survival from prehistoric times. Moreover the *ḏd*-pillar must primarily have been fashioned from some vegetable material, and in its earliest function it seems to have been used as a support of a nameless deity.

[4] Cf. Emery, *The Tomb of Ḥor-Aḥa*, p. 31, which shows the aspect of the early enclosures of the Falcon; see also below, p. 328.

which the primaeval deities lived and founded their resting-place. Apparently the ideas already known from the myth about the *Island of the Egg*[1] underlie also the conception of the nature of the first sacred place in the tradition we are outlining: the birth-place of the gods assumed the function of their first cultus-place. If our equation be correct, it would appear that the primaeval domain of the *ḏd*-pillar or *ḏd*-pillars would be equivalent in its significance to the Hermopolitan pool enshrining the lotus. The picture of this sacred domain of the primaeval age will provide further evidence to support the hypothesis that the Egyptians definitely imagined the spot of creation as a genuine, though very primitive, cultus-place of the Creator.[2]

In the myth about the *Island of Trampling* there is mentioned yet another deity who lived in the vicinity of the realm of the Falcon. This one is said to be the Earth-Maker (*ỉr-tꜣ*), who was believed to have dwelt in the field of reeds in the company of some other deities. These were two creators of the waters whose names were the *Divine of Heart* (*ntrỉ-ỉb*) and the *Ptḥ-nwyt, Creator-of-the-primaeval-water*; then two protecting deities whose names were *Sẖm-ḥr* and *Pꜣ-sgmḥ.*[3] The physical appearance of all these divine beings is never described in our sources, and their names are very rare as names of gods; in fact, they are known to us only from this narrative. Nevertheless, in this myth they represent a group of deities who seem to be closely associated with the Creator of the Earth. Since the Earth-Maker is said to have lived in the place where another creative power was present, it may be surmised that the Edfu account refers to a somewhat modified version of the original myth of creation; consequently the Earth-Maker and his fellows are substituted for the second divine generation of gods who were believed to have lived in the *Island of the Egg*. There are definite points of contact in the description of the sacred domain in the *Island of the Egg* and the account of this sacred spot. There is, too, on the other hand, a striking resemblance to the *domain of the ḏd-pillars*. The Earth-Maker would appear, therefore, in an equal position with the *Pn*-God. Further resemblance can be noticed in their companions. As the *Pn*-God appears to be associated with the divine being described as the *Ḥtr-ḥr*, the Earth-Maker seems to be

[1] Cf. pp. 84–7. [2] Cf. p. 85. [3] Cf. pp. 19–20.

connected with the *Divine of Heart.*[1] At this point, too, our document reveals a new fact. Certainly this companion of the Earth-Maker is not the same god as the *Divine Heart of Rēᶜ*, who is Thoth.[2] No adequate picture is given of this *Divine of Heart* in our narrative. It is highly probable that he was one of the original inhabitants of the *Island of Trampling* and that he was connected with the creators of the Earth, the Shebtiw. The Edfu narrative tells us also that the *Divine of Heart* created the *mw*-water.[3] It is not stated how he did, nor is he said to have interfered in the creation after the Shebtiw appeared on the scene. This *Divine of Heart* is also mentioned in connexion with the *pāy-land of Djeba.*[4] There, too, he does not appear as an acting divine power. Since evidence is that this available *Divine of Heart* was associated with the *ḏdw-Ghosts of the Island of Trampling*, he was probably conceived as an intangible deity, and was regarded as an Ancestor-god whose role was essentially symbolic when the new phase of creation dawned. Consequently he must have been regarded as one of the original dwellers in the island of creation.

The group of deities associated with the Earth-God is, on the whole, new and certainly these creators are of an order different from the original creative powers whom we know from the myth about the *Island of the Egg*. All of them are described in the Edfu account as intangible deities, but it is evident that they all had their resting-place in the field of reeds. We suspect that there is preserved the account of yet another early sacred domain of remote age, and that, perhaps, the Edfu account alludes to the place in which the Earth-God was duly worshipped in prehistoric Egypt. We can reconstruct, with a reasonable degree of probability, a coherent picture of the sacred place in which the Creators of the primary matter, Water and Earth, were believed to have been first adored. This sacred domain will then be the third sacred place in the history of the Egyptian sacred domains of which it was believed that they had existed in the 'primaeval age'.

This primaeval sacred domain seems to have existed on the ground in which the symbols of the creating powers were believed

[1] E. VI. 177,2.10; 181,12; 183,2 (= III. 7,10); 329,2.9.

[2] E. VI. 174,17; I. 289,4; Junker, *Götterglaube*, pp. 45–7.

[3] Cf. p. 21.

[4] E. VI. 177,2.10.

to have been hidden.[1] We are told that it was there that the *ìr-tꜣ*, the Earth-Maker, had lived with his companions. Our narrative does not preserve a picture of the Earth-Maker himself; he is, in fact, only mentioned in the text. On the other hand, however, the description of the Earth-Maker's domain is detailed. It seems that it resembled a primitive sacred domain which was fashioned from some light materials. A *nht*-shelter is referred to in the description; its function seems to have been to shield the symbols of the Progenitor.[2] In its surroundings, perhaps encircling the shelter, stood an enclosure which our text describes as the *ḥwt-ìsdn*, the *Mansion of Isden*.[3] This *Mansion* appears to be the Earth-Maker's dwelling-place, and, perhaps, the four other deities who seem to have played the role of his fellows in this drama of creation rested there. The text does not tell us what the real resting seat of the Earth-Maker and his fellows within this Mansion was, but describes several sacred emblems which seem to have been kept in the Mansion, and which are said to have been the emblems of the Earth-Maker himself. These are: his mace, described as the *ḥḏ-wr*, the *Great White*, the *ḏd*-pillar and the *Image-of-the-Front-of-the-God*.[4]

This tradition is completely unknown elsewhere, but we do not doubt that it preserves a detailed picture of a constructed, though primitive, sacred place of the type of the later enclosures described as *ḥwt*, mansion, and that this tradition reveals an entirely different conception of the nature and appearance of a sacred place in which the Earth-God was believed to live.

The primaeval resting-place of the Earth-Maker seems to have been imagined as a square structure fashioned from reeds. This was a properly fashioned enclosure. Perhaps this enclosure was erected on the edges of the pool of creation, encircling and protecting it because, it might be surmised, it was believed that the concrete shape of the elementary creating powers was concealed in the pool. Perhaps at a somewhat advanced stage another light structure having the form of a mere shelter was made within this

[1] Cf. p. 89. [2] E. VI. 183,4 and above, p. 22.

[3] E. VI. 183,4; the meaning of the name *ìsdn* in this context remains unsolved.

[4] Some resemblance might, perhaps, be seen in a representation on a sealing from the Archaic Period where beside a *ḥwt*-enclosure there is the *ḥḏ*-mace, cf. Petrie, *The Royal Tombs of the Earliest Dynasties*, I, Pl. V, 7.

ḥwt-enclosure to protect the symbols of the elementary creative powers and thus to mark the most sacred part of the ground of the enclosure. In the midst of the courtyard there might eventually have been the *ḏd*-pillar, which, perhaps, was the resting-place of the Earth-Maker, and was protected by the two other symbols, the *Great White* and the *Image-of-the-Front-of-the-God.* This is inevitably a hypothesis for which no parallel can, at present, be quoted. Nevertheless, we may hazard a guess that around this presumed seat of the Earth-God there were assembled the four other creators, and probably these were believed to have acted at his command. It is true that we cannot claim that the Earth-God was exactly the first deity who ever had a place of worship of such an appearance as is described in our Edfu sources. No single piece of archaeological evidence can be cited to reveal the appearance of the early sacred places in which the Earth-God might have been adored. Moreover, no memory is preserved of an early sacred domain bearing the name *ḥwt-ỉsdn.* But the way in which this primitive enclosure is pictured at Edfu, does not appear to us unnatural. It shows logical features of organization which may well be those of the early sacred domains constructed from reeds. We incline to the opinion that the Edfu account once again gives a clear idea of the characteristics of a primitive enclosure as well as of its inhabitants, as it might once have existed in predynastic Egypt. We think that we meet here exactly the same situation as is already known from the two other accounts concerning the place in which the Creator was believed to have dwelt first. As far as the myth is concerned the fact which is of real interest is that the divine inhabitants of the *Island of Trampling*, too, are described as having founded their cultus-places in it before the rest of the world was created.

Compared with the Hermopolitan evidence, the idea of the cultus-place within the island of creation is, undoubtedly, more prominent in the Edfu myth. For the purpose of our study, however, it is significant that the earliest known allusion to a *ḥwt*-mansion occurs in connexion with the Creator of the Earth, and that there are definite hints of a belief that a *ḥwt*-mansion was the dwelling-place of the Earth-God himself in the first period of existence of the original island. Moreover, this cultus-place of the Creator contained sacred symbols which are said to have been stored within the *Mansion of Isden*. It is, therefore, most likely that this primaeval mansion was conceived as a real place of worship.

The situation in the *Mansion of Isden* shows, on the other hand, one feature similar to that in the two preceding accounts. The Earth-God does not seem to have lived alone in his primaeval enclosure, but it is highly probable that he was believed to have lived there in the company of other creative powers. We had in the first myth the Sun-God with the *pꜣwtyw*, the *Primaeval Ones*; in the field of reeds the *ḏrty*-falcons associated with the *Pn*-God; finally in the first *ḥwt*-mansion the Earth-God with other creators of the primary matter.

The two accounts disclosed by the first Edfu cosmogonical record are valuable pieces of evidence, and their detail adds a great deal to the Egyptian conception of the *Homeland of the Primaeval Ones*. These views are, at present, found expressed only in the inscriptions of the Temple at Edfu. This fact does not necessarily mean, however, that the Edfu inscriptions reveal only a tradition which would solely apply to the site of the Edfu Temple or to another sacred place in Upper Egypt. These three accounts are probably a part of a much wider, perhaps even of a general theory concerning the primary appearance of the mythical world in which the Egyptian gods were believed to have come into existence, to have lived and to have created their own sacred domains.

It is inherently possible that at Edfu we find a hitherto unknown, but certainly a genuine tradition which has its roots in facts, experiences and beliefs which lead us far beyond the limits of historical times, since these two sacred domains of the primaeval age are said to have existed before the first sacred place that survived in historical times was created.

The three accounts of the Creator's domain have apparently a common ideological background, but differences can be noticed when we examine their physical details. Unlike the Hermopolitan tradition, according to which this *Homeland* was merely a pool containing the lotus, the seat of the Creator, around which were assembled the creative powers, the description preserved in the first cosmogonical record shows a somewhat more developed and advanced stage of the primitive resting-place of the Creator and his fellows; it hints also at a somewhat more elaborated conception of the primitive sacred domains. The Hermopolitan primaeval domain in the island of creation is in essence a natural outcome of the elementary phases of creation. In contrast, the two domains described as having existed in the *Island of Trampling* contain elements which were fashioned. Yet the *ḏd*-pillar of the *Pn*-God must have been tied up from the stalks of the reeds, and the *ḥwt, enclosure*, of the Earth-Maker with its shelter (*nht*) must have been constructed. The account preserved does not permit us to discern who was the power who might have created these resting-places. Hence, what can be suggested, with all due reserve, is that the first divine beings to occupy the *Island of Trampling* during its first period were believed to have created them themselves after they settled on the first piece of solid land.

In the last account of the Creator's sacred domain which we have been analysing the primitive *mansion* (*ḥwt*) with its shelter (*nht*) is paralleled by the sacred place represented by the lotus-pool and the field of reeds containing the *ḏd*-pillar. We are of the opinion that this account preserves the memory of a primitive cultus-place which once existed. It follows that the origin and the existence of the first *mansion* (*ḥwt*), the first properly constructed enclosure, the most basic feature of the complete 'House of the god' of later historical times, was included in the first period of the existence of the primaeval island and was linked with the process of the creation of the Earth. This point, undoubtedly, is of prime importance. It follows that the *ḥwt-mansion* was not only the dwelling-place of the Earth-God; it was also the result of his creative activities. It seems to us most likely that in the speculation implicit in the Edfu records, the act of 'fashioning' a resting-place of the god came to be regarded as part of the process of the creation of the Earth; it formed only a part of all the acts of creation which were believed to have taken place within the island during its first period. It seems to be the final act that had happened in the island. We imagine that the Egyptians believed that after the first phases of creation in general were completed, the creators fashioned for themselves their resting-places in the very place where the existence of the world started, and thereby they fulfilled the first phase of the creation of substances.

The mythological situation pictured in the first Edfu cosmogonical record seems to have produced yet another interesting fact.

If we admit that in describing the creation of the Earth the texts record the stages of evolution of the Egyptian sacred places, it is evident that the Egyptian tradition was that the earliest cultus-places were founded near, or even enshrined, the piece of earth in which the symbols of the creative powers were believed to have been concealed. This is a valuable piece of evidence which will show that the connexion between the creation and the origin of the sacred place was most probably a tradition of remote date. A further deduction that can be made is that in Egypt the earliest cultus-places were founded exclusively for the worship of the Creator and the natural creative forces. The fact that the first Edfu cosmogonical record preserves on the one hand the account of the primaeval realm of the Sacred Falcons, and on the other hand that of the Creator of the Earth, is significant enough to suggest where these traditions may have been at home. We imagine that in this part of Egypt these traditions and beliefs were made into a myth of creation which became familiar to other religious centres of predynastic or protodynastic Egypt. Another fact peculiar to this tradition is that the deities residing in these domains bear specific names. The tradition may point to a somewhat later stage of the 'mythical age', when the worship of nameless creative powers was followed by a period in which, near the original sacred spot, the more advanced type of sacred places developed. If we recall that the *Pn*-God appears to be on a par with the Sun-God, it is evident that the first Edfu cosmogonical record discloses the tradition of an early cultus-place which adopted the original belief to its local needs. It seems definitely to reflect the final stage of the development of the *Homeland* of the Primaeval Ones, which is here the sacred domain of the *ḏd*-pillars where the *ḏrty*, the sacred falcons of the primaeval age, were believed to have rested. In what follows our documents seem to point to the times when the Egyptians began to associate the original nameless powers with animate beings. It should be recalled that in our creation story the principal deity, though he is a physical personality conceived as a bird, is still nameless and is described only as the *Pn*-God, *This One*. His fellows then bear specific names, but all these names contain the component *ḥr*, *face*, *countenance*. It looks as though the tradition implicit in the Edfu record alludes to the time when Egyptian belief gave importance to the countenance of the being in which the divine power was believed to dwell. Similar features can be seen in the tradition of the third primitive domain. There is also a deity whose name contains the element *ḥr*. The names of the other deities appear to be derived from their creative activities; thus the Earth-God is described as the *ỉr-tꜣ*, the Creator-of-waters as the *Ptḥ-nwyt*. These two names characterize the creative activities which these two divine powers were believed to have completed, and from which resulted the land where they founded their resting-place. It appears that at that stage of the belief there seems to have been a need to mark out in a somewhat more prominent way the place where the concrete likeness of the divine powers was believed to dwell. Supports were fashioned for them from light material, and finally fences were erected around their private realm.

The views expressed in the Edfu accounts, therefore, render it highly probable that the belief in the Creator's private domain was of general application. They demonstrate that this belief must have been familiar to several cultus-places of prehistoric times, and that, consequently, it is likely that the Creator's cultus-places were among the first that were founded. As far as our instances go, this tradition applies to the cult of the Sun-God as well as to that of the Earth-God.

The ideological background that can be discerned in the descriptions of the three domains of the Creator confirms that there was originally a single myth about his primaeval domain. This myth seems to have been taken over by many other religious centres of the early historic Egypt, each of them bringing such modifications as might have been dictated by local beliefs and traditions. The mythological situation in the *Island of Trampling* can be considered as a proof of what we have very tentatively suggested,[1] that each of the principal religious centres of Egypt claimed for itself the honour of being the first sacred place in which the Creator dwelt with his fellows before he had created the world.

The existence of the domain of the Creator is interpreted as

[1] A closely related idea is contained in the Karnak Creation Myth, cf. *ASAE*, XLIV, 52. Thebes came into existence before any other land because the Earth-Maker was hidden in its ground, and in the same place there was also concealed the *Arm* (ʿ).

forming a definite era in the creation of the world; it has, too, a vital significance in the history of the Egyptian temple, as will be seen below.

A further consequence is that the idea inherent in this creation story is that only from the *Homeland of the Primaeval Ones* could the domains of the gods of historical times have been created. The existence of a small and primitive sacred place on the edges of the island of creation at the dawn of this world appears to be the prerequisite of their coming into existence. A study of the *Myth concerning the Origin of the Temple of the Falcon* will justify this statement. It seems to indicate that the origin of the genuine sacred places of the Falcon was directly linked with the domain of the Creator.

It is, however, evident that the creation of the lands for the new sacred domains did not proceed from the domain of the Creator in a direct and continued line. Between the time when the sacred world of the Creator and his primaeval fellows existed within the island of creation and the time when it was believed that the lands for the domains of other gods began to be created, there was a long period of darkness.

CHAPTER 8

The Decay and Resurrection of the Primaeval Island

Nothing is known about what happened to the *Island of the Egg* after the Sun-God was born, and after the world in general was brought into existence.[1] None of the texts deriving from the Hermopolitan doctrine affords an explanation of the eventual fate of the original island of creation; nowhere is there any account to tell us of the gradual growth of the *Seat of the Sun-God* within the pool of the island.[2]

Nevertheless, at Edfu there are a number of data that enable us to reconstruct the consecutive periods as well as to trace the fate of the *Homeland of the Primaeval Ones,* after they founded their resting-places in it, and after life developed within the island. Although these data seem to apply to the *Island of Trampling* in the first place, yet their significance implies that the Edfu records yield views of general application. Certainly, it will be wrong to think that the story about the fate of the island of creation was only a local Edfu tradition.

As has briefly been mentioned above, it is noteworthy that the beginning of the first Edfu cosmogonical record refers neither to the origin nor to a previous existence of this island such as can be discerned in the texts of the *Offering of the Lotus.*[3] The first picture recorded appears rather to allude to a primaeval world which already existed, and which was in darkness.[4] This situation provides a reasonable ground for theorizing. It may be surmised that the first era known by our principal sources was a period which started from what existed in the past. The general tone of the beginning of the first record seems to convey the view that an ancient world, after having been constituted, was destroyed, and

[1] Cf. p. 74.

[2] All the known texts that derive from the Hermopolitan doctrine end with the description of the lotus as the seat of the Sun-God, the Creator of the world, cf. pp. 86–7.

[3] Cf. p. 62 ff.

[4] Cf. pp. 12–13.

as a dead world it came to be the basis of a new period of creation, which at first was the re-creation and resurrection of what once had existed in the past.

There are hints of another mythical world of which the island seems to have been a survival. In the preceding chapter we discussed the allusions to the other mythical world, and we attempted to outline its features. It was believed that two sacred domains were constituted within the *Island of Trampling* during the first period of its existence, one of them being the domain of the Creator of the Earth, the other that of the *Pn*-God and his fellows, who rested on the *ḏd*-pillars. If our reconstruction be accepted, it would follow that the domain of the Creator was destroyed.

This hypothesis receives some support at first from the fact that the island is said to have been in darkness before the creators of the lands for sacred domains, the *Shebtiw*, were introduced into it.[1] Another argument can be seen in the significance of the names which the island was given in our creation story. The name *Island of Trampling* itself suggests that when the first phases of creation had been completed, and the primaeval 'Lord of All' was resting on his primaeval seat, such as the lotus or the pillar of reed, life developed within the island; this then became the scene of various mythical events, such as, for instance, the *ṯiṯi*. Theoretically *ṯiṯi* can be interpreted as *trampling* or *aggression*.[2] It may, therefore, be surmised that there was a fight in the island. The exact nature of this fight is difficult to explain. That a time of combat was, indeed, connected with the early history of this island, is quite clear when we refer to the subsidiary names of the island: *Island of the Combat* and *Island of the Peace* appear to reflect the same situation. These names might hint at the main mythical events which were believed to have come to pass in the island after the domain of the Creator of the Earth and the *Pn*-God were constituted. Both of these domains might have been assailed by an enemy, and this might have led to a fight between the original inhabitants and the enemy. The result was that both of the early

[1] E. VI. 181,12–13 and above, p. 13.

[2] *Wb.* V, 244 (1.2); cf. above, p. 34, the *Myth about the Solar Temple*, where allusion is made to the *bw-ṯiṯi*, which was the battlefield; the idea of the fight will be plausible here also.

domains were destroyed and that the Sound Eye fell.[1] This event is, in fact, the mythological picture with which the Edfu text begins. The mention of the *Sound Eye* in this creation story appears a little strange. The function of the *Sound Eye* is, in fact, not clear here, for it is never referred to in the ensuing narrative. Except for one rather vague reference to the light,[2] this myth of creation never mentions any astral body, nor alludes to the Sun Disk. The *wḏꜣt*, *Sound Eye* might in this tradition have been the name of the centre of the light which illumined the island. This is, however, somewhat hypothetical. All that can be said, with due reserve, is that it looks as though there is an allusion to a disaster which caused the fall of the *Sound Eye*,[3] with the result that complete darkness fell on the sacred domain of the Creator. In this darkness the island was found when a new period of creation dawned.

The view that it was a fight that brought the first sacred domain of the Creator to an end can furthermore be supported by the evidence of the name which the primaeval water surrounding the island of creation is given in this context. It has been said at the beginning of chapter 5 that in this myth the primaeval water from which the Earth was believed to have emerged, bears the name *ḥbbt*.[4] In the opening words of this narrative, however, the *ḥbbt*-primaeval water is given the name *wꜥrt*.[5] We do not think that *wꜥrt* has in this context the same meaning as is known from the tradition about the primaeval falcon-like deities, the Sages.[6] In this tradition *wꜥrt* seems to describe the pool in which the falcons were born. This interpretation, indeed, appears to be unlikely here. In contrast, the occurrence of the word *wꜥrt* in the first Edfu record may hint at a rather gloomy situation that might surround the island; eventually it might hint at the probable fate of the island. *wꜥrt* might describe the water lying on the primaeval world after this was brought to an end. In support of this view we can refer to another and well-known mythological event. In the Osiris-myth *wꜥrt* was the name of that part of Nun in which

[1] E. VI. 181,11.

[2] E. VI. 181,13.

[3] This tradition may show a somewhat earlier aspect of the myth about the fallen Eye than that which is preserved in *Pyr.* 2050 and in *BD.* chapt. 17, spell 17; cf. Müller, *Eg. Mythology*, pp. 89–91.

[4] Cf. p. 55. [5] Cf. p. 13, n. 4. [6] Cf. p. 81.

the dead body of the god was found and in which his grave was.[1] Using this evidence one is tempted to imagine that a closely similar situation was believed to have existed in the history of the *Island of Trampling* and that this is the very beginning of the period of the island known from the main Edfu record. The primaeval water might have submerged the island as a consequence of a fight, and the island become the tomb of the original divine inhabitants; thus the *ḥbbt*-water became the *wʿrt*-water. That it might have been interpreted in this way is highly probable. The beginning of the first Edfu record does not tell us that the new generation of creators arriving in the island would perceive the island itself when the sun shone once more on the primaeval waters. It is stated that they saw only the reeds on the surface of the water.[2]

The mythological situation we attempted to outline appears admissible in view of the fact that in the first records there are, indeed, frequent allusions to the 'death' of the first creation. It is, in fact, its general tone. It should be recalled once again that one of the subsidiary names of the island is *the Island of Combat*, a name which shows a link with the title of a mythological narrative which was incorporated in the text of the first record. This title reads: *The Place (bw) of Uniting of the Company (ḏꜣjsw) which passed by.*[3] There is much that is uncertain in the interpretation of this expression, for no parallel can be quoted and the text gives no further information in this respect. The use of the verb *sni*[4] in this context suggests that this 'Company' of divine beings was, perhaps, believed to have perished. If we accept this explanation, it would appear that the original divine inhabitants of the island, the presumed company of the *Pn*-God,[5] while fighting against the enemy, were killed. If this surmise be correct, there may be a link

[1] E. I. 216,8; 223,12; Junker, *Götterdekret über das Abaton*, p. 41 ff. It may be suggested that this idea finds realistic expression in the structure of the Cenotaph of Seti I at Abydos, cf. Frankfort, *The Cenotaph of Seti I at Abydos*, II, 25–9.

[2] Cf. p. 13; for the text in E. VI. 181,14 we suggest the following interpretation: 'The radiant water was the name of the *wāʿret* at that moment. The reed was perceived (*ḫf*) by those who were on the water (*mḥ*) (= Shebtiw) when they recognized the (image ? of the) *Ḥeter-ḥer*.'

[3] Cf. p. 16.

[4] *Wb.* III, 455 (2).

[5] Cf. p. 94.

with the idea that the island might become the 'tomb' of its own inhabitants.

Indeed, in this connexion reference should be made to a mythical place which is described in this tradition as the *dwꜣt n Bꜣ*, *the Underworld of the Soul.*[1] The existence of an 'underworld' in the vicinity of an island of creation is most significant for the study of the ideas that underlie this creation story. Since we can quote evidence that Osiris was believed to have been *pre-eminent in the Underworld of the Soul,*[2] and that he is the *ḥtpy*, *the reposing, the pre-eminent in the Underworld of the Soul, who partakes of the meal* (*smꜣ iḫt*),[3] it is evident that there is a clear allusion to a burial place, which was possibly, it may be suggested, that of the Earth-God. The Edfu inscriptions preserve the memory of a belief that the Earth-God, the *Mesenty*, who brought everything into existence and who founded (*smn*) the Earth, has his *Ba*. This *Ba* of the *Mesenty* then is *The Pre-eminent in the Underworld of the Soul.*[4] These quotations, though brief, are of real interest. They seem to allude to the belief that a chthonic deity was the first deceased god in Egyptian mythology; they, too, disclose the belief in the Soul of the Earth-God.[5] The Soul who appears in the Edfu myth about the time when the first sacred domain was revivified,[6] might have been the very Soul of the deceased Earth-God. This Soul was related to the *Pn*-God and if our conjecture be accepted, it would follow that the *Pn*-God too might primarily have been an Earth-God. This is not explicitly stated in our text but we know that this *Pn*-God was regarded as being the *ḏrty*-falcon, and this brings to mind the *myth about the Sages* according to which the Creators of the Earth were imagined in the form of the *ḏrty*-

[1] Cf. p. 15, n. 8, for references in the Edfu texts.

[2] E. v. 291,15.

[3] E. v. 67,6.

[4] E. v. 253,6.

[5] For the Soul of the Earth-God see Theb. T. 79*b*; Piehl, *Inscr.* I, 160*c*; Sethe, *Amun*, p. 26; the Souls of the Earth-God (*Ḳmꜣtf*) are referred to in E. II. 1–2; v. 202,6–7; *Urk.* VIII, 76, 2; 141, 4; *Temple of Opet*, p. 167; *ASAE*, III, 55. We suspect that this Soul of the Earth-God is the Soul who came into being at the Beginning (E. IV. 1, 14), who emerged from Nun (Theb. T. 84*h* = de Buck, *Oerheuvel*, p. 71) when the Earth was still in darkness and who is found equated with the Earth-Maker in *Urk.* VIII, 97, 10; 66, 7–8.

[6] Cf. p. 16; since in the tradition of a later date this Soul is equated with the Ka, our surmise appears admissible.

falcons.[1] This tradition is known to us only from the Edfu textual evidence.

Further allusion to the 'death and decay' of the first mythical world can be seen in the mention of the *relic* (*iḫt*) *of the Pn-God.*[2]

As far as the description preserved permits us to reconstruct the situation, the name *relic* seems to apply to the reeds which grew on the marginal land of the island. In the first mythical world reeds were used for making the resting-places of the gods, specifically for the making up of the *ḏd*-pillar.[3] Thus the reeds used for such a purpose and remaining *in situ* appear to have been regarded as the *relic* of the sacred domain that once existed there but had perished. Words such as *wāᶜret* and *iḫt*, *relic*, and *Underworld of the Soul* suggest that closely connected with the island of creation there was a place that had obvious funerary associations, a place which was conceived as the burial place of a deity who died, whose soul had flown to the sky and whose material form remained in the same place: this Ka who dwelt among the reeds of the island.[4] The tradition of a god who was brought out of Nun by a pre-existing power, but who died thereafter, whose soul went to the sky and for whose embodiment the underworld then was created, can be discerned in another text preserved at Edfu. In a description of the *August God who came into being in the Great Pool*,[5] and who is the Sun-God born in the lotus, we read that

> for his soul the sky was uplifted so that he may shine therein, the underworld being mysterious to conceal his body.

This short text seems to emphasize the Egyptian belief that the life of the Creator, in this particular instance the solar deity, was limited. Although we have no evidence from the Hermopolitan texts that the Sun-God, after having created the world, was killed, it may be assumed with reference to our Edfu texts that this belief was derived from a general doctrine.[6] The death of the Creator seems to have been regarded as the starting-point of a new phase of creation, or a new period of existence. This view

[1] Cf. p. 77. [2] E. VI. 182,2.
[3] Cf. p. 102. [4] Cf. p. 16. [5] E. III. 186,4–5.
[6] Cf. *BD*, ch. 17 = *Urk.* V, 6 ff. which illustrates the connexion between death and creation.

agrees with the Heliopolitan doctrine concerning the daily rebirth of the Sun-God. Referring to our Edfu myth, we can see definite points of contact with the fate of the *Pn*-God. As has been said, the *Pn*-God appears on a par with the Sun-God as regards his function in the first sacred domain of the island. That he was believed to have died is equally admissible, because the myth speaks of his *Ba* and *Ka* who appear on the scene at the opening of the new era in the existence of the island, but they are never said to be tangible divine beings.[1]

To supplement the theory concerning the *death of the first mythical world* it must be emphasized that the first cosmogonical record contains yet another allusion to the decay of a former state and describes its remains. A very brief mention is made in the second part of the first record of an *Entering in that which was in decay*.[2] This sentence is closely linked with the description of the domain of the Earth-Maker.[3] We may hazard a guess that this sentence describes the state in which the new generation of gods arriving in the island found the Enclosure of the Earth-Maker and his fellows. It was reduced to debris.

To explain the reasons for the death and the destruction of the first sacred domain of the Earth-Maker several interpretations are possible. In referring to what has been said about the fate of the domain of the *Pn*-God, it may be suggested that this was, indeed, the general Egyptian theory: the first sacred domain that ever existed was believed to have been limited in time, and its decay was merely the normal course of events. In the same way in which the domain of the *ḏrty*-falcons resting on the *ḏd*-pillars had disappeared, the Enclosure of the Earth-Maker vanished. In support of this view we can refer to another Edfu inscription revealing the belief that the life-span of the first generation of gods, the *Primaeval Ones* (*pꜣwtyw*), was limited in time. After they completed their task in the creation of the world they were believed to have been buried, and the other generation of gods came to their grave to perform the funerary rites on their behalf.[4] This quota-

[1] Cf. p. 16.
[2] E. VI. 183,4; cf. above, p. 22.
[3] Cf. p. 97ff.
[4] E. I. 289,6–8: 'He (= Thoth) adorned the Primaeval gods after they completed their life-span. He ferries with them towards the Nome of the West, (even) *Djême*, the Underworld of the *Ḳmꜣt.f*. Shu crosses to them while carrying the

tion concludes all the previously mentioned allusions to the death of the first sacred world, and appears only as a somewhat modified interpretation of the trends of thought that underlie our creation story.

We suggest that the Edfu myth gives a somewhat more dramatic context for the general theory. There was perhaps a storm in which the first sacred domain, represented by the *Mansion of Isden*, was thought to have perished. There are, in the same Edfu source, hints of a mythological situation that could only result from an aggression against the island of creation. This hypothesis receives some support from a clear allusion to the defeat of the *Ḥeter-ḥer*. The description of the domain of the Earth-Maker contains 'words of a god' which the Earth-God seems to have told to his successor, his son, and who is in this myth the Falcon.[1] He seems to have described to him what had happened in the dwelling-place of the Earth-Maker. He refers to a snake, the *nhp-wr*, the *Great Leaping One*, who appears to be the chief enemy of the god. He explains that the arms of the enemy oppressed the head of the *Ḥeter-ḥer*, who was defenceless; his feet were pierced, and the ground of the domain was split. This is a clear picture of a disaster. From the narrative preserved it would appear as though the words of the Earth-God yield the fate of the domain of the Earth-Maker and what had happened in the domain of the *ḏd*-pillars. This description, though short, is explicit enough for us to reconstruct the Egyptian belief connected with the destiny of the *Homeland of the Primaeval Ones*. This sacred domain, having been constituted by the creators themselves, came to its end at a definite moment of the primaeval age. A storm, perhaps, came over the island during which an attack was made by an enemy pictured as a snake. The aggression was so violent that it destroyed the sacred land with

ḥtp-offerings daily and (?)...at the beginning of the week. The Living Soul, the overlord of all the gods, reaches them at its (due) time of the Festival of the Valley.'

[1] E. VI. 183,5: 'The *nhp-wr*-snake has approached. The Father spoke to the child.' We suspect that this text alludes to what had happened after the enclosure of the Earth-God was reconstructed. Perhaps there occurred then what had once happened during the first time-period of the existence of this domain. When the gods settled down, the enemy-snake appeared on the scene. He reappeared once again after the enclosure was reconstructed, and was ready for a new attack.

the result that the divine inhabitants died. This interpretation accords with other parts of the first Edfu record which alludes to the death of the *Company* (*ḏ3jsw*) to which we have referred above,[1] and to the darkness that covered the primaeval island.

There is substantial evidence to attest the theory concerning the 'death' of the first sacred world in the mythical age in which the Earth-God and a nameless deity ruled. The mythological situation which we attempted to outline shows points of contact with the myth of Osiris and fits in with the allusion to the fall of the *Sound Eye* which seems to mark the beginning of the new era in the history of the *Island of Trampling*. On the other hand, this mythological situation once more recalls ideas included in the Heliopolitan doctrine. The Primaeval Hill at Heliopolis was the place of birth, but it was at the same time the place of death which then became the place of rebirth. Probably our Edfu document discloses a somewhat earlier conception of this idea. In the Heliopolitan doctrine the rebirth was manifested by the appearance of the Soul of the Sun-God. Here too the Soul of the Creator was present in the island when the new phase of creation dawned. Its emergence would mean the rebirth and renewal of the island. This Soul is in our creation story the *Flying Ba* (*B3 ḥ3tty*).[2] This *Flying Soul* thus returned to its original place, the field of reeds in which the domain of the *ḏd*-pillar was once created and then buried.

A further important fact that emerges from the Edfu account is the allusion to the underworld. The Edfu narrative makes it clear that the underworld was believed to have existed before the world was created. It does not preserve a description of this underworld of the primaeval age; it gives only its name: *dw3t n B3*, the *Underworld of the Soul*.[3] Nevertheless it seems to disclose an interesting view of the origin of the underworld. From the mythological situation described we conjecture that the underworld of the primaeval gods might have been conceived as a direct outcome of the existence of the first sacred domain, the cultus-place of the Creator. It was thought, perhaps, that the underworld resulted from the destruction of the cultus-place of the Creator of the Earth, and that during the period of darkness

[1] Cf. pp. 16–17. [2] Cf. pp. 15–16. [3] Cf. p. 15, n. 8.

the underworld became the resting-place of all the original inhabitants of the *Island of Trampling*. This underworld was regarded as a place concealed underneath the field of reeds in which the original deities arrived in their spiritual appearance and there found their new home. There is no authority to give further details. We can only add the common statements that the underworld was created by the Creator at the same time as the water, earth and sky.[1]

Our deduction from the Edfu account, however, may be supported by a number of allusions bearing on the 'revelation' of the original dwellers of the *Island of Trampling*. We already know that the beginning of the first Edfu record alludes to the arrival of a divine being described as the *Ka*.[2] The narrative suggests that he lived among the reeds, and that there he had his own resting-place pictured as the *ḏd*-pillar.[3] As will be seen below, this divine being was the former ruler of the lands adjacent to the island.[4] It is likely that this deity was regarded as the inanimate form of the nameless God, the *Pn*-God, and consequently the counterpart of the *Flying Ba*. We can refer to an Edfu text which, though undoubtedly an interpretation of a later date, is significant as probably indicating the Egyptian view of the nature of this *Ka*. We are told that *the Ka arrived in the capacity of the Flying Ba*.[5] We know that the *Flying Ba* was the spiritual likeness of the nameless god and the text cited refers to their relationship. Hence, it is evident that there was a belief in a nameless deity, who, after having died, could appear in the form of his *Ba*. A further implication of this belief is that this deity must have had his *Ka*. Since he does not bear any specific name we may suppose that his posthumous forms bore names describing only their appearance. This *Ka*, as the likeness of the defunct *Pn*-God, was probably the *Ka of the Creator of the Earth*. Further support for this hypothesis may be seen in the fact that the *Ka* appeared in the island at the moment when the new period of creation of the Earth dawned. We suspect that he was thought to have dwelt in the underworld during

[1] For instances see the statements in *Urk*. VIII, 65. 94. 111. 138.

[2] E. VI. 182,3; the text reads: 'the Ka has arrived, the reed having been removed'; cf. also above, p. 14.

[3] Cf. pp. 27–8.

[4] Cf. p. 215 ff.

[5] E. VI. 15,1 and above, p. 14.

the period of darkness and to have emerged when the light shone once more on the island. Since we are told that he appeared on the scene after the reeds were removed, the *Underworld of the Soul* was probably believed to have been concealed underneath the field of reeds in which the domain of the *ḏd*-pillars once existed.

This *Ka* is said to be present in the island throughout the whole period of its development. It appears that a part of the work of the creation was effected at his command,[1] but he is never described as a physically real divinity. This confirms that he was believed to have revealed himself from a place of funerary nature and this statement seems to accord also with a belief of which we are acquainted by an interpretation of a later date. It was believed that the voice of the *Ka* was heard, but that no man could see him.[2]

Following the *Ka* yet another deity appeared on the scene, and seems also to have come forth from the *Underworld of the Soul*. He is described as the *Sanctified Ruler* (*ḥḳꜣ ntrỉ*) who resembled the *Nefer-ḥer*.[3] We already know this deity. The first Edfu record showed that this god most probably lived in the island during its first era, and was believed to be a falcon and one of the companions of the *Pn*-God.[4] This god, though mentioned in the narrative, is never said to be a living god who would intervene in the process of the creation of the Earth. We conclude that he was present only in his spiritual appearance, and this, perhaps, we may say, gave him a new function in the island. He was regarded as the protection of the *ḏd*-pillar.[5] We know that the *ḏd*-pillar was the seat of the *Pn*-God, and that this *ḏd*-pillar was regarded as the relic (*ỉḫt*) of the former domain when the new period of creation dawned. Therefore, the *Nefer-ḥer* revealed himself in the island in the capacity of the protector of the sole remainder of the former sacred domain of the *ḏd*-pillars.

Further evidence of the same belief is afforded by the presence of the god called *Ḥeter-ḥer*.[6] The beginning of the first record makes it clear that *Ḥeter-ḥer* was in the island before the creators landed in it. As will be seen below, *Ḥeter-ḥer* was there throughout the whole period of development of the new world of the

[1] Cf. pp. 27–8.
[2] Cf. E. vi. 15,3.
[3] E. vi. 182,4 and above, p. 94.
[4] Cf. p. 110.
[5] E. vi. 182,7 and above, p. 15.
[6] Cf. pp. 94–5.

gods, but he is never said to have acted. Since it is known that *Ḥeter-ḥer* was one of the former rulers of the *Island of Trampling* and the text does not say that he was a living god, it is possible that he, too, was conceived as an intangible divine being, and in his nature was equal to the *Ka* and *Nefer-ḥer*. Perhaps the Egyptians thought that there remained in the island, in the very place in which his resting-place once stood, an image to which he returned in his spiritual appearance when once more the sun shone on the island.

The way in which the appearance of the original inhabitants of the island at the commencement of the new sacred world, is described, as well as the nature of the place from which they seem to have come, makes it unlikely that they were supposed to be in the island in their original nature. They seem to have been present not as deities acting in the creation, but as the ancestor gods. This would seem to be an argument in favour of the hypothesis concerning the origin of the underworld: it was created to house the Creator of the Earth and his companions after their resting places in the island were destroyed.

A further deduction that can be made is that the field of reeds assumed a new function when the second period in the existence of the island dawned; it became an ancestral territory. So much is suggested by the name which qualifies this field of reeds in which a new sacred domain was to be created: *the (field of) reeds that restores the Ancestors* (*tpyw-ᶜ*).[1] The fact that the land in which the creation was to be effected was at the same time a territory of the Ancestors can be illustrated by a passage in the Karnak Myth of Creation. The *place of the origin* is the *s3t3w*, the *ground of the Ancestors*.[2] The same tradition is known from the texts of the Temple at Philae. The *Sanctified Territory* which Ptah founded, and which men call the *Beginning of the Earth*, was at the same time a burial place in which Osiris was believed to rest.[3]

There are, therefore, solid reasons for supposing that the domain of the *ḏd*-pillars and the Enclosure of the Earth-Maker were regarded as ancestral lands when the new period of creation

[1] E. VI. 183,3 and above, p. 21.

[2] *ASAE*, XLIV, 126, 143 and Sethe, *Amun*, IV, 70.

[3] Cf. Junker, *Der grosse Pylon des Tempels der Isis in Philae*, *Amun*, p. 45, l. 7.

began. This would offer an undeniable argument in favour of the hypothesis that the first sacred world, the domain of the Creator of the Earth, was believed to have been brought to an end, and that from its decay the underworld of the gods resulted.

The name *tpyw-ʿ*, *Ancestors*, can, in this tradition, only apply to the original divine dwellers of the field of reeds. There is a good deal of evidence from the Edfu inscriptions to demonstrate that the first generation of creators was regarded as the *Company of gods, the Ancestors of the First Occasion*,[1] as the *Ancestors who created the Primaeval Ones (pꜣwtyw) and who brought into existence all that exists*,[2] and that the Earth-God, too, was believed to be the *First among the Ancestors*.[3] This brings to mind the situation in the *Island of the Egg*, which in our Edfu texts bears as a subsidiary name the *Fiery Place of the Ancestors*.[4] In addition we find at Edfu a number of isolated instances which prove the theory concerning the *Place of the Ancestors* or the *Field of the Ancestors*. They tell us of the *Field of the ḏrty-Falcons, the blessed territory of the Primaeval Ones*,[5] a name which appears to be used in the Edfu geographical lists as synonymous with the *District of the ḏdw-Ghosts which enshrines the reeds*[6] and the *Field of the Ancestors*.[7]

We cannot deny the logic of the theory implicit in the Edfu accounts though it is the only source of its kind. It refers to the death from which results the rebirth: the resurrection of the island and of its inhabitants. The divine beings who were first to found the resting places in the island of creation are now the *tpyw-ʿ*, the *Ancestors*, of the new world of gods. They, too, bear the name *ḏdw-Ghosts*.[8] In their spiritual form in which they came forth from the *Underworld of the Soul*, they seem to have attended the creation of the lands for new sacred domains which were the continuation of their own cultus-place. The idea of 'ancestry' evidently governs the creation theory implicit in our Edfu documents.

A new phase of creation began when once more the light shone on the primaeval island and waters. It is to this precise mo-

[1] E. VI. 174,12.14.
[2] E. V. 85,3.
[3] E. IV. 103,10; C.D. V, 44, 11–12.
[4] E. IV. 140,2; 393,16; VI. 247,11.
[5] E. IV. 43,12; VI. 224,4.
[6] E. III. 158,5–6 = IV. 338,14–15.
[7] E. III. 102,4.
[8] E. VI. 184,10; similarly in E. IV. 266,6; V. 85,9–10; 181,10; VI. 12,7; 177,1; 183,16; VII. 15,2–3.

ment, when a new period dawned, that it would seem that the beginning of the first Edfu record refers. Thus it would refer to a renewal or revival of what had previously existed, and from this renewal there developed a new period of creation which altered the original aspect of the island. There thus appears to be a strong reason for supposing that our Edfu records are concerned in the main with the second phase in the existence of the island of creation.

This picture of the beginnings of the sacred world is unknown elsewhere. In the main, however, it makes allusion to a very common fact: the light brings new life to the world which must have lain in darkness as a consequence of the aggression made by the enemy on the domain of the Earth-God. The record is silent about the causes, or the power which dispelled the darkness and brought out the light again. It is only briefly stated that the primaeval water grew radiant.[1] Then the creator gods appeared on the scene. These creators are two divine beings who are described as the *Companions of the Divine of Heart*[2] whose names were *Wa* and *ᶜAa*. They were members of a divine family which we know from the Edfu texts only under the name *šbtyw*, the *Shebtiw*. The text does not indicate from where they had come. We are reduced to speculation. It is unlikely that they were among the original dwellers of the island who died. Also the record does not provide a single hint that they might have been among the fellows of the Earth-Maker in his primaeval Enclosure. On the other hand, however, there is at Edfu evidence of a tradition that these Shebtiw were the second generation of the creators of the Earth. They were, in fact, regarded as the offspring of the Earth-God. In a separate study devoted to this family of creators[3] we came to the conclusion that it was believed that these Shebtiw were born in Nun, probably in a region called *wāᶜret*, from which they emerged to create this world.

Our creation story makes it clear that the Shebtiw were in no way connected with the creation of the original island, but that, on the contrary, their sole concern was the creative work during the second period of the creation of the Earth: the time when the

[1] E. VI. 181,13.
[2] Cf. p. 13.
[3] Cf. *ZÄS*, LXXXVII, 41 ff.

lands adjacent to the island were created.[1] They were the only deities who were believed to be able to complete the creation described as *sw-iḫt-tȝ*.[2] From this point of view it is clear that their creative work was not, by its nature, the organic process, but an action of metamorphic and magical order.

Our chief sources proceed to tell us that the Shebtiw emerged from the water and were brought by an unnamed power to the edges of the island. They perceived the reeds and recognized the god *Ḥeter-ḥer* over and above them.[3] There is also allusion to the god named *Divine of Heart*, who, however, does not seem to have acted at the time when the Shebtiw emerged. The Shebtiw were possibly within the *wāʿret*, and perhaps they were born during the period of darkness. When the light shone once more on the dead and silent island, they emerged on the surface of the waters.

The appearance of the Shebtiw, the creators of magical nature, on the ground of the dead world seems to be the first step towards the opening of a new period of creation. From the order of the accounts preserved in the first record it is obvious that the new phase of the creation of the Earth did not instantly follow the landing of the creators. In the first place the Shebtiw seem to have founded their own settlement on the marginal land of the island which is described as the *gs-wʿrt*.[4] Although this name occurs only once in our record, it is certain that *gs-wʿrt* was believed to be a place-name since it is provided with the determinative ⊗. However, nothing has survived from which to reconstruct the Egyptian idea of the aspect of this place. But we can cite evidence of a tradition of a probably somewhat later date, which is known also from the Edfu sources only. *Wa* and *ʿAa* are described as the *Lords of the Island of Trampling* who established (*smn*) this place and who first lived there in the company of Rēʿ.[5] Doubtless they were regarded as the first living deities who occupied the Island of Trampling and who lived there close to the spot where the image of *Ḥeter-ḥer* stood. Around their home, however, the former world of the Creator and the domain of the *ḏd*-pillars was still dead. Their dwelling-place appears in this tradition to be

[1] Cf. p. 187ff.
[2] Cf. p. 161.
[3] Cf. p. 13.
[4] E. VI. 181,16.
[5] E. VI. 358,13–14.

the centre from which the new phase of creation, the resurrection of the first sacred world, was disseminated.

The narrative proceeds to give a number of facts which make it possible to reconstruct the Egyptian views of the way in which *Wa* and *ᶜAa* acted while revivifying the dead sacred world.

In the development of events the stage next to the foundation of a very primitive settlement of the creators on the marginal land of the island was an event described as the *sḏdỉ ḏbꜣ*, *Planting the ḏbꜣ-Perch.*[1] Some account of this mythological event has already been given in our separate study. It is, however, important to repeat the essential features of this event, which is unique of its kind. This event is doubtless, from the Egyptian point of view, vital in the development of the creation story, in particular, the revivification of the dead world and the origin of the new sacred domain which replaced it.

It is stated in our record that after the Shebtiw settled in their home, the reeds came floating by; then

> the reed was split in two, and a half of it came to them. A slip (*ḏbꜣ*) of reed which was in the primaeval water was planted, so that the Winged One who marches around might perceive (it). The name of the reed which is in the primaeval water is djeba (perch). Protection (was established). That which was made by the two (divine beings), the Ka having arrived and the reed having been removed. The relic (*ỉẖt*) of This One, the *ḏrty*-falcon upon the *ḏd*-pillar, is the reed that uplifts the god (*wṯs nṯr*). The slip (*ḏbꜣ*) of reed is the name of the Perch in Wetjeset-Neter. Thus Djeba in Wetjeset-Neter became the name of this domain, great being the inundation in the fields that surround the marginal land (? *gs*) of reeds.[2]

It is evident from this account that the *Perch* (*ḏbꜣ*) was set up by *Wa* and *ᶜAa* on the edge of the Island of Trampling, within the field of reeds, of which the principal function is defined by the expression *wṯs-nṯr*, *to uplift the god.* It is inherently possible that the Perch was erected in the same place as that in which the *ḏd*-pillar of the *Pn*-God once stood, probably close to the *ḏd*-pillar supporting *Ḥeter-ḥer*, and also near the place where the

[1] Cf. p. 133, and *ZÄS*, LXXXVII, 47, n. (*z*).

[2] E. VI. 181,16–182,2 and above, p. 14; this is the first attempt to translate this part of the first cosmogonical record.

symbols of the Creator were hidden.[1] This tradition makes it clear that the *Perch* is not the self-created seat of the god which emerged from Nun like, for example, the lotus, the Seat of the First Occasion of the Sun-God. The seat of the chief deity in our creation story, though in essence a slip of reed, was erected by the two creators of the Earth, and is, in fact, the first result of their creative capacity.

The abbreviated versions of this myth help to fill out the picture of the *Planting of the Djeba-Perch*.[2] It is explained that the Falcon had arrived thereafter, alighted on the Perch and was uplifted by the reed. We attempted to explain in our previous study[3] that in these statements there seems to be preserved some of the general Egyptian theory concerning the beginnings of the earliest sacred domain that survived in historical times. This idea receives some support from the fact that our document tells us that at that stage of the primaeval age the great inundation was still lying around the Perch.[4] The meanings which belief and tradition connected with this primaeval *Perch* are doubtless many and varied.

If we recall that the reed was the sole relic of the former domain of the *Pn*-God and his fellows, it is evident that only the reed as such was believed to have contained the power of uplifting the god; the relic of the early domain was the only means through which the dead world might have been brought to its former state. The reed was the material from which the *d̲d*-pillar was made, and as the relic of the first sacred world that vanished, provided the essential element for the creation of a new sacred domain that succeeded the former in a direct line.

The essential idea implicit in the description of this event was undoubtedly the idea of the resurrection of the former world of the gods, and this idea can be emphasized by what followed thereafter. It is clearly stated that the reeds having been removed, the *Ka* of the dead ruler arrived at the place of the Perch. We may suggest that by virtue of the action of removing the reeds and planting the slip on the marginal land of the island the inanimate

[1] Cf. p. 94 ff. [2] Cf. p. 15.
[3] Cf. *JEA*, XLVIII, 84–7.
[4] E. VI. 182,3.

form of the dead ruler was re-animated, and brought him out of the darkness to the very place where his former domain had once existed. It would appear that the erection of the Perch was the vital act in this process and this act made it possible for him and for all the other deities of the early sacred domain to reveal themselves. All these actions occurred in a field which was sacred prior to the erection of the Perch, and if we recall that in this creation the *Ka* is said to be the first to come from the company of the divine Ancestors, this circumstance, therefore, provides decisive evidence that only through the erection of the Perch could the former sacred nature of that particular place be revivified. Hence, it is evident that the Perch is in this tradition the manifestation of the resurrection of the first holy world. It is the symbol of its new era and represents in a somewhat altered form its antecedent: the *ḏd*-pillar. The *ḏd*-pillar, the most sacred emblem of the perished world, would appear to have imparted the sanctity to the specific slip of reed. Consequently, the sanctity that was conferred on it would appear to have had its manifestation in the power which is defined in our sources as the action of *wṯs-ntr*, the *uplifting of the god*. This sacred act, which is known to us from the Edfu narrative only, is the resurrection of a divine being. The rebirth of the divine nature of a god was the starting-point in a new phase of creation of the Earth from which this world was believed to have developed.

It follows that the Egyptian belief was that the existence of the Perch was the principal means by virtue of which the island could gradually be brought to a new life and to its former state. The Perch was believed to impart sanctity to its nearest surroundings, and thus it was believed that the first sacred domain (*niwt*) was created on the marginal land of the island of creation. This first domain created at the dawn of the new period of creation bears the name *Wetjeset-Neter*. The manner in which it was created proves that it assumed and bore the function and the characteristics of its antecedent, the sacred domain of the *ḏd*-pillars that vanished. Then, after the Perch had been erected and the new divine being in the island had alighted upon it, the ancestral *ḏrty*-Falcons were awakened from their slumber. They returned to the place where they formerly ruled in their spiritual forms. This is evident from the presence of the Soul described as the *Flying Ba.*[1] Our hypothesis can furthermore be illustrated by the part which the ancestral deities played in the re-created domain of *Wetjeset-Neter*. The narrative makes it clear that they came to appoint their successor, the Falcon, and to protect him in his new home.[2] The circumstances described reveal the importance of the field of reeds in Egyptian mythology. It was in a field of reeds that the first sacred domain was created and existed. When this domain vanished the field of reeds was believed to have protected the funerary abode of its rulers. It was again in a field of reeds that life was renewed. In our creation story it was in the field of reeds that the early divine generation of gods revealed themselves after its sanctity was revivified by the creation of the Perch. In the same field of reeds the first domain for the new divine being was founded. It follows that the field of reeds had vital significance in the origin of sacred places. Further illustrative evidence of the same thought can be found in the geographical list of the Pronaos at Edfu. The field of reeds is described in the following terms:

> He (= the King) brings the meadow of the divine dwellers, (even) the district (*ww*) of the *ḏdw*-Ghosts which enshrines the reed that gives new strength to the Weak One.[3]

There is a striking resemblance between the definition of the field of reeds in this short text and the description of the domain of the Ancestors in our creation story. The idea that the reed gives new vigour to the Weak One seems to accord with the characteristics of the Domain of *Wetjeset-Neter*, which is said to be *twꜣ tpyw-ꜥ, uplifting* (or: restoring) *the Ancestors*. The idea evidently was that the field of reeds as a place with funerary associations was the only part of land in which the revivification of all that was dead could be effected. In connexion with the text in the Edfu geographical list we have to remember that the field of reeds in the *Island of Trampling* contained primarily the *ḏd*-pillars upon which rested the deities governing the island. These are now the

[1] Cf. p. 16; certainly the Flying *Ba* is a divine being other than the Ruler of the Wing, because it is stated in the text that the Flying *Ba* came close (to the Perch ?) after the Ruler of the Wing, the *Nefer-ḥer*, was already in the place.

[2] Cf. p. 116ff.

[3] E. III. 158,5–6 = IV. 338,14–15.

Ancestors of the re-created sacred domain. As Ancestor gods residing in their images on the *ḏd*-pillars they are the *ḏdw*-Ghosts. There is, therefore, reason for assuming that all these statements were inspired by the same tradition.

A further deduction that can be made from these texts is that both allude to a deity who does not bear any specific name. Therefore, if our equation be correct, the *Pn*-God from the main Edfu document is to be linked with the *gnn*, the *Weak One* in the spell quoted above. Here once again we think of a tradition concerning a nameless deity who was believed to reside in a field of reeds, who died there and whose mortuary image was hidden in the same field of reeds. He was subsequently re-animated by another divine power also in the field of reeds. This brings to mind one of our hypotheses expressed above, that the first defunct deity in Egyptian mythology seems to have been an Earth-God.

In view of all the evidence in the Edfu texts we have no doubt that one of the vital thoughts of this cosmogonical theory is the idea of a revival and resurrection. The analysis of our document makes it clear that the first act of creation which the two Shebtiw completed in the *Island of Trampling* was solely an act of re-creation of a divine world which once existed and which ended in darkness.

At the beginning of this chapter we suggested that it looks as though the Egyptians believed that the historical domains were founded on what existed in the past, on the grounds of a sacred world that perished. The facts yielded by the analysis of our sources confirm our surmise. Since it is known that the original inhabitants of the *Island of Trampling* were the *ḏrty*-falcons, and moreover, since there is at Edfu explicit evidence that their realm was regarded as the 'territory of the Ancestors', it is, therefore, clear that a land of ancestral tradition was the only place fitting for the foundation of a new sacred domain. The new phase of creation of sacred domains, however, was possible only after the vanished world was resurrected and was brought to its former state. There is, consequently, no doubt that the period of the primaeval age in which the sacred domains which survived in historical times originated, was definitely not regarded as the first period in the existence of the island of creation. It is also clear that the Edfu narrative starts at the moment when the second period of the primaeval world of gods dawned.

For the Egyptians the re-creation of the domain of the Ancestors does not seem to be the result of a supernatural power which would act in a latent manner. The Edfu account shows that another creative power was needed in the revival of the domain of the Ancestors. And it was this power that actually 'fashioned'. It is evident that at the beginning of this act of re-creation it was necessary to constitute means which could bring the god, in the form of his living substitute, to his former state. Then and only then could the creation of further sacred domains be carried out.

The revivification of the other primaeval domain which was believed to have existed in the *Island of Trampling* during the first period of its existence is also placed in the field of reeds described as the *Wetjeset-Neter*. This act was probably assigned to the same creative powers, the Shebtiw; it proceeds, however, on a somewhat different scale. It was, in fact, a real re-creation and reconstruction of the former state of that domain, as will be seen below. This episode is said to have happened after the revelation of another Earth-God, who is Tanen. We have no doubt that in the brief allusions with which the first Edfu record begins there is enshrined a myth about the restoration of the sacred domain of the Creator, an act which culminated in the origin of sacred domains of other divine beings.

The analysis of the beginning of the first Edfu record shows that it enshrines a composite and manifold tradition. It permits us to gain a fairly clear idea of the essential parts of Egyptian cosmological doctrine. It enables us to reconstruct the picture of a very ancient domain which the Egyptians looked on as that of the Creator of the Earth, and believed that it once existed in the island of creation, but was destroyed. The narrative explains a good deal of the mythological circumstances with which the Egyptians seem to have surrounded the part of land in which the creation of this world began.

It emerges from the Edfu accounts that the Egyptians believed in two distinct eras in which the Earth was created, each of which represented, on the other hand, a definite part in the history of their sacred places. Strictly speaking it was in the first period of the creation that the foundation ground of this world was created; this then was conceived as being the sacred domain of the Creator of the Earth. The second phase of the creation was then the restoration of the domain of the Earth-God and the era of the origin of the historical domains. Our records proceed to give a quite detailed account of the means which brought the domain of the Earth-God to its former state.

Our main Edfu sources undoubtedly convey views of general significance and application. The statement that a first world, created when light was first made, was destroyed, accords with one of the major ideas of Egyptian cosmogony. At this point we see a link between the fate of the island as it is known from the Edfu sources and a thought expressed in the *Book of the Dead*, Spell 175; according to the latter, the Earth, after it was created, disappeared beneath the primaeval waters. The Edfu account, therefore, adds many details to this view and, moreover, gives it a dramatic context.

The first creation can be regarded, from the point of view of the tradition implicit in our documents, as the history of the *Homeland of the Primaeval Ones*. In the history of this domain the allusions to the fall of the Sound Eye, the *wāᶜret*, the *Underworld of the Soul*, and the revelation of the Ancestor Gods, are all valuable pieces of evidence that this *Homeland* ended in darkness and beneath the primaeval waters.

It is of interest that in the second period a new generation of the Creators of the Earth appeared on the scene. The Creator of the Earth does not seem to have acted himself, but he was replaced by other deities who are described as his 'progeny'. The main, indeed the exclusive, concern of the creation performed during the second phase was again the creation of the Earth. The interpretation of the origin of animate beings appears definitely foreign to this doctrine. Hence, it is not unreasonable to conclude that the Edfu Myth of Creation was inspired by a doctrine whose sole concern was the origin of terrestrial substances and their intimate derivatives.

PART III

The Second Era of the Primaeval Age

CHAPTER 9

The Origin of the Lands used as Sacred Domains

BEGINNINGS OF THE CULT OF THE FALCON

The primaeval domain (*niwt*) created on the marginal land of the *Island of Trampling*, the *Wetjeset-Neter*,[1] appears to be the principal outcome of all the actions of creation which the Shebtiw completed in revivifying the island. And from this spot developed a new phase of creation which altered the aspect of the primaeval world of gods. It is obvious from the Edfu account that the Shebtiw re-created the original sacred domain neither for the *Pn*-God and his fellows nor for the Earth-Maker and his company. Another divine being had appeared in their place. The newcomer in the *Island of Trampling*, after this was revivified, is the Falcon, the *Winged One* (*ndb*) by his first name.[2] As has been said, there are, in our myth, definite hints of another mythical world of which the island was the survival; it is, therefore, a logical deduction from the facts that the world of the dead deities became the actual foundation ground of a new holy world of which the Falcon became the ruler. The place of origin of the first Falcon's domain was not a freshly created land, but a land which originally was that of a nameless god who had funerary associations, and who, though represented as a Falcon (*ḏrty*), seems to have been an Earth-God.

In this respect all the events which are described at the beginning of the first record, i.e. the emerging of the Shebtiw, the revelation of the *Ka* and the other *ḏrty*-falcons, then the erection of the *Perch*, are incidents and decisive moments concurring in the constitution

[1] Cf. pp. 15–16, 109 ff.

[2] E. VI. 182,1, and above, p. 16, n. 3; *ndb* is in this tradition the name of the deity for whom the first temple was constructed, therefore also a nameless divine being who was described according to his physical appearance. Only once is his name written in full, in the first occurrence in our text; the following instances show the sign used for writing *ntr*-god. Therefore the conception of a deity was at that stage of history closely associated with a bird.

of the first sacred place of the *Winged One*, the later Falcon, in the *Island of Trampling*. The idea inherent in the account of this mythological situation is that the cult place of the divine being who is the god (*ntr*) of historical times, derived from the events by virtue of which the vanished world of the Creator was revivified. Only the Edfu texts make known these trends of thought and interpret the circumstances in which it had happened. Nowhere else do we know of a text explaining the reasons and conditions that led to the creation of the cult of the *ntr*-god, as well as the foundation of a sacred place for the newly created cult. For the cult of the Falcon, too, the Edfu sources are the only evidence.

That the Falcon arrived in the land of another and earlier divine generation, and that in that land his first sacred domain was afterwards founded, is asserted in the texts of some ritual scenes found at Edfu. They allude to the belief that the Falcon, at Edfu the Falcon Horus, arrived in (*sꜣḥ*)[1] the land (*tꜣ*) of the *First Generation* (*ẖt tpt*);[2] he assumed the protection of some sacred substances described as the *iḫt* only.[3]

This idea is also expressed in the text of the ritual episode of *Bringing the ꜥankh-bouquet of the išd-tree* which is engraved on the outer wall of the Pronaos of Edfu.[4] The spell to be recited by the officiant reads:

Take to thyself the *ꜥankh*-bouquet for thy Soul, O, Atum, Horus the Beḥdetite, great god, lord of the Sky. May thy heart unite with joy, may Thy Majesty abide in *Nedjem-ꜥAnkh* in thy form of Horus-with-uplifted-arm. When thou hast reached the land of the First Generation in Beḥdet,[5] thou hast awakened the gods on their seats (*wṯst*).[6]

---

[1] Cf. pp. 21, n. 7, 23, n. 6.

[2] E. IV. 356,13–14; V. 64,11; VI. 136,3; for the allusions to the First Generation of gods (*ẖt tpt*) see E. VI. 174,11; *ASAE*, XLIV, 143 and Sethe, *Amun*, p. 48; cf. also above, p. 76, the Edfu evidence concerning the original inhabitants of the island of creation.

[3] For the expression *nd iḫt*, cf. pp. 27–8.

[4] E. IV. 355,7.

[5] *ẖt tpt n Bḥdt*, the *First Generation of* (or: *in*) *Beḥdet*, this is evidently an Edfu tradition which replaced the primaeval land by the site of Edfu.

[6] It looks as though in the Edfu tradition the term *wṯst*, lit. *litter* (cf. Blackman and Fairman, *Misc. Greg.* p. 412), was used to describe the resting-place of the god in the primaeval age.

We have no doubt about the possible points of contact with our myth because the mythological situation that can be deduced from this spell fits in with our narrative; it is concerned with the appearance of the Falcon on the mythical scene, and reflects the same belief, the interpretation of which was only slightly modified under the influence of views and traditions current in historical times.

In the ritual formula Horus the Behdetite is described as being equal with the Soul of Atum; we see here a parallelism with the condition of the primaeval Falcon, who is said to have been equated with the *Flying Ba*.[1] There is much that is similar to the description of the arrival of the god in the new land. Horus is said to have reached the land in which another earlier divine generation lived. His appearance awakened them on their seats. The *Winged One* in our creation story is found in the same circumstances. He came to the island, which was sacred prior to his arrival, and in which was the sacred domain of the *ḏrty*-falcons that had vanished. The arrival of the *Winged One* is, in fact, concomitant with the resurrection of the former sacred domain, which was performed and completed by the Shebtiw. We imagine that the Egyptians believed that after the domain itself was revivified and its sanctity restored by the erection of the Perch, the *Winged One* appeared. This was precisely one of the reasons why the ancestral *ḏrty*-falcons were re-animated, were awakened from their slumber, and, as intangible divine beings, came out of the *Underworld of the Soul*. The emergence of the *Winged One*, therefore, can be interpreted as completing and consecrating the significance of the erection of the Perch. The awakening of the *ḏrty*-falcons and the erection of the Perch[2] are the starting-point of a new era, the second, in the existence of the *Island of Trampling*. For the Falcon, however, this was the earliest part of the history of his cult. It was the time of his *Seat of the First Occasion*,[3] as we learn from the tradition of a later date.

Some account of the *Planting the Perch* (*sḏḏi ḏbꜣ*) has already been given.[4] We read in the narrative that *The name of the reed* (*nbi*) *which is in the primaeval water is djeba*.[5] This statement can be

[1] Cf. p. 115 ff. [2] Cf. p. 121 ff. [3] Cf. *JEA*, XLVIII, 81–91.
[4] Cf. p. 14. [5] E. VI. 182,1–2.

taken as decisive evidence that the slip of reed was thought to be planted on the marginal land of the island, and that the first sacred place of the Falcon in its primary state was believed to have been surrounded by waters.[1] This description appears to reveal one of the fundamental ideas of the myth: the creation of the god's seat, that seat which followed the former domain of the *ḏd*-pillars, came to pass on the margin of the primaeval waters.[2] This seat was erected within a field of reed which by its nature was a sacred land prior to this action; its principal function was believed to be the power *wṯs nṯr*, *uplifting (restoring) the god.* Hence, it is legitimate to conclude that the *ḏbȝ*-Perch of the Falcon was made in the same place as that in which the *ḏd*-pillar of the defunct *Pn*-God once existed, and that it had the same function as the *ḏd*-pillar. The *ḏbȝ*-Perch is actually the substitute for the most sacred emblem of the former domain of the *Pn*-God and *Ḥeter-ḥer*. That it was believed to have happened in this way is possible because the record does not mention that the *ḏd*-pillar would also have been restored in the same site after the domain was revivified.

The significance of the name which the first domain of the Falcon bore since then, the *Wetjeset-Neter*, stresses the idea that the creation of the first sacred domain of the Falcon was conceived as the rebirth and restoration of the vanished sacred place of the Creator. From this point of view it is entirely clear that the sanctity of the place in which the first cultus-place of the Falcon was to be created was imparted by what had existed in the past and had perished. We do not doubt that the first era in the history of the primaeval domains of the Falcon can be defined as the time of the re-creation of a destroyed world. This mythical event of settling down on the ancestral land is what the interpreter of a later date described as the *sȝḥ*, *coming close to the land of the First Generation of gods.*

Our record preserves a unique picture of the way in which the first resting-place of the god whose cult survived in historical times was founded. Allusions are known, indeed, to the 'Seat of

[1] This is moreover confirmed by the expression *bw-ḥbbt* occurring in E. VI. 184,13.

[2] Cf. p. 68, allusion to the belief that everything was created on the marginal land of the island of creation, and Gardiner, *AEO*, II, 158.

the First Occasion',[1] but nowhere is there any explanation of its nature and appearance or of the manner and circumstances under which the resting-place of the god was created in the primaeval age. In contrast, our creation story describes in great detail the origin of a very primitive domain[2] that was believed to have been established on the marginal land of the island of creation.

We can attempt to draw an outline picture of the first sacred place of the Falcon in the *Island of Trampling*. We imagine that the name *Wetjeset-Neter* applies to the whole field of reeds, representing probably the extent of the former domain of the Earth-God,[3] and in the midst of which was the *Perch*. The Falcon lived in it together with the ancestral deities, the *ḏrty*-falcons. It follows that the first domain of the Falcon was regarded as being at the same time the place of the worship of the Ancestors. This feature is of prime importance for, as will be seen below, the connexion with the Ancestors is a vital element in all the phases of creation of the primaeval domains of the Falcon. It was there, in the realm of the Ancestors, that the Falcon was adored for the first time as a god by the powers who created his domain, the creators of the Earth known in our story as the Shebtiw.[4] Hence, the offspring of the Earth-God are in our creation story the first beings who completed a ritual act of adoration.[5] That this might have been the Egyptian idea of the 'Seat of the First Occasion' of the Falcon can be demonstrated by referring to the reliefs which at Edfu accompany the first cosmogonical record.[6]

The Falcon ruled in the *Wetjeset-Neter* as the *Lord of the Perch* (*nb ḏbꜣ*). Except for the ancestral deities, the Shebtiw were the only companions in his first home. The description of the field

[1] E. IV. 358,3 giving this as the definition of the Perch; see also *JEA*, XLVIII, 86–7.

[2] E. VI. 182,3: *kꜣ Ḏbꜣ m Wṯst-nṯr ḫpr Ḏbꜣ ḫpr Wṯst-nṯr ⟨m⟩ kꜣ niwt tn*, 'The name is Djeba in Wetjeset-Neter. Thus Djeba and Wetjeset-Neter became the name of this domain', occurs as the final statement in the description of the first *niwt*-domain of the Falcon; cf. above, p. 14; the literal meaning of this sacred name will be: the Perch in (or: of ?) the Uplifter of the god.

[3] Cf. p. 14, n. 3, the supplementary quotations in the Edfu texts indicating that the whole field of reeds was regarded as the 'uplifter', the place in which the god was restored to his former state; cf. p. 118 ff. for the explanation of this act.

[4] E. VI. 182,4 and IV. 358,16.

[5] Cf. p. 120 ff. for the role of the creators of the Earth in the constitution of sacred places.

[6] E. XIV. Pl. 561.

of reeds in our record may well reflect the aspect of a genuine, though primitive, domain or enclosure in which the sacred falcons were reared in a far distant past. This can be demonstrated by the picture of an enclosure on a seal from the Archaic Period.[1] We can see some points of contact between the *ḏbꜣ*-Perch of our myth and the supports depicted on the seal, which might well have been fashioned from reeds or other light material.

The description of subsequent events makes it likely that his first sacred domain was regarded as a real centre of creation of new lands in which other sacred domains were founded thereafter. All the acts of creation that occurred in the domain of *Wetjeset-Neter* are the eras in which the sacred world of the Falcon in the primaeval age came into being. The bringing into existence of these new domains was also effected by the Creators of the Perch, the Shebtiw *Wa* and *ᶜAā*. These periods of the creation of the Earth seem to have occurred only after the Falcon was definitely established as the ruler of the original *Wetjeset-Neter*. It is quite evident that this mythical episode formed an integral part of the long-drawn-out drama of the creation of lands. The record proceeds to describe a mystic act by virtue of which the Falcon, as the Lord of the Perch, consorted with the Soul of the *Pn*-God, the *Flying Ba*.[2] We suspect that the picture of this event conceals the explanation of how it happened that the Falcon was equated with the former deceased ruler. The abbreviated version of the myth confirms this view. It is stated that by means of this mystic act, the Falcon was enabled to unite with the sky of *Him-whose-command-is-unknown*.[3] It was believed that only through this act did the Falcon become the real successor of the deceased *Pn*-God. Only when this had happened could the creation of the new lands for the Falcon's domains be carried out.

The account of the events connected with the original domain

[1] Petrie, *Royal Tombs*, I, Pl. IV, 8 showing a slip of reed beside which is the Falcon, and underneath which is the sign ⊗ *niwt*, domain. There is therefore textual as well as archaeological evidence for believing that the earliest sacred places had a rounded form. For another representation of an early domain of the Falcon in the open field see Petrie, *Royal Tombs*, II, Pl. V, 3.

[2] Cf. p. 16; E. VI. 182,8 furnishes unique evidence of this event.

[3] E. VI. 15,2–3; perhaps this act was interpreted as the rebirth of the original nature of the god; for the Falcon as a symbol of rebirth cf. *BD*, ch. 77, 78, 81, 83, 85, 86, 87 and also a brief allusion in P. dem. Pamonth, III, 1.

of *Wetjeset-Neter* in the second era of the existence of the *Island of Trampling* has every aspect of being a complete history of a primitive cultus-place. If we recall the name of the divine being for whom it was created, the *Winged One*, we may venture to suggest that there is preserved either an extract or an abbreviated version of what might well have been a single myth about the origin of the place of worship of a sacred bird. This bird might have been later identified with the Sacred Falcon, and thus the story of his cultus-place was adopted and adapted for the explanation of the beginnings of the cult of the Falcon.

One must not, however, imagine that the domains of the Falcon were created in a single action. The narrative enables us to discern several periods succeeding the time of the resurrection of the earlier domain of the *ḏd*-pillars and the constitution of the *Wetjeset-Neter*.

The second period of the creation in the Falcon's primaeval domain meant an extension of the actual territory of the island: the origin of the first plot of land adjacent to it, which is described as a *pāy*.[1] At this point the text is silent about the way in which the actual land of this *pāy* was created. It is only briefly stated that the *pāy*-land *dj-ᶜ ḥr.s, appeared on it*.[2] From this description it can be deduced that a land called *pāy* might have been created in a way other than the island itself. There was certainly a connexion between the emerging of this *pāy*-land and the activity of the two Shebtiw, since they were in the island when the *pāy*-land emerged, and are said to have uttered sacred names on that occasion. This picture of the emerging of the *pāy*-land may allude to the symbolic and magical manner of creating the Earth, the *sw-iḫt-tꜣ*, of the nature of which a preliminary account has been given.[3] Since there is no allusion to the making of the Earth for the actual land of that *pāy* by an organic process, the Earth, as the substance, must have been created prior to this action of uttering names, and must have lain beneath the water. Our document would seem to describe, therefore, only the second phase of the creation: the emergence of the Earth hidden beneath the primaeval water.

[1] E. VI. 182,10 and below, p. 171; the etymology of the word *pᶜy* is unknown, therefore we use only the phonetic rendering of the word.

[2] Cf. p. 17. [3] Cf. p. 27.

This event was believed to have been caused by the uttering of the sacred names. This hypothesis receives some support from a brief allusion occurring at the beginning of this narrative. It is stated that there was a great inundation in the fields (*iḥw*) that surrounded the marginal land of the island where the reeds grew.[1] The first *pāy*-land to emerge at the edges of the island of creation might well have been one of these *iḥw*-fields, since the major idea of this creation myth is not to create something anew, but to re-animate what already was. The Egyptians clearly believed that the actual land of the sacred domains that survived in historical times was brought into existence in a way unlike the origin of the island, and resulted from the activities of divine powers who were not the same as those who created the Earth as a substance. This will accord with our previous hypothesis concerning the *foundation ground* which the island seems to have been.[2] In the subsequent parts of the narrative there is other evidence to bear out the theory that the island was a real foundation ground for the lands needed for the creation of sacred domains.[3]

The aspect of the newly created *pāy*-land was apparently made similar to that of the original domain of *Wetjeset-Neter*. No detailed description of it has been given. The Falcon was subsequently greeted as the lord of that *pāy*-land.[4] Therefore, he must have had his divine seat there, which we imagine to have been again a *ḏbȝ*-Perch. A slight indication in favour of this hypothesis might be seen in the allusion to intercourse between the *Ka* and the Falcon, during which the *Ka* was believed to reveal to the Falcon some secret things.[5] That this event had happened in the *ḏbȝ*-Perch is found to be explained in the tradition of a later date.[6] This *pāy*-land had its own name which seems to have derived from the greeting formula which the Shebtiw addressed to the Falcon.

It appears that following this action other *pāy*-lands originated. In the Edfu version, however, this part of the narrative is presented in a very concise way. Nevertheless, the occurrence of the expression *in rn, to say name(s)*,[7] preceding a series of names which

[1] Cf. p. 15, n. 1, 2.
[2] Cf. p. 84.
[3] Cf. p. 142ff.
[4] E. VI. 182,11.
[5] E. VI. 182,17.
[6] E. VI. 17,11.
[7] E. VI. 182,12.

we suppose were recited by the two Shebtiw, then the exclamation *arrive at this place*,[1] suggest that this part of the narrative conceals another allusion to the same magical process of creation. The result of this action would thus be the appearance of other *pāy*-lands alongside the marginal land of the island, where other domains were founded in which again the Falcon became the ruler. The interpretation suggested will accord with the allusion to the *nis ḏ3jsw, reciting the learned spells*,[2] an action which seems to have been followed by what is described in our document as *sni m ḫf, passing by in view*.[3] This expression may describe the appearance of the new plots of land emerging in the sight of the inhabitants of the island.[4]

Strictly speaking, the Egyptian theory appears to be that in the second period of the existence of the revivified island, plots of land, the *pāy*-lands, were believed to emerge alongside the marginal land on which the reeds grew (*gs nbi*).[5] Their coming into existence is represented as the result of a properly symbolic and magical action.

In the third period of this creation story the *ḥᶜy-wr*, the *great primaeval mound*, is said to have originated.[6] It appears that the *Shebtiw* were believed to bring this mound into existence, and again by virtue of uttering spells. On this mound there seems to have been created a single sacred domain, also described as a *niwt, domain*, which, however, bears three names. These names may possibly reveal the significance of the mythical events which were believed to have happened in it. From these names we infer that this mound was also believed to be the territory of the Ancestor (*M3*),[7] who might have been the deity who is described as *He-who-*

[1] E. VI. 182,13.

[2] E. VI. 182,11; we suspect that this part of the narrative describes the same event as that which occurs in E. VI. 184,11, cf. below, p. 160ff.; the word *ḏ3jsw* is perhaps here used as the general term describing all the sacred spells which the Shebtiw uttered while creating the lands.

[3] E. VI. 182,12; this expression may, very tentatively, be compared with *ḫf bs* occurring in E. VI. 183,11.

[4] Cf. p. 18.

[5] E. VI. 182,3 and above, p. 15, n. 2.

[6] Cf. p. 18, n. 6.

[7] Two readings are possible: either *mspr m3wi, New Territory* or *mspr n M3*, the *Territory of the Ancestor*; of these we would prefer the second because it accords with the following event.

is-great-of-arm.[1] The mound seems to be the place in which the enemies of the god were believed to have been annihilated. The existence of the mound does not seem to have any special significance in the development of the domain of the Falcon, but may be connected with the subsequent event. It is explained that a deity emerged from the mound because danger was approaching. A snake appeared near the domain of the Falcon, who was defenceless, and, in fact, unprotected while resting on the *Perch*.

The divine newcomer in the *Island of Trampling*, which is now extended in size by the *pāy*-lands, and also has a mound, bears the name *Ḥn-ntr, Protector God*. This name is known to us from the Edfu records only.[2] It is not obvious from the account of the main cosmogonic record whether this deity might have been one of the gods from the vanished world of the Creator. The tradition tells us only that

> the Protector God came forth thereupon in this place to protect the God within the Wetjeset-Neter in the capacity of the Segemeḥ.[3]

From the fact that this deity is portrayed as an acting god but in the capacity of another deity who is not represented as a physical personality, we conjecture that the *Ḥn-ntr* was conceived as a physically real deity. He may have been born in Nun like the Shebtiw[4] and may have emerged in connexion with the appearance of the new terrestrial configuration.[5] This hypothesis will accord with an interpretation of a later date telling us that the primaeval mound having been created, the protecting god of the Falcon came out of it, and he, too, acted in the capacity of another deity who is obviously an intangible god.[6] The *Protector God* in our story seems to be related to the *Ḥeter-ḥer*; perhaps he was his offspring since he is described as the *likeness of the Radiant One with a face like unto the Ḥeter-ḥer*.[7] We suspect that he might

[1] This deity is not mentioned elsewhere in the narrative; we suspect that there might be a connexion between this place and the symbol of the Creator, the *Arm*; cf. p. 22.

[2] Cf. p. 19.

[3] E. VI. 15,3–4.

[4] Cf. p. 120ff.

[5] Cf. p. 166.

[6] E. IV. 358,17.

[7] E. VI. 182,17.

reveal himself in the resurrected island to act in the place of the *Ḥeter-ḥer*, who was an Ancestor at that time, and that his main function was to exercise protection over the successor of the *Pn*-God.

Following him another deity enters on the scene. It is the *God-of-the-Temple*.[1] His original nature is described by the name *Ptḥ-nwyt*,[2] a mythical name which is known to us only from this narrative. Hence the God-of-the-Temple must also have been a creative power. He, too, was possibly related to the *Ḥeter-ḥer*. We are told that he was brought out of Nun as the *likeness of the Radiant One with a face like unto the Ḥeter-ḥer*.

The circumstances under which the appearance of these two divine beings occurred are relevant. We are inclined to suggest that their revelation showed the characteristics which might be enshrined in the type of Earth created at the end of the period when the *pāy*-lands of the Falcon originated. We know that the primaeval mound was believed to be the territory of the Ancestor, who is not named in our text, but who might have been an Earth-God. If this surmise be admissible it would result that the revelation of the two divine beings was regarded as being the manifestation of the power that was enshrined in the earth of the mound. The God-of-the-Temple was most probably a creator. His task in the newly created world might have been to create the protection of the Falcon. What is said to have happened thereafter accords with this suggestion.

As a consequence of the danger, the protection of the god seems to have been made: an enclosure described as *sbẖt* seems to have been erected.[3] The text is concise. This *sbẖt* may perhaps have been a simple fence erected around the Perch of the Falcon. The next stage was the origin of a new kind of water, which in our document is described as the *mw*-water. It appears as though this myth of creation distinguishes the *mw*-water from the primaeval

[1] Cf. pp. 19–20.

[2] E. VI. 186,3–4; there is no other information to throw more light on the significance of the name *Ptḥ-nwyt*. If we take it literally it would mean that this god was in his essential nature the creator of the water; but this suggestion cannot be justified. We know only that in the Edfu tradition this god was represented as a falcon-headed deity.

[3] E. VI. 183,1 and above, pp. 20–1.

water (*nwyt*) in general. If this view be correct, it would mean that the *mw*-water appeared later after the terrestrial world was in existence, but when it was still in its primary shape.

How this *mw*-water was created is not stated in our document, though the text indicates its creator: it is a deity called *Ntr-ỉb*, *Divine of Heart.*[1] Although this view sounds a little unusual, the only interpretation we can suggest for the sentence *Ntr-ỉb ptḥ mw* is that *The Divine of Heart created the water.*[2] This *mw*-water seems to have been created for a special purpose and was believed to contain a power which prevented the snake from coming near the sacred domain of the Falcon. It is stated that this water was sanctified (*sntr*) against the snake. We imagine that this *mw*-water may have formed a circle around the domain of *Wetjeset-Neter*, perhaps resembling the channel which was made around sacred places later on. At any rate the narrative alludes to a 'channel',[3] but, unfortunately, does not give further information in this respect.

The *sbḫt*-enclosure, eventually surrounded by the channel of the *mw*-water, may have been the first means by which the protection of the *Perch* against evil was ensured. No description is given of the constructing of this enclosure. This enclosure seems to be connected with the revelation of the two protecting deities, whose main function in the island seems to be to protect the sacred place and its divine occupier. It may be suggested that the origin of the first enclosure that was ever made in the island was believed to be the material projection of their presence.

Three important facts seem to derive from the description of this event. The *sbḫt*-enclosure appears as the name of the earliest type of enclosing wall that was made in Egypt around the sacred place in the dim past. We cannot verify this information elsewhere, and we do not know to what real type this *sbḫt*-enclosure may correspond; we imagine it as a mere fence fashioned from light material.

It should be borne in mind that the *sbḫt*-enclosure is said to have originated at the end of various episodes of creation of the Earth.

[1] E. VI. 183,2.

[2] The parallel text on the Pronaos doorway shows exactly the same wording, cf. E. III. 7,7.

[3] E. VI. 183,1.

This circumstance suggests that its construction might have been interpreted as an act of creation equal in its significance to the other act of creation which occurred earlier in the island.[1] Consequently, it was included in the order of the creation of the *pāy*-lands. The two Shebtiw may have been responsible for its construction because they are the only acting creators on the site. Hence, the idea inherent in the description of these events is that the first constructed enclosure of the god resulted from the orders of the creation of the Earth. Its origin is the reflexion and projection of a creating power who revealed himself as a god.

The two protecting deities, the Shebtiw, seem to have acted at the end of all these events jointly with the *Divine of Heart*, who is referred to at the very beginning of this myth and whose *Companions* were these two Shebtiw. It appears that it was believed that the intervention of their presumed leader completed the normal course of all the acts through which the first sacred place in the history of the Falcon's domains reached its final stage.

It is likely that the emergence of the primaeval mound ends the myth about the creation of the actual lands needed for the domains of the Falcon, and that the history of their development closes with the revelation of the two protecting deities and with what resulted from their presence in the island. We incline to the opinion that the creation of the Falcon's domains as evolving from the former realm of the *ḏrty*-falcons who rested on the *ḏd*-pillars, was completed in the setting up of the *sbḫt*-enclosure and in the digging of the channel.

There will be some doubts whether this form of a primitive sacred place consisting of a vegetable seat of a god and surrounded by a mere fence of reeds was erected on the freshly created plots of lands, the *pāy*-lands, or whether this simple construction was made around the original Perch in the *Wetjeset-Neter*. Since the description of the creation of the sacred place of the god within the *pāy*-land, as will be seen below, does not refer to a fence described as *sbḫt*, we may assume that a sacred place of such an

[1] If this be correct it would mean that the origin of the *sbḫt*-enclosure was the principal outcome of all the orders of creation of the lands.

aspect was made in the original *Wetjeset-Neter*, the first domain created on the ground of the ancestral territory.

The following part of the narrative seems to bring us to the original field of reeds, apparently to a spot within it other than that in which the *Perch* was. We suspect that there is a clear allusion to another myth of creation about the primaeval domains of the Falcon. This myth might have originated in another place, and might in the original version of the *Sacred Book of the Specification of the Sacred Mounds* have primarily formed a part independent of the first myth, which we have already analysed. The presumably second myth about the origin of the primaeval domain of the Falcon might have been simply juxtaposed to the first myth only later, perhaps even in the Edfu editing. In the study of the second myth several facts appear which make this surmise inherently possible; thus, for instance, the *Perch* in the domain of *Wetjeset-Neter* was in existence but is not mentioned in the second part of the Edfu narrative. Several *pāy*-lands already existed together with the primaeval mound, but there is no reference to them. We suppose that the second part of the first Edfu cosmogonical record might have been based on another ideological background, and be, consequently, the result of a tradition which originated in a place other than that in which the tradition concerning the *djeba*-perch was at home. Nevertheless, one feature is common to both, and this is precisely the idea of the revivification which, too, underlies the events recorded in the second part of the first Edfu record. This tells us about the resurrection of the domain of the Earth-God.

In our exposition of facts concerning the *Island of Trampling* in its first period we suggested that it seems that two primitive domains might have existed in it side by side. The order of events in the creation of the primaeval domain of the Falcon seems to indicate another possible interpretation. We suspect that the name *Wetjeset-Neter* may be of general significance and that it may describe any place in which, on a ground of an earlier sacred place, a new sacred domain started; for in this creation story the same name applies to two originally distinct primaeval areas, each of which shows an entirely different physical aspect. The Edfu account gives a clear idea of the belief that a *Wetjeset-Neter* was the place in which the Earth-God described as the *Earth-Maker* dwelt, and that an early domain of such a nature and such a name was the starting-point in the constitution of the first cultus-place of the Falcon. While comparing the way in which these two earlier domains were revivified and restored, we find further arguments that there are two distinctly different trends of thought, and consequently two originally independent myths.

If these deductions be accepted, it will follow that the theory concerning the origin of sacred lands which we have attempted to reconstruct, might originally have formed a single myth about the resurrection of the domain of the *Pn*-God and his divine fellows, in short, the deities who dwelt on the *ḏd*-pillars. This myth included, so far as we are aware from the Edfu evidence, the constitution of a place of worship of the Ancestors, which is described as proceeding step by step with the origin and growth of the first phase of the place: the creation of the first sacred domain of the Falcon. Supposing that this was the Egyptian idea, we can attempt to outline the final aspect of the first primaeval realm of the Falcon in which his cult was established and which existed side by side with the place of worship of the Ancestors during the second era of the 'primaeval age of the gods'.

It appears that the centre of the first sacred realm was a cultus-place of the Ancestors that is said to have borne the name *Wetjeset-Neter*. In its physical aspect this domain (*nἰwt*) was in fact the replica of an earlier sacred place which consisted of a small number of supports, made from vegetable material such as reed and to which, in this tradition, the form of the *ḏd*-pillar was given. These original supports were substituted by a slip of reed named *ḏjeba-perch*. Along and around the boundary of this ancestral domain there were created lands in which the domains of the new god were founded thereafter. The period of their creation seems to have ended in the origin of the mound. Then followed the consolidation of the protection of the early domain. During this period there seems to have originated the first constructed enclosure.

The Edfu records do not enable us to state where these domains existed, which according to this tradition were sacred to the Falcon. It is a possibility that in these lines there is recorded the history of Damanḥur or other sacred places of the Falcon Horus in the Delta.[1] No authority can be cited to support such a hypothesis, and this research is outside the framework of our study.

Nevertheless, it is tempting to imagine that a sacred realm of such an aspect and extent as is described in our record, may have represented for the Egyptians of historical times the *ỉ3t n p3wt tpt*, the *Sacred Mound of the Primaeval Age*. This hypothesis will accord with the significance of the title of the Sacred Book which we are studying,[2] and is supported by the secondary name of the *Island of Trampling*: *the Sacred Mound* (*ỉ3t*) of *Ḥeter-ḥer*. This second name does not occur in the main record but appears in a text which must have been written in accord with it some time later in historical times.[3] We conclude that the first part of the Edfu record preserves most probably an originally single myth about the origin of the domains of the *Winged One*. These *pāy*-lands may have been the sacred domains on which the tradition looked as on the first *ỉ3t*, *Sacred Mound*, of the Falcon. It may, consequently, be suggested that the following part of the same record yields the 'mythological history' of another *ỉ3t*, *Sacred Mound of the Primaeval Age*.

We have already pointed out[4] that the sentence *Coming close to the (field) of reeds of Wetjeset-Neter that restores the Ancestors* appears to have originally been the title of a single myth. This myth, too, might have been adopted and used as an explanation of the origin of the primaeval domains of the Falcon. The Edfu tradition, however, looks upon this event and all the succeeding actions as following the three acts of creation through which the sacred world of the Winged One came into existence. In the general history of the origin of the domains of the Falcon, therefore, all that follows presents the fourth phase of their creation. And this fourth phase of creation involved again an act of re-creation of what once had existed in the past but had died.

No accurate description is given of the arrival of the divine beings in this field of reed, and the text does not tell us to whom

[1] Cf. Gardiner, *JEA*, xxx, 23 ff.

[2] Cf. p. 12.

[3] E. vi. 11,5.

[4] Cf. pp. 21–2.

the word *sꜣḥ*, to *come close* refers. This word may refer to the arrival of the two Shebtiw, who, as will be seen, are the main acting power in the new episode of creation.

Before the early sacred domain had been re-created, the narrative tells us about the revelation of a god who is not mentioned in the beginning of the episode. This deity is Tanen, the *Lord of Creation* (*ptḥ*). He is said to have appeared on the scene as a 'protection'[1] after the Shebtiw pronounced a spell. The occurrence of the word *ptḥ*, unknown to the first part of this creation story, may indicate that in this part of the Edfu narrative there are enshrined fragments of another tradition. The revelation of Tanen as a protective divine power perhaps made it possible for the former domain of the Earth-Maker to be re-created and made similar to its former state. If this be correct, Tanen would appear here in a position equal to that of the *Ka* at the beginning of the re-creation of the domain of the *ḏdw*-pillars. It is worthy of note that in both of these traditions the creation was initiated by the revelation of the Earth-God. It should be remembered that here also the scene is placed in the field of reeds. The fact would attest the important part that a field of reeds played in the origin of any sacred place.

In this part of the narrative there is no allusion to the *Pn*-God, nor to the *Ka*, who were the prominent personalities of the first creation story. This is another and valuable argument to support our hypothesis that the Edfu tradition here associated two originally distinct myths.

The picture of the field of reeds of *Wetjeset-Neter* which is preserved in the second part of the record, affords further support for the theory that the creation of the domain of the Falcon was, in the first place, an act of resurrection through which an earlier sacred world came to its former state. This description of the field of reeds is of importance because it exemplifies the conception of the nature of a place in which a sacred domain was created at the dawn of the history. Emphasis is again laid on the idea of the *Ancestor* in connexion with the Creator and creation. This field of *Wetjeset-Neter* is pictured as a place of ancestral tradition which was in decay. In the preceding chapter we have attempted to

[1] Cf. p. 23.

outline the appearance of the sacred domain which was believed to have existed there prior to the arrival of Tanen.[1] We suggested that this spot was regarded as the very place in which the Earth-God dwelt during the first period of the island's existence. This domain was believed to have been destroyed when the island was attacked by a snake.[2]

We are told that the first act in the restoration of the domain of the *Earth-Maker* followed at once the revelation of Tanen. A shelter (*nht*) was erected as a 'protection' (*sꜣ*)[3] of the symbols of the creating powers which are described as the *Member of the Progenitor*. The narrative indicates the dimensions of this shelter, which are 5 by 15 cubits. We suspect that at this point the Edfu record might give us the idea of the extent of primitive shrines that might once have existed in Egypt. The erection of this shelter is described as being the first act of creation which the creators completed in the field of reeds. For this reason, we suggest that this act may be linked with the *Planting of the Perch*. If this be correct, we see here, in spite of the similarity of the general thought, a definite hint of an entirely different tradition from that which underlies the myth already analysed.

The next stage is described as *Constructing what was planned.* The use of the words *ḫws* and *wḏꜥ* confirms the idea of a reconstruction. It has been suggested in the preceding chapter that the Egyptians believed that the *Earth-Maker* founded a Mansion for himself and that this Mansion also housed his companions. It is likely that the statement *Entering that which was in decay by the God-of-the-Temple* describes the state in which the Mansion of the Earth-Maker was found after the creators entered into this area. There is much that is similar to the account of the restoration of the domain of the *ḏdw*-pillars. We have here the two Shebtiw whom we suppose to be responsible for the erection of the *nht*-shelter, then the God-of-the-Temple who is said to have attended the construction of the *sbḫt*-enclosure. It seems that it was believed that when the *God-of-the-Temple entered* the ground of the former dwelling-place of the Earth-God that site was revivified, and as a result the *Mansion of Isden* was restored. The

[1] Cf. p. 97ff. [2] Cf. p. 113.
[3] Cf. p. 22.

close link with the event described as the *Planting of the Perch*[1] is furthermore borne out by the nature of the land in which these actions of restoration happened. This was again a land of ancestral tradition in which an Earth-God was believed to have dwelt. Only a place with such a tradition could make it safe for a new sacred domain to be founded there. The action of restoration is here again described as a decisive step in the forthcoming period of creation.

Another point of similarity with the myth about the domain in *Wetjeset-Neter* is that the original inhabitants of the *Mansion of Isden*, though mentioned in the narrative,[2] are never said to be present as physically real deities. It is highly probable that they had there the same function as the ancestral *ḏrty*-falcons in the first *Wetjeset-Neter*.

When the *Mansion of Isden* was reconstructed the Falcon seems to have entered into it. No description is given of what may have been his resting-place within this enclosure. What, however, appears quite certain is that he was told by Tanen of the way in which this domain was destroyed.[3] Tanen seems to be the prominent personality in the following episodes, which we suppose came to pass within the *Mansion of Isden*. He created from staffs protecting symbols in giving them the names of the companions of the *Earth-Maker*.[4] The creation of the protection appears to be a preliminary act of a ceremony by virtue of which the Falcon became the successor of the *Earth-Maker*. It is explained that Tanen presented the Falcon with sacred symbols such as the spear described as the *Great White* (*ḥḏ-wr*), the *ḏd*-pillar and that which is described as the *Likeness of the Front of the God*; meantime yet another symbol was brought in the presence of the *God-of-the-Temple*.[5] The narrative describes an episode of offering symbols by a god who was a creator, to another god. This act shows, in its general significance, a striking resemblance to the episode of presenting the *iḫt* by the *Lord of the Wing* to the Falcon resting on the Perch.[6] In dealing with the first mythical episode we suggested

[1] Cf. p. 133 ff. [2] Cf. p. 99 ff. [3] Cf. p. 23. [4] Cf. p. 97.

[5] It looks as though this list indicates the sacred objects that might have been kept in the primitive enclosure. This information, though very interesting, cannot be supported by archaeological evidence.

[6] Cf. p. 16.

that it has every appearance of being an act by virtue of which the Falcon was equated with the deceased ruler. It may, therefore, be suggested that this episode performed on the grounds of the Earth-God had the same consequence. In receiving the emblems of the Earth-Maker the Falcon might have been believed to assume the power of the former ruler of this Mansion. He might have been regarded as his successor then. These emblems, together with the two staffs in which the companions of the Earth-God were embodied, ensured the protection of the Falcon in his new home. The performance of this ceremony and its completion appears as the principal means that resurrected the sanctity of the destroyed domain of the Earth-God.

We have no detailed account of how the shelter was erected and the *Mansion of Isden* was reconstructed; as an act of creation it can be compared with the description of the Planting of the Perch.[1] Nevertheless, we imagine it as a simple courtyard open to the sky within which the most sacred part was marked out by the shelter. It is likely, though it is not clearly stated in the text, that the Shebtiw were responsible for all these actions of construction and reconstruction. At that stage there is no allusion to other creators of sacred places who could do so. The only difference that can be noticed from the first narrative is the presence of the *God-of-the-Temple*, who does not appear in the first event at all, but seems to intervene in this process of re-creation. One could not read these two episodes of re-creation without being struck by the strongly pronounced parallelism of ideas as far as the function of the *Mansion of Isden* and the significance of all the actions are concerned. They are the same as those which we have in the first myth about the domain of the *ḏd*-pillars, only projected into and applied to another sacred place. In both narratives we have an account of the physical work of restoration which was followed by the performance of a symbolic episode, and which was the presenting of special offerings by one god to another. The result was that the domain of the Earth-God was revivified and was brought to its former state. In both myths the

[1] We suspect that in this myth the *nht* in fact replaced the original *ḥwt*, mansion. If we agree with the hypothesis that the shelter replaced the mansion, it would result that the first enclosure was in its dimensions 5 by 15 cubits.

resurrected domain was the nucleus of the creation of new lands for other sacred domains. In the first myth the Shebtiw performed all the actions of creation resulting from the revivification of an earlier sacred domain; here, too, they are the main actors in the forthcoming stage of creation which would, consequently, appear as the direct outcome of the restoration of the *Mansion of Isden*.

It has been noticed that with the exception of the Falcon and the acting creators there appeared divine beings completely unknown to the first part of this record. Moreover, the structures in this second *Wetjeset-Neter* show somewhat more advanced and developed features than the domain of the *ḏd*-pillars.[1] The difference in the physical appearance of these two early sacred domains is enough to show that the first Edfu record enshrines traditions of two early cultus-places. We suspect that the mythological situation which we have been analysing discloses a tradition which originated in another place, but was associated with the idea of the revivification of a former state. These facts will enhance the general significance of the *Wetjeset-Neter* in the history of the early Egyptian cultus-places. They will show that the tradition concerning the resurrection of the domain of *Wetjeset-Neter*, though unidentified by archaeological evidence, must have been familiar to several early cultus-places, and was modified to suit local beliefs. Thus it might happen that this myth was taken over by a place consecrated to the Falcon and was used as an explanation of the origin of the first enclosure of the Falcon in the primaeval age. Here once again the predominant thought of the episode of foundation is that the first enclosure of the Falcon was erected on the grounds of an earlier sacred domain, which was that of the Earth-God.

In the fifth stage in the history of the primaeval domains of the Falcon, according to the Edfu tradition, new lands needed for further sacred places of the Falcon were created. These are again the *pāy*-lands that were created from the *Mansion of Isden*. In the description of their origin no hint is made of any organic work

[1] The first domain consisted only of a group of supports; on the contrary, the second domain shows a planned, though primitive, structure, and dimensions are given.

which the Shebtiw would complete. We are told that following the ceremony in which the Falcon was instituted in the rulership, the God-of-the-Temple summoned the two Shebtiw, and apparently instructed them in the manner of creating. At this point we can see a difference in that the first myth does not speak of the God-of-the-Temple as being present in the island when the *pāy*-lands began to emerge.[1] We see here a clear allusion to another conception of the act of creation of the *pāy*-lands. Since the Shebtiw created the *pāy*-lands, but only in the second part of the first record are they said to have been instructed in the manner of creating, it is evident that the description of the fifth period in the creation of Falcon's domains discloses a tradition that originally was distinct from the first episode. These facts accord with our hypothesis that the myth about the resurrection of the domain of the *Earth-Maker* might well primarily have been an independent myth which at a definite moment was adopted and adapted for the interpretation of the origin of Falcon's domains. This moment is never and nowhere indicated.

The meaning of the instructions which were believed to have been issued by the God-of-the-Temple before the start of the new phase of creation of the Earth can only be guessed at, for they are recorded in the most enigmatic way,[2] and no parallel text can be cited. What appears to be quite certain is that the Shebtiw were inducted in the creative activity described here as *nḥp*, *to fashion* and that they were sent to visit a certain place named as the *bw-ẖnm*.[3] As has been said, the meaning of this name remains obscure. We imagine that all that came to pass in this *bw-ẖnm*, which, eventually, might have been a place near the enclosure of the Earth-God. The Shebtiw proceeded to specify the *iḫt*, *substances*, at a definite moment which is indicated in the record as the time in which the *Arm* was invoked by the *praise of Rēʿ*.[4] Although there is one common point with the first episode of creation of the *pāy*-lands, the allusion to the *Arm* does not occur in the first myth. The event described may have been what the Egyptians regarded as a 'rite of creation', which began with the

[1] Cf. p. 18. [2] Cf. p. 24. [3] Cf. p. 24, n. 1.

[4] Cf. p. 24, n. 4; it looks as though the expression *ḥsi Rʿ* replaces the word *ḏ3jsw*, cf. p. 18, n. 3, but only in this context.

worship of the Creator, who is here represented by the symbol of the *Arm*. This then, as has been suggested, was the physical form of the elementary creative power which was believed to have been concealed in the ground of the enclosure.[1] The immediate outcome of this event renders the suggested interpretation reasonably possible. The result of this action was the emergence of the *pāy*-lands which we imagine appearing around and along the field of *Wetjeset-Neter* where the *Mansion of the Earth-God* was.

This description of the beginning of the creation is undoubtedly more accurate than that in the first myth, and is of prime importance for the Egyptian idea of how the creative forces acted on the emergence of the *pāy*-lands. We suspect that we have here an extensive account of what is described in the first myth only as the *dj-ᶜ*, *appearing*, of the *pāy*-lands.[2] The adoration of the symbol representing the power which was believed to have brought into existence the plots of land, was regarded as being the prerequisite to effect the emergence of the *pāy*-lands. The expression *sw-iẖt-tꜣ*, *to endue the substances with power*, does not occur here, and moreover the nature of the *iẖt*, which undoubtedly must have played an important part in this episode, is not determined. We suspect that these *iẖt* might represent the symbols of the lands to be created. The use of the word *dm*, *to name* or *to specify*, confirms the importance of the *word* in this action of creation. We imagine that the Shebtiw while naming the *iẖt* indicated the lands to be created, and thus through this procedure they made it possible for the lands to emerge from the primaeval waters.

The text proceeds to give a long list of names introduced by the word *pᶜyw*, *pāy*-lands.[3] There is much that is similar to the first myth and we have no doubt that this part of the Edfu narrative yields exactly the same situation. We think that these names are the sacred spells (*ḏꜣjsw*) which the Shebtiw pronounced at the adoration of the *Arm* by the 'praise of *Rēᶜ*'. These names may be considered as revealing the proper sense of this kind of rite.

[1] Cf. p. 89.
[2] Cf. p. 137.
[3] E. VI. 183,12–18.

It would follow that these sacred names were pronounced over the *iḫt*, *substances*, and that, consequently, this act meant the giving of names to the *iḫt*. These *iḫt*, *substances*, having been named, caused the Earth hidden beneath the waters to emerge. If our reconstruction of this mythical situation be correct, we suggest that this part of the narration reveals the characteristics of the 'rite of creation' that was believed to have been performed in the *bw-ḫnm* at the dawn of history. This *bw-ḫnm* may have been the place in which the *iḫt* were stored, and so the nucleus of the creation of lands of which the nature and functions are strictly defined. Undoubtedly these newly created lands had the same function as in the first instance and were the grounds for the foundation of the Falcon's domains. They appear to have been originally domains subsidiary to the *Mansion of Isden* in the field of *Wetjeset-Neter*. We suggest that each name listed in the record is that of a single *pāy*-land which was made into a sacred domain of the Falcon. This part of the record does not, however, reveal anything which can help to describe the eventual development of all these *pāy*-lands. Another difficult point is that the narrative does not permit us to discern whether a *djeba*-perch was created in these *pāy*-lands or whether a *ḥwt*-mansion was constructed there imitating and repeatedly re-enacting the Mansion of the Earth-Maker.

This list of names of the *pāy*-lands suggests that in it there may be preserved the names of the original sacred domains of the Falcon. Since all these domains are projected into a mythical plane, it follows that these names may be those of sacred places earlier than historical times. This is, of course, a speculation for which, at present, there is no clear textual or archaeological evidence.[1]

This period of creation also led to the appearance of the *ḫʿy-wr*, *great primaeval mound*. Its emergence represents the sixth era in the history of the primaeval domain of the Falcon. According to our document no special tradition seems to have been connected with this mound.

We have seen that the centre of the creation is in this episode

[1] We do not claim that these names preserved the names of the cultus-places of the Falcon on the *Great River*, cf. p. 168.

fundamentally different from the domain of the *ḏd*-pillars, and that other deities, unknown to the first narrative, came on the scene; the actual creators, however, are the same, and the manner in which the new domains were created shows obvious affinities with what is described in the first myth. It is, therefore, suggested that this episode of creation discloses the history of the origin of another *iꜣt*, the *Sacred Mound of the Primaeval Age*, which was believed to be sacred to the Falcon.

In the stages of the creation of the Falcon's domains the seventh phase is apparently an act of re-creation, and this event seems to bring us, once again, back to the original island.

This part of the narrative bears the title *ḥḥ bw-ẖnm*, *Visiting the bw-ẖnm*,[1] an expression known from the account of the fifth phase in the creation of the Falcon's primaeval domain. Apparently another allusion is made to the same mythical place. As we have seen, the interpretation of the name *bw-ẖnm* meets with difficulties and there is no authority to clarify the explanation only very tentatively suggested in our summaries.[2] *ẖnm* is a problematic word. It may be used here as an infinitive qualifying the word *bw*, which is, in fact, a very frequent construction in our texts. On the other hand, however, *ẖnm* may be a noun; if so it is to be taken either as *ẖnm*(*t*) with the meaning *well, cistern*[3] or as the masculine noun *ẖnm*, *water*. The latter is frequent in the administrative documents of New Kingdom.[4] It appears in the same documents as a formative of place-names. In this respect attention should be drawn to an instance in a stela from Abydos,[5] which speaks of a *ẖnm* which is in Abydos. Furthermore, we find on two wine-jars from El-Amarna[6] inscriptions with a mention of a source of wine described as *pꜣ-ẖnm n iw Mšd*, the *Water of the Island-Meshed*. The last instance appears to be relevant to our problem, since in both cases we can see a close connexion between the *ẖnm* and an island. Our record is, however, silent about the location of this place and about its eventual connexion with the two other sacred spots. The description preserved tells us only that this *bw-ẖnm*

[1] E. VI. 184,2 and above, p. 25. [2] Cf. p. 161.

[3] Cf. Gardiner, *AEO*, I, A 29.30.

[4] Cf. Gardiner, *P. Wilbour*, II, *Comm.* pp. 30–1.

[5] Cf. Mariette, *Abydos*, II, 37, l. 12 = Gardiner, *JEA*, XXVII, Pl. 11, l. 12.

[6] Cf. *City of Akhenaten*, III, no. 75, 183.

enshrined the *Place of Wa*, which, we may conjecture, was his original resting-place.

Nevertheless, it is significant that here as well as in the account of the creation of the *pāy*-lands that departed from the Enclosure of the Earth-Maker, we meet the same deities: Tanen and the two Shebtiw. If we recall that at the beginning of the fifth phase in the creation of Falcon's domain Tanen emerged after the Shebtiw recited a spell, it may, very tentatively, be suggested that this *bw-ẖnm* was a place of water, perhaps a still water within the island. The text does not state that Tanen would emerge in the midst of Nun, and that from there he reached the island. This *bw-ẖnm* might have been, perhaps, equivalent to the Hermopolitan pool in the island of creation. Perhaps this *bw-ẖnm* was the place from which the subterranean water welled out, whereupon the creative powers might eventually have been brought out of Nun, in the first instance Tanen. Although the text does not say it, we imagine that perhaps the water coming out of this well brought him to the field of reed, the *Wetjeset-Neter*. We know that the Shebtiw, too, suddenly emerged near the edges of the island of creation, but the narrative does not indicate the exact place from which they would emerge. As this account refers to a place described as the *bw W3*, the *Place of Wa*, we are tempted to suggest that they dwelt also in this primaeval well, before they landed in the dead domain of the *Pn*-God.

We know from the account of the fifth phase of creation that the Shebtiw visited this *bw-ẖnm* before they started to create the actual land of the *pāy*-lands. It may, therefore, be surmised that this primaeval spring brought out not only the creative powers but also the constituent elements in the creation of the Earth, the *iḫt*.

This is, inevitably, a hypothesis for which there is no textual evidence. If, however, we assume it, it would follow that this *bw-ẖnm* was regarded as being the place of origin and the realm of the creative powers acting in the second period of the creation of the Earth. The Edfu account would seem to disclose how the Egyptians imagined that this particular place was made into a sacred domain.

It is highly probable that this part of the first record introduces us to a part of the primaeval island other than the field of *Wetjeset-Neter*, and in spite of the similarity of the general ideas that underlie the story, the account makes us familiar with traditions and beliefs distinctly different from the two previous ones. We notice a fundamental difference in one of the essential features of this *bw-ḫnm*. In the description of the appearance of the *bw-ḫnm* no mention is made of reeds, but on the contrary, the willow is said to be its centre. This appears as a starting-point for an attempt to reconstruct, at least theoretically, the physical aspect of the *bw-ḫnm*. The picture of a willow standing near a well gives a clear idea of a primitive sacred place as it might once have existed in Egypt. We imagine that it might have been believed that a primaeval creative power, after having emerged from the water, could dwell among the branches of a willow, and that there he was adored.

What happened around the willow, according to our mythical episode, appears to be another instance attesting the existence of an earlier sacred place which for this reason was associated with the island of creation and was believed to have existed there during the first period of its existence. Since the willow is said to have been there when the creators arrived, and no allusion is made to its being planted and growing, it is possible that the Edfu tradition associated with the two preceding accounts yet another myth about the resurrection of a sacred place which was in decay and which became the centre of creation of lands for new domains. In spite of the differences concerning the concrete aspect of the place, the close parallelism of thought between this story and the two other myths already discussed is apparent. We incline to the opinion that in this part of the first Edfu record there is enshrined the early history of yet another, the third, *ỉ3t*, *Sacred Mound*, of the Falcon. We think that we have here beliefs in another sacred place linked with the idea of the revivification of an earlier sacred domain which was brought to death. This myth too was adopted for the explanation of the origin of the primaeval domains of the Falcon.

It seems to result from this account that when the two Shebtiw arrived in this area, Tanen revealed himself.[1] Afterwards they

[1] E. vi. 184,2; *dj-ʿ* seems to be used here with the meaning *to reveal*, cf. above, p. 17, n. 7.

came to a place described only as a *bw*, *place*; *ʿAā* then created, again by the mere pronouncing of a name, a sacred domain (*niwt*), the name of which was *bw-ḥmr*, *the Place of the Throne*. This *Place-of-the-Throne* seems to be the only place which was believed to have been created there. As far as the rather obscure text permits us to reconstruct the situation, it appears that the willow was included within this place. Some sacred objects were brought in and placed in the presence of the *Arm*. These objects are described as *iḫt*; these *iḫt* may have been the substances already mentioned in connexion with the creation of the *pāy*-lands, which was performed from the *Mansion of Isden*.[1] This ceremony having been completed, an enclosure (*sbty*) seems to have been erected, which we imagine as surrounding the *Place-of-the-Throne*. Subsequently a new generation of Creators appeared on the scene. These are the *Builder Gods*, who are unknown to the earlier mythical situation. Perhaps they were responsible for the constructing of this enclosure.

What follows is an episode of adoration. The text is, however, silent about the deity who might have been adored or as to who might have been the eventual performers of this act. The result of all these incidents seems to be the constitution of a domain of which the Falcon became the ruler. At this point we notice a certain resemblance to the two previous accounts of the formation of a sacred domain within the island of creation. It is said that the willow grew radiant, and that subsequently the Falcon was uplifted. Hence, this account propounds the idea that the willow was the Seat of the First Occasion in the cult of the Falcon. This seat came into being also on the ground of an earlier sacred domain which needed to be revivified. It was, in fact, revivified at the time when the Falcon arrived and settled down on the willow. Consequently, the willow growing radiant was the symbol of resurrection in this creation story.

The text alludes to the *Arm* but does not specify whether this *Arm* was brought by the Shebtiw to the site or whether it was concealed in the ground of that place. If the second suggestion be admissible, we have here, once again, convincing evidence that a primitive sacred place was founded on the ground in which

[1] Cf. p. 22.

a nameless creative power represented by the symbol of the *Arm* was believed to have dwelt. The belief in the *Arm* is already known from the second myth about the *Wetjeset-Neter*, and this evidence confirms its significance and importance in the foundation of a sacred place. Another similarity to the first narrative can be seen in the mention of the *nht*-shelter, which we imagine to have been erected underneath the willow, then the mention of two deities described as *Šḥm-ḥr* and *Ḥḏ-wr*. Both these names are already known from the description of the Enclosure of the Earth-Maker, and we suppose that we have here the same divine beings, and that they played the same part in this episode as they did before.

When the Falcon rested on the willow, the protection of the place was constituted in a way closely resembling the already known order of creation, which involved a 'magical protection' of an early cultus-place. The text is unusually obscure, but what appears quite certain is that the protection was constituted by means of symbols. The magical power of protecting was conferred upon them by a giving of names. This account ends in the statement *To be done according to that which has been done.* We suspect that there is only a summary indication of what was believed to follow; there may have been an allusion to the procedures of creation which occurred in the two other early sacred domains after they were brought to a new life.

Viewed as a whole, this order of creation, as far as it can be reconstructed from this enigmatic text, recalls the situation known from the history of the domain of the *ḏd*-pillars as well as from the episode of the restoration of the *Mansion of Isden.* We have no doubt that we have here the same theory of the re-creation and reconsecration of a primitive cultus-place, only associated with beliefs and traditions of another sacred place.

When this domain was re-created the Falcon again became its supreme lord. We meet here the same creative powers, Tanen and the two Shebtiw, then two protecting deities from the earlier stage of existence of this domain. No allusion is made to the other deities who were prominent personalities in the two preceding episodes. Neither the *Pn*-God, nor the *Ka*, nor the *God-of-the-Temple* are mentioned or described as intervening in the process of actions through which the *Place-of-the-Throne* came to be a sacred domain of the Falcon. This circumstance makes it likely that we have here decisive evidence of yet another, third myth about a creation and re-creation of a sacred place in the island of the primaeval age of gods. The theory that this episode was, indeed, an act of restoration and reconsecration is supported, in the main, by what is said about the willow. The willow is described as growing verdant after several ceremonies were completed underneath it. We suspect that these episodes had the effect of bringing the willow to a new life. The picture of the willow, therefore, gives a clear allusion to the revivification of what was in decay.

A further similarity that can be seen between the *Place-of-the-Throne* and the *Wetjeset-Neter* is the part which this place seems to have represented in the subsequent stage of the history of Falcon's domains. As has briefly been pointed out above, it is evident that the domain of the willow, after it was restored, was a nucleus of creation of further grounds for the foundation of Falcon's domains. This last, the eighth, phase in the creation of the primaeval domains of the Falcon is interpreted in this tradition as evolving from the domain of the *Place-of-the-Throne*.

In this ultimate stage of creation two *pāy*-lands are said to have come into existence. They bear the name *Wetjeset-Neter* and *Djeba* respectively.[1] These two names do not occur in the long list of the *pāy*-lands, as mentioned above, but they are identical with the name of the original domain in the island. This circumstance can be purely incidental. On the other hand, these two *pāy*-lands, believed to have emerged at the end of a long-drawn-out drama of the creation of sacred domains, may have been given these names to commemorate the existence of the very sacred place in which the cult of the Falcon had its origin.

The description of the origin of the *pāy*-land of *Wetjeset-Neter*[2] is detailed and supplements the Egyptian view of the emergence of the plots of lands adjacent to the island of creation. It is stated in the text that the Shebtiw were assembled in a place of special

[1] E. VI. 184,14 and 176,12.
[2] E. VI. 184,10 ff.

nature before the start of a new phase of creation. This place is described as the *bw-sw-iḫt-tꜣ-im, the Place in which the substances of the Earth were endowed with power.*[1] No detailed picture of its appearance is preserved. Moreover, this name does not occur in connexion with the two previous periods of creation of the *pāy*-lands. We are reduced to speculation. We have to remember that in all the three instances known of the beginning of the creation of the *pāy*-lands a sacred domain of an earlier date was revivified and brought to its former state. It is fairly clear from the account that the existence of such a renewed sacred place was regarded as the pre-requisite to the performance of the rite of creation through which the *pāy*-lands were brought out of Nun. We may hazard a guess that this *bw-sw-iḫt-tꜣ* might have been a special place within the renewed sacred place; there might, perhaps, be a place in which these *iḫt-tꜣ* were kept, and where, eventually, the rite of *endowing with power* was performed. This is, inevitably, somewhat hypothetical, for no relevant texts can be cited. If this view, however, be admissible, it would follow that only the place which was destroyed could assume the potentiality of becoming the centre of a new creation through the act of revivification as has been described above.[2] Such an interpretation assumes that in this episode of creation the name *bw-sw-iḫt-tꜣ* applies to the *Place-of-the-Throne.* And the interpretation would appear possible if we recall that at the beginning of this account allusion is made to some *iḫt* which were brought in, and that a ceremony was performed in front of the *Arm.* We imagine the two Shebtiw as being within the *Place-of-the-Throne* and performing the magical rite of *sw-iḫt-tꜣ*. We suspect that the name *bw-sw-iḫt-tꜣ* is only another name of the sacred place described as the *bw-ḫnm.* We have attempted to interpret the significance of this place.[3] If we recall its function in the fifth phase of the creation of the Falcon's domain and then its real nature in the seventh phase, it is highly probable that the creation of the *pāy*-lands derived from the *bw-ḫnm.* This is, in this seventh phase of creation, the very place that was restored and from which the new creation started. This shows that the place of ancestral tradition was regarded as the real centre of creation of the Earth, and that the name *bw-sw-iḫt-tꜣ* qualifies the function of the *bw-ḫnm.* It was therefore believed that only in the place in which the primary creative power rested could the *substances of the Earth* be endowed with power.

Doubtless, this last instance of the creation by magical procedure is the most illustrative evidence that is furnished by the Edfu record. If we agree that in all the instances of the word *iḫt* the same substances are referred to, it is clear that they represent, as symbols, the lands to be created because in this account they are defined as the *iḫt* of *tꜣ*-Earth.[1] A further important fact that can be deduced from this account is that it sets out clearly that the Egyptians imagined the creation of the Earth as a mere emergence of the plots of land from the water. We read in our document that in the meantime the Shebtiw recited the sacred spells (*ḏꜣjsw*), the water gradually receded from the edges of the island and the actual land of the *pāy*-land was brought out (*bs*).[2]

This part of the record is explicit enough to enable us to reconstruct the physical aspect of the *pāy*-land and to reveal the Egyptian view of how the freshly emerged Earth was made into a sacred domain. It is highly probable that they believed that the creators of the Earth made it into a sacred land and made it similar to the original domain of *Wetjeset-Neter*.

Mention is made of *arriving in a bw-ḥbbt*[3] after the *pāy*-land came into existence. The expression *bw-ḥbbt* occurs only in this third account. Theoretically the interpretation *the place of the primaeval water* may be suggested. We suspect that this name may describe a specific place on the marginal land of the *pāy*-land in which the reeds grew. The Shebtiw apparently recited further sacred spells, then the *Ḥeter-ḥer* is said to have appeared on the scene.[4] What follows has every appearance of being a march of the deities present in the *pāy*-land at which perhaps the image of the *Ḥeter-ḥer* was carried in front of the procession to a special place within this presumably small area. The place to which this

[1] Cf. *ZÄS*, LXXXVII, 43, n. (*f*).

[2] It will be noticed that each of these three instances of creation is described in a somewhat more explicit way than the preceding one and that the definition by *sw-iḫt-tꜣ* occurs only in the last; there will be another hint of three different traditions in each of which the same process of creation found a somewhat altered definition.

[3] E. VI. 184,12–13.

[4] This suggestion is based on the occurrence of the word *ḏꜣjsw*, cf. E. VI. 184,13.

procession led is described as the *bw-ḏd, the place of the ḏd-pillar.*[1] We think that in this point lies the essential feature of this creation story, for this *bw-ḏd* is described as being equal to the place of the *djeba*-perch of reed. The *ḏd*-pillar is not pictured here as a real object which would stand in a definite part of the marginal land. It is highly probable that on the *pāy*-land also the *ḏd*-pillar, as a relic of a sacred domain that once existed but had vanished, determined the very place in which the seat of the Falcon, the *Perch*, was to be erected. Therefore, the sanctity of the site of the sacred place of the Falcon was, once again, imparted by what had existed in the past. The Perch was again the first thing which was to be created in the *pāy*-land; hence, once again, the Perch is the manifestation of the renewed sanctity of the land.

One could not read this account without being struck by the close resemblance of events and actions to what had happened on the marginal land of the island when the first *Wetjeset-Neter* was resurrected. The Falcon is said to have come thereafter and was lifted up by the reeds. The *pāy*-land then received the name *Wetjeset-Neter.*[2] The beginnings of the sacred life in the newly created *pāy*-land were thus conceived to be a mere re-enactment of the procedures by virtue of which the first sacred domain in this history was constituted.[3]

The explanation of the origin of the *pāy-land of Djeba* adds in great detail to the picture of the initial phase in the life of the primaeval domains of the Falcon.[4] This second account is in many ways more explicit than the description of the origin of the first sacred place in the *pāy*-land of *Wetjeset-Neter.* We imagine that in the first instance there were repeated all the acts of creation already known from the history of the original domain of *Wetjeset-Neter*; then the procedures by which the *pāy*-land of *Wetjeset-Neter* was created were repeated. The contents of the second Edfu record have every appearance of indicating that the Egyptians believed that any *pāy*-land in which the sacred domain of the Falcon was to be founded, had the same commencement. There was therefore one unique way in which all the primaeval domains of the Falcon came into existence.

[1] E. VI. 184,13.
[2] Cf. p. 145.
[3] Cf. p. 93 ff.
[4] E. VI. 176,12 ff.

In the *pāy-land of Djeba* the Falcon seems to have ruled as the *Child of the Ḥeter-ḥer.*[1] The description of the magical rite of creation as well as that of the emergence of the *pāy*-land are not included in this narrative. The text starts with a greeting formula addressed by the crew to the Falcon. Then the speech of the god seems to follow. We incline to the opinion that the god told his crew of the manner in which the ground and his domain too were created. The important fact is that the narrative alludes once more to the reed and describes it as *the reed that restores* (*twꜣ*) *the place in which the ḏd-pillar was.*[2] Then the text proceeds to tell us of various actions which the Shebtiw were believed to complete there while making the bare land of the *pāy*-land into a sacred domain. They are said to have arrived in the field of reeds and performed there a rite of adoration of the *ḏd*-pillar of the *Ka.*[3] As a result the *Ka* himself seems to have revealed himself and to have instructed the Shebtiw how to erect the Perch. We find here the same trends of thought as are known from the history of the *pāy*-land *of Wetjeset-Neter.* The erection of the Perch is the chief means to revivify the sacred nature of the *pāy*-land. This Perch was to be planted in the same place in which the *ḏd*-pillar formerly stood. In this account the event of the *Planting of the Perch*[4] is recorded in a somewhat modified way. It is stated that the primaeval waters became calm. The Shebtiw then performed an act which is described as *sḫꜣ iḫt, Recalling the substances.*[5] No explanation is given of the characteristics of this episode. We think that there is allusion to the same *iḫt* as are known from the preceding episodes of creation, and that the expression *sḫꜣ iḫt* describes the rites of creation to be performed over the *iḫt*. This ceremony was usually performed before the start of the creation of the Earth. Unlike the preceding accounts, this narrative seems to indicate that a ceremony concerning these substances was also included in the procedures of the creation of the resting-place of the Falcon.

[1] Cf. p. 30.

[2] E. VI. 177,3 and above, p. 146.

[3] E. VI. 177,4–5.

[4] Cf. p. 121.

[5] E. VI. 177,7; this episode is mentioned only in this narrative.

The event which follows is similar to what had happened in the other *pāy*-land. The Shebtiw came close to the edge of the land when the reeds were floating by. When they reached a certain place they divided the reeds and a slip of it was planted. This slip of reed then assumed the function of the seat of the Falcon, who was uplifted as the *Lord of the Perch*, and thereby the land was sanctified.

It is clearly stated in this account that after the Perch was erected, then the domain (*niwt*) of *Wetjeset-Neter* came into existence.[1] The Falcon was greeted and a *silent rite* (*sgr*)[2] seems to have completed the series of actions by virtue of which the domain of the Falcon in the *pāy*-land was believed to have been created.

What follows is expressed in a very enigmatic way. Nevertheless it seems that the next episode is concerned with the protection to be set around the Perch. This does not occur in the first account. The text seems to allude to a protecting power which was adored and invited to enter into this area.[3] As a result, it is stated that the Perch grew bright against evil. Another allusion is made to the *Divine of Heart*, who in this connexion seems to be described as the *overlord of the image* (?).[4] It is not clear to whom the word *ḥ*ʿ*w*, for which we suggest the interpretation *image*, may refer. The narrative may well allude to the image of one of the ancestral deities which might have been brought in the *pāy*-land as the symbols of protection. Perhaps we have here, instead of the image of the *Ḥeter-ḥer*, that of the *Divine of Heart*. Nevertheless, the mention of the *Divine of Heart* is interesting when we recall that he is the first deity mentioned in connexion with the emergence of the Shebtiw on the edges of the island. It would appear that at the end of this long-drawn-out drama of creation of the Falcon's domains the *Divine of Heart* reappeared on the scene to fulfil the normal course of events. He might assume the same functions as the *Ḥeter-ḥer* had in the *pāy*-land of *Wetjeset-Neter*.

1 E. VI. 177,10.

2 The sole evidence in our texts; that there might be a connexion with a foundation act is indicated by a document from Old Kingdom, cf. Sethe, *ZÄS*, LXX, 51–6; this was also the first rite to be performed in the early Osiris cult place, cf. E. I. 221,1.

3 E. VI. 177, 9 interpreting as *mi s*(?), *s* for *sꜣ* (?), protection.

4 Reading *ḥry ḥ*ʿ*w* (?), the expression is very problematic and there is no parallel.

At the stage of the primaeval age in which the sacred domain of the Falcon was founded in the *pāy*-land of *Djeba*, the Edfu account of the periods in which the lands for the domains of the successor of the Earth-God were created comes to an end.

The Edfu sources permit us to gain a fairly clear idea of all the stages of creation from which was derived the sacred world. The Falcon was believed to rule there in the primaeval age; his domain replaced the *Homeland of the Primaeval Ones* and the cultus-place of the Creator. The Edfu documents give convincing evidence that it was believed that the primaeval domains of the Falcon were not created in a single action. We can discern eight stages in the history of their development. Each stage in the creation was basically a restoration, though on a somewhat different scale, of something that had previously existed. Each stage resulted in an increase in size of the island and marked a further step in the formation of the domains of the god who was believed to have succeeded to the Creator. In every instance the creation of the sacred domain proceeded on the same plane. The actual land for the domain was created on the marginal land of the island of creation after this was brought to a new life. On the new piece of earth a slip of reed was planted representing the first resting-place of the god. The place of the god's seat seems to have been determined by a pre-existing object which is, in this tradition, always the *ḏd*-pillar. Sanctity was imparted to the Falcon's domain by that which had existed in the past. The sacred nature of the place of the god was manifested in the uplifting of the Falcon. There was, it seems, only one act by which the actual land of the domain was created, and there was only one act by which this land was sanctified.

We have seen that our document yields, in fact, three times the beginnings of the first cultus-place of the Falcon, and that in each instance the commencement of his cult is associated with the resurrection of an earlier sacred domain; each such domain shows another physical appearance. In this sequence we have the domain of the *ḏd*-pillars, on the other hand the *ḥwt*-mansion of the Earth-Maker, and, finally, the domain of which the centre was the *sbty*-enclosure enshrining the willow. Of these the first, the former domain of the *ḏrty*-falcons, seems to be the most important in the constitution of the Falcon's domain. Primarily there must have been a single myth about the restoration of a vanished sacred domain which became the base for the creation of a new sacred world. It is, therefore, evident that there was a single theory concerning the origin of the later historical domains, and that this tradition was familiar to several cultus-places of a remote date. But in the Edfu editing of these myths all these traditions were regarded as forming a single history of the origin of the Falcon's sacred places.

The history of the creation of the primaeval domains of the Falcon comprises three great eras of creation of the *pāy*-lands which departed, all of them, from a pre-existing sacred centre. It looks as though the primaeval realm of the Falcon was pictured as consisting of three terrestrial units, each of which was described at a later stage of history as *i3t, Sacred Mound.*

While using the Edfu textual evidence it is possible to sketch out the general appearance of the sacred world that resulted from the various actions of creation that emanated from the original island. The centre of the primaeval realm of the god seems to have been formed by a cultus-place which existed prior in the island, and which, after the island was revivified, assumed the function of a place of worship of the Ancestors. These ancestral cultus-places seem to be a vital element in the origin and development of the later historical domains. Our document describes three, of which two were within a field of reeds, the *Wetjeset-Neter* and the *Mansion of Isden*, and the third, the *Place of the Throne*, around a willow; each of them was encircled by an enclosure; each enclosure erected in the island bears another name and must, consequently, have been of another type, but all of them seem to be constructed from light material. Within these enclosures of Ancestors the first resting-place of the god was erected. On the boundary of these ancestral enclosures there were, eventually, the *pāy*-lands of the Falcon, in which, at that stage, all that existed was the *djeba*-Perch.[1] From all this evidence an important fact emerges: before the actual land of the later historical domains came into

[1] Cf. p. 165; it appears as though the images of the original divine inhabitants of the *Island of Trampling* were brought into the newly created *pāy*-lands; it will be noticed too that each new *pāy*-land seems to have its own Ancestor god.

existence the Egyptians believed that there existed centres for worship of the Ancestors.

Naturally the question arises where was the region in which these ancestral cultus-places existed together with all the domains said to be sacred to the Falcon. Several tentative suggestions can, of course, be made, but we do not claim that the Edfu accounts enshrine the history of the *dmjt*-sacred places of the Falcon Horus in the Delta.[1]

[1] Cf. Junker, *Die Politische Lehre von Memphis*, 70 and *ZÄS*, LXXV, 72; Gardiner, *AEO*, II, 152, 160–1.

CHAPTER 10

The Pāy-land and its Development

The attempt to understand the Egyptian theory concerning the origin of the actual land in which the historical domains of gods were founded, is beset with many difficulties. The Egyptian documentary sources provide no other relevant texts; there are no similar narratives to cite in illustration of the statements that can be deduced from the first and second Edfu cosmogonical records.

Between the revivification of the earlier domains that were believed to have existed in the island and the creation of the actual land for the new domains of the second generation of gods, there was a period of time during which the sacred life developed around the substitute of the vanished world. The text speaks of the constitution of sacred places for the worship of the Ancestors in which the new generation of gods found their first home.

The Edfu accounts suggest what might once have been the general history of the origin of sacred domains in historical times. This view is in particular supported by the manner in which the name of the god for whom all these domains were created was written. His name was never written in full, but only the sign 𓅆 occurs in the texts. As already mentioned, there is no evidence that the god described as a 𓅆 could only mean the Falcon Horus.[1] This sign reads *ntr* too,[2] and it has been noticed that once in our narrative this sign is replaced by the name *ndb*, the *Winged One*.[3] Considering this, and in view of all the points of similarity in the three accounts that form the first Edfu cosmogonical record, we conjecture that in the background of this creation story lies the tradition concerning the origin of sacred domains of the *ntr*-god. A further argument that can be found in our document is the definition of the field of reeds which played the most important part in all the actions concurring in the constitution of the sacred domain. We can cite an instance showing the name of the field written in full *wṯst-ntr*.[4] This evidence, though of a later date, is

[1] Cf. pp. 5, 12, 44, 45.
[2] Cf. *ASAE*, XLIII, 225.
[3] Cf. p. 16.
[4] E. VI. 224,10.

significant for it confirms that the Egyptians interpreted the name of the field as the *Wetjeset-Neter*. It is inherently possible that the successor of the Earth-God was conceived as a divine being in the form of a bird, and that originally he was also a nameless god, and that, for this reason, he was described only as the 'Winged One'. This, we may say, might have been the original conception of the *ntr*-god, at least as far as this tradition is concerned. Perhaps even at an early date this sacred bird was equated with the Falcon, then the Falcon Horus. That the tradition concerning the *Djeba in Wetjeset-Neter* was familiar to several cultus-places and consequently might have been modified and associated with other beliefs can be seen in the explanations of the meaning of the name *Djeba*. We find them in the lists of the *Mythological names* of the Edfu Temple incorporated in the *Building Text* of the Enclosure Wall.[1] These are summaries of traditions which were attached to the name *Djeba*. We read in the first instance of the *Djeba* created by the Shebtiw; then the text alludes to the *Djeba* in which the evil-doer was punished; the third entry refers to the *Djeba* in which Horus protected the relic of his father. There is therefore illustrative evidence that the myth about the primaeval *Djeba* was only associated with the Myth of Horus son of Osiris at a somewhat later date. Supposing that the Edfu text reflects the stages in which the original *myth about the Djeba* was taken over from one place to another and consequently modified under the influence of local beliefs, we see here additional support for the theory that the *Djeba* was originally a place sacred to a *ntr*-god represented in his primary appearance as a bird. This suggestion accords with the title of the sacred book in which the myth seems to have been recorded first.[2] The origin of the *Djeba* was then an event of the time of the *Early Primaeval Ones*. Further evidence of this interpretation can be found in a ritual text at Edfu telling us that the Egyptians linked the early part of the history of *Wetjeset-Neter* with the belief in the *Sanctified God who came into being at the First Occasion*.[3] In view of these hints we incline to the opinion that the Edfu cosmogonical records reveal a

[1] Cf. p. 6.

[2] Cf. p. 12; the title of the book alludes only to the *Primaeval Age* and does not mention the Falcon.

[3] E. IV. 181,10 and *JEA*, XLVIII, 87.

tradition of a cultus-place which was earlier than the time in which the cult of the Falcon or of the Falcon Horus was constituted.

Having abstracted the facts and beliefs which can reasonably be considered as specific to the cult of the Falcon, we may now embark on an 'outline history' of the *foundation ground* for the sacred domain of the god (*ntr*) who was believed to have come into being at the First Occasion. The new fact borne out by the study of the Edfu texts is the conception of the origin and the primary nature of the land in which the first domain of the god of historical times was believed to have originated. Our document does not deal with one plot of land but, on the contrary, mentions a number of them which appeared around the edges of the original island. These lands are said to have emerged gradually, one by one on the surface of the primaeval waters. Each of them was regarded as representing a definite terrestrial unit which, in our document, is described by the term *pᶜy*.[1] We are told that in all these *pᶜy*-lands the sacred domains of the Falcon were founded. Our text does not mention a god, a high supernatural power, who would issue a command with the view to effecting the foundation of the domains of the Falcon. It seems to us most likely that the creators of the Earth, the Shebtiw, were believed to be the founders of Falcon's primaeval domains.

The Edfu accounts permit us to gain a fairly clear idea of all the phases of the history of the *pᶜy*-lands that evolved on the marginal land of the domain of the Creator, and were, in all probability, subsidiary to it in the first phase of their existence.

The word *pᶜy* is known to us, in the main, from the Edfu texts, but it would be wrong to think that its use in describing the essential unit in the constitution of a sacred domain was a tradition confined to Edfu. This may be shown by reference to the Karnak Myth of Creation. A *pāy*-land is said to have originated after the Creator dried up the water around his place of origin.[2] From such a land he seemed to have created the world in general, then he constituted his domain in it.

[1] Cf. *Wb.* I, 504 (2), which translates only as 'shore'; in the Edfu texts this word occurs in: E. IV. 357,17; VI. 17,8.9–10; 176,12; 181,1 (used in plural); 182,10 = III. 31,13; 183,12.14.18: also *Urk.* VIII, 91, 11; *ASAE*, XLIV, 114–15; Junker, *Abaton*, pp. 32, 74; *ZÄS*, XLII, 20; Gardiner, *P. Wilbour*, II, *Comm.* pp. 26–7 and p. 27, n. 1; *AEO*, I, 12–13.

[2] *ASAE*, XLIV, 114.

Another allusion to a *pāy*-land being again the essential unit in the constitution of a sacred domain, can be found in the inscriptions of the temple at Philae. The text is very brief. Nevertheless, it discloses an interesting view of the function of the *pāy*-land. The word *pāy*-land describes a land that emerged from the water in which the cultus-place of Osiris was founded. This *pāy*-land is defined in the text as a territory which was decreed to Osiris in the *Beginning*.[1] Although there is no further explanation in the Philae text, this allusion probably hints at the same theory as that enshrined in our Edfu texts. In both, in the myth about the primaeval domains of the Falcon as well as in the Osiris myth, the *pāy*-land is the final type of land in which the cultus-place of the god was to be founded.

The etymology of the word *pᶜy* remains unsolved. We know only that apart from its occurrence in quotations made in the later religious texts this word occurs in administrative documents of New Kingdom.[2] No certain answer can be given to the question what was the nature of the land named *pāy*. The part of the Edfu account devoted to the description of the origin and functions of the *pāy*-land is, therefore, of real interest; it sets out clearly that the name *pāy* applies to a specific plot of land. This, then, appeared only after having been formed beneath the primaeval water, and emerged on the margin of another and earlier terrestrial configuration such as the island (*iw*). In the myth the emergence of these *pāy*-lands is connected with actions of symbolic order. It is explained that the *pāy*-land emerged (*bs*) after a rite was performed over certain *iḫt* which, in our document, are never accurately described; they appear to be portions of the primary matter symbolizing the Earth which is to be created. The *pāy*-land, therefore, resulted from two factors: in the first place, there was need of a magical rite which is said to have consisted of uttering sacred spells; this was followed by the adoration of the *Arm*, which we suppose to be the concrete shape of the elementary creative power. These rites performed over the *iḫt*, substances, were believed to have caused the receding of the water from the edges of the island. It was in this way that the actual land of the future sacred domain came in sight. From the description preserved in

[1] Cf. Junker, *Abaton*, p. 32. [2] Cf. Gardiner, *P. Wilbour*, p. 27, n. 1.

our document the *pʿy* was originally a plot of irrigated land which was believed to have appeared at a definite moment of development by virtue of the activities of supernatural powers. That the *pāy*-land might have been conceived to be a mere plot of land appears possible if we recall the beginning of our creation story. This alludes to some *iḥw*, fields, which are said to have been near the island, but hidden beneath the waters. These *iḥw*-fields seem to have been in the same places as those in which the *pāy*-lands emerged thereafter. It may, therefore, be conjectured that the *pāy*-lands were marginal fields of a somewhat more solid piece of land. For the god (*ntr*) this *pāy*-land represented the primary extent of his domain in which his first cultus-place was to be founded thereafter; and which became the centre of the subsequent development of the sacred area. The Edfu account makes it clear that the god's realm was not represented by one single *pāy*-land but that, on the contrary, his realm was constituted by several lands of this type.

The emergence of the *pāy*-lands marks the final stage of the creation of the world of the gods in the primaeval age which we imagine as the starting-point of the physical world of men. The *pāy*-lands themselves were the means by which the actual world developed. The narrative, however, does not go as far as to include the appearance of men on the lands created for the gods. It appears as though this narrative aims at proving that the Earth created during the second era of creation was the land created only for the new generation of divine beings. It is inherently possible that the Edfu narrative hints at a progressive creation of the Earth. We may say that after the appearance of the original series of *pāy*-lands around and along the edges of the primaeval island there was a process of what might be called a continuous creation by the emergence of a progressive series of plots of lands on the edges of the already existing *pāy*-lands as the water of the primaeval flood slowly subsided. As has already been pointed out above, the claim of this doctrine of creation is not to describe the organic process of creating the substance of the Earth, but it is quite evident that its main concern was to interpret the manner in which the surface of the world was constituted. The Hermopolitan creation doctrine teaches that the surface was created by the activity of solar energy. In the theory implicit in the Edfu records this was the outcome of a *magical rite of creation.*

The *pāy*-lands were thus the realm of the *ntrw*-gods, who are represented as tangible deities and who were believed to have succeeded the *pꜣwtyw*, the *Primaeval Ones*, in the rulership over the world of the primaeval age. It is of interest to refer once more to the text incorporated in the Building Text of the Pure Ambulatory of the Edfu Temple, which we have already discussed above. This text gives us a clear proof that the Egyptians believed in a succession of several divine generations. Our main source suggests that it was believed that the appearance of each new generation of gods was connected with the emergence of new plots of lands which meant the increase in size of the original plot of land in which the Creator dwelt first, and which became the home of the new generation of gods. It will be noticed that in these accounts the origin of the new generation of gods is never described; their appearance is simply mentioned as being concomitant with the emergence of the Earth. To illustrate this view we can refer to a series of descriptions in our Edfu records telling us about the appearance of a deity or of a group of deities who were unknown to the preceding episodes of creation, but who entered on the scene at the moment when the original island was found increased in size. Simultaneously with the emergence of the primaeval mound, the *Protector-God* and the *God-of-the-Temple* entered the domain of *Wetjeset-Neter.* After the enclosure of the *Place-of-the-Throne* was erected, the Builder Gods then arose within the island. In the final stage of the history of this creation there appeared the *Crew of the Falcon* on the scene of the *pāy*-land.

The Edfu account preserves a detailed description of the way in which a freshly created land was believed to be made into a sacred domain. We can rightly claim that in this respect the Edfu sources furnish the sole evidence in the present state of our knowledge. No description is given of special rites performed by the creators through which the newly created land would be consecrated so that a foundation of a sacred domain could be effected there. On the contrary, the account seems to be concerned with what proves to be the sacred nature of the *pāy*-land. This was the action *wṯs-ntr*, in other words the moment when the Falcon was uplifted. The Egyptians apparently believed that at any place where the god represented by the Falcon in our myth arrived, he was subsequently uplifted by a stalk of reed or a tree; there was the very site in which his cultus-place should be created.

While outlining the era of the creation of the Falcon's domains, we described this episode and we said that this act was exactly the procedure through which the original island was revivified. Since the narrative does not mention any other rite which might accompany this *wṯs-nṯr* action, the Egyptians, doubtless, believed that there was only one act by virtue of which a freshly emerged land acquired the nature of a sacred land. The fact that an episode special to a land having funerary associations is described as the starting-point in the life of the *pāy*-land seems to indicate that there was, most probably, a close resemblance between the original nature of the island and that of the *pāy*-land. Consequently, the *pāy*-land was conceived of as being a sacred land prior to its emergence. The uplifting of the god was then a mere manifestation of the sacred nature of the land that was brought out of Nun by a magical rite of creation, and this uplifting proved that the genuine sacred nature of the new piece of land was restored.

On two occasions only is a somewhat more detailed account given of the development subsequent to the initial act of 'uplifting'. This is the history of the *pāy*-land of *Wetjeset-Neter* and *Djeba* that was believed to have been created from the *Place-of-the-Throne*. These two accounts show a striking resemblance in the interpretation of the events which were believed to have come to pass in the *pāy*-lands. It is precisely this that suggests that the beginnings of any *pāy*-land listed in our sources might have been explained in the same way. This is, of course, largely a theory. No document referring to the early history of all the other *pāy*-lands known from the Edfu records has been preserved.

In discussing the creation of the *pāy*-land of *Wetjeset-Neter* we have seen that after all the divine beings entered the newly created land they proceeded to a place within the *pāy*-land which seems to have been given a special significance, and which is described in our document as the *bw-ḥbbt, place-of-the-primaeval-water*.[1] This *bw-ḥbbt* has every appearance of being the centre of

[1] Cf. p. 162.

the *pāy*-land though it was on its marginal part, and was, most probably, regarded as the most sacred part of the *pāy*-land because the *Perch*, as the first seat of the Falcon, was erected there. The two accounts do not mention that a resting-place of another type would be erected in the new sacred land, such as, for instance, the *ḥwt*, *mansion*, or that a tree like the willow would be used in the *pāy*-land for this purpose. We incline to the opinion that in any place sacred to the Falcon the slip of reed represented the original type of his resting-place and was, consequently, in all the *pāy*-lands the essential step in the foundation of his domain. The *bw-ḥbbt* with the *Perch* shows the Falcon's domain in its primary appearance. This picture indicates that the Falcon's domains were believed to reflect in the early stage of their existence the aspect of the *Homeland of the Primaeval Ones*. It follows that not only was the choice of the ground for the first domain in the *pāy*-land determined by the conditions in the original island, but also the physical aspect was likened to the place of worship of the Ancestors.

Unlike the situation in the original domain in the island, the sacred places created in the *pāy*-lands seem to have been provided with sacred symbols or images which are said to have been brought from the *bw-ẖnm*.[1] These were three. We imagine that they were used as protecting symbols of the earliest type of the god's resting-place in an open field. They were probably displayed around the Perch to mark out that the place was sacred or to intimate who was the lord of that part of the land. These symbols might have eventually been placed on the boundary of the *bw-ḥbbt*.

It is of prime importance that the first protecting symbols that were in the *pāy*-land were believed to have been brought from a centre of creation of the Earth. We see here points of contact with the creation of the means of protection in the *Enclosure of the Earth-Maker*, where Tanen made from staffs the protecting emblems of the god.[2] It looks as though it was believed that only the power which created the terrestrial substances could ensure the safety of the god in his new home. In addition to these symbols there might have been also displayed in the *bw-ḥbbt* the image of one of the Ancestor gods. In both documents a brief allusion is

[1] Cf. p. 165.

[2] Cf. p. 149.

made to the *Ḥeter-ḥer* and the *Divine of Heart* as being present *in situ.*[1] On the other hand, however, the narrative does not say that at that stage of history an enclosure resembling the *sbḫt* or the *sbty*-fence that were made in the field of the Ancestors[2] would be erected around the Perch within the *pāy*-land.

The first sacred place that was made in the *bw-ḥbbt* may be imagined as a muddy area at the water's edges in which there was nothing more than the support of the god and a small number of protecting symbols. There the god was believed to have lived first in the company of the creators of the Earth. It must be remembered that his companions were the divine beings who constituted the means of his protection. The Shebtiw, after they created the land for the domain and erected the resting-place, completed the last phase of the constitution of the domain. It is worthy of note that in the land that derived from the island of creation Tanen's progeny are the divine beings who were primarily responsible for the safety of the Falcon.

The *pāy*-land seems to be the region in which the successor of the Creator settled down in the company of some divine beings who, unknown to the earlier stages of this history, are described as the *crew of the Falcon.*[3] The origin of this *crew* is not explained in the text, nor is any description given of their appearance. This fact accords with what has already been said, that nowhere is there any allusion to the origin of the gods who acted in this drama of creation or for whom the lands were created. This circumstance confirms our opinion that the sole concern of this myth is to interpret in a direct and continuous line the origin of the Earth and its intimate offspring.[4] Since the first allusion to the *crew*[5] is made in connexion with the origin of the *pāy*-land of *Wetjeset-Neter*, it is tempting to suggest that the crew consisted of the divine beings who appeared on the scene at that time or were brought out of Nun simultaneously with the *pāy*-land. If this

[1] Cf. p. 165.

[2] Cf. pp. 21–2.

[3] The word used for describing the god's companions in the *pāy*-land is *ist*; cf. E. VI. 17,7.9; 176,3.12; 179,10.12; 181,2; 184,12.17; 185,1; 329,10.13; 332,1.6.7; see also *Wb.* I, 127 (17).

[4] Cf. p. 274 ff.

[5] E. VI. 184,13.

surmise be correct we have here another indication to demonstrate the Egyptian theory that as soon as a new shape of land was created a new divine generation was brought into existence; this then formed the company of the god, the lord of the *pāy*-land, in his new home.

Nothing is told of the manner in which the Falcon came to be the lord of the *pāy*-land. The accounts of the history of the *pāy*-lands *Wetjeset-Neter* and *Djeba* do not allude to the *episode of consorting* between the *Flying Ba* and the Falcon which is known from the history of the original domain of *Wetjeset-Neter*,[1] and by virtue of which the Falcon was equated with the Creator. The consequence of this episode was that the Falcon assumed the function of the ruler of the island. It may, therefore, be surmised that the Falcon, having once acquired this capacity, was then able to become the ruler of any land which evolved from the domain of the Creator. His overlordship over the *pāy*-lands would consequently be natural and derived from his right of succession. The fact that in the original domain of *Wetjeset-Neter* an act of creation is said to follow this mystic episode of consorting, may accord with this hypothesis. It would follow that the *pāy*-land could only be created after its apparent ruler was in existence.

It is, however, of interest to mention that after the Falcon was uplifted by the Perch within the *pāy*-land, he was greeted by the creators, the Shebtiw, in the first place. Then followed a silent rite, further acclamations, and offerings were presented. Thereafter the *Place* (*bw*) was declared as the Falcon's property.[2] This episode does not occur among the ceremonies connected with the restoration of the original *Wetjeset-Neter*. It would follow that this solemn act referred exclusively to the actual situation in the *pāy*-land. It seems most likely that the word *bw*-place describes here the ground in which the *Perch* stood. After that *bw*-place was consecrated, there was a need of yet another sacred act through which the *Lord of the Perch* was enabled to enter definitely into possession of the ground of the *Perch*.

The narrative does not mention the authority who could make this declaration and does not assert that this declaration might have been the 'words' of the *Ka* or the Flying *Ba*. It may, very

[1] Cf. p. 16.

[2] E. VI. 177,13 and above, p. 30.

tentatively, be suggested that the divine beings who were present in the *pāy*-land, who were the Shebtiw, the Builder Gods, and the 'crew' of the Falcon, did so. One may recall a scene from the creation of the *pāy*-lands which departed from the former domain of the *Pn*-God. The Shebtiw, after they have created the lands by reciting sacred spells, stated: 'Do come into this place.'[1] We suspect that in this way they addressed the Falcon resting on the original Perch and that this exclamation was the reason why the Falcon left the ancestral territory and entered into the land created for him. It would seem that the divine beings who formed the god's company were believed to foretell the decisive moments in the development of the sacred life. A similar situation can be found at the end of the description of the origin of the *pāy*-land of *Wetjeset-Neter*. This indicates that the Falcon while resting on his Perch was acclaimed by the crew in an act which looks like being an act of recognition of his overlordship. The crew greeted him as their *ndm*. The word *ndm* is new. As far as our instances go this word occurs only in connexion with this act of proclamation in the *pāy*-land.[2] We suggest that in this tradition the word *ndm* has a special meaning and describes the deity who was to become the legitimate lord of the *pāy*-land. The natural right of the Falcon to be the ruler of the *pāy*-land thus required two additional episodes; in the first place a declaration to the effect that the ground of his Perch was his imminent property, then an act of recognition of his overlordship. These statements were not made by a higher divine power but it is clear from the text that both were issued by the deities who were the companions of the Falcon in his new home within the *pāy*-land.

The Falcon then, having been recognized as legitimate ruler of the *pāy*-land, seems to have addressed his crew. At this point the text is written in a very difficult and almost enigmatic manner, and its meaning can only be guessed at with the help of an interpretation of a later date. The god's words may have been the words which the *Ka* was believed to have communicated to the Falcon in the Perch of the original island.[3] Hence, these words might possibly have formed part of a set of divine regulations for ordering life in the sacred place; this, however, is inevitably somewhat hypo-

[1] E. VI. 182,13. [2] Cf. p. 28. [3] Cf. p. 19.

thetical. If, however, it be correct, it provides additional support for the theory that the sacred life on the *pāy*-land was envisaged as being similar to the life on the primaeval island.

The *crew of the Falcon*[1] appears now, apart from the *Lord of the Perch*, to be the chief divine inhabitants of the *pāy*-land. Their function in the *pāy*-land is not clear from the first. But that the Shebtiw, after the *pāy*-land was consecrated and the protection of the god was constituted, sailed away and that the crew took their place in the *pāy*-land, seems to be possible if we recall the end of the first cosmogonical record. It is stated that the

> crew had approached. The Shebtiw sailed (away ?). The crew of the Falcon came close having perceived the *pāy*-land of the Falcon.[2]

With the help of an interpretation of a later date we can reconstruct a rounded picture of that moment in the history of the *pāy*-land. Although the beginning of the later record is damaged, we can read in the remaining part of the text *sacred spells while passing by according to the words of the Ka.*[3] Thereafter the text alludes to the arrival of the crew. We suggest that in the damaged part of the secondary record the name of the Shebtiw may be restored. We imagine that the Shebtiw, while reciting sacred spells, perhaps spells for the protection of the sacred domain for which they created the actual land, left the *pāy*-land at the command of the *Ka*. They went, perhaps, according to his orders to another part of the mythical world to continue their creative task.

If we accept this reconstruction of the mythical situation in the *pāy*-land, it would follow that the Egyptians believed that when the elementary phases of the creation of sacred domains came to an end, the part which the Shebtiw played in its origin was thereby completed. It ended at the moment when the protection of the Perch was constituted. The crew might have replaced them in the forthcoming stage of the history of the *pāy*-land. They, perhaps, made their settlement there. The tradition reveals that the Falcon himself invited them *to settle down beside him.*[4] Their duty is described by the expression *nḏ iḫt n pᶜy*, *to protect the iḫt of the*

[1] E. VI. 17,7 reads *ìst n bìk.*

[2] E. VI. 184,17–18.

[3] E. VI. 17,6.

[4] E. VI. 17,9 reads: *in bìk n ìst.f (s)nḏm.sn r-gs.f*; apparently *snḏm* means here that the land was occupied as a definite settlement.

pāy-land in which the god dwelt.[1] It is clear that the crew was since then regarded as the main protecting force in the *pāy*-land. What, however, the *iḫt* of the *pāy*-land were is not stated in the text. It may be surmised that these *iḫt* might have been the same *iḫt* used as constituent elements in the creation of the *pāy*-land.[2] If so, it would follow that the substances needed for the creation of the actual earth of the *pāy*-land, the symbol of the Earth, represented the first sacred objects of the domain of the Falcon. This may explain why a special guard of them was constituted in the domain and this task seems to be the duty of the new company of divine beings described as the *crew of the Falcon.* In view of these allusions we may say that the substances which caused the *pāy*-land to be, were believed to form an integral part of its existence, and, perhaps, on their presence within the *pāy*-land depended further development of the area sacred to the Falcon. The mention of the *iḫt* as being present in the *pāy*-land after this was definitely occupied by the gods recalls the scene in the *bw-ḫnm, the Place of the Well,* where the *iḫt* were stored underneath a willow and were adored before the start of a new period of the creation of the Earth. Nevertheless, these *iḫt* seem to be of prime importance in the life of the *pāy*-land, as will be explained below.[3]

It is likely that after the initial phases of the foundation of the Falcon's settlement, there developed in these *pāy*-lands a new type of place of worship. In the primaeval island all that the evidence permits us to say is that the place of worship was primarily a simple, primitive type of enclosure. On the *pāy*-land, in contrast, the use by the crew of the Falcon of such words as *ḫnm, to construct* and *nḥp, to fashion,* suggests that a much more developed place of worship, a duly constructed building of more solid materials, perhaps existed.[4] The record explicitly indicates the circumstances and conditions that underlie the origin of the new type of sacred places created in the *pāy*-lands.

The *pāy*-land was regarded as the imminent realm of the Falcon, for it is defined as the *pʿy n bik,* the *pāy-land of the Falcon.*[5] The choice of the exact site on which the first properly con-

[1] E. VI. 17,10; similarly 184,18.
[2] Cf. pp. 156, 161.
[3] Cf. p. 286 ff.
[4] Cf. p. 148.
[5] E. VI. 185,2 and 176,4.

structed sacred place of the god was to be erected, however, depended on the will of the dead god. Unlike the situation in the original *Wetjeset-Neter*, the speech of the crew discloses yet another belief distinctly different from the tradition of the earlier domain. It is stated that the part of the *pāy*-land in which the Perch stood, was to be constructed (*ḫnm*) because this place (*bw*) was bequeathed to the Falcon by the *Ka*. This is an entirely new idea unknown to the previous orders of creation. The origin of the first sacred place of the Falcon in the *pāy*-land was not only a rebirth and restoration of a sacred domain that vanished. The Egyptian theory evidently was that the first sacred place which was in its physical appearance different from the usual type of the primaeval resting-place of the god created in the original island, was not brought into existence by the procedure of revivification. The first sacred place in the *pāy*-land was to be constructed. This domain was believed to have originated on grounds which were decreed in bequest to the god at the beginning of the world by the *Ka*, who was in fact an Earth-God.

Unique as the Edfu evidence is, we do not doubt that our documents disclose a genuine tradition concerning the essential nature of the original sites on which the later historical domains evolved. The belief in the *Ka*, too, is a new fact. Evidently our records intimate the view that this belief was familiar to several sacred places of a remote date. The divine being described as the *Ka* might have been regarded as the founder of the original Egyptian domains. We may think of a part of Egypt, of a district which, unfortunately, we cannot identify, but in which it was believed that all the sacred places that existed there were foundations made by the Earth-God himself at the beginning of the world.

It has been noticed that throughout the development of the mythical history of the *Island of Trampling* as well as that of its offspring, the *pāy*-lands, the dead ruler, the *Ka*, seems to have played a prominent part. This mythical personality is known to us only from the first and second record. As has been pointed out above, he seems to be related to the *Pn*-God, *This One*.[1] He is the first divine being to appear in the island of creation following the arrival of the creators of the Earth. It was he who gave the

[1] Cf. pp. 14, n. 5 and 115–16.

instructions to the Shebtiw as to how to fashion the Perch of the Falcon. As the ground of the Perch was originally his own domain, it becomes now logical that he did so. At the end of this series of acts of creation he determined by his bequest the exact site on which the first domain that survived in historical times was to be founded. Although he is never pictured as a physically real deity, he was regarded as the chief authority who issued commands for the foundation of mansions in which the gods of historical times were to be housed; he was believed to have stood behind all the phases of development of the sacred places that took origin in the island of creation. These beliefs seem to have inspired the view expressed by an interpreter of a later date who described the *Ka* as the *Ka whom no man has seen, (even) this God, the Ka who established (smn) the Temples.*[1]

We mentioned that a part of the *pāy*-land was believed to be of special significance because the *Ka* resided there. This is sufficiently clear from the statements of the assembly of gods who attended the consecration of the *pāy*-land.[2] The former dwelling-place of the *Ka* is described only as a *bw*, *place*;[3] no detailed account of its eventual appearance is preserved in the Edfu text; this *bw-Place of the Ka*, however, is another new fact that has emerged from the study of our documents. It is hardly possible that the *Place of the Ka* would be the same place as the *Underworld of the Soul* mentioned in connexion with the revivification of the original domain in the island.[4] The account of the origin of the *pāy*-land does not allude to the underworld at all. On the other hand, if we recall once again the beginning of the first record telling us that the *Ka* revealed himself after the reeds were removed on the marginal land of the island, it will follow that the original realm of the *Ka* was not believed to be on the island itself, but nearby, perhaps beneath the primaeval waters at the moment when the new period of the creation dawned. This would seem to indicate that he appeared exactly on the brink of the earth which was still beneath the waters and that he came from the *iḥw*-fields, which at that time are said to be submerged. Since it is highly probable that these *iḥw*-fields were the later *pāy*-lands in

[1] E. VI. 17,6–7.
[2] Cf. p. 26.
[3] E. VI. 184,18.
[4] E. VI. 185,2.

which the domains of the Falcon were founded at the command of the *Ka*, the emergence of the *pāy*-lands must have entailed the appearance of the actual land of the realm of the *Ka*. The *pāy*-land probably represented the realm of the *Ka*, and so perhaps all the *pāy*-lands which are mentioned in our documents. The marginal part of it on which the Falcon rested later on might have been the centre of the realm of the *Ka*. It is known that the place on which the Perch was erected is described as the *bw*, *place*. But it is less likely that this *bw*-place may apply to the whole *pāy*-lands; it would be too small and would represent only the nearest surroundings of the Perch. It seems to us more likely that the *bw*-place describes the ground of the former dwelling-place of the *Ka*.[1] Further arguments in favour of this interpretation can be seen in the allusions to the place of the *ḏd*-pillar already known from the account of the origin of the *pāy*-land of *Wetjeset-Neter*.[2] The narrative concerning the origin of the *pāy*-land of *Djeba*, too, speaks definitely of the *ḏd*-pillar of the *Ka*, at the front of which a ceremony of adoration was performed before the Perch of the Falcon was erected.[3] Its purpose was, most probably, to restore the sacred nature of the place so that the Perch could be planted. The following order of actions makes it clear that only on the marginal land of the *pāy*-land recurred what once came to pass in the original domain of the island. We have here once again the *ḏd*-pillar as the resting-place of a defunct deity who determines what was the most sacred part of the *pāy*-land which was to be used as the foundation ground for the new domain. Hence, the origin of the first domain of the *ntr*-god, here the Falcon, in the *pāy*-land was determined by the same beliefs, specifically, by the tradition of *what once had existed but had died*. The first domain to be created in the new land, therefore, is nothing more than the re-creation of a vanished sacred place and was physically equal to the ancestral sacred place. The obvious affinities which we can notice in the two accounts prove that all the episodes which happened in the *pāy*-lands of the Falcon were derived from the acts of creation which once occurred in the original island.

1 E. VI. 17,6–7. 2 Cf. p. 163.

3 Cf. p. 18, the list of the *pāy*-lands sacred to the Falcon. The tradition concerning the bequest of the Ka must have been at home in all these early cultus-places.

We may here recall the text already quoted from the Philae inscriptions telling us that the place of the cult of Osiris in the *pāy*-land was decreed to him at the beginning of the world.[1] The power which did so is not mentioned in the Philae text, but we cannot deny the similarity of thought in both instances. We can conclude that there was a belief in a divine power who assigned to the gods the final site of their permanent home.

The general significance of the theory which we have been outlining can be seen in the fact that the same process of creation of the actual land for the sacred domains is interpreted as emanating from three different parts of the original island, each of which shows an entirely different physical aspect.[2] This is undoubtedly convincing evidence that there was one single theory which was familiar to at least three early cultus-places.

In imitation of the original sacred domain in the *pāy*-land that resulted from the command of the *Ka*, other domains came into existence, but each such domain claimed that it was built on the original sacred land. Thus the historical domains came into existence with their temples and thus it came about that so many temples could claim to be the actual site on which the creation first took place.

At Edfu, for instance, the *pāy*-land was sacred to the Falcon Horus, and the sacred domain of Horus was considered as the first to have been created when the original island was brought to a new life.[3] The historical temple at Edfu is therefore the first temple that was built on the original *pāy*-land. It was, in the Egyptian belief, the *Mesen in the golden pāy-land*.[4]

It has been noticed how strongly pronounced in this creation theory is the association of the creation with death and decay. We may say that this is the leading idea of the history of the early sacred domain in the island as well as of that of the *pāy*-lands. Although the Edfu narratives preserve the account of the origin of only two *pāy*-lands sacred to the Falcon, we incline to the opinion that the bringing into existence of all the *pāy*-lands listed in our sources, their making into sacred domains, proceeded in

[1] Cf. p. 172. [2] Cf. pp. 166–7.

[3] Cf. p. 17, where we pointed to the possible interpolations made in the original text by the Edfu tradition. [4] E. VII. 35,9; 179,1.

the same way. We would suggest that the mythological situation that can be reconstructed from these two accounts may be applied to any *pāy*-land. We have already pointed to the characteristics of this creation theory in describing the importance of the cultus-places of the Ancestors in the creation of historical domains. These trends of thought could hardly be the result of a derivative or local tradition such as, for instance, the Edfu tradition may be. While looking over all the phases of creation interpreted in our records, we sense the influence of much deeper reasons. In all the eras from which the sacred world of the gods resulted death was only the first step towards a new phase of creation. We have also seen that in our drama of creation the progress and development of the sacred places was always assisted by ancestral deities. Nothing is known about what might have happened to their enclosures within the original island after the Falcon was definitely settled in his own domains. But their places of worship were *in situ* prior to the creation of the domains for the new divine comer to the island. Their decay seems to be conceived of as the main cause of the origin of the new domain. This circumstance attests and emphasizes their role in the creation. We conclude that their existence appears as only a part of the history of the latter.

Strictly speaking, the idea inherent in the history of the *pāy*-lands is that the death of an entity is the cause of the origin of a new phenomenon. The dead domain of the Creator was reborn after it was destroyed, and its rebirth meant the origin of a new sacred world. Our documents show, in a modified form applied to a particular case, one of the major thoughts of Egyptian wisdom in general: death formed only a part of the creation of the world because the creator did so when he created life and death.[1] These trends of thought are associated with the existence of the primary matter and implicated in the conception of the nature of the land which was the starting-point in the existence of a sacred domain from which the temple derived later on. These thoughts, therefore, underlie the origin of sacred domains and their temples.

In all the stages of the history of the *Island of Trampling* and in

[1] Cf. Shabaka Stone, l. 57. Cf. Junker, *Die Götterlehre von Memphis*, p. 59 and Gardiner, 'Life and Death' (*Hastings Encycl.*).

the initial phase of the history of its adjacent plots the divine beings called *Shebtiw* are those who are primarily responsible for any action of creation which came to pass there. They were creators who by virtue of a magical rite re-created and brought to a new life what once had existed and had vanished. In a separate study[1] we attempted to interpret the nature of these creators. It emerged that these Shebtiw were creators who effected the creation of the world by transforming the substances. They seem to have been concerned with the creation of the lands for the sacred places. It was they, the first inhabitants of the *Island of Trampling* at the dawn of its second era, who re-created the domain of the *Pn*-God and that of the *Earth-Maker*.

It was they who created the lands for the domains of the successor of the Creator and the successor of the *Ka*. They made them similar to the former sacred world. When fashioning the seat of the god in the *pāy*-land the Shebtiw repeated the same creative act which they performed first in the island. They were, in fact, creators of the places of worship of the Ancestors.

In the execution of the creation, however, the Shebtiw seem to have been subjects of a higher power. The power of fashioning (*nḥp*) was conferred on them by the *God-of-the-Temple*. Their work was carried out according to the commands of the *Ka*, for it was the *Ka* who instructed them in the manner of fashioning the *djeba*-Perch. The *Place-of-the-Throne* only was re-created by order of Tanen. The facts suggest, though our sources do not clearly say so, that the Shebtiw may also have been considered as responsible for the building of the enclosures in the original island.

The resurrection of the *Island of Trampling* and the creation of the *pāy*-lands of the Falcon appears to be the main part of their activities, but surely not the sole one. An Edfu text discloses a tradition, completely unknown elsewhere, that the Shebtiw, after having created the domains of the Falcon, left the *Island of Trampling*. They were believed to have sailed to another part of the primaeval world in which they created Heracleopolis.[2] No detailed account of their activities in that region has come down to us.

[1] Cf. *ZÄS*, LXXXVII, 44 ff. [2] E. IV. 358,18.

CHAPTER II

The Secondary Pāy-lands

The situation in the *pāy*-lands in which the primaeval sacred domains of the Falcon were founded first, and all the traditions connected with these domains, are to be considered as solely applying to the lands which evolved in the vicinity of the realm of the Creator. The narrative proceeds then to allude to an event which has every appearance of being yet another action of creation, only performed under different circumstances. It seems that after the Falcon was established on the grounds of the former domain of the *Ka*[1] other sacred places came into existence. These, eventually, might have also been the *pāy*-lands, but evidently they were subsidiary to the already existing sacred domains of the Falcon.[2]

It would seem that during the following stage in the history of the primaeval domains of the Falcon the scene was removed to another part of the *Island of Trampling*. A *pḥwi-wᶜrt* is mentioned at the beginning of this part of the narrative.[3] The interpretation of this name meets with difficulties, for no parallel can be quoted in our sources. Theoretically, if we assume that there might be a connexion between this *wāᶜret* and the *wāᶜret* mentioned at the beginning of this story,[4] it would follow that now the development of events leads us to the opposite side of the island. Indeed, we can quote evidence that in the tradition of a later date the area to which the *pāy*-lands of *Wetjeset-Neter* and that of *Djeba* belonged was regarded as the *wᶜrt ḫnty, the Foreland of the wāᶜret.*[5] It may therefore be suggested, with all due reserve, that this part of the myth may describe what was believed to have happened in the *Hinterland of the wāᶜret.*

The occurrence of the word *ḫpr, to come into being,* makes it clear that we have here a series of sacred places which were to be created on the *Hinterland of the wāᶜret.* If we agree that the order of the actions of creation as it is recorded in the Edfu account yields their chronological order, it is evident that the events on the

[1] Cf. pp. 178–81. [2] E. VI. 176,9–11. [3] Cf. p. 31.
[4] Cf. p. 13. [5] E. VI. 14,14.

Hinterland of the wāʿret were believed to be of a later date than the origin of the domains of the Falcon on the grounds of the *Ka*.

The result of this ultimate act of creation was the origin of a sacred domain described as *iw nšni*, *Island of Fury*. The way in which this *Island of Fury* was brought into existence is not recorded in the text, nor is there any mention of the creators who did so. No relevant text can be cited to confirm that the Shebtiw acted there, and that they perhaps repeated the acts of creation which they performed on the other side of the primaeval island.

The real nature of this *Island of Fury* is not clear. We suppose that there might be a link with the *Island of Trampling*, but exactly what connexion it had with the latter is problematic. Theoretically, there appear to be two possibilities: either it was another name of the *Island of Trampling*[1] or it was a *pāy*-land that was created on the other side of the *Island of Trampling*. In connexion with the second hypothesis, it should be pointed out that on occasion the *pāy*-land could be called *island* (*iw*), and that one of the lists of the primaeval *pāy*-lands bears the name *Island of Rēʿ* (*iw Rʿ*) and is connected with the *pāy*-land named the *ḏd-Pillar of the Earth*.[2] The name *iw nšni*, *Island of Fury*, however, occurs only once in our document and is not included in the main list of the *pāy*-lands in the first record.[3] This seems to be another argument in support of our hypothesis that the following narrative describes a new episode of creation which was performed from the *Island of Trampling*. Supposing that this might have been the Egyptian idea, we might infer that the 'mythical history' of the primaeval domains of the Falcon involved yet another act of creation of the Earth, which can reasonably be described as the origin of the 'secondary' *pāy*-lands; these, eventually, might have been subsidiary to the Falcon's domain in the *Wetjeset-Neter* and *Djeba*.

The beginning of this record does not tell us who was the deity for whom all these domains were created. Two place-names, however, should be stressed because they appear to be relevant in this respect. The names *Maa-Ḥor* and *Ḥotep-Tanen*[4] can be taken as a clear evidence that both the Falcon and Tanen, the

[1] Cf. p. 13, the Island of Trampling shows a subsidiary name.

[2] Cf. p. 25. [3] E. VI. 183,13. [4] E. VI. 328,17–18.

principal deities of the *pāy*-land of *Djeba*, had their resting-places in the presumably new area, and that probably they were also the chief deities of that part of the primaeval world. From this point of view it is possible that there was a direct connexion between the main part of the *Island of Trampling* and the newly created region. As Tanen is here mentioned as the principal deity, it is tempting to suggest from the first that this particular act of creation might have emanated from the *bw-ḥmr*, the *Place-of-the-Throne.*[1] On the other hand, however, this view would appear doubtful, because it was the creation of the *pāy*-land of *Wetjeset-Neter* and that of *Djeba* that seem to have started from the *Place-of-the-Throne.*[2]

No document is preserved to tell us of how the mythical situation might have evolved in the original *pāy*-lands sacred to the Falcon after the creation of the original settlement was completed. It may, however, be surmised that the Falcon, after he spent some time in his own domains, journeyed; probably the company, including Tanen and the deities who constructed his first enclosure,[3] followed him. Their journey perhaps led to the 'Hinterland' of the island, which we imagine might have been unoccupied at that time. The hypothesis that the Falcon and Tanen were believed to undertake a journey through the primaeval *wāᶜret* seems to receive some support from the beginning of the third Edfu record.[4] Allusion is made to the *smd*, *wandering*,[5] of a company of gods. Who exactly the members of the divine company are is not stated in the text. We venture to suggest that, in this context, the word *psḏt* may describe the company of the deities from the original *pāy*-lands of the Falcon. This 'company' of divine beings is said to have wandered *in their train*. The text does not explain to whom the suffix *-.sn* refers. Since, however, Tanen and the Falcon seem to be the leading personalities in this episode, it is possible that the suffix *-.sn* refers to them. If so, Tanen and the Falcon travelled from the *pāy*-land of *Djeba* ahead of the company of the creators through the primaeval region. Perhaps it was believed that in any place in which they settled they founded new sacred domains. And these sacred domains might

[1] Cf. p. 158. [2] Cf. p. 160 ff. [3] Cf. p. 236.
[4] E. VI. 328,18–329,1. [5] Cf. p. 33.

have been the ones named at the end of the second Edfu narrative.[1] Among these the names *Maa-Ḥor* and *Ḥotep-Tanen* are significant, for they can be linked with the previous situation in the *pāy*-lands as well as with the following development.

The Edfu record does not preserve a detailed picture of the acts of creation which might have occurred in the *Hinterland*. But this does not necessarily mean that the original version of this sacred book did not include a detailed account of all that happened in the *Hinterland*. That lands for sacred domains were believed to have been created in that part of the primaeval world is highly probable. It is also of interest that we read in the beginning of the third record the name *ndm, lord.*[2] It is known that this name was the title of the Falcon after he had been proclaimed lord of the original *pāy*-lands. In this very point there is, probably, an allusion to the situation which had occurred in the original *pāy*-lands. Although the occurrence of the word *ndm* is a fragile argument, it tempts one to consider it as a supplementary indication to support our hypothesis that the situation described in a concise manner hints at yet another phase of creation of the *pāy*-lands for the Falcon and at another episode of proclaiming him lord of these *pāy*-lands. Although we cannot cite any precise textual evidence, we imagine that these secondary *pāy*-lands might also have been created by virtue of *sw-iḫt-tꜣ* action, and that on the whole there was only repeated the order of creation which is well known as emanating from the original island.[3] But the text says nothing in this respect and speculation is vain. If we assume that the Falcon was the lord of these *pāy*-lands, there also might have been performed an act of recognition of his overlordship, perhaps in the same way as was done in the original *pāy*-lands. This brings to mind the allusion to the *pꜥyw*, the *pāy*-lands, of *Djeba* which we find in the Edfu preamble to the set of the cosmogonical records.[4] Since the origin of one single *pāy*-land is interpreted in the main sources, but on the other hand it is stated that later other sacred domains were created, these might have been the *pāy*-lands of *Djeba* only briefly referred to in the introduction. It will follow

[1] E. VI. 176,9–11, a list which continues in the beginning of the third record, E. VI. 328,17–18, cf. above, p. 39.

[2] Cf. p. 28.

[3] Cf. p. 24.

[4] E. VI. 181,1.

that the history of the primaeval domains of the Falcon involved yet another phase of the creation, and that *pāy*-lands were created as lands subsidiary to those in which the Falcon ruled first. We may imagine that each of the original *pāy*-lands was surrounded by a number of plots of land in which further sacred places for the Falcon were founded. If this interpretation be admissible, yet another meaning of the expression *pḥwi wʿrt* is possible. It may indicate in this context the very end of the terrestrial extent of the original *pāy*-land. Consequently, the *iw nšni*, *Island of Fury*, would be one of the *pāy*-lands subsidiary to the original *pāy-land of Djeba*.

This *Island of Fury* seems to have had special significance among the new *pʿyw*-lands of *Djeba* since the text speaks only of cultus-places which were believed to have been founded in it, including the *Mansion-of-Shooting*, *Maa-Ḥor*, *Nbwt*, *Mansion-of-Mystery*, *House-of-Combat*, *and Ḥotep-Tanen*. It is doubtful whether a Perch for the Falcon would be erected in that region. The narrative does not allude to the eventual fashioning of the seat of the god. It proceeds to give the name of a sacred place which is described as the *Seat-of-the-Two-Gods*.[1] This may be imagined as a joint resting-place of Tanen and the Falcon, but the text says nothing of its eventual aspect, and we do not know whether it was a sacred place in an open field or a properly constructed enclosure. If we recall that some of the names occurring in the narrative contain the term *ḥwt*, *mansion*, it would seem that the first settlements that were founded in this region were made similar to the *Mansion* of the Earth-God in the island.[2] Consequently the *ḥwt*, *mansion*, would appear to be the first type of resting-place that was constructed in the secondary *pāy*-lands.

The account does not reveal anything more of the history of the sacred places listed, nor does it allude to their eventual fate. What follows is an allusion to the arrival of the gods in a part of the *Island of Fury* in which was a place of special significance in the development of the sacred life in that region.[3] This place appears to have been connected with a divine being who bears the name *'Ir-iḫt*,[4] and might, consequently, be the most sacred part of the *Island of Fury*.

[1] E. VI. 328,18. [2] Cf. p. 23. [3] E. VI. 329,2.

[4] The name occurs in Edfu texts in E. VI. 329,2, cf. *ZÄS*, XCII, 117; also E. VI.

The sudden appearance of a deity unknown to the earlier history of this primaeval world is a little strange. One must, however, bear in mind that the events described at the end of the second, and at the beginning of the third record are in the Edfu version presented in a concise form. One cannot judge in all details what connexion this *'Ir-iḫt* might have had with the sacred places in the original *pāy*-lands, and with those in the secondary *pāy*-lands. A suggestion may be sought in the fact that the creation of the original *pāy*-lands was the resurrection of the *Home* of the *Ka*. Although the narration does not state it clearly, we may surmise that perhaps this phase of the creation might mean also the restoration of the original homeland of yet another Earth-God. The secondary *pāy*-lands might have been, in their essential nature, the former realm of this *'Ir-iḫt*.

Naturally, no relevant texts can be cited to confirm our deductions from the beginning of the third record. Theoretically the name *'Ir-iḫt* may be interpreted as the *Maker-of-substances*. The occurrence of the word *iḫt* tempts one to suggest that these *iḫt* might describe the 'substances' required in the creation of the *pāy*-lands.[1] We may have here an isolated allusion to a tradition unknown elsewhere in which the Creator of the Earth was known only as an *'Ir-iḫt*. But the text says nothing about the appearance of this deity. We imagine that he might have been conceived as an intangible divine being rather like the Earth-Maker who is connected with the *Wetjeset-Neter* in the second myth. That this *'Ir-iḫt* was regarded as the creator of the Earth is confirmed by the abbreviated version of this myth, in which, instead of *Maker-of-substances*, we read the name *Earth-Maker*.[2] Moreover, this *Maker-of-substances* seems to have played the role of the *Mꜣ-Ancestor*[3] in these secondarily created *pāy*-lands. It is, therefore, likely that he, as an Ancestor God, had his resting-place there, and that this might be the *bw*, *place*, to which the assembly of gods came and

182,12 (= III. 7,2), E. III. 199,12 and is replaced in E. IV. 169,15 by *ir-tꜣ*. If this be correct, it will indicate that the word *iḫt* is to be taken as *substances of the Earth*.

[1] Cf. pp. 172–3.

[2] E. VI. 17,13.

[3] *Mꜣ* with the meaning *ancestor* is known from the Edfu texts: E. III. 32,10; 33,13; 201,6; 202,12; E. VI. 169,10; 175,8; 186,8; 312,1. The meaning *ancestor* finds its confirmation in E. IV. 304,9.

which was the scene of the ensuing event. Since this *bw*, *place*, is described as the *bw tpy*, the *First Place*, or *the Place of the First One*,[1] we think that the narrative alludes, once again, to the already known situation, and that we have here a clear allusion to an early settlement of an Earth-God which had disappeared, and which was the home of the *Maker-of-substances*. The emergence of this subsidiary *pāy*-land may be imagined as entailing the appearance of the land of the former resting-place of the Earth-God, which, undoubtedly, was in decay.

No description is given of the eventual appearance of this *First Place*, and no allusion is made to the probable process of its revivification. What appears certain is that we have here again a definite hint of the belief that the land of an early settlement of a divine power who was an Earth-God, after having been destroyed, became the foundation of a new sacred domain. The general situation is admittedly described in a somewhat altered manner. But the choice of the land for the foundation is again determined by a pre-existing resting-place of an Earth-God. Thus the Egyptian theory concerning the origin of the domains that survived in historical times was that such a domain could originate only in the place in which the Creator of the Earth first dwelt.

We have already pointed out that it is highly probable that the Egyptians believed that the Earth was created in three successive periods, each phase of creation being in fact a re-creation of previously existing grounds that disappeared beneath the primaeval waters; each phase of this long-drawn-out process of re-creation resulted in the origin of a new sacred domain which, in its primary aspect, was a mere re-enactment of what once had existed. In this order of events we have the revivification of the enclosure of the Earth-Maker, the *Mansion of Isden*; then followed the re-creation of the realm of the *Ka*, which was manifested in the origin of the first series of *pāy*-lands along and around the edges of the island of creation; at the end there appeared further *pāy*-lands which brought to a new life the former homeland of the *Maker-of-substances*.

In the tradition we have been outlining, however, the ancestral nature of the place does not appear to be the only means which

[1] E. VI. 329,2.

made it possible for a new sacred domain to develop there. We find in the description of the following events ideas and facts which are unlike the history of the origin of the *Wetjeset-Neter* and that of *Djeba*.

The narrative seems to be concerned with describing the actual situation when the company of gods of Tanen and the Falcon arrived. The *First Place* of the *Island of Fury* was apparently in danger, for the *rꜣ*-snake appeared on the landing stage of the island. The danger of his attack was undoubtedly the reason why preparations were made to consolidate the safety of that place. The way in which the protection of the place in which a divine power was believed to have been enshrined was arranged, shows a tradition of an entirely different order from that in which the protection of the sacred places in the original *pāy*-lands was made.[1] It is said that in the first place a *bw-titi*, *Place for Crushing*,[2] was planned. Then appeared on the scene a large company of divine beings who resembled animals such as falcons, lions, snakes, and bulls.[3] They were sanctified by Tekh and Seshat to become the god's protectors. The whole company (*ṯt*)[4] was then divided into four groups (*sꜣ*); each group was placed along one side of the *bw-titi*, the *Place-for-Crushing*. In the midst of them the Falcon stood. These four groups of protectors seem in their function to have replaced the Protector God from the original field of reeds[5] and the two staffs of Tanen mentioned in connexion with the 'Enclosure' of the Earth-Maker,[6] for no allusion is made to them in this part of the myth. According to a view of somewhat later date which we find in the abbreviated version of this myth, these four groups of protectors are described as the *Soldiers of Tanen*,[7] whom Tanen called upon to protect the god because the domain (*niwt*) of the gods was created by the command of the Earth-Maker.

A decree of protection was promulgated by Tanen against the enemy of the god. Thereafter the snake was overthrown and the victorious gods are said to have settled (*snḏm*) beside him.[8] It can

[1] Cf. pp. 19–20. [2] Cf. p. 34. [3] Cf. pp. 34–5.

[4] E. VI. 329,9; *ṯt*, cf. E. III. 33,15; VI. 17,2; 18,9; 329,3.6.9.10.13; 332,1.5, is used in these texts as a synonym of *ist*; cf. also E. V. 161,7; VII. 19,15; 41,17.

[5] Cf. p. 20. [6] Cf. p. 23. [7] E. VI. 17,12–13.

[8] E. VI. 328,15–16.

be supposed that the expression *snḏm ⟨r-⟩ gs, to settle beside someone,* implies the Egyptian idea of the victory over an enemy. Settling down on the ground of the battlefield means here most probably that the land was conquered and definitely liberated from the enemy. This appears to be a very old custom, perhaps a custom of predynastic Egypt since, in our creation story, it is projected into a mythological plane; nothing more is known of it.

This mythical battlefield was then purified with a view to founding a sacred domain there. At that very moment of the mythical history another deity appeared on the scene, completely unknown to the previous narrative. It is Rēᶜ.[1] The description of the arrival of the gods in this region does not give a single hint of the presence of the Sun-God in the company of Tanen and the Falcon. He is also not mentioned in the episode of the fight. Consequently, it would appear that the Sun-God was believed to have joined Tanen and his fellows at the moment when the area was cleared up from the enemy.

This account sets out clearly that the final stage of preparing the grounds for sacred domains in the secondary *pāy*-lands was determined by events distinctly different from what happened in the history of the *Wetjeset-Neter* and *Djeba*. In the history of the former the foundation ground of the sacred domain was determined by what had once existed there. In the secondary *pāy*-lands, in contrast, though allusion is made to a place of ancestral tradition, this does not appear to be the sole and essential means which could make it possible to create a sacred domain. Moreover, in this account it is not expressly stated that any of the acts of revivification were performed in order to bring the former dwelling-place of the god to its former state. The ground of that early settlement, however, assumed another function. It was the scene of a fight. Thus only through the fight and its victorious outcome was the god enabled to enter into possession of the ancestral place.

Another difference from the history of the original *pāy*-lands can be seen in the part played by the Falcon in the development of events. The Falcon is not interpreted as a mere successor of the dead ruler, but, instead, he acts and leads the combat. In this

[1] E. VI. 328,16.

tradition, the Falcon conquered the place of ancestral tradition so that a new sacred domain could be founded there.

It is evident from this exposition that the third record describes a somewhat later and more advanced stage of the primaeval age. This is demonstrated by the type of sacred places that were founded there. There is no allusion to the making of a primitive resting-place as in the original *pāy*-lands. This account refers to *enclosures* which were earlier than the time of the fight. It introduces us definitely to two consecutive episodes occurring in the same region; in each of these a sacred domain was created, though on the same land, under different mythological circumstances. These domains arose near the original domains of that region, and do not seem to have been created for the original gods of these *pāy*-lands. New divine beings are said to have come into that region after it was made safe from the enemy, and these newcomers appear to be the lords of the secondary sacred domains. These domains would not be created on the marginal land of the water; on the contrary, it appears as though they were founded in the mainland of the *pāy*-land.

With the creation of these settlements on the former battle-field a definite era of the primaeval age comes to an end. The gods are now found settled in their proper domains. What follows has every aspect of a new phase of creation. Its main concern, however, appears to be the development of the inner area of the sacred domains themselves.

CHAPTER 12

The Characteristics of the Site of the Temple

We have seen that the decisive moment in the history of both the earlier and the later *pāy*-lands occurred when the deities reached an area which, though included in the *pāy*-land, was in its nature distinctly different from the rest of the land. Then started a new period in the development of the primaeval domains.

This area, described by the common word *bw*, *place*,[1] was the site of the first enclosure to be erected in the *pāy*-land. In both of the accounts, behind the choice of the final site for the god's home lies the same tradition concerning the ground of the dwelling-place of the *Ancestor*. This only was regarded as the fitting place to effect the foundation. The circumstances that surround the choice of the site are distinctly different in each of these accounts. There is no similarity between the development of the events in the original *pāy*-lands after the Falcon became its supreme lord and all that happened in the *pāy*-lands of a somewhat later date. We may, eventually, speak of two theories concerning the characteristics of the site of the first enclosure of the god in which the later historical temples were believed to have developed, and suggest that these theories vary according to what was the real nature of the ancestral territory and whether it existed in the original *pāy*-lands or in the secondary ones.

The original *pāy*-lands are described as being the realm of the deceased Earth-God, the *Ka*. Naturally there must have been one single place where the private residence of the *Ka* was during the first era of the primaeval age. This is said to have been on the marginal land of the territory, and was believed to have enshrined the relic of the resting-place of the defunct ruler. This, then, is never described as being a real object; it is only said to have been replaced by another type of resting-place after the *pāy*-land was restored to its former state. The Perch, the natural outcome of

[1] We can agree that in our records the word *bw* is used as a technical term and describes any original place, a place of creation or the site in which a sacred domain was to be founded.

what once existed, marked out the scene of the new phase of creation.[1]

We could not state dogmatically that a closely similar situation existed also in the secondary *pāy*-lands in the early period of their existence. All that we know from the Edfu texts is that there were erected enclosures of the type of the *ḥwt, mansion*, but how and under what circumstances the text does not reveal. That Tanen and the Falcon were believed to have founded resting-places resembling the later *ḥwt, mansions*, we can only guess at with the help of the place-names.[2] These enclosures might have been erected shortly after the actual land of the *pāy*-land was created. It is quite clear that these enclosures were earlier than the period of the fight and that a tradition other than the myth of the fight was probably connected with their foundation ground. But the text says nothing nor does it describe their eventual development and their destiny after the *First Place*, the residence of the *Maker-of-substances*, was conquered by the Falcon. This point seems to be without importance in this tradition and speculation is vain.[3]

The main concern of the preserved part of the narrative is, therefore, the history of the *First Place* in that region. This was primarily the dwelling-place of the Earth-God described as the *'Ir-iḫt*. The text does not explain what his resting-place was. Certainly, the tradition concerning the *ḏd*-pillar is foreign to this mythical episode. Moreover, there is no hint of the eventual restoration of this seat. It looks as though the fight, specifically the metamorphosis of the ground into a *bw-tỉtỉ, Place-for-Crushing*,[4] was the means of revivifying its former sacred nature. All that happened after the gods conquered the area of the Ancestor is described as being an act of purification (*twr*) of the battlefield. It appears logical and natural that the battlefield should have been cleansed from the vestiges of the fight so that the assembly of the gods could enter into it. The natural needs are interpreted here as a ritual ceremony enabling the deities to make their settlement. But with the exception of this act there is no allusion

[1] Cf. p. 121. [2] Cf. p. 192.

[3] We may imagine that these *ḥwt*-mansions were founded in the same way as the *Mansion of Isden* in the island. There is no evidence to confirm the suggestion.

[4] Cf. p. 34, n. 1 for references.

to other rites to be completed before the foundation of the enclosure was laid out in the *First Place*.

If we return to the lands which were the gift of the *Ka* to the god, precisely to the moment after the nearest vicinity of the Perch was declared as the imminent property of the Falcon, it is evident that the record alludes to a series of actions distinctly different from what had happened in the *Hinterland*. The two Shebtiw are described as performing yet another act of creation. Allusion is made to a ceremony which has every appearance of being an invocation of the *iḫt, substances*.[1]

What follows is a description of a scene strongly resembling the procedure of the creation of the *pāy*-land itself. The Shebtiw are said to have sped to an already known place which in our records is described as the *bw-sw-iḫt-tȝ-r.r.w-im, the place-in-which-the-substances-of-all-the-lands-were-endowed-with-power*.[2] The text is again silent about the location of this very centre of creation. We are reduced to a speculation. It may, very tentatively, be suggested that it was probably the place from which all the *pāy*-lands were created. If this be correct, we must assume that the Shebtiw once again returned to the centre of creation in the original island, from which this ultimate act would also have to start. This would show that it was believed that there was in the primaeval world one sole place from which all the succeeding phases of creation of the Earth emanated and that the Egyptians believed that the terrestrial world was, indeed, created from a single centre. This, as far as our document tells us, was the *bw-ẖnm, the place*, for which we suggested, very tentatively, the interpretation *the Place-of-the-Well*. This hypothesis receives some support from the fact that this second instance of the name *bw-sw-iḫt-tȝ*, unlike the first occurrence, contains the expression *tȝw r-r.w, all the lands*. We suspect that this expression applies to all the *pāy*-lands listed in the first cosmogonical record.

The description of this episode of creation seems to indicate, on the other hand, that when all the *pāy*-lands had been brought into

[1] E. VI. 177,13: *ȝt sbi itn šwy nis šbtyw iḫt m ḥf, The moment having passed and the disk having shone, the Shebtiw called the substances which were in sight*; we suspect that this is a description of the situation in which the magical rite was performed; consequently this moment occurred at sunrise, cf. E. VI. 183,12; allusion is made to the *praise of Rēʿ*, cf. p. 25.

[2] E. VI. 177,14.

existence, there followed yet another act of creation, perhaps performed on a somewhat reduced scale. Under these conditions the magical rite of *endowing the substances with power* caused the primaeval water to *recede* from the edges of the existing *pāy*-land. But no *pāy*-land is said to have emerged thereafter. The outcome of this action is described only as *wḏꜥ bw*, *the place has been delimited.*[1]

It is clear that we have here only the re-enactment of the rites of creation which were performed on the edges of the original island[2] and that here also a submerged land came into sight as the result of it. But nothing more is said of the nature of this *bw*-place. As the Perch was already in existence, and is pictured as standing on the marginal land of the *pāy*-land, this *bw*-place may well be the nearest surroundings of the Perch. We know from the account of the origin of the *pāy*-land of *Wetjeset-Neter* that the Perch was erected in what is called the *bw-ḥbbt*, the *Place-of-the-Primaeval-Water*.[3] The *bw*-place in the episode which we have been outlining must have lain beneath the water at the time when the Falcon was proclaimed *ndm*-lord of the *pāy*-land.[4] Consequently, this ultimate performance of the *sw-iḫt-tꜣ* would mean nothing other than the bringing of this particular *bw-ḥbbt* into a fitting state, so that the command of the *Ka* could be effected.[5]

The actual site of the enclosure to be constructed, therefore, required a special act of creation which occurred only after the mainland of the *pāy*-land was in existence. We deduce that this circumstance depended on the original nature of this *bw*-place. We know from the account of the origin of the *pāy*-land of *Djeba* that the *ḏd*-pillar of the *Ka* was enshrined exactly in the *bw*-place to which this performance of the magical rite of creation was applied. It follows that this ultimately created piece of land was the site of the former *Home of the Ka*, which represented the foundation ground of the first enclosure of the Falcon in the *pāy*-land. Yet another point is to be stressed in the description of this episode of creation. It is not stated that the ground of the *Home*

[1] E. VI. 177,14.
[2] Cf. pp. 14, 137 ff.
[3] Cf. pp. 162 ff., 176.
[4] Cf. pp. 178–9.
[5] Cf. p. 183.

of the Ka was *bs*, 'brought out' of Nun,[1] but the text describes this action as *wḏ*ᶜ. We conjecture that in this particular instance the magical rite was performed on a somewhat altered scale and might have been used with a view to drying out the muddy area and restoring the eventual boundary of the former *Home of the Ka*. The lay-out of the foundation ground was thus believed to restore the exact extent of the former domain.

The text proceeds to tell us that after the neighbourhood of the *Perch* was made into solid land, the Sages, the Builder Gods and the crew of the Falcon came close to their lord. We suspect that this very brief description indicates that the assembly of the gods entered into the very ground of the *Perch*. Then, after an episode of greeting and adoring, the *nḥp*-action was foretold.[2] From this order of events it is entirely clear that in the land which was inherited by the Falcon, only one specific place could be the site of what was about to happen, and this was only the part of the land which enshrined the relics of the *Home of the Ka*.[3] Only to this part of the *pāy*-land did the *wḏt nfr*, the *blessed command* of the *Ka*,[4] apply, making it safe for the god to found his settlement there. The occurrence of the term *nḥp*[5] makes it clear that since the very moment when the ground of the *Home of the Ka* was restored, the nature of the creative activities was altered. We have here a clear allusion to the constructing of the first enclosure of the Falcon that was ever made in the original *pāy*-land as soon as the process of creating the Earth was completed.[6] The first account of the origin of the *pāy*-land adds further details to the statements by the assembly of gods on the ground of the *bw*-place in the *pāy*-land of *Djeba*.

[1] Cf. above, p. 161 and E. VI. 184,12, the description of the emergence of the *pāy*-land on the edges of the island.

[2] E. VI. 176,4; *nḥp bw ḫr.k*, *May the place that carries thee be fashioned*.

[3] E. VI. 176,5; from this point of view the *ḏd*-pillar of the *Ka* mentioned in VI. 177,5 would not appear to be a real object; probably there are the same circumstances as in the island, cf. above, p. 14, for the *ḏd*-pillar of the *Pn*-God.

[4] E. VI. 176,5; we suspect that this sentence specifies what is enshrined in the place which was to be constructed.

[5] It appears that in these records the word *nḥp*, to *fashion*, is used with special reference to the constructions of the early sacred enclosures, cf. E. III. 42,14; 186,5–6; IV. 7,6; 19,9; 73,12; VI. 18,6.7.9.10; 168,14; 173,3; 176,4; 183,11; 320,11; 322,14; VII. 24,4; 27,11; 49,14.

[6] Cf. p. 177.

The description of the origin of the *pāy*-land of *Wetjeset-Neter*[1] alludes to a closely similar situation and explains yet another belief connected with the early stage of the existence of the *pāy*-land of the Falcon. This *pāy*-land, or a part of it at least, is equated with what is described as *snbt*,[2] which is said to have been *šb*, transformed, to protect its lord.[3] The ensuing narrative alludes to an event described as the *Entering* (*into the place* ?) *in which the ḏd-pillar of reeds was*.[4] The word *snbt* can be used here as a noun, and if so, it would seem to qualify the whole *pāy*-land, which might have been regarded as a piece of land placed over and above the level of the primaeval water and which could ensure the protection of the god; therefore, the *pāy*-land was described as being equal to the *snbt*.[5] If, on the other hand, *snb* is here used as a verb,[6] an alternative interpretation may be suggested: *Constructing what was transformed to protect its lord.* We incline to the opinion that this very brief description conceals an allusion to the magical rite of creation which was ultimately performed on the marginal land of the *pāy*-land. In this context the verb *šb*, *to transform*, may have replaced the expression *sw-iḫt-tꜣ*, *to endow the substances of the Earth with power*, well known from the description of the origin of the additional piece of land on the edges of the *pāy*-land of *Djeba*. Since the ultimate episode that is said to have occurred in the *pāy*-land of *Wetjeset-Neter* is placed in the *bw-ḥbbt*,[7] we suggest that the term *snb* refers only to a part of the *pāy*-land. We think it describes the ground of the former *Home of the Ka* which was to be transformed so that a construction of somewhat more solid material could be erected.

The interpretation suggested seems to accord with the allusion to the episode of *Entering* (*into the place of*) *the ḏd-pillar*.[8] The gods are said to have reached that area only after it was *šb*, *transformed*. Only after the neighbourhood of the Perch was made into solid

[1] Cf. p. 160 ff. [2] E. VI. 184,14.

[3] This passage is discussed in detail in *ZÄS*, LXXXVII, 44–5.

[4] E. VI. 184,15; we suspect that this sentence describes the final act of the episode interpreted in VI. 184,10–15.

[5] Cf. *Wb.* IV, 161 (8).

[6] Cf. *Wb.* IV, 161 (7).

[7] E. VI. 184,13 and above, p. 162.

[8] Here also it is doubtful whether the *ḏd*-pillar would be a real object remaining on the site.

land was it thus possible for the gods to enter into the most sacred part of the *pāy*-land, *the Home of the Ka*.

These two accounts show much similarity and prove that the Egyptian idea was that in the whole *pāy*-land there was one particular spot which came to be regarded as enshrining the protective powers that made possible the foundation of the Falcon's domain. The special nature of that piece of land was derived from the relic of the vanished world, the *ḏd*-pillar. Here again there is disclosed the belief that a territory of ancestral tradition was the only land fit for the foundation of a sacred domain, and that it was determined by the relic of the earlier sacred place. We are convinced that the Egyptians believed that the foundation plot of the first enclosure to be constructed in the original *pāy*-land, which was the starting-point in the existence of the historical temple, was not laid out on the mainland of the *pāy*-land, but beside it. Apparently the foundation plot of the first enclosure was conceived as being later in origin than the *pāy*-land itself. Its origin, however, entailed yet another act of creation which was a mere repetition of the procedure through which the *pāy*-land came into existence. The Edfu account gives us conclusive evidence that by the emergence of the *bw, foundation plot*, the long-drawn-out drama of the creation of the Earth was definitely completed and this ultimate *bw, foundation plot*, became the scene of a new phase of creation which resulted in the origin of the temple.

The record discloses the belief that the first enclosure was believed to restore the former residence of the *Ka*, but it does not contain a description of how this enclosure was erected on the *pāy*-land. Since, however, the Builder Gods are mentioned in the second record as being present in the *pāy*-land,[1] it is legitimate to suggest that they may have been responsible for its construction. The description of the constructing does not seem to be the interest and the purpose of the narrative, but on the contrary, its main concern seems to be to interpret another episode connected with the foundation of a primitive enclosure: the constitution of the *magical protection*. This, apparently, was the duty of Tanen, and his function in this site recalls the situation which seems to have existed in the *Enclosure of the Earth-Maker*, the *Mansion of*

[1] E. VI. 176,3.

Isden, after this was restored in the original island.[1] We know that Tanen provided that enclosure with *magical protection* when he created protective symbols which are described as his staff and the likeness of the god. Since Tanen is said to have been present on the site of the enclosure of the Falcon and to have placed his arms around the god, it is, therefore, tempting to suppose that the same situation occurred there though the text does not explain this episode. It does not give details of what might have been included in this sacred rite. It seems to us most likely that, in consequence of this episode, a procession was performed by the creators in which the Lord of the *pāy*-land was conducted to his legitimate place within the enclosure. This seems to be one of the most interesting points of the narrative. The god was believed to have entered his house in the company of the creators of the Earth. This episode was followed by an act of fumigating which, as far as this tradition is concerned, seems to have closed the ceremony of entering the enclosure.[2] Unfortunately the text is exceptionally obscure, and one can only guess that the following narrative might contain spells which were to be recited at an act of consecration of an early sacred place. This is, of course, largely an hypothesis for which no relevant texts can be cited. Nevertheless, we incline to the opinion that in these very brief descriptions, there is interpreted the starting-point in the existence of the Falcon's first mansion. It is of prime importance that in the development of the events of the *pāy*-land, specially after the final *bw*, *foundation plot*, had emerged, no allusion is made to the *Protector God* and to the *God-of-the-Temple*.[3]

The analysis of the Edfu records furnished decisive evidence that the Egyptian cosmogony did not contain a single theory concerning the origin of the site of the first properly constructed enclosure of the god, and consequently that of the temple. Some points of contact have been noticed in the background of these two theories; both stress the idea that the site of the first enclosure derived from a place of ancestral tradition. It is also evident that Tanen was the chief authority who made the site safe so as to

[1] Cf. p. 148 ff.

[2] E. VI. 176,6; this suggestion is based on the occurrence of *ꜣm*; it looks as though the *Divine of Heart* would perform this act but this is somewhat hypothetical.

[3] Cf. p. 262 ff. for their functions.

house the god there. At this point, however, a distinct difference can be seen in the order in which the protection was effected. No staffs provided with magical power were used, but the *Soldiers of Tanen* are said to have appeared on the scene, and they then performed the duty of protecting the god. Moreover, it is to be borne in mind that the site, though of ancestral tradition also, was included within the mainland of the *pāy*-land.

As has already been pointed out above, at the time when the victorious company of gods took hold of the site, a new divine being appeared on the scene. The sudden appearance of a god who is not described as being a member of the divine family who lived in the original island, and who did not take part in the fight, makes it obvious that, originally, the second Edfu myth might well have been another interpretation of the origin of the Falcon's sacred places. This tradition either interprets the manner in which the secondary sacred places of the Falcon were created later on or acquaints us with the Falcon's original domains in a place other than that in which the belief in the *Ka* was at home. The presence of the Ancestor *'Ir-iḫt* may support the second interpretation suggested.[1] This myth might have been at a definite moment connected with the first myth, in which the *Ka* plays a prominent part, and consequently might have been used as the interpretation of the origin of the Falcon's enclosures in the secondary *pāy*-lands. These lands were occupied by Tanen and the Falcon, but apart from their original dwelling-places there might have been relics of other sacred domains from an earlier world which needed to be restored. The restoration and revivification of their sacred nature seems to have entailed procedures other than those known from the sacred places that derived in a direct line from the creation of the Earth. The situation interpreted in the third Edfu record may apply to the origin of the domain of almost any god. It may be surmised that when this myth became familiar to places other than its home, further modifications of the original version might have been effected and thus it happened that this myth was adopted and adapted for the interpretation of the origin of the first domain of other divine beings and in a way which is demon-

[1] The *'Ir-iḫt* is not mentioned in connexion with the *bw-ḫnm*, cf. p. 155; this would be another hint of an entirely different tradition.

strated by explanation of the origin of the first Solar Enclosure. If we decide in favour of this interpretation we must point out that emphasis is laid on the presence of Tanen and the Falcon in the places in which a sacred domain of another god was to be created. In our opinion it seems that this belief had resulted from the transferring of tradition from one place to another. Tanen and the Falcon travelled through the primaeval world. In places where they stopped they prepared the way for the creation of sacred domains of which they were not the sole occupiers. Other gods seem to have been believed to join them and to share the enclosures with them. From this belief a theory might have been derived that the sacred domains of the gods could only originate in places in which Tanen and the Falcon had dwelt first. A further support of this explanation can be seen in the fact that the second myth does not preserve an account of the creation and of the early stages of development of the lands primarily belonging to the Sun-God. It contains no allusion to the creation of the *Seat of the First Occasion*. We conclude that according to this theory the first Solar domain was not believed to have originated in lands specially created for the Sun-God, but on lands originally belonging to other deities. This view seems to accord with what our text tells us, that after the sacred settlement had been made by Tanen and the Falcon the site was *twr*, *purified* (= sanctified or consecrated) for Rēᶜ. It is equally admissible that our Edfu records disclose a tradition entirely different from the Hermopolitan myth of creation. This doctrine does not claim that a *pāy*-land would be created from the island of creation in which the first enclosure of the Sun-God was to be founded. On the contrary, the Hermopolitan theory is that the first temple of the Sun-God was created in the place where the god was born; therefore, this could only be the pool of the primaeval island. Moreover, the Hermopolitan sources do not describe the way in which the first Solar Temple was believed to have been created at the beginning of the world. The idea of constructing a temple is not in line with Hermopolitan trends of thought. The Edfu records, therefore, acquaint us with a tradition concerning the origin of the sacred enclosures of the type *ḥwt* or *inb* which were believed to have been created only in places which had a direct connexion with the Earth-God.

This brings to mind the picture of the *Mansion of Isden* in the original island, of which the enclosures created at a somewhat later stage of the primaeval age were only a projection and reflexion. The Egyptians believed that to such sacred enclosures divine beings came from other parts of the mythical world and found their final home there. These statements seem to be confirmed by the idea disclosed by the title of the myth about the origin of the Solar Temple, which reads: *Coming of Rēᶜ to his Mansion* (*ḥwt*) *of Ms-nḫt.*[1]

The descriptions of mythological situations which are enshrined in the third Edfu cosmogonical record prove that the myth about the origin of the temple of the Falcon was most probably the earliest document concerned with the origin of an Egyptian temple. It is the only known source that enables us to illustrate the stages that preceded the foundation of the first constructed enclosures, and to ascertain the Egyptian views about how the actual site of the temple was believed to have been created. Consequently it would seem that the Egyptian theory was that originally there was only one temple, the foundation ground of which derived in a direct line from the process of the creation of the Earth. This was on the *pāy*-land which was the gift of the dead deity.[2]

The Edfu records make it clear that the origin of the site of the temple varies according to whether it was the site of the temple of the Falcon or that of the Solar Temple. The site of the second sacred domain is the result of mythical events which came to pass only after the sacred world was constituted. It was not specifically created for the Sun-God, it was not a bequest of an earlier and higher power, but a battlefield. The sanctity of the first sacred domain of the Sun-God was not given to it by what had existed in the past, but appears, in part at least, to have been due to the victory of the gods.

The history of the site of the second mythical temple therefore suggests that, originally, there was one sole domain in which the

[1] Cf. p. 188 ff.

[2] The result accords with our suggestion that in the background of this story is the myth about the origin of the domain and the temple of a *nṯr*-god who originally might have been nameless, cf. p. 169 ff.

Mansion of the God originated as an entity. On the other hand, it seems to exemplify the theory concerning the expansion of constructed domains of gods outside the original area of the *Mansion of the God*.

It follows that the other myths about the origin of sacred places which are known to us[1] can reasonably be regarded as derivative traditions. The majority of them emphasize the idea of the *fight*, and the fight of the god against his enemies appears to be the essential condition that enabled the god to found his domain. The main Edfu record made it possible to investigate the origin of this tradition. To illustrate this view reference should be made to the myth about the *Fight of Horus against Seth*.[2] The mythological situation is placed in the *House of Rēᶜ* which was to the south of the *Wetjeset-Neter*. Rēᶜ-Harakhte is said to have given Beḥdet with its sacred mounds (*iꜣwt*) to Horus. Horus then was bound to fight against his adversaries before he assumed the function of the lord. This short narrative does not seem to claim to explain the origin of Beḥdet or describe the creations of the mounds (*iꜣwt*).

The same trends of thought prevail in the *Myth of Horus*.[3] The situation is again placed in the *Wetjeset-Neter* in which Rēᶜ arrived. The myth is not concerned with the interpretation of the origin of this *Wetjeset-Neter*. It existed when Rēᶜ with his fellows arrived there. On this *Wetjeset-Neter* was based the fight against the enemies of the god and it was led by Horus. In every place in which the enemies were overthrown, there a sacred place was founded. We suspect that in this myth the principal reason for the founding of sacred places was the celebration of the victory. There is an obvious similarity of ideas between the second part of the third Edfu cosmogonical record and this myth. The close link is borne out by the fact that the fight again appears as the essential condition for the origin of a sacred place.

It has been noticed that in these derivative myths the original aspect of the sacred domain is generally described as *iꜣt*, *mound*. Evidence can be quoted to show that most probably the word *mound* was generally used in describing the original island with its adjacent *pāy*-lands.[4] We can refer to the title of the sacred

[1] Cf. p. 50.
[2] Cf. p. 51, n. 2.
[3] Cf. *JEA*, XXI, 26–36.
[4] Cf. p. 167.

book in which the origin of the sacred domains was recorded. Although the title contains the word *ỉ3t, mound,*[1] the contents interpret the origin of the *pāy*-lands and their enclosures. Yet supplementary evidence can be cited from the Edfu texts to show that the word *ỉ3t* could be used in describing the original piece of land that emerged from Nun at first.[2] It appears as though the *ỉ3t, mound,* would represent for the Egyptians of later historical times the picture of the original world of gods in the primaeval age.

The study of the Edfu cosmogonical records enabled us to reconstruct a series of mythological events concerned with the origin of sacred places. Generally we find the statement that the Creator, after he had emerged from Nun, created his *nỉwt, domain.* The Edfu texts are, at present, the only source which makes it possible to reconstruct phase by phase the succeeding events which occurred between these two poles of Egyptian mythological tradition: the emergence of the Creator and the creation of his domain.

It has also been seen how prominent is the part played by Tanen in this mythological sequence from the very moment when the first step was made towards the revivification of the site and the restoration of the *Mansion of Isden.* He is also the main personality in all the events which came to pass on the marginal land of the *pāy*-land of the Falcon as well as in those which happened in the secondary *pāy*-lands. For this reason, it seems to us most likely that this long period of time was regarded, at least in the tradition of a later date, as the *reign of Tanen.*[3] On the other hand, Tanen is not mentioned in connexion with the origin of sacred places in the *ỉ3wt, sacred mounds.* This would seem to be further evidence to support our hypothesis concerning the *original land of the Mansion of the God* to which divine beings were believed to come from other parts of Egypt.

[1] Cf. p. 9. [2] E. VI. 22,7. [3] Cf. p. 293.

PART IV

The Creation of the Temple

CHAPTER 13

Reconstruction of the Theory concerning the Origin of the Temple of the Falcon

A comprehensive account is given of the manner in which the site of the Falcon's first enclosure in the original *pāy*-land was believed to have come into existence. It looks as though at the moment when this enclosure was erected and was occupied by the gods, a definite time of evolution came to an end. The site with the most elementary type of enclosure seems to have become the scene of a new phase of creation which was regarded as a new and important period in the *reign of Tanen*. The traditions connected with the last created piece of Earth seem to be the factors that determine the characteristics of the forthcoming phase of creation. We think that it is of interest to summarize the ideas that lie behind the creation completed on the land of the *Home of the Ka*. An important feature in this narrative is the *ḏd*-pillar.[1] We can follow this in a direct line from the very moment when the creators reached the desert island and when the first sacred domain was re-created as far as the foundation of the first enclosure in the *bw*-place of the *pāy*-land.[2] The *ḏd*-pillar is never described as a physically real object on the site; only the memory of it seems to have remained in the knowledge of the creators. This is, in particular, demonstrated by the episode of adoration which the Shebtiw were believed to perform on the edges of the *pāy*-land of *Djeba*.[3] They are said to have *recalled the substances*, *sḫ3 iḫt*, on the former site of the *ḏd*-pillar. From this rite developed a new phase of creation which resulted in the origin of the temple. The *ḏd*-pillar, therefore, as an unreal symbol seems to have had the function of determining land of a specially sacred nature. This seems to indicate that the Egyptians believed that where the *ḏd*-pillar was, there the sacred nature of the Earth was eternally vital, but needed to be revivified by the creation of a new entity closely resembling in its physical appearance that which had once existed there.

[1] Cf. pp. 96–7, 184, 203. [2] Cf. p. 205. [3] Cf. p. 30.

The site on which the restoration was to be effected was conceived as deriving from the orders of creation of the Earth. It was the direct, though ultimate, outcome of the long-drawn-out drama of the creation of the Earth. Only a land of this nature was believed to be capable of assuming the function of a foundation in the forthcoming phases of creation which were manifested in the origin of a new sacred unit: *the temple*. The divine powers who were believed to have acted in this phase of creation were the deities who took part in the former process; they were the *Progeny of the Earth-God*. The Edfu texts seem to intimate the view that as soon as the process of the creation of the Earth came to an end, then followed what is described as *nḥp, to fashion*;[1] again therefore, an act of creation, only performed on an entirely different scale and under other circumstances. The action *nḥp* seems to replace the former process, which was of a magical and symbolical nature, and was believed to have been performed for the first time on the land which was the gift of the deceased Earth-God.

It has been noticed how closely parallel the beginnings of the Falcon's enclosure are to those of the other and earlier divine beings. The setting up of the Perch on the marginal land of the *pāy*-land is equivalent to the setting up of the resting-place in the original domain of the *Wetjeset-Neter* in the *Island of Trampling*.[2] The first enclosure could thus be laid out on land which resembled in its nature the piece of Earth on which the creation started and on which too the first resting-place of the god was erected in the beginning of the world. This belief is parallel to another tradition. In imitating the physical appearance of the first sacred domain that ever came into existence in the island as the resurrection of the vanished realm of the *Pn*-God, the first enclosure of the Falcon in the *pāy*-land restores the *Home of the Ka*. However, neither the earliest enclosure of the Falcon nor the private residence of the *Ka* must be imagined as resembling in detail the developed *ḥwt-ntr*, the *Mansion of the God*. They were undoubtedly much simpler and more elementary structures; but it was from them that eventually the temples of historical times evolved.

While discussing the situation in the *pāy*-land we indicated the

[1] Cf. p. 202. [2] Cf. p. 121.

probable physical appearance of the first sacred place that was believed to have been founded in an open field and in a muddy area.[1] With a view to sketching the phases of development of the Falcon's primaeval domains, it is only necessary to return to the marginal land of the *pāy*-land of the Falcon. As has been said, the text is very brief and enigmatic. Nevertheless, our sources contain a number of facts which make it reasonably possible to reconstruct all the phases of evolution from the humblest type of place of worship in an open field to the final stage of the *ḥwt-nṯr*, the *Mansion of the God.*

The primitive enclosure enshrining the Perch of the Falcon that was erected on the water's edges, seems to illustrate an early stage of evolution. We have mentioned above that the creation of sacred places which the creators of the Earth were believed to have completed, has every appearance of being based on real facts. All the sacred domains which are described in our story, starting with the most primitive resting-place of the god in the island, not only reflect and reproduce the original sacred places of the Egyptian gods but also indicate the manner in which these places were founded. Hence, the place which was believed to have been fashioned for the Falcon on the land of the *Home of the Ka* is only an additional element in this series. The description only conceals another manner of creating a sacred place as it might have been done in the dim past of predynastic Egypt. The fact that in the *pāy*-land the Perch was erected before there is any trace of the site of the enclosure proves that the same type of resting-place has symbolized the resurrection of the sacred domain of gods within the original island. The revivification of the Home of the *Ka* marks the starting-point in the creation of the new type of sacred abode: *the temple.* The delimitation of the foundation ground was clearly regarded as being the second episode in the constitution of primitive sacred domains according to the beliefs and customs of a remote date. In default of any precise textual or archaeological evidence we have to return to the myth. The site of the enclosure may, perhaps, have been delimited by the Shebtiw themselves, who may be imagined as walking in procession along the boundary of the former *Home of the Ka,*

[1] Cf. p. 328; see also Petrie, *Royal Tombs*, II, Pl. 3, no. 4.

thus indicating where the reed fence should be erected.[1] It looks as though, in the early stages of history, the planning of the foundation ground was regarded as a secret act since it is projected into a mythical plane and is interpreted as a rite of a magical order. The narrative is concerned with the description of the ceremonies which followed the delimitation of the ground and which have every appearance of being rites performed with a view to establishing the *magical protection* of the sacred place to be. Of these the rite of fumigating[2] seems to be the most important. It is clear that at this stage of the history of the Falcon's domains the spear does not seem to play any special part. At the end of this episode a procession seems to have been performed. We imagine that all the deities present *in situ* were believed to have walked in procession around the ground of the enclosure. This may indicate that in the early stage after the ground was delimited statues or images of the deities for whom the enclosure was to be erected were carried in procession around the ground before the construction began. The order of ceremonies may well preserve a memory of the earliest rites of foundation. In this connexion no allusion is made to any of the usual episodes of a *foundation ritual*, in particular, to the performance of the *Stretching of the Cord* and the *Setting out of the four sides*.[3] The point is of importance for the general history of the primitive enclosures.

As we have seen, nothing is said of the way the enclosure might have been erected around the Perch;[4] the text does not give its name. The narrative contains some hints of its existence, but these are unusually obscure, and when we can expect the description of physical work to start, the mythical scene comes to an end.

The first enclosure that was made in the *pāy*-land was probably a mere fence fashioned from the reeds. This fence formed a courtyard open to the sky, at the rear of which was the Perch as a mark of the most sacred part of the site. Naturally such a primitive enclosure must have contained a symbol or symbols to indicate that the place was sacred or to intimate who was the god who resided there. At this point we may recall the sacred symbols which the

[1] Cf. pp. 31, 203. [2] Cf. p. 205.

[3] Cf. p. 239 for the order of ceremonies in the foundation of the first Solar Temple.

[4] Cf. pp. 31–2.

Shebtiw were believed to have brought from the *bw-ḫnm*.[1] These symbols, in all probability, represented the earliest type of sacred objects that might have been kept in the primitive enclosures. They included also the image of an Ancestor god. We cannot cite archaeological evidence to confirm that this type of emblem was really the earliest symbol used in predynastic cultus-places of the Falcon. We do not know to what real objects they may correspond. Nothing more is said about the *iḫt, substances*, for which, as we know, the crew of the Falcon was responsible in the *pāy*-land.[2] They might have been kept within the newly erected enclosure, but the text does not mention that, eventually, a shelter or any other light construction was made above them. The lack of information on this subject appears at first surprising, especially if we recall the situation on the edges of the *pāy*-land before the land for the new foundation was created.[3] But the presumed absence of the creative matter prompts a suggestion. As there is no allusion to them since the moment when the first enclosure was erected, it may be surmised that these *iḫt, substances*, were believed to have been infused into the structure of the first enclosure.[4]

The first important fact that can be deduced from the Edfu account is that the earliest enclosure of the Falcon is said to have been founded on the water's edges. This appears to be also a custom of the early ages, for we can add further textual evidence indicating the river-bank as the foundation ground of sacred domains.[5]

To show that the Edfu evidence reveals the aspect of a genuine sacred enclosure as it might once have existed, we may recall representations of enclosures of sacred animals and birds which we find on objects from the Archaic Period.[6] They show close similarity with what is known from the Edfu texts. In view of

[1] Cf. p. 31. All the primitive enclosures described in our sources contained protecting symbols which are not, with the *exception* of the *ḥḏ*-spear, known from the representations on the sealings from Archaic Period. Two interpretations are possible: either the symbols described in our records did not survive in the Archaic Period, or our texts allude to the traditions of a site from which no archaeological evidence has come down to us.

[2] Cf. pp. 180–1.

[3] Cf. pp. 202–3.

[4] Cf. p. 294 ff.

[5] E. III. 167,2; Naville, *Bubastis*, Pl. 46 and Gardiner, *AEO*, pp. 158, 160.

[6] Cf. Emery, *Tomb of Ḥor-Aḥa*, pp. 31, 32, and below, p. 330.

these points of contact in the essential features of the structure we suggest that in both we have the same traditions and the same conception of the appearance of an early sacred place. At Edfu there is preserved the memory of a genuine enclosure of sacred birds. We also find at Edfu two instances of reliefs that depict the appearance of the early cultus-place of the Falcon. These two representations might have been inspired by the contents of the cosmogonical records and can only be regarded as a pictorial expression of the thought contained in the records. Their resemblance to the original drawings on the archaic objects, however, is striking.[1] We see in the relief a thicket of reeds representing the primaeval Perch. The Falcon is seated on it, and on the right and left of the seat there stand the creators of the Perch in a position of adoration. Beside this scene there is the spear of the Falcon bearing the name *Sḫm-ḥr* and believed to have emerged from Nun;[2] it is the embodiment of the Protector God.[3] We can see the *God-of-the-Temple*[4] in the scene, but no allusion is made to the *Protector God*. His function seems to be limited to the time when the Falcon lived only in the ancestral place of the original island.[5] The myth refers to *Ḥeter-ḥer* and to the *Divine of Heart* as being present on the *pāy*-land when the Perch was erected; no evidence can be quoted to show that they were present also in the enclosure.

The artificially made support of the god, the Perch, could eventually be replaced by a tree. This is clear from the interpretation of the origin of the *sbty*-enclosure in the *Place-of-the-Throne*.[6] A number of additional instances can be quoted from the Edfu texts which show that the willow, indeed, was regarded as the original seat of the Falcon.[7] We can thus follow two traditions as far as the nature of the resting-place of the Falcon within the enclosure is concerned.

The text says nothing about what might have happened between the erection of the oldest type of a sacred enclosure in the original *pāy*-land and the final stage of the *ḥwt-nṯr*, *Mansion of the God*,

[1] E. x. Pl. 105 and xiv. Pl. 561.
[2] E. vi. 358,2; iv. 185,15–16.
[3] Cf. pp. 97, 149–50.
[4] Cf. E. xiv. Pl. 561.
[5] Cf. p. 140.
[6] Cf. p. 158.
[7] E. iii. 10,15; 187,4; iv. 358,16; vi. 15,3.

the first temple of the Falcon according to the Edfu tradition. No record is preserved elsewhere which would enable us to reconstruct the subsequent phases of development. Nevertheless, our sources proceed to give a description of a temple (*ḥwt-ntr*) which is said to have been founded in *Wetjeset-Neter* in the *reign of Tanen.*[1] This date, in spite of its abstract meaning, is of importance and shows that the Egyptians believed that the temple as an entity originated beyond the limits of historical times. We can see in this mythological date a further hint of the tradition concerning the continuity and relationship between the creation of the Earth and the origin of the temple, at least as far as the foundation of the primitive temples is concerned.[2] We have already pointed to the Egyptian belief that the time when the *pāy*-lands were created is described in the late sources as the *reign of Tanen*. Hence, the title of the fifth Edfu record seems to indicate that the event described in our sources as the *nḥp*, *fashioning*, which refers to the foundation of the enclosure from which the temple evolved later on, was believed to have been included in the same era of the mythical age. This agrees also with a technical fact that the interpretation of the origin of the lands as well as that of the first temple was included in the same sacred book.[3] It will follow that in the fifth Edfu cosmogonical record survives the memory of the final stage of development of the divine settlement which resulted from the command of the *Ka*.[4] This is said to have happened in the place named *Wetjeset-Neter*. We suspect that the name of *Wetjeset-Neter* in this account is the name of the place where the temple was believed to have been founded. Although the text does not say it, it is tempting to suggest that

[1] We have already pointed to the problems raised by the reading of this sacred name. The suggested reading *Wṯst-ntr* finds confirmation in E. VI. 224,10. *wṯst* is, generally, the word for the carrying-chair of the Lower Egyptian King, cf. Blackman and Fairman, *Misc. Greg.* p. 414 and Gardiner, *JEA*, XXVII, 44, n. 1, and the common name for the town and the temple at Edfu. Our text shows distinctly a somewhat earlier tradition connected with the word *wṯst*; it describes the seat of the god, his first resting-place, then the temple which developed around this seat; further occurrences of *wṯst* meaning the first seat of the god are found in the Edfu texts: E. IV. 229,9, the temple is the god's *wṯst*-seat since the primaeval time; VI. 18,3; in III. 186,4–5 *wṯst* applies to the willow.

[2] Cf. p. 208 ff.

[3] Cf. pp. 8–9.

[4] Cf. pp. 202–5.

this *Wetjeset-Neter* might be the *pāy*-land of *Wetjeset-Neter*. The first *ḥwt-nṯr* of the Falcon may thus be that of the *pāy*-land *Wetjeset-Neter*; it originated in the reign of the Earth-God and was founded on the land which the deceased Earth-God determined in his bequest to the Falcon.[1]

Some account of the aspect of the *Temple in Wetjeset-Neter* has already been given.[2]

The record speaks of an enclosure described by the term *inb* of which the dimensions are in part lost, but which might well have been of 300 cubits from west to east, and at least 400 cubits from north to south.[3] Within this enclosure there was a second enclosure of which the name is not given in the text; this second enclosure included a number of halls and rooms that eventually composed the first *ḥwt-nṯr, Mansion of the God.* The second enclosure was erected at a distance of 105 cubits on each side of the outer enclosing wall. Within the interior of the inner enclosure was a small chamber of 30 by 20 cubits which was, as has been mentioned, the *ḥwt-ḳni* of the temple.[4] This chamber was erected at the rear of the north wall of the inner enclosure. The exact dimensions of the inner enclosure are unknown. It was 90 cubits from east to west because its east and west walls were each of them 105 cubits from the outer enclosing wall. The exact north–south dimension is lost.

At the south end of the inner enclosure were further sacred rooms. The text mentions a central hall named as the *wsḫt-ḥw* of 50 by 45 cubits, flanked to east and west by smaller rooms of 30 by 30 cubits, described as a *booth* (*sḥ*) and having to the south of it a small hall named the *wsḫt-šms-ib* and measuring 30 by 15 cubits.[5] It seems that further buildings were included in the great enclosure, but the text of the following description has disappeared.[6] In its final stage, therefore, the inner enclosure representing the real temple consisted of four rooms or halls at the south, and an open court of uncertain dimensions, at the north end of which, and presumably on the axis, was a small chapel, the earliest building on the site.

[1] Cf. p. 28. [2] Cf. pp. 28–9.
[3] E. VI. 326,2–3; the missing part of the text extends over a half of the original line.
[4] E. VI. 326,4–5. [5] E. VI. 326,7–8. [6] E. VI. 327,2.

No supplementary documents can be cited to fill the lacunae in this account. Nevertheless, an analysis may be attempted of the surviving description of the mythical temple from the *reign of Tanen*. We can discern in the text several stages of the growth of the temple, which may duly reproduce the phases in the development of this complex.

At the beginning of the description emphasis is laid on the constructing (*ỉr*) of the outer enclosure wall (*ỉnb*), though, obviously, this term *ỉnb* must apply to a mere fence of great dimensions, fashioned from reed and other light material, and not to a wall of bricks and stones. The description is brief and reads:

How to know the foundation ground (*snṯt*) of the enclosing wall (*ỉnb*). To be made around beforehand.[1]

Apparently the *ỉnb*-enclosure was laid out on the *pāy*-land in order to protect the sacred area and to separate it from the world outside. It may, perhaps, be imagined that this wall or fence described as the *ỉnb* was pictured as marking the limits of the *pāy*-land itself, but there seems to be no reason why it should do so, and if the ground of the enclosure and the *pāy*-land were the same, the latter would be very small and there would be no room for anything but sacred buildings. On the other hand, it may be thought that the outer enclosure was set up in a more or less arbitrary manner along the most convenient line. It should be pointed out that in the myth about the temple of the Falcon no special meaning seems to be connected with the foundation of the *ỉnb*-enclosure. This point seems to have been of no importance to the Egyptians, and speculation is vain. It is completely unknown whether the area embraced by the outer enclosure corresponded to any concrete entity, for the record is silent on this point. We know only that this enclosure extended from south to north.

[1] E. VI. 326,2; an alternative interpretation of this sentence can be suggested; *ỉr.tw* may be here for the infinitive frequently occurring in the instructions; on the other hand, it can be used as a participle; then the second interpretation will be: the *foundation of the enclosure that was made around before it.* We suspect that *ḥr-ḥȝt.f* is used with temporal meaning specifying that the enclosure is to be made or was originally made before any other building was constructed; the occurrence of the suffix *-.f* is problematic. We suspect that it has a rather impersonal meaning and refers to the constructing, the action *ỉr* or *nḥp*.

The term *inb* is new in this tradition, unknown to the previous descriptions of the erection of the fence around the Perch, where we come across terms such as *sbḫt*, *ḥwt* and *sbty*.[1] As none of these terms occurs in the description of the temple it is highly probable that there might be an influence of another tradition, perhaps even of a later date. We are inclined to suggest that this description might refer to a somewhat later stage of the 'Primaeval Age' of gods than the end of the accounts in the second Edfu record. There might have been a long period of time between the type of sacred enclosures fashioned on the *pāy*-lands first and the stage of which the Edfu record gives an interesting account. That in the instructions for the building of the temple the *inb*-enclosure is said to be made in the first place before any other sacred building had been erected on the site seems to indicate an order of constructing different from what is known from the situation in the *pāy*-land. The preserved description of the organization of the temple in *Wetjeset-Neter* must therefore refer to a much later stage in the development of the primitive temples, if not even to the final stage of their growth and history. It clearly shows an order of construction which is unlike what is known about the order which prevailed in the *pāy*-lands.

The following part of the record is very damaged, and there is no other relevant source which might help to sketch the subsequent development of the buildings eventually constructed within the area delimited by the outer enclosure. What appears, however, to be quite certain is that in the encircling outer enclosure there was erected yet another enclosure; the distance between the walls of these two enclosures was 150 cubits on both sides, on the west as well as on the east side. The preserved part of the text does not give the name and the dimensions of the second enclosure in which the temple eventually evolved. Thus it appears that at a definite moment there were two enclosures fashioned from light materials like reeds which formed the early *Mansion of the God*.

The text then proceeds to give the 'specification' of the ground plan (*snṯt*) of the interior of the second enclosure.[2] It is of impor-

[1] Cf. pp. 20, 22, 26.

[2] E. VI. 326,5.

tance that in this connexion the term *ḥwt-nṯr* is not used.[1] The text seems to give the impression that, at that stage, a distinction was made only between the enclosing wall and its interior.

It will be noticed that in the first stage of construction made within the interior of the inner enclosure a sanctuary described as *sḥ*, *booth*, is said to be erected, and that the Perch (*ḏbꜣ*) is not mentioned at all as enshrined within the inner part of the enclosure. Since the Perch was definitely in existence, it is legitimate to theorize and to suggest that this *sḥ*, *booth*, originated in a shelter primarily erected to protect the Perch, and that, in fact, it became the first and most important part of the primitive temple. It is known that in the earliest stage of its history the Perch of the Falcon stood in a courtyard open to the sky.[2] It is natural that there was a need to shield the god's seat. Yet the form of the sign for *sḥ*  makes it evident that a simple light structure resting eventually on three pillars was erected above the Perch. This type of primitive shelter became the elementary form of the first sanctuary of the primitive temples, the *sḥ*, *sanctuary*.[3] The suggestion that the sanctuary in our record may represent the place in which the Perch was believed to stand in the original construction, is supported by the stress laid on this sanctuary in the description. Since this sanctuary is mentioned in the first part of the description of the inner part of the enclosure, it was perhaps considered to be the most important part of the complex. At this point, too, the description may hint at a definite stage of the development. The text indicates that the sanctuary was erected at the north rear wall of the enclosure[4] and in its middle. Although this sanctuary is

[1] The suffix -*.s* in the expression *m-ẖnw.s* suggests that the inner enclosure must have borne a specific name; but we cannot say whether this was the *ḥwt-nṯr* or *sbḫt* because of the state of the preserved source.

[2] Cf. p. 330.

[3] The term *sḥ* is used in this tradition to describe the most elementary sanctuary constructed within an enclosure. It does not give an accurate idea of its aspect. We may imagine a primitive shelter like the representation of Ptah's sanctuary on a bowl from the First Dynasty, cf. Petrie, *Tarkhan I and Memphis V*, Pl. 3. On the contrary in E. VI. 170,4; 171,1; 171,5; 172,2.2 *sḥ* seems to describe a rectangular sanctuary of much bigger dimensions, cf. below, p. 241.

[4] *sḥ mtr.s r-gs sꜣwi n inb mḥty*, *a sḥ-sanctuary is in its middle at the wall of the northern enclosing wall.* This description is interesting. We come again across the suffix -*.s*, which makes it quite clear that in the damaged part of the text there must have been the name of the inner structure which was composed of *inb*-outer walls.

given the name *ḥwt-ḳni*, it is described by the term *sḥ*, and it is this, perhaps, that hints at the original aspect of the inner enclosure which was made in the *Wetjeset-Neter*. Originally the *Temple in the Wetjeset-Neter* was probably a mere courtyard having at its north wall very little more than a simple, light structure of reeds[1] erected round the Perch to screen and protect it with its lord and to mark the most sacred part within it. This 'booth' might have been the starting-point of the construction of the interior in the primitive temples, and it was from it that the 'Holy of Holies' of the later temples eventually developed.

Nevertheless, it is legitimate to doubt whether the name *ḥwt-ḳni* was the original name of the first sanctuary that was ever constructed in the primitive temples of the Falcon. *Ḥwt-ḳni* might be translated *Mansion of Valour*[2] or *Mansion of Throne*.[3] All the spellings known from the Edfu texts[4] support the former rendering. But the ideas inherent in the name *Mansion of Valour*, with its associations with the fight between Horus and Seth, are foreign to our cosmogonical texts. There is no evidence in the description of the events occurring on the *pāy*-land of *Wetjeset-Neter* and that of *Djeba* which would testify a connexion between these *pāy*-lands and a very early sanctuary of the Falcon bearing this name. Moreover, such a name does not occur among the names of the sacred places of the Falcon listed in our sources.[5] It is known that *Mansion of Valour* is one of the names of the secondary sanctuary in the historical temple of Horus the Behdetite at Edfu.[6] Probably the priestly redactor of our text automatically gave the mythical sanctuary the name borne by the sanctuary he knew. We cannot cite an instance or refer to a tradition according to which an early sanctuary or shrine consecrated to Horus would bear the name *ḥwt-ḳni*. Certainly, our record is affected by later editing. Considering the name of the main sanctuary of this mansion, then the fact that the construction of the outer enclosure is mentioned in the first part of the account, we do not doubt that this record discloses

[1] Cf. p. 330, c.
[2] *Wb.* v, 45 (1–3).
[3] *Wb.* v, 51 (15).
[4] E. IV. 86,7; 262,14; V. 10,7; 86,3; 104,7; 155,2; VII. 2,2; 10,9; 29,21; 188,17; 202,5; VIII. 120,9; 133,5; 155,13.
[5] Cf. p. 25.
[6] E. IV. 5,1; VII. 2,2; 10,9; 29,21.

views of a primitive temple which was constructed according to the pattern of a much earlier prototype.

Nevertheless, it is inherently possible that this type of building consisting of a courtyard with one single sanctuary in its northernmost part represented a definite stage in the development of Egyptian temples in general,[1] that this construction was repeated in several places, and that the aspect of the back central sanctuary might change according to local traditions. Later an extension might have been made to this temple-courtyard and further buildings might have been constructed in its front part. This might have been the third phase in the development. This extension might have been made with a view to meeting the requirements of the service in the primitive temples, and this was, perhaps, what gave rise to a smaller courtyard in the front of the enclosure. Our document indicates that off the south wall of the inner enclosure a hall described as *wsḫt* was added at a time which is not indicated. Nothing in the tradition can be linked with this front hall, nor do we know its function. The text alludes to an act described as *ḥw*. Tentatively, the interpretation *to sanctify* may be suggested. But there is no evidence to clarify the meaning of the episode *ḥw* in the service of the primitive sanctuaries. This *wsḫt*-hall has two side chambers described as the *sḥ*-sanctuaries, then a smaller hall at its front which might resemble the hypostyle hall of the later temples. But nothing more is said of their eventual significance, and moreover, the record is completely damaged in this part. We know nothing of what other extensions might have been made to this complex or what other sacred buildings might eventually have been enshrined in the same enclosure.

Two facts emerging from this account can be considered important. The temple appears to have developed in its buildin from north to south. Nowhere is there in the preserved pa of the text mention of brick or stone being used as material fc the construction of the *Mansion in Wetjeset-Neter*.

[1] At this point we can refer to further representations on the seals from Arch Period; cf. Petrie, *Royal Tombs*, II, Pl. 10, no. 2; Jéquier, 'Les temples primi et la représentation des types archaïques', *BIFAO*, VI, 25–41; Badawi, ' première architecture en Égypte', *ASAE*, LI, 25–6 and *A History of Egyp Architecture*, pp. 33–6.

The development of the temple in *Wetjeset-Neter* appears to include four stages. In its primary stage the temple was a simple courtyard in the northernmost part of which was erected the resting-place of the god who was adored there. This seat might eventually have been surrounded by protecting symbols and images of Ancestor gods. In the second stage a roof was made over the seat and this gave rise to the first sanctuary within the enclosure, which is described in our text as the *sḥ*-sanctuary. In the third stage an extension was made at the south end in building a hall with a number of side chambers. It remains doubtful whether at that stage other chambers were built within the original enclosure along its sides. In the fourth stage this structure was surrounded by yet another wall of much bigger dimensions.

It may be suggested that what is described in our record as the *ẖnw*, *interior*, acted as the original nucleus of the physically real temple, and that this original nucleus has preserved the genuine features of the primitive enclosure in which the god was first adored. We see here points of contact with the mythological narrative. What was believed to have resulted from natural needs in the *bw-ḥbbt*, *the place-of-the-primaeval-waters*, formed the original nucleus of the normal type of the Egyptian temple. In the Edfu tradition, however, this was the genuine type of enclosure of the Sacred Falcon, and consequently the fundamental unit of the earliest type of his temple.

Having said this, we must point out that these words are in no sense intended to imply either that the prototype of such a temple was a temple of the Falcon Horus, or that it ever actually existed at Edfu in prehistoric or archaic times. There is neither archaeological nor textual evidence to confirm that an archaic cultus-place called *Wetjeset-Neter* or *Wetjeset-Ḥor* ever acted as the first sacred place consecrated to the Falcon Horus in Upper Egypt. The fact that in the Edfu texts this temple is associated with the cult of the Falcon Horus seems to be due to the later Edfu propaganda. It has been noticed that nowhere is there an allusion to the constitution of the cult of the Falcon Horus in connexion with this temple. We do not claim, either, that these records reveal the history of the early shrines and primitive temples that might have been founded in the districts of Lower Egypt, in the Lower Egyptian

Djeba,[1] or in the *Dmỉt-n-Ḥr* or on the 'Shore of the Western River'.[2] Although it is tempting to compare the mythological situation in the Edfu records with the geographical conditions of the Falcon's cultus-places to the north of Memphis, this problem is outside the scope of the present study.

When we confront the archaeological account of the organization of the temple in *Wetjeset-Neter* with the mythological narrative concerning the events in the *pāy*-lands, it appears that the Edfu records present the view that a temple of this structural development was believed to have been founded as the renewal of the *Home of the Ka*. This type of temple is, in fact, the sole one which the Edfu tradition derives from the creation of the Earth; consequently it is the first mythical temple that was consecrated to the Falcon. As far as the myth is concerned such a temple might have been believed to have existed on any *pāy*-land which was sacred to the Falcon. We may surmise that on all the *pāy*-lands which we find listed in our documents the same type of sacred building was believed to have been erected, and that in all these *pāy*-lands the development of the sacred place proceeded in the same manner from the simplest type of place of worship to the complete *ḥwt-ntr*, the *Mansion of the God*. Therefore, the type of sacred building described in the tradition as the *Temple in Wetjeset-Neter* was regarded as the structure specific to the original *pāy*-lands. The history of this temple will then illustrate the characteristics which might have been common to all the early temples. If we agree that in the account concerning the original *pāy*-lands is recorded the history of the development of an early religious centre, and that these *pāy*-lands represent the earliest cultus-places of Egypt, it will follow that this type of temple was the oldest type of the Egyptian temple in general. This would show that there was a unique type of temple, and a unique plan of organization according to which all the sacred enclosures and temples were constructed during one of the prehistoric ages. We may, perhaps, see here a point of contact with the fact that the Edfu record does not indicate who was, in fact, the lord of the *Temple in Wetjeset-Neter* for whom this temple was primarily founded.

[1] Cf. Gardiner, *JEA*, xxx, 59.

[2] Cf. p. 171, n. 1.

We cannot state dogmatically that this was only the Falcon, for an early temple of an appearance such as is described in our records could, of course, be constructed to apply to almost any god. If we agree that a more general significance is intended, this may explain why the Perch is not mentioned in the description. Nevertheless, from the point of view of the myth, this temple was created for the successor of the Creator, the *Winged One*.[1] It is tempting to assume that this temple was primarily consecrated to the cult of the *Winged One*. We know, on the other hand, that later on the Falcon was equated with the Winged One, consequently he was regarded, at least in some parts of Egypt, as the first divine occupier of the *Temple of Wetjeset-Neter*, and this tradition was adopted later on by the Edfu temple.

Although the Edfu sources have preserved a detailed account of all that had happened before the temple was founded, here, on the contrary, the description is very brief and it is concerned with the bare physical appearance of the temple. There is no extensive account of the successive phases of development which can easily be discerned in the final stage of the history of the temple, no interpretation of various mythological events which might accompany the growth of the temple and might help to explain their abstract significance. The narrative does not allude to the creative powers who fashioned the first temple. This point appears surprising. It may be thought that this part of the original narrative was omitted in the Edfu editing, and that the original version contained a detailed description of the work completed by the Progeny of the Earth-God in fashioning the temple for the successor of the Creator. Moreover no indication is given at all of the ceremonies which were connected with such an early temple. Nothing is said in the fifth record of the foundation rites, nor is there a picture of the consecration ceremony which must have existed at a remote date since evidence is given of its elementary aspect in connexion with the creation of the earliest type of the enclosure of the Falcon. The text reveals nothing of the ritual service which was celebrated in such an early temple, and what was the use of the sacred chambers named in the Edfu record. This lack of information might be a hint of a very old tradition of the

[1] Cf. p. 169 ff.

temple in *Wetjeset-Neter* in which the ritual service comprised simple episodes of adoration and presenting offerings. This accords with the fact that the Edfu record does not reveal the name of the deity to whom this temple was primarily consecrated.

It is, therefore, logical at this stage of our study to enquire whether the temple said to be that of the Falcon in the *Wetjeset-Neter* was solely a myth, a product of speculation, or whether the Edfu accounts have preserved the memory of a temple that had once really existed in the dim past of predynastic Egypt.

It must be admitted that there is no scrap of archaeological evidence that such a temple ever existed at Edfu, nor have remains of such a primitive shrine as yet been found elsewhere in Egypt. With the exception of the isolated pieces of evidence which we duly quoted in the course of this study, there are no data to confirm our deductions and to illustrate in a connected way the development of the temple. As against this, the account of the appearance of the temple and of its eventual expansion is clear and specific, and certainly built on real facts. The temple developed in a way that seems logical and natural, and detailed dimensions are given, though it must be borne in mind that in myths numbers and dimensions are among the least reliable data. We incline to the opinion that experiences of a far distant past lie at the heart of the Edfu myth of creation. It has been noticed that the description indicates four succeeding stages of development, and that, consequently, there must have been a long period of time between the elementary structure, the later original nucleus, and the complete *Mansion of the God*. Thus if we take the earliest and simplest unit in this temple, the sanctuary *ḥwt-ḳnỉ*, *Mansion of Valour*, and its enclosure, there is a distinct resemblance to the drawings of sacred buildings on the objects of Archaic Period, a resemblance that even extends to the placing of the main sanctuary apparently at the end of the reed enclosure and against the wall—a fact to which we have already pointed in our analysis. The Edfu evidence is probably based, in part at least, on facts, and it may well describe a primitive temple which is now completely lost, but which once existed in Egypt.

It is inherently possible that a structure such as that of the *Temple in Wetjeset-Neter* was constructed and reconstructed in many places of predynastic Egypt, and perhaps it is only the memory of the final stage of its appearance that survives in the Edfu records. This view appears admissible if we recall the way in which the title of the record[1] is written. This makes it clear that there was a temple constructed in the far distant past and that another was made on exactly the same pattern but still during the period regarded as the mythical age of the gods. Strictly speaking, the Edfu record appears as the summary of a long development of a temple, beginning with the first temple, the existence of which remained only in the memory. Again, it will be noticed that the text never mentions materials such as bricks and stone in connexion with this temple but always refers to light materials such as reeds which must surely have been the materials of the earliest structures. The fifth Edfu record has preserved a part of the history of an Egyptian temple as it existed in a definite region and in a definite period; this, in our opinion, can hardly be much later than the late predynastic period, though possibly it may extend into Archaic Period. If this be so it would indicate that, though the great funerary monuments of the early dynastic period were built from brick, the temples might still have been constructed from light materials as was the custom of somewhat earlier times.

In support of the theory that the Edfu account has disclosed traditions of a very ancient site it is of interest to draw attention, once more, to the tradition concerning the *ḏd*-pillar. It is known that the sacred places in which the pillar was regarded as a sacred object were the earliest cultus-places that ever existed in Egypt.[2] We have clear evidence that the origin of the *Temple in Wetjeset-Neter* was determined by a pre-existing sacred place which had as its centre the *ḏd*-pillar.

There is, of course, the problematic question of where the tradition concerning the early *Temple in Wetjeset-Neter* had its home. The allusion to the time described as the *reign of Tanen* points, naturally, to a site in the Memphite region or, at least, in Lower Egypt. Further support for this hypothesis may be seen in a fact derived from Edfu. We find that in the relief representing a scene of adoration in the primitive *Wetjeset-Neter*, the king, as

[1] Cf. p. 28.

[2] Cf. Mond–Myers, *Temples of Armant*, pp. 1–2; Kees, *Götterglaube*, p. 96 ff.

an officiant who was believed to enter freely into the *Wetjeset-Neter* to adore its lord, bears the title of *ʿḏ-mr*.[1] This title, as is well known, appears in the texts of the Old Kingdom associated with the royal functionaries of Lower Egypt.[2] We suspect that this scene of worship in an early sanctuary, as it is depicted on the wall of the Edfu temple, may preserve the memory of a Memphite or Lower Egyptian tradition. It cannot, however, be proved that this *ʿḏ-mr* represented in the institutions of predynastic Egypt the chief priest appointed to the early sacred places of the Falcon. Nevertheless, the strongly pronounced Memphite tone in which the Edfu records are written, cannot be denied. It is highly probable that these records have preserved Memphite traditions concerning the origin of sacred places and the temples which were founded there later on. That these traditions and beliefs are most probably of Lower Egyptian origin can be confirmed by the fact that nowhere in the whole narrative is there a single hint of a distinct connexion with Upper Egypt. It is the Edfu tradition solely that used this myth for explaining the origin of the temple of their local god, the Falcon Horus. It associated its local cult with a tradition of much earlier date, which was probably foreign to Upper Egypt. Consequently, the temple of the Falcon Horus in Upper Egypt is the first house of the god that came into existence on land that emerged from the primaeval waters close to the actual spot on which the creation of the world commenced. On the mythical plane the building of the first house of the Falcon was undertaken at the command of a defunct deity, and was fulfilled during the period when the Earth-God ruled.

This mythical temple resembled in many respects the primitive sacred enclosures that once existed in Egypt not later than the First Dynasty. The Edfu tradition, and so, perhaps, the tradition of many other temples, evidently looked on this far distant temple as the work of the gods themselves in which the creation of the Earth was completed. This temple was, undoubtedly, regarded as the starting-point in the development of the actual historical temple.

[1] E. VI. 181,6.

[2] Cf. *ZÄS*, LXXV, 72; a functionary of Old Kingdom who was a prophet of Horus bears the title of *ʿḏ-mr*.

CHAPTER 14

History of the Primaeval Temples of the Sun-God

There are good reasons for assuming that the first Solar Temple was also founded on a *pāy*-land. This *pāy*-land in which the Sun-God was believed to have settled down first, so far as we are aware from the Edfu tradition, bears the name *Island of Fury*.[1] The *Island of Fury* was not the original plot of land that emerged on the edges of the island of creation, but on the contrary, this *pāy*-land was a secondary creation, a land which was believed to have originated after the Falcon was established in his own domains.[2] In view of these facts it is natural that the secondarily created *pāy*-lands had their own tradition concerning the origin of their temples. But nothing has been preserved from the history of the early *mansions* (*ḥwt*) that were founded there by Tanen and the Falcon.[3] The narrative is solely concerned with the period of the fight and with the subsequent development of the sacred place that was created in the *bw-tpy*, the *Place-of-the-First-One*.[4]

The antecedents of the foundation of the first Solar Temple are very different from those connected with the first mansion of the god, the Temple of the Falcon in *Wetjeset-Neter*. This has already been seen in the study of the characteristics of the site of the first enclosure to be created. To outline only briefly the main differences which have been noticed in the history of origin of these two temples, it may be recalled that the first Solar Temple did not originate on the private domain of the Sun-God, on a land specially created for him, but in a region which was first occupied by Tanen and the Falcon. The site of the Solar Temple does not show obvious funerary associations; no emphasis is laid on what was in the past and died; there is no evidence of an act of revivification to be performed on the site with the view to restoring the former sacred nature of the land; there is no allusion to a direct connexion

[1] Cf. p. 189.
[2] Cf. p. 193 ff.
[3] Cf. p. 192.
[4] Cf. p. 199.

with the process of the creation of the Earth; moreover, the tradition concerning the *ḏd*-pillar as a pre-existing sacred object enshrined *in situ* is definitely foreign to this myth. It is clear that the Solar Temple was founded first and developed on a site that was in its essential nature a *bw-titi*, *Place-for-Crushing*,[1] where the enemies of the god were killed. It is therefore evident that the origin and the growth of the first Solar Temple was associated with other ideas than the history of the temple in *Wetjeset-Neter*, and that it was, in all probability, of a later date, created at a somewhat more advanced stage of the primaeval age than the Temple of the Falcon. A hint of this theory was seen in the title of the myth about the Solar Temple, which we find in the text of the Pure Ambulatory and which stresses the idea of *coming* of the god to his Mansion.[2]

Two other passages from the Edfu records can be quoted in support of our statements. The preamble to the set of the cosmogonical records alludes to a mythical episode in which Rēᶜ is said to have arrived in a new region and invited an unspecified divinity to settle down (*snḏm*) beside him in the *pāy*-lands of *Djeba*.[3] It is known that these lands were sacred to the Falcon and that he was the *nḏm*-lord there.[4] Hence, this short text records only in a somewhat different manner the arrival of the Sun-God in the original domains of the Falcon. A further hint of a closely similar mythological situation can be seen in a scene of consecration of a mythical temple which is preserved on the walls of the Edfu Temple. In this scene are seated figures of Horus the Behdetite, Hathor and Ptah, and, facing them, stand the king, Rēᶜ-Harakhte, Ptah-Tanen, Thoth, Seshat the Great and thirty other gods.[5] Rēᶜ-Harakhte has one hand raised as he adores the *Great Seat* (*st wrt*) by its names and recites:

O, Thou, Place (*st*) in which Apopis was pierced. As the Ka-of-the-Earth lives for me, I have made thee as my (?) Per-Khāᶜw in the Mansion of the God that I may hide myself within thee. I have also made thee as my (?) Great Place (*bw-wr*) in the First Shrine (*sḫm ḫnty*). I made thy glories, I made beautiful thy places, I embellished thy

[1] Cf. pp. 36–7.
[2] Cf. pp. 31, 208.
[3] E. VI. 181,1 and above, p. 6.
[4] Cf. p. 191.
[5] E. VI. 319,1–16; 321,6–323,5 = XIV. Pls. DCIII–DCV.

chapels (*sḥw*), (even) the Ḥetep-nebwy, the ʿAḥ-m-ḥerit, the Mansion-of-Eternity and the House-of-Everlasting.[1]

Thereafter is added a gloss that in this way the temple acquired certain of its names.

The remarkable fact is that here Rēʿ-Harakhte is in a subordinate position, adoring not only Horus the Behdetite and his protector Ptah, but also a temple called the *Great Seat*. He also speaks of constructing a part or parts of the temple within a previously existing building which is described as the *Mansion of the God* or the *First Shrine*. Although this text is obviously affected by later editing, it is definitely connected with the series of cosmogonical records, and therefore it seems not unreasonable to suggest that the facts briefly noted above obtain their real significance as a record that the Solar Temple was built later and on land initially devoted to another god. The principal new fact that emerges from these allusions is that the temple as an entity was believed to have existed before the Sun-God. We suspect that the name *sḫm ḫnty*, the *Sanctuary of the First One*,[2] may allude to shrines or enclosures existing before the foundation made in the *bw tpy*, the *Place of the First One*, or it may describe the sacred building in the *Place of the First One* which Tanen and the Falcon founded there before the Sun-God appeared in the *pāy*-land.

Another feature distinctly different from the first myth is that before the Sun-God could himself lay claim to any part of the *Island of Fury*, it was necessary to fight against the snake, and only after the snake had been overthrown, was the battlefield made into a sacred place by a rite described as the *purification* (*twr*).[3] Then, and only then, was it possible for the *Ancestor*[4] to arrive and settle down in the company of divine beings whose task was now to construct the mansion for the Sun-God. Examining the early part of the history of the *pāy*-land called *Island of Fury*, we can see in this order of ideas the influence of another tradition. The tone of the narrative seems to change. It is stated in the first part of the third record that the *Ancestor* was in the place which became the

[1] E. VI. 319,3–8.

[2] The word *ḫnty* may be merely an epithet of *sḫm*; on the other hand, it may describe the first deity who rested here.

[3] Cf. p. 207.

[4] Cf. p. 36.

scene of the subsequent events. It is unlikely that he could remain in that place during the period of the fight; he was, perhaps, believed to have returned to his original place, in either his abstract or concrete form, after the place was cleansed in consequence of the fight. We suspect that in the reference to the presence of the Ancestor in the foundation ground of the enclosure of the Sun-God there might be an allusion to the customs of the early ages. Perhaps there was a custom to display the statue or the image of an Ancestor God on the site where a sacred place was going to be founded. And this itself seems to be another hint of the theory that this mythical story refers to a somewhat later and more advanced stage of the mythical past. It is true that in the presence of the *Ancestor*, described in this part of the narrative also as a *Mꜣ*,[1] a point of similarity can be seen to the history of the Temple of the Falcon. Moreover, the *Ancestor* of the Solar Temple seems to be the *Maker of the Substances*,[2] therefore an Earth-God too. On the other hand, however, the foundation of the first Solar Temple does not appear to have been conceived, in the strict sense, as the revivification and restoration of the vanished domain of this form of the Earth-God. It is possible that the tradition follows another trend of thought. The presence of the *Ancestor* was required on the site of the foundation with a view to ensuring and reinforcing the protection of the sacred place. This is already well known from the history of the domains of the Falcon. Were the element of ancestry in this mythical story genuine, there would not be a stress on the episode *snḏm ỉm m-ꜥb Mꜣ*, *settling down there together with the Ancestor.*[3] We suspect that at this point there are associated two traditions of distinctly different date. In the background of this episode is the belief in the origin of a sacred place in the *bw-tpy*, the genuine resting-place of the deceased Earth-God. This belief was, most probably, combined at a somewhat later date with the common tradition concerning the origin of the sacred enclosure in a battlefield where stress on ancestry was no longer natural, and, therefore, there was need of making an indirect reference. This might have been a procedure of a rather artificial order, such as, for instance, a procession in which the statue of the *Ancestor* was

[1] Cf. p. 193, n. 3. [2] Cf. p. 192.
[3] Cf. above, p. 36, n. 4, and E. VI. 169,9–10.

carried into the site while magical spells of protection were uttered. For an analogy, it is of interest to refer to what happened in the *pāy*-land of *Wetjeset-Neter*, where the image of the *Ancestor Ḥeter-ḥer* was carried before the Falcon.[1] We know that *Ḥeter-ḥer* was not at home in this land, but his presence made the foundation possible.

Further differences from the way in which the first Temple of the Falcon was created can be seen in the procedures of fashioning the mansion in the later *pāy*-lands. The creation of the first Solar Temple does not start in erecting the seat of the god. Nothing equivalent to the Perch of the Falcon is mentioned in this myth. Although the text is very brief and obscure in this part of the story, it is likely that following the initial rites, once more a magical rite of protection was performed, presumably by Tanen.[2] Then the text seems to allude to a scene of encounter between Tanen and Rēʿ.[3] The constructors of the mythical temples, the Builder Gods with the Sages, conducted by Tekh and Seshat, then arrived on the scene in the presence of the *Ancestor* and Tanen. After a ceremony of presenting some kind of unspecified offerings, the chief gods of the site went around in procession, and the foundation was laid out.[4] Probably they were believed to walk around the boundaries of the foundation ground, and perhaps there is allusion to a ceremony which seems to have been also performed in the original *pāy*-lands.[5] It is stated thereafter that the foundation of the enclosure was made in the presence of the *Eldest One* (*wr*) of *Wetjeset-Neter*, *Tanen*, *the Ogdoad and Rēʿ*.[6] This short list of deities is important for the history of the temple. It mentions the god of the first temple according to this tradition, who is described as a nameless god, save that he is qualified by the name *wr*, the *Eldest One*; then the text refers to the Ogdoad, who are completely unknown to the earlier episodes. This list seems to suggest

[1] Cf. p. 31. [2] E. VI. 169,10.

[3] Cf. p. 36. But the whole passage is unusually obscure.

[4] E. VI. 169,10, where an alternative reading can be suggested: either *prỉ r-rwt ỉn nbw*, *coming outside by the lords*, or *prỉ r-ḥꜣ*, *coming forth in procession by the lords*; the first suggestion would seem to indicate that all the gods had there another and earlier dwelling-place from which they came out to the foundation; the second interpretation suggested would seem to make our theoretical reconstruction possible.

[5] Cf. pp. 204–5. [6] E. VI. 170,1.

the modification of the original version of the myth about the sacred settlement in the secondary *pāy*-lands under the influence of local beliefs and traditions. The order of the divine names in our document appears unusual, but it may be explained if we admit that the names of the Ogdoad and of Rēᶜ were incorporated in the original text at a somewhat later date, when the myth we are studying became known in the early cultus-places of the Sun-God. If this surmise be accepted, there will be no doubt about our theory concerning the originality of the myth about the Temple of the Falcon. We incline to the opinion that originally this myth dealt with the creation of the subsidiary mansions for the original god of *Wetjeset-Neter*, the *Wr, Eldest One*. After having become familiar to other religious centres of predynastic Egypt, the secondary mansions of the Falcon and Tanen came to be regarded as the earliest enclosures of the local god or gods. Their names might have been simply associated with those of the original occupiers of these mansions, just as we find in our document. This view may explain why in the majority of texts concerned with the origin of sacred places the fight against the enemy-snake is described as the essential condition that enabled the god to make a settlement, a view to which we have already referred.[1] We may say that the Edfu evidence seems to illustrate the way in which the Solar cult adopted the myth about the mansions of gods created in the secondary *pāy*-lands.

The view that the Solar cult may have used, as an explanation of the origin of its primaeval enclosures, traditions originally connected with sacred places of the Falcon or of another god seems to be logical when we refer to the spell translated above.[2] A further argument can be cited from the title introducing the description of the temple in *Wetjeset-Neter*.[3] It is clearly stated that the construction of the mansion which was originally made in *Wetjeset-Neter* was made once again at a somewhat later stage of the primaeval age in the presence of Rēᶜ. It is therefore suggested that the description of the ground plan of that temple as it is preserved in the Edfu record reveals the final stage of the appearance of the original temple, and may eventually have been drawn

[1] Cf. p. 209. [2] Cf. pp. 233–4.
[3] E. VI. 326,1, and above, p. 221.

according to a structure made in a place sacred to the Sun-God. Two important deductions can be made. It is inherently possible that at the beginning of the history of Egyptian temples there was one unique type of temple which was constructed and reconstructed in many places of predynastic Egypt, and that, secondly, the Solar cult did not have its own type of structure. Evidently the early sacred enclosures were made on the pattern of somewhat earlier structures specific to sacred places other than those of the Sun-God, as, for instance, the original sacred places of the *Eldest One*.

We may imagine, therefore, that the first sacred enclosure of the Sun-God was regarded as equal in its organization to the *Temple* in *Wetjeset-Neter*. Consequently the fourth record concerned with the origin of the Solar Temple describes the creation of the *second* primaeval temple of the Falcon. These secondarily created temples were not thought to have been constructed in exactly the same way as the original *Wetjeset-Neter*. We have already seen differences as regards the initial ceremony preceding the foundation.[1] Another and essential difference is that the account of the origin of the second temple speaks definitely of a *foundation ritual*, and gives clear evidence of the episode of *Stretching the Cord*.[2] This is the earliest allusion to it in our creation story. While referring to the creation of the temple of the Falcon, it appears that this foundation rite replaced the *wḏ*ᶜ *bw*, the episode in which the site of the enclosure was delimited.[3] Since in the first story the foundation ground was believed to have been determined by the extent of an earlier sacred place, it is evident that later on there was no need of other special rites. On the contrary, the nature of the ground of the later enclosure seems to have required a procedure of a special order. It may be surmised that the later enclosure was of the same dimensions as the original one. This is confirmed by the numbers given in our texts, which indicate

[1] Cf. p. 216ff.

[2] E. VI. 170,1, the first allusion in our sources; see also Kees, *Untersuchungen zu den Reliefs aus dem Re-Heiligtum des Rathures*, where a study of the rites used during the Old Kingdom can be found; the Edfu evidence makes it clear that these rites were of much earlier origin, and certainly used during the time when the temples were still constructed from reeds.

[3] Cf. p. 201.

that the original great enclosure and that of the second temple were identical in space.[1]

There is no similarity in the following phases of construction. We have seen that the temple of the Falcon grew phase by phase around the most sacred part of the area in which the Perch of the Falcon was.[2] The account of the physical appearance of the Solar Temple tells us that the first act to follow the *Stretching the Cord* was the setting out of the outer Enclosure Wall (*ỉnb*).[3] It is, therefore, clear that the enclosure was erected before any other sacred building on the site. The narrative explains the reason of this action: the enclosure had the function of protecting the sacred area from the evil coming from outside.[4] It is evident that a construction that started in the erection of an enclosure was not made on the water's edges, but, most probably, on the mainland. There was no longer the sacred water that had the power of preventing the enemy from coming near the sacred area;[5] therefore, there was a need to find another means of protection. And these facts are only another argument in favour of the theory that now the records refer to a much later and more advanced stage of the primaeval age.

The account of the *Temple in Wetjeset-Neter* does not disclose any tradition which might, eventually, be connected with the outer enclosure (*ỉnb*). Here, on the contrary, the erection of the outer enclosure is described as a mythological scene. The Builder Gods are said to have established a square construction (*ỉfdw*); then all the other divine beings who were present celebrated a festivity.[6] It is to be noted that the enclosure as a structural unit is here described by the term *ỉfdw*, which is unknown to the first myth.[7]

The description of the building and the set-up of the Solar Temple is the most interesting and extended document known about the organization of the primitive temples. It is not possible,

[1] Cf. pp. 333, 335.

[2] Cf. p. 223 ff.

[3] E. VI. 170,2: *(s)d̲d̲ỉ ỉfdw*.

[4] E. VI. 170,3–4.

[5] Cf. p. 141.

[6] E. VI. 170,2 and above, p. 37; we suspect that following the erection of the enclosure a procession was performed around the four walls.

[7] E. VI. 170,2; *ibid.* 170,5.6; most probably indicating the elementary structural unit; for the meaning 'four sides of a building', consequently 'enclosing wall' or 'enclosure' see *JEA*, XXXII, 77–8, where the majority of the Edfu instances are discussed.

at present, to give as precise a description of this Solar Temple as we have given of the temple of the Falcon. The text gives us an equally detailed account of the Solar Temple, with precise measurements in cubits, but the narrative is so concise and cryptic that it is not yet possible to present a description of the temple as a whole that gives a satisfactory explanation of all the exceedingly puzzling dimensions which occur in a concise narrative.

What is quite certain is that there was an outer enclosure (*ỉnb rwt*) measuring 400 cubits from south to north and 300 cubits from west to east, and that inside this vast enclosure was built the Solar Temple. It is also certain that the foundation of this enclosure represented the first step in the building of the temple, and that its foundation was an act by itself. There is no clear statement about the existence of an inner enclosure such as existed in connexion with the temple of the Falcon, but that such an inner enclosure must have existed, seems to be a logical deduction from the facts. It seems probable that the temple consisted essentially of three units. Probably this record hints at several subsequent stages of development of the Solar Temple which in this version, however, are presented as a composite whole. The study of the record permits us to discern them; probably each unit reflects the aspect of a definite stage of development in the history of the Solar Mansion.

The first unit to be built within the vast enclosure is described as a *sḥ*-sanctuary, and measured 90 cubits from west to east by 20 cubits from south to north.[1] It was probably divided into three rooms, each of which was 30 cubits by 20 cubits. If our suggestion that the Edfu record has preserved several succeeding stages of development is correct, this rectangular sanctuary would appear to be the earliest type of the cultus-place of the Sun-God. We thus picture a vast enclosure enshrining one single building, the *sḥ*-sanctuary, which comprised three cultus-rooms. Such a construction seems to have been the nucleus of the mansion of the Sun-God. No archaeological evidence can be cited to confirm this view.

The second unit was a square structure erected to the south from the first *sḥ*-sanctuary.[2] It appears as though Tanen performed

[1] E. VI. 170,4–6 and p. 334.

[2] E. VI. 170,6; from the order of the description it is certain that this *ỉfdw* must have been other than that mentioned in 170,2.

a 'magical rite'[1] before the foundation ground was laid out. It is certain that a new ceremony of *Stretching the Cord* was performed before the second unit was erected. This is then described as a *ỉfdw* 'enclosure' being 90 cubits long, and 110 cubits wide. It is not certain, however, whether an ambulatory separated this unit from the *sḥ*-sanctuary or whether its overall south-to-north dimensions included the 20 cubits of the north-to-south dimension of the *sḥ*-room. It looks as though we have, at this stage of the building, to imagine a court with three rooms of 20 by 30 cubits along the north side. A construction of this type might then be the second stage in the development of the Solar Temple.

The third period in the development seems to be the construction of various rooms and halls within this courtyard. This second unit seems to have had two cultus rooms also described as a *sḥ*-sanctuary, rooms which were built from west to east within the courtyard. One of them bears the name of *ḥwt-ḳnỉ*, *Mansion of Valour*.[2] It appears that a hall (*ḥ3yt*) was erected in front of them.[3] In the remaining space between this hall and the front of the enclosing wall there seem to have been built two other halls (*ḥ3yt*), presumably on the axis of the courtyard.

The third unit is even more uncertain. It is possible that it was again a *ỉfdw*, an enclosure with an ambulatory 15 cubits wide.[4] The joint measurement of all the three units is 240 cubits,[5] but the width apparently varied. Therefore, as it is known that the north-to-south dimension of the second unit was 110, and as, in addition to it, we have the 20 cubits of the first sanctuary, it results that the north-to-south dimension of the third enclosure must have been also 110 cubits. A gate seems to have led from the first hall (*ḥ3yt*) of the second unit into the third one.[6] The third unit seems to have had three sanctuaries described as *sḥ* which were erected along the east wall; possibly the same number of sanctuaries were constructed along the west wall.[7] In the centre between the eastern and western rows of sanctuaries there seem to have been erected

[1] E. VI. 170,6: *ḫt n Tnỉ*: the exact meaning is not clear.

[2] E. VI. 171,1.2.

[3] E. VI. 171,3–4, but the text is exceptionally enigmatic.

[4] E. VI. 172,1.

[5] E. VI. 172,6.

[6] E. VI. 171,7.

[7] E. VI. 172,2–4.

a number of halls (*ḥ3yt*). Unfortunately the description is very cryptic at this point.

The essential features of this type of building are thus a rectangular sanctuary described as a *sḥ*-room which eventually might have been divided into three cultus chambers, then the square courtyard called *ỉfdw*. The way in which this type of sacred building developed into a composite whole shows no similarity to the original mansion once constructed in *Wetjeset-Neter*. It presents us with a much more complicated and elaborated aspect. There would be, therefore, little doubt that such a scheme of constructing a sacred enclosure must have evolved at a much later date, and that the development must cover a long period of time. Nowhere in the description is there any allusion to what might have been the seat of the god who was adored in this temple. Moreover, except for the opening words, nowhere is there evidence that the Sun-God was the first deity to be worshipped in this temple.

It is certain, on the other hand, that this complex of sacred buildings formed in its final stage two distinct *ḥwt-ntr*, *Mansions of the God*, each of which measured 110 cubits from north to south.[1] A single enclosing wall (*ṯsm*) surrounded them at a distance from the main enclosure (*ṯsm wr*).[2] This distance, however, is not specified in our text.

The account seems to end with an allusion to yet another temple (*ḥwt-ntr*) which might have been included in the vast outer enclosure.[3] This temple seems to have been founded to the west from the main complex; it was a temple of 90 by 105 cubits. The document, however, does not give further information as to its form and its eventual connexion with the main temple.

No name is given to this complex of sacred buildings, nor is there allusion to a tradition of a mythical locality where such a temple might have been first constructed. In the whole account only one sanctuary has a specific name; this is the *Mansion of Valour*, a name which is identical with that of the main sanctuary

[1] E. VI. 172,5–6: the text reads: *s3wỉ ṯsm m ḥwt.wỉ ntr*, 'the wall of the enclosure of the two temples'.

[2] E. VI. 173,1; it will be noticed that at the end of the record the word *ṯsm* substitutes for the term *ỉnb*.

[3] E. VI. 173,1–2; the description appears as a mere additional note.

of the temple in *Wetjeset-Neter*. As this name is used in the description of two temples of an entirely different tradition, it appears as though this name might have had, in the organization of the early temples, a special significance.[1]

The Edfu records proceed to give an account of yet another primitive temple of the Sun-God, which seems to have been constructed according to a similar scheme. The fifth Edfu record preserves the description of a temple of which the overall dimensions were 110 by 90 cubits.[2] A decisive argument in favour of the view that this is a temple other than the complex of sacred buildings which we have been outlining, is the fact that this second temple appears to be almost a construction by itself, which had no outer enclosing wall. Much important evidence is furnished by the aspect of its front portion.

The Edfu account indicates that the nucleus of this temple was formed by an enclosure of 110 by 90 cubits, but does not explain to what real entity these dimensions apply, whether it was a *ỉnb*, enclosure, or a *ḥwt-nṯr*, *temple*. Moreover, no allusion is made to the foundation episodes which must have existed at that period; the account does not even include the description of the organization of the inner part of the structure. On the contrary, the part of the account which has survived in the Edfu inscriptions seems to be concerned with the *wḏᶜ ḫnt*, *planning the front part*.[3] This word *ḫnt* occurs twice in the text;[4] only in the second instance is it accompanied by the name *Place-for-Piercing*, whilst in the first instance we read the suffix *-.s*. We conjecture that there is an allusion to a mythical place named *Place-of-Piercing* in which a *mansion* was founded since the feminine suffix applies to this construction. The name of the mythical locality makes it quite clear that there was a tradition that in any place the Sun-God arrived at, he had to fight against the snake. After the enemy-snake was overthrown, only then was the Sun-God believed to be able to settle down and found his temple. It is likely that this mansion, too, was created on a ground which became sacred by virtue of the fight. In its elementary aspect this mansion might resemble the main constituent unit of the great temple, since we are told that

[1] Cf. pp. 195–7.
[2] E. VI. 323,6.
[3] E. VI. 323,9.
[4] E. VI. 323,9.11.

its overall dimensions were 90 by 110 cubits. This enclosure probably contained one or two sanctuaries of the type *sḥ*, eventually erected in its northernmost part. Then after a certain time another structure was made at its front. Two halls (*ḥꜣyt*) seem to have been added, one being 15 by 50 cubits, the other 45 by 50 cubits. A construction which was in all 60 by 50 cubits does not seem to fit easily into the plan of the great temple of the Sun-God. This itself is an argument in favour of the theory that this account records a part of the history of another mythical temple of the Sun-God.

The eventual connexion of this mansion with the great temple of the Sun-God is not defined in the text. It may be suggested that this enclosure might have been erected in the vicinity of the great temple; it might eventually represent a reconstruction of a part of the earlier building, or an additional structure erected at the front of the south wall of the great temple. As against this, it should be borne in mind that this enclosure as a whole is defined as a *ḥwt-ntr*;[1] therefore it must have been an entirely independent construction. It may also be surmised that this enclosure was even earlier than the great temple because it shows a much simpler construction. The text refers neither to an outer enclosure nor to other sacred buildings which might have been connected with this type of temple. This interpretation is, however, eliminated by the fact that the history of the temple does not show any connexion with the orders of creation which can be discerned in the history of the Great Solar Temple. We incline to the opinion that this account discloses the Egyptian theory on the origin of the derivative mansions of the Sun-God which were created later in the 'mythical age' after the main temple was completed. Stressing the significance of the name *Place-for-Piercing*, we may imagine that the Egyptians believed that the Sun-God, after spending some time in the main temple, departed for a journey through the mythical world. In any place in which he and his company of gods fought against the enemies, an enclosure was founded in commemoration of their victory. Whenever the enemy had been killed, the battlefield was purified and another temple was founded. And each new temple imitated in its appear-

[1] E. VI. 324,3.

ance the elementary structure which was made in the original *bw-tỉtỉ*, *Place-for-Crushing*. Thus the earliest constituent element in the creation of the Solar Temple, the *ỉfdw* with the *sḥ*-sanctuary, occupying a space of 90 by 110 cubits, came to be the essential unit of the derivative mansions of the Sun-God. These buildings, being originally simple courtyards, might have developed later. Other structures might have been erected in front. And this seems to be the moment of the primaeval age to which the short account incorporated in the fifth record alludes. Apparently there were interpretations of these derivative mansions of the Sun-God which do not, however, survive in the Edfu records. These describe only the ultimate stage of their development, which seems to have been the planning and constructing of their front part, an era in the history of the Egyptian temple which resulted in a new type of temple.

A further argument in support of the theory that the myth about the origin of the Solar Temples deals with more than one temple is the fact that the final name of this apparently later temple was *ḥwt-Ms-nḫt*, the *Mansion of Ms-nḫt*.[1] This name does not occur in the account of the origin of the great temple.

The Edfu tradition concerning the origin of the temple of the Sun-God involves, therefore, the foundation of two temples. The first of these was a large building of 240 by 110 cubits made up of three units, each of which was a complete entity in itself. This building stood in a vast enclosure of 300 by 400 cubits. The second type of temple was much simpler in aspect and was in its overall dimensions 170 by 90 cubits. There is, of course, no shred of evidence that any of these temples described in the Edfu records as the primaeval temples of the Sun-God ever functioned as the earliest places of worship of Rēᶜ, nor is there any evidence of the existence of such an early temple near Heliopolis.[2]

The type of the 'House of the God' said to be that of the Sun-God started, therefore, with the erection of the outer enclosure (*ỉnb*). This seems to be the specific feature of the constructions erected in the secondary *pāy*-lands. It is entirely clear from the Edfu account that in the pattern of the original building the outer

[1] E. VI. 324,4, and above, p. 40.

[2] Cf. lately Roeder, *Hermopolis*, pp. 36–7.

enclosure (*inb*) was the last to be constructed. This circumstance seems to confirm that in the history of the Solar Temples we have a later type of sacred building which was constructed about that time, or somewhat later after the original type of the temple reached its final stage of evolution. A further argument to support our theory can be seen in the fact that the accounts of the Solar Temples show clearly that these mansions were founded near to another sacred place which had already been constructed. Moreover, the organization of the interior of the later mansions manifests a distinctly different conception. Although there are connexions in the main structural features of the organization, these later mansions are, strictly speaking, different in type, plan and tradition; their foundation was most probably influenced by religious ideas other than those involved in the origin of the temple of the Falcon, because the site of these temples was the place in which the god fought with and defeated his enemy, and on which, after it had been purified, he settled down in the company of the Ancestor god and the Creators.

We have no doubt that the accounts which have survived in the Edfu redaction cover a very long period of development. This fact is apparent when we give more attention to the type of the main sanctuary within the enclosure, and to the question of whether this sanctuary was erected before any other building on the site or subsequently to the construction of the outer enclosure. In the second manner of building a temple we clearly see constructions of a much later date, but, surely, they were structures made during the predynastic time, since the only materials that can be postulated were reeds.

As for the *Mansion of Ms-nḫt*, the text discloses a tradition unknown from other narratives and tells us that the Sun-God did not dwell there alone but with a company of deities. Since at that stage of the mythical age the only divine beings who are said to have been present were the creators of the sacred places and temples, we conclude that they were the companions of the Sun-God in his house. It would follow that when the creation of sacred places and temples came to an end, the Egyptians believed that all the deities who were engaged in the creation assembled and made their home in the temple which was created last. The Mansion of *Ms-nḫt* seems to have been regarded as their final resting-place, and this view finds confirmation in one of the subsidiary names of this temple: it bore the name *The Domain of the Gods* (*niwt nṯrw*).[1] The word *nṯrw*, *gods*, probably refers here to all the groups of the creators. The Heliopolitan tradition does not know of a temple near Heliopolis in which Rēʿ resided, together with the creators of the Earth. It is, therefore, suggested that the name of Rēʿ replaced the name of the deity to whom this enclosure was primarily sacred. Perhaps the memory of a primitive temple in which the creators of the Earth were adored survives in this account; the tradition might have been assimilated by Heliopolis later in historical times. No equivalent can be quoted from the Hermopolitan tradition either. These trends of thought are foreign to the Hermopolitan tradition concerning the origin of the temple of Rēʿ. As has been said,[2] the Hermopolitan doctrine has no claim to interpret the circumstances under which the first temple of Rēʿ was created, and to describe its growth and physical appearance. The traditions to which we have referred in this discussion seem to indicate that in the background of this myth of creation are the beliefs of a single region.

[1] E. VI. 324,5, and above, p. 40, n. 7.
[2] Cf. p. 48.

CHAPTER 15

The Bringing to Life of the Temple

In contrast to the coherent picture of the structural development, very little is known about the life and rites which were performed in the Temple of the Falcon. As stated, the temple in *Wetjeset-Neter* seems to have been founded and constructed prior to the constitution of the foundation ritual as known to us from historical times.[1] We incline to the opinion that this account may preserve the memory of customs connected with the foundation of sacred places which were in use in predynastic Egypt and from which derived the later foundation and consecration ritual of an Egyptian temple. The account of the laying out of the first sacred enclosure of the Falcon alludes to a simple rite which may be considered as a 'magical rite of protection'.[2] Unfortunately the text of the record is at this point very brief and the significance of this rite may only theoretically be reconstructed from the general meaning of that part of the narrative. Moreover, the text does not give any definite title of this rite. We may, perhaps, doubt whether this mythical rite was, indeed, a foundation rite in the strict sense, or whether it was a rite performed with a view to consecrating or re-consecrating the foundation ground of the enclosure. We recall that the Shebtiw brought in sacred symbols from the *bw-ẖnm* and that the Egyptians believed this piece of land to have been sacred prior to the creation of the Falcon's sacred place.[3] The extent of his enclosure was believed to have restored the ground of a pre-existing sacred place of the Earth-God; it results that this rite aimed at ensuring the sacred nature of land which was believed to have been naturally delimited. It follows that in remote times there were no foundation rites in the strict sense, only acts which might appear obscure even to the Egyptians of historical times, and therefore they were conceived

[1] Cf. p. 219.

[2] E. VI. 177,11–12; the text is too enigmatic to establish a satisfactory translation, and parallels are lacking.

[3] Cf. pp. 203–4.

to be a ceremony of a magical order which the creators performed themselves. It can be added from our text that following this act some kind of offerings which are not described were presented, presumably to the god.[1] These *iḫt* are possibly the same substances as those required at the creation of the Earth. The text, however, says nothing more, and speculation is vain.

A somewhat more explicit account is given of the ceremony which was performed after the construction of the enclosure. Tanen played the prominent part; allusion is made to the safeguarding of the god,[2] then to a procession which is said to be *bs, to conduct.*[3] We suspect that the record refers to the moment when the god was carried into the enclosure; then the ceremony of fumigating was performed.[4] It seems that we have in this very brief account the earliest evidence of the *Festival of Entering the Temple.* If this interpretation be accepted, it would mean that this particular ceremony formed only a part of the creation of the temple, and that this final act was exclusively the duty of Tanen. Tanen seems to play here the part of the protector of the god and of his resting-place, and in this capacity he fulfilled the creation of the temple. If we recall the belief that Tanen was brought out of Nun as a 'protection',[5] it becomes now logical that he did so. Hence, his function in the history of the temple was determined at the beginning of the world.

Nothing is known of other rites and ceremonies which might have been performed in this early temple. We may think of very simple scenes of adoration (*iꜣw*) which were once performed in front of the Perch within the original domain of *Wetjeset-Neter*;[6] perhaps, there was performed a 'silent rite' (*sgr*);[7] certainly there were completed various acts of presenting offerings which are described only by the common expression *ir iḫt*, and possibly

[1] E. VI. 177,12.

[2] E. VI. 176,5.

[3] This interpretation is based on the expression *bs.sn⟨r⟩bw.f*; but no parallel can be quoted.

[4] E. VI. 176,6, *ꜣm* is certain as a reading; what follows is unusually obscure; probably we have here spells to be recited at this ceremony.

[5] Cf. p. 21.

[6] E. VI. 182,5 is the first allusion in our sources.

[7] E. VI. 177,9 gives only the word *sgr* without any interpretation; next to it the episode of *ḥsi Rꜥ* seems to be performed.

the acts of *ḥw*-sanctifying to which the description of the physical appearance of the temple[1] seems to allude briefly.

The myth about the origin of the Solar Temple introduces us to an entirely different situation. This circumstance is important both for the history of the Egyptian temple in general and for the origin of the ritual. We have already pointed to some of the rites connected with the Solar Temple.[2] It is only necessary to refer to these rites with a view to filling in the picture of the 'bringing to life of the Solar Temple'. We learn from the history of its origin that rites were already performed before the foundation of the outer enclosure of the temple was laid out.[3] This, of course, might have been entailed by the fact that the foundation ground was a battlefield, and there was an urgent need to cleanse the site. It was also believed that in the secondary *pāy*-lands the foundation of a sacred domain began with the rite of purification, and that, consequently, this was the custom of a somewhat advanced stage of prehistoric times. The purification might have been regarded as an act of consecration through which the land reached its final sacred nature. The text does not reveal how it was done; only the title of the ceremony (*twr*) has survived in the record.[4] The text is unusually concise, but it seems that the initial ceremony was followed by one or several processions in which the statues and images of gods were carried around the sacred area, then assembled in its midst. This might, perhaps, have been the episode which is described in our text by the expression *snḏm im*, *settling down there*.[5] The account seems to indicate that this procession of gods included also the image of an ancestral god who might, eventually, have been carried in front of the procession and been placed first on the foundation ground.[6] This

[1] Cf. p. 225. [2] Cf. pp. 233, 240–1.

[3] Cf. pp. 234–5: the magical protection performed by the Soldiers of Tanen; but in this part of the narrative these soldiers are no longer referred to.

[4] E. VI. 169,8; perhaps through this act, the pouring out of water, the foundation-ground was believed to have acquired the sacred nature equating it with the land which was naturally sacred.

[5] This act, while performed on the ground of the foundation, might re-enact the original 'settling down' in the *bw-titi* as the sign of victory, cf. p. 36. Very little is known of the significance of the processions performed in the early temples; for some preliminary remarks, cf. Kees, *Das Re-Heiligtum*, pp. 22–4.

[6] E. VI. 169,10 and above, p. 206 ff., for the mythological significance of this scene.

preliminary ceremony seems to have ended in a rite which might, eventually, have been an act bearing on the constitution of a 'magical protection' of the foundation ground. But the text is concise again and we can only suggest that this final episode was performed by Tanen. Then occurred, perhaps, yet another procession of gods. All this is, perforce, a theoretical reconstruction. On the other hand, with reference to the situation in the temple of the Falcon, this order of ceremony does not appear unnatural. It may be surmised that at that stage of the development of sacred places the customs connected with somewhat earlier sacred places were in part re-enacted, in part replaced by ceremonies of a rather artificial kind in order to imitate what was believed to have been essential in the history of the earlier sacred domains. Episodes of earlier date were probably used as rites preliminary to the foundation ceremony. What is certain is that in what follows the history of the Solar Temple is entirely different from the sequence of creation in the temple of the Falcon.

It is legitimate to claim that the foundation of the Solar Temple gives the first definite evidence of a duly performed foundation ritual, the *Stretching of the Cord.*[1] This was followed by the episode of *sḏdi ỉfdw*, the *Setting out of the four sides of the Enclosure.*[2]

A detailed picture is preserved in our Edfu sources of what can be described as the 'rites of consecration' of a temple. Here again the ritual episodes are interpreted as mythical events in which the gods themselves enacted the consecration of the temple. It seems that the Egyptians believed that Rēʿ and Tanen were not on the site when the temple was constructed. But they were told by Thoth and Seshat that the *temple was fashioned in its (proper) place.*[3] They arrived at the site together with the assembly of deities who were engaged in the creation of the temple.[4] The first act to be per-

[1] E. VI. 170,1, and the ritual of foundation of the Solar Temple of Rathures, cf. Kees, *Das Re-Heiligtum*, pp. 3 ff., considered as the earliest evidence known.

[2] E. IV. 353,6–7; both of these rites are interpreted as mythical episodes performed by the gods.

[3] E. VI. 32,6: *ẖnm pr pn ḥr nḥp.f*; id. in E. VI. 18,6 and 173,6.

[4] That this mythological scene was included in the original version of the myth is confirmed by the fact that the title of this scene occurs at the end of the fourth record, E. VI. 173,3, and is repeated in E. VI. 320,6.

formed then was the naming of the enclosing wall.[1] This appears to have been the duty of Rēʿ. The assembly of gods proceeded to what is described as the *Place* (*bw*). In this context the word seems to define the main part of the enclosure, since the text proceeds to tell us that *the temple is in the place where the snake was pierced.*[2] Thereafter another ceremony was performed by Tanen, and it was precisely by virtue of this act that the temple acquired its names.[3] This situation is unknown from the history of the temple in *Wetjeset-Neter*. The tradition connected with this temple seems to propound the idea that the temple was given this name after the land in which it was created. By way of contrast, in the history of the Solar Temple the ceremony of giving the temple names is dealt with as an independent act which appears to be of prime importance in the life of the temple. It would seem to result that in the secondary *pāy*-lands the temples, while physically existing, were regarded only as an entity. There was need of a special act to bring them to their real function.

The relief that accompanies the fifth cosmogonical record furnishes further scenes to illustrate the 'consecration rites' that might have been performed in the Solar Temple following the episode described above. This scene manifests the belief that after the temple was given names by Tanen, the assembly of the Creator gods performed a procession at which they sang hymns and recited spells of adoration. The short texts incorporated in this scene appear to describe an early *Festival of Entering* (*ḥb n ʿḳ*). This ceremony was opened by Tanen, who seems to have invited the god, the lord of the temple, to enter his sanctuary.[4] Then Seshat was believed to utter a proclamation: *The Earth-Maker has been brought into the presence of Rēʿ in the Seat-of-the-two-gods.*[5] An act of adoration of the temple itself, described a sthe *Great Seat*, was

[1] E. VI. 320,12; here again the main enclosing wall is described by the term *ṯsm-wr*, cf. above, p. 242.

[2] E. VI. 320,13; this evidence only confirms the tradition, but no textual or archaeological evidence confirms that this was the name of the first Solar Temple.

[3] E. VI. 321,1–5; the names listed seem to have been believed to be the utterances of Tanen; the passage ends in words *kꜣ ḥwt-nṯr in Ṯnì, name(s) of the temple, so said Tanen.*

[4] E. VI. 321,16.

[5] E. VI. 321,14–15.

believed to have been performed thereafter by the lord of the temple. He adored the sacred entity which came to be his home, and adored it by the names which Tanen had given to the temple.[1] In this way we learn that the joint Solar Temple was believed to have as its chief name that of *The House-of-Appearance in the Mansion-of-the-Throne*.[2] There is no evidence, however, to confirm that this was the name of an archaic temple of the Sun-God. This name might well have been formulated in the tradition of a later date with a view to describing the significance and purpose of the temple. The important fact is that an early ritual of consecration of the temple seems to have included a ceremony of adoring the temple itself.[3] Thereafter a procession seems to have been conducted along the four sides of the enclosure, the participants being the deities who were engaged in the construction of the temple. It is of prime importance that during this ceremony mention is made of the Earth-Maker.[4] We imagine that perhaps there is an allusion to the image of the Earth-Maker which was carried in front of the procession, then brought into the main sanctuary of the temple. We are inclined to see in the presence of the Earth-Maker in the ceremony of the 'Consecration of the Temple' further evidence of the close connexion between the Earth-God and the temple as an entity.[5]

A closely similar situation emerges from the account of the *Temple of Ms-nḫt*. Its construction having been completed, a procession was performed around the enclosure. After a greeting episode performed by Rēᶜ, in which the temple is invoked as the *sbḫt-enclosure of the divine company*,[6] there followed what appeared to be an act of *blessing the iḫt* (*ḥsi iḫt*).[7] This episode is not mentioned in the description of the consecration of the joint temple. It recalls, however, the ceremonies performed over the *iḫt*, sub-

[1] E. VI. 319,3–8.

[2] E. VI. 319,4–5 = 421,1; it will be noticed that the first instance gives *Mansion of the God* as opposed to the *Mansion of the Throne* in the second instance.

[3] Cf. pp. 233–4.

[5] Cf. p. 235.

[4] E. VI. 17,13.

[6] E. VI. 324,1 and 325,3; *psḏt* must refer to the Creator gods, who seem to represent the first co-templar deities of the Sun-God.

[7] E. VI. 324,1 gives the only evidence in our documents.

stances in the enclosure of the Falcon.[1] The gods proceeded once more in procession around the enclosure; then Tekh and Tanen gave names to the temple. From this ceremony we learn that the temple seems to have consisted of two parts, of which one was the *ḥ3yt*-hall bearing the name of *Great Seat*, while the other is described as *ẖwyt, sanctuary*, and bears the name *Ms-nḫt*.[2] A spell was recited by Rēʿ in which he ordered the gods of his company to settle (*snḏm*) there.[3] Since then the enclosure seems to have borne the name *niwt ntrw*, the *Domain of the Gods*.[4] The following narrative alludes to the association between the god (*ntr*), most probably the lord of the temple, and his *Ancestor*, who is said to be Tanen.[5] It appears that a mystic act was believed to have ended the order of the ceremonies. This, however, is the sole evidence occurring in our document. The tradition seems to imply the belief that the temple was constructed not only to house the god, but also as the dwelling-place of other divine beings, especially as the resting-place of the Ancestor god. It would follow that after the temple had been constructed and was given names, it was necessary for the Sun-God to issue a command in order to occupy the temple. The deities who took part in the creation of this temple seem to have constituted the first company of the co-templar deities of the god.

The last ceremony to be performed was again a procession. The Sun-God and his fellows are said to have proceeded along the four sides of the temple.[6] They entered into the temple and took their rightful position within it. Then a magical rite seems to have been performed by Tanen to ensure the protection of the house of the god. Although these texts are, in part at least, affected by later editing and by the Edfu tradition, their close connexion with the

[1] Cf. p. 200.

[2] E. VI. 324,4–5 and above, p. 40.

[3] E. VI. 324,5; but the tradition of the *snḏm* of the gods is not known elsewhere.

[4] E. VI. 324,6 and above, p. 40, n. 7.

[5] E. VI. 324,6, the sole evidence of an association with the *ḏfn*-Ancestor, perhaps an allusion to his permanent presence within the temple, but we do not claim that this uniting is of the same nature as the 'consorting' with the Soul of the Creator.

[6] E. VI. 325,1–2; undoubtedly this procession was performed after the ceremony of giving names.

set of cosmogonical records is obvious and gives them the value of a document. We suspect that we have in these short texts hints of what once was a complete set of rites which were duly performed in the sacred enclosures of remote times. There perhaps existed a record of a high date that preserved the consecration ritual in the use of primitive temples.[1] This record might have been, in the Edfu redaction, broken into short sentences and modified for a descriptive purpose. It does not seem improbable that the Edfu pictorial evidence has preserved an account of the order of ceremonies which were real and were enacted in the early temple of protodynastic Egypt, if not even during the late stage of the predynastic period.

This early ritual of consecration, therefore, seems to begin with the ceremony of *giving names* to the temple.[2] Thus it was believed that only through such a procedure could the temple acquire its essential functions and assume its final nature as the dwelling-place of the god.

By virtue of this ceremony the temple was believed to have been brought to its real life. Since this ceremony is said to have been performed before the god, the lord of the temple, entered it, it is evident that only through this ceremony could the temple be handed to its legitimate lord. The purpose of this ceremony of *giving names* was to confer the power of 'magical protection' on the temple so that it could ensure the protection of the god. At this point lies the essential difference in the history of the two mythical temples. It has been noticed that the name of the first temple that was believed to have been created in the mythical past, the *Wetjeset-Neter*, derived from the means through which the foundation ground of the temple re-acquired its sacred nature. Since the ground of the first temple was sacred prior to the foundation, and since the Mansion of the Falcon re-enacted in its existence a sacred abode of an earlier date, the name of the temple only commemorates the restoration of the deceased world. There was, therefore, no need of a consecration rite, nor of a ceremony of *giving names*. In contrast, the Solar Temple did not restore in the strict sense the Home of the Earth-Maker; it was the memorial of

[1] Cf. Sethe, *Untersuch.* III, 131.
[2] Cf. Kees, *Götterglaube*, p. 171.

the victory of the gods, and this, too, is manifested in the names of the temple, which show an entirely different conception. On the whole, they appear to define the significance of the temple and to specify the purposes for which it should be used after it was handed over to its legitimate lord.

It is worthy of note that in this tradition also the god who was believed to be the only authority to give the temple names and to conduct the final episodes of the 'creation of the temple' was again Tanen. His task appears to have been the completion of the 'creation of the temple'. If we recall the detail that Tanen, after he revealed himself in the *Island of Trampling*, conferred the power of protection on two staffs by giving them names,[1] it is likely that the tradition of the Solar Temple took the beliefs of an earlier sacred place and adapted them to its purpose. There is much similarity in the general significance of these two events; only the manner of completing them is somewhat different. In the first instance the creation of the magical protection by naming was completed before the Falcon entered the Enclosure of the Earth-Maker.[2] Here, in the tradition of the Solar Temple, the 'giving of names' was performed before the temple was handed to its lord. A further resemblance can be seen in that in both the name, once pronounced, conferred on an entity its final characteristics.[3] The temple, once having been given names, was believed to have been filled with life like the spear, and then and only then could it act and exercise its main function, the protection of the god. The constitution of the *magical protection* by the means as described, is, therefore, the elementary but essential act of the early *Ritual of Consecration of the Temple*. The second act was the *Festival of Entering* (*ḥb n ʿḳ*).[4] We picture it as consisting, in the main, of a procession performed by the divine occupiers of the temple alongside the four walls of the Enclosure. During this procession hymns were sung and further acclamations recited. This procession led to the main sanctuary of the temple, at the front of which, probably, the final act of the festival was performed: the *Handing*

[1] Cf. p. 23.

[2] Cf. pp. 142–4.

[3] Cf. pp. 24–5, the creation by naming performed by the Shebtiw.

[4] E. VI. 321,17, but we do not claim that this term was already in use in the early temple.

over the Temple to its Lord. It is most significant that Tanen, the Earth-God, who initiated the life of the temple by giving names to it, seems to be again the sole divine power who was believed to be capable of performing the ultimate rite. Thereafter, as the third act of this ceremony, the presiding god adored the gift of the Earth-God which was given to him as the only means of his protection on the Earth.

There are, of course, no relevant sources to confirm our reconstruction according to the Edfu evidence. It is unknown where and when this type of ritual originated. From the fact that the Edfu evidence projects this ritual into a mythical plane, it is evident that such a ritual must have existed in the organization of the early temple of at least protodynastic times. The character of this ceremony, when compared with what is known from the Consecration Ritual which was in use in historical temples, is readily understood.[1] It is, therefore, suggested that the Ritual of Consecration which we have been outlining was the basis of the ceremonies performed later on in the historical temples.

The Edfu records prove that the episode of *bringing to life of the temple* was included in the order of the creation, and that it was, in fact, the integral part of the history of the origin of the temple since the divine powers who acted in the ultimate phase were the Creators themselves. A further deduction that can be made is that the temple, after having been completed in its construction, required a special act to reach its final significance as a temple housing and protecting the god. This ceremony might derive from what was the antecedent of the creation of the temple. The history of the Solar Temple proves it. Since the first evidence of a duly formulated ritual is connected with the Solar Temple, the Edfu documentary sources offer, therefore, one argument more in favour of the theory that the ritual of the Egyptian temple was Heliopolitan in origin.[2]

[1] E. IV. 330,12–331,16 and Blackman and Fairman, 'The Consecration of an Egyptian Temple according to the Use of Edfu', *JEA*, XXXII, 75 ff.

[2] Blackman, *PSBA*, XL, 57–66, 86–91; 'Sacramental Ideas and Usages in Ancient Egypt', *RT*, XXXIX, 44–8; and *JEA*, V, 118–24; 148–65.

CHAPTER 16

The Homeland of the Temple

The facts that can be deduced from the Edfu texts enable us to gain a fairly clear idea of the development and conception of the primitive temples in Egypt. They render it inherently possible to conclude that at Edfu we have only fragments, a selected number of accounts, from a great and important history of the Egyptian temples. They furnish decisive evidence that two distinctly different types of temple were believed to have been created in the primaeval age in the subsidiary parts of Earth pictured in our sources as the *pāy*-lands. Strictly speaking, the first and most primitive of these temples is the Mansion attributed to the Falcon which is conceived as developing around the *Perch of the Winged One* which was regarded as the result of the creation of the Earth. The second type of temple is said to be that of the Sun-God. It is a much more developed structure, artificial in many respects, and was certainly not founded until after the creation of the world and the first temple was completed. The bringing into existence of the temples is interpreted in a different way. We have no doubt that the origin of each of these two temples was influenced by different streams of religious thought, and that these two types of temple refer to different eras of the mythical age. One of the main arguments in support of our statement is the fact that the first temple to be built existed before there is any mention of the Sun-God himself or of his temple, and that one text actually describes the Sun-God as adoring and praising a temple which already existed, the *Great Seat*, and thereby acting in a junior and subordinate capacity.[1] In addition to the mythological situation that can be sketched from the narratives the title of the description of the *Temple in Wetjeset-Neter*[2] confirms the view

[1] Cf. pp. 233–4; the Edfu documents make it clear that this tradition is earlier than the time when the Heliopolitan doctrine was formulated. The result of this study is definitely against the theory put forth by Anthes, cf. *JNES*, XIII, 21–51, 191–2; *JAOS*, LXXIV, 35–9; *ZÄS*, LXXX, 81–9, LXXXII, 1–8; *MDIK*, XV, 1–2; *JNES*, XVIII, 169–212.

[2] Cf. p. 12.

that the temple as an entity did not originate in the region where the Solar cult was at home. It follows that there was a tradition of a temple of a remote date which was associated with the belief in the *wr*, the *Eldest One*.[1] This temple must have been constructed from reeds, and after it had reached the final stage of its development, was constructed and reconstructed in many other places. From this type of temple other sacred enclosures were derived, and this secondary type of sacred building is connected with the cult of the Sun-God. It is most likely that the Edfu records contain an attempt to describe the succeeding phase in the creation of the temple in a definite region. The sole concern of the theory implicit in the Edfu records seems to be the temple itself as an entity; its connexions with various deities appear to be the work of the tradition of a later date or the result of local beliefs. The creation story of the temples attributed to the Sun-God, therefore, would represent what can reasonably be described as the second part of the history of the Egyptian temple in general. It is likely that in the creation of the second type of temple the development of genuine native sacred buildings was fulfilled. In our opinion this time seems to refer to an important epoch in the history of Egypt.

The continuity of traditions and the theory of two important periods in the history of the Egyptian temple seems to be plausible if we remember the situation in the secondary *pāy*-lands. In a land occupied by the Falcon and Tanen, near to the earlier structures described as the *ḥwt*-mansions, the new type of sacred building originated in the *bw-titi*, the *Place-for-Crushing*. In spite of the differences in the beliefs connected with the origin of each temple concerned, and the differences in the details of their constructions, we must admit, on the other hand, that there are affinities in their general structural development. These seem to accord with the continuity of tradition to which we have pointed above. If we take the main structural units of these two temples we can demonstrate a connected line of development which seems to have occurred in a single region. The fact that in all the stages of this history the same divine beings acted as creators of the sacred places and temples may be further support for our hypothesis.

[1] Perhaps the *wr* is the name given to the *Winged One* in the tradition of a later date.

We had in the first stage the resting-place of the god in an open field which at a definite moment was surrounded by a fence. This type of sacred place seems to represent the place of worship of the Ancestors. The text says nothing of its eventual development. This type of primitive sacred enclosure produced the elementary unit of the mansion of the god, in which the first properly constructed sanctuary was made as the protection of the god's seat. To this courtyard further constructions were added at its southernmost end; this then gave the first *ḥwt-ntr*, *Mansion of the God*, which at a definite moment was enshrined within a much greater outer enclosing wall. The original nucleus of this complex appears to be the starting-point in the construction of other mansions (*ḥwt*) of which a definite part might have been sheltered, thus imitating the original type of sanctuary. The text does not describe their eventual development. But it alludes to a type of building which seems to reflect the appearance of the original courtyard of the first temple, which, though on somewhat different scale, developed at its southernmost end through the addition of two front halls. In great detail is described the stage of evolution which produced the final phase of the original temple. The record gives decisive evidence that at a particular moment of the mythical age the building of the temple began with the erection of the outer enclosure (*inb*). Here again, in spite of the differences in details, we find that the dimensions of the outer enclosures are equal, and that even the first courtyard to be constructed within the enclosure shows a breadth of 90 cubits, i.e. the dimension of the original structure. It is true that each of the two main temples shows an entirely different appearance in the organization of its interior; but we must bear in mind that the development which we have been outlining covers a very long period during which much might have been altered and modified to meet the needs of the ritual service to be performed in these temples. Having said this, we must point out that these words are in no sense intended to prove that all the phases of this long development occurred on the same site. On the contrary, temples of such a physical appearance and various degrees of development were constructed and reconstructed in very many places of pre- and protodynastic Egypt. Nevertheless, in considering the resemblances in the general structural units of these buildings made from reeds or other light material, there are points of contact that render it reasonably possible to conclude that there was a single centre in which this type of sacred building originated. The Edfu records thus preserve the memory of an early religious centre where the places of worship were constructed first.

Having analysed the Edfu documents and having attempted to trace the main line of the structural development of these sacred buildings, we must naturally enquire where was the region in which these two types of temple originated. From the point of view of the myth this region was the private realm of the Earth-Maker.[1] The records do not explain what real land is denoted by this mythical domain. They scarcely give precise geographical data. The names of the sacred places which we can read in the texts are not confirmed by archaeological evidence from historical times.

It is inherently possible that in the Edfu tradition the origin and growth of the temple complex and the events which determined and affected its creation are projected into a region which is described as the *First Province of the Falcon*.[2] This name is known only from the Edfu texts, and evidently it replaced the name of the cultus-place of the Creator, the island of creation. We do not claim, however, that this name is to be considered as equal in significance to the name of the *Island of the Egg*.[3]

It is difficult to state dogmatically where this *First Province of the Falcon* was situated, for there is no definite geographical evidence. But we must recall that our principal sources incorporate the local Edfu tradition, and that for the temple of Horus at Edfu the primaeval island was the site of the temple itself. As has already been indicated above, every temple throughout the country probably claimed to be the original temple and the site of the creation and would thus adopt the original form of the myth for its own purposes. Thus when the Edfu records speak of the *First Province of the Falcon*, that term may well mean the district of

[1] Cf. pp. 183 ff., 198 ff.

[2] E. VI. 11,1; for the tradition concerning the *First Province* in general cf. above, p. 304.

[3] Cf. p. 65 ff.

which the historical site of Edfu and its temple formed part; but it does not by any means imply that in the original version of the myth the region was also called the *First Province of the Falcon*; on the contrary, in that version it very probably bore another name which would undoubtedly have been suppressed in the Edfu redaction.

In spite of editorial activities, the Edfu texts still retain sufficient pointers to render it possible to state with confidence where the original version of the myth was formulated and set down. It is impossible to read the principal Edfu records and not be struck by the very pronounced Memphite background and tone which is still preserved in them. The emphasis on the role of Tanen, who attends the 'birth' of the temple complex, and who is present during the whole period of the development, especially if we recall the allusion to the *reign of Tanen*, as well as the Memphite connexion of the creative deities, all point to the Memphite region as the source of the original form of the myth. Consequently, it may be expected that in the formulation of this myth there are reflected traditions attached to the early sacred places of that region. In fact a well-known text on the inner face of the enclosure wall of the temple at Edfu tells us that the temple was built at the dictates of the Ancestors according to what was written in *this book which descended from the sky to the north of Memphis.*[1] We believe, therefore, that the basis of the Edfu tradition concerning the origin and nature of the temple complex was Memphite. In fact, we venture to suggest that the basis of the conception of the Egyptian temple was formulated at Memphis, just as Heliopolis and its temples were the basis of the ordinary daily ritual of the temple.[2]

If we are to seek the cradle of the Edfu traditions in Memphis, we can hardly go far wrong in linking it with protodynastic times. Some hints of this may, perhaps, be seen in the geographical lists on the east and west inner faces of the enclosure wall of Edfu.[3] The lists of the historical names are preceded by long, unfortunately much damaged, lists which contain many of the names

[1] E. vi. 6,4; quoted by Blackman, *JEA*, xxviii, 36. [2] Cf. p. 257.

[3] E. vi. 34,2–38,3; 194,13–208,13. We do not claim that our records describe the history of 'Ankh-tôwi, cf. Petrie, *Tarkhan*, i, Pl. 35.

recorded in the cosmogonical texts; this, we suggest, is a hint that the names in question refer to sacred places such as once might have existed in the Memphite region during prehistoric or protodynastic times. We are of the opinion that the Edfu records preserve the memory of a predynastic religious centre which once existed near to Memphis, on which the Egyptians looked as on the *homeland* of the Egyptian temple.[1] It must be admitted that there is no scrap of archaeological evidence that such temples ever existed in Memphis. Nothing is, so far, known from archaeology about the organization of the early Memphite sacred places and the early Memphite constructions. Nowhere can we find evidence that in the Memphite region there existed an early sacred domain called *Wetjeset-Neter* in which the Falcon was adored first, and yet the Edfu tradition emphasized the idea that his sacred domain and its temple were closely connected with Tanen.

It is perfectly true that no precise predynastic or protodynastic parallels to the type of the temple of the Falcon and the Solar Temples that can be deduced from the Edfu texts have ever been found. Nevertheless, there are definite points of contact between the shrines depicted on archaic sealings[2] and the theoretical reconstruction made from the Edfu material.

In view of the Memphite influence that can be detected in the Edfu tradition, it is natural and legitimate to ask whether the Archaic Cemetery at Sakkara can provide us with useful material. In the first place, in view of the notorious lack of precision in the Egyptian indications of orientation, there is nothing that need necessarily render it impossible to ask whether Sakkara, and more particularly the Archaic Cemetery, could not be the place to the north of Memphis where the mythical book was believed to have descended from the sky. Sakkara, in fact, is slightly to the north-west of Memphis. If, however, one examines the Archaic Cemetery at Sakkara, there are certainly some features that im-

[1] It is of interest to mention that closely analogous facts can be discerned in the funerary ritual of Old Kingdom. Blackman has pointed out (*JEA*, v, 160) that the old Egyptian funerary rites as they are known from Saqqara Mastabas show marked differences from the funerary ritual of the Vth Dynasty.

[2] Cf. Petrie, *Royal Tombs*, II, Pl. 7, no. 8; Pl. 10; Ricke, *Bemerkungen*, I, 37; Vandier, *Manuel*, II, Pl. 556–61.

mediately attract attention, in particular the regular provision of an ambulatory around the superstructure. Tomb 3505[1] is of special interest, for in addition to the ambulatory, we find the tomb and a small temple together within the same enclosure. Tomb 3505, in fact, presents us with the same combination of temple and place of funerary cults, in addition to an ambulatory, that we have already noted was one of the essential features in the constitution of the original temple of the Falcon.[2] We do not for a minute suggest that the earliest temples in any way resembled the tombs of the Archaic Cemetery, but we do consider that there are undeniable points of contact between the actual constructions of the Archaic Cemetery and the theoretical reconstructions that can be made on the basis of the Edfu records. It may be that at Sakkara and Edfu we have, in the one in brick and in the other in hieroglyphic, aspects of what was essentially the same Memphite tradition. We think, however, that the mythological records of Edfu reflect an earlier phase of this tradition than what is represented by the temple or chapel in Tomb 3505, since at Edfu there is not the slightest justification for postulating any constructional material but reed in so far as the first temple, that of the Falcon, is concerned.

In support of this theory further archaic sanctuaries can be cited. At Hieraconpolis[3] and at Heliopolis[4] there is definite evidence of the existence of archaic structures on relatively small oval mounds, which may, without undue difficulty, be imagined as imitations of the mythical mound or island.

Regarding Heliopolis another interesting fact can be cited. A tablet preserved at Turin (Turin 2682)[5] shows a plan of an early shrine or temple at Heliopolis. The plan of this early Heliopolitan temple may perhaps be typical of the early temples of Heliopolis. The temple represented on the Turin tablet consists of three juxtaposed units of which the central unit had a sanctuary against its rear wall. This sanctuary is called *msn* and was used for the cere-

[1] Emery, *Great Tombs of the First Dynasty*, III, Pl. 2, 40.

[2] Cf. p. 220.

[3] Cf. Quibell, *Hieraconpolis*, II, Pl. 72–3.

[4] Cf. Petrie, *Heliopolis Kafr Ammar and Shurafa*, Pl. 1, 2.

[5] Cf. Ricke, 'Der "Hohe Sand in Heliopolis"', *ZÄS*, LXXI, 116, Pl. III; for the explanation, cf. p. 111.

mony of *Erecting the willow*.[1] Here, there is perhaps some connexion with the primitive rites performed underneath the willow as described in Edfu records.[2] The general position of the *msn*-sanctuary and its significance appear to be very close to the description of the archaic shrines. Moreover, the appearance of the sanctuary itself seems to be like that of the legendary shrine described in the Edfu records.[3] It consists of a hall which is surrounded by small side sanctuaries on three sides. Possibly the central part of that temple preserves the aspect of an early enclosure to which other smaller halls or cultus-rooms have been gradually added. It is tempting to think that the set-up of the temple as it is represented on the Turin tablet might comprise elements surviving from the prehistoric enclosures and temples constructed in the Heliopolitan region.

At Armant,[4] also, there appears to have been a protodynastic temple below the New Kingdom temple. A sondage by Myers in the west forecourt of the temple revealed that below the layer of foundation sand of the New Kingdom were several floors associated with a not inconsiderable number of sherds and a few pots and other objects of protodynastic date.[5] On the uppermost floor, Myers found, *inter alia*, two pits which have every appearance of being foundation deposits, and which he dates S.D. 78. No objects from the lower levels of the deposit could be dated earlier than S.D. 63. Unfortunately, the excavation covered too small an area to enable any comparison to be made; it is impossible to tell whether this apparently protodynastic temple at Armant was a mound, real or artificial, nor to tell of what materials the temple was built, nor whether there was an enclosure. All that can be said is that it is highly probable that there was a protodynastic temple at Armant below the New Kingdom temple, thereby indicating a continuous tradition, and that already at this early date the foundation deposit existed.

The last primitive temple to which reference can be made is that at Medamud excavated by Robichon and Varille.[6] It is a most

[1] *Ibid.* p. 113. [2] Cf. p. 158 ff. [3] Cf. p. 333.
[4] Cf. Mond and Myers, *Temples of Armant*, I, 1–2, 29. [5] *Ibid.* Pl. 10.
[6] Cf. Robichon and Varille, 'Description sommaire du temple primitif de Médamoud', *Recherches d'Archéologie*, XI; Vandier, *Manuel*, II, 575–81.

unusual and remarkable building with features that cannot yet be explained with complete satisfaction. The characteristic feature of this temple is two mounds in each of which is a small rectangular chamber approached by a passage. It is immediately evident that this temple, primitive though it is, is the expression of a tradition entirely different from that of the temples on the *pāy*-lands which is at the heart of the Edfu tradition. The temple at Medamud might have associations with the funerary cult but this is not certain and it is a question that lies far outside the scope of the present study.

At the end of this exposition of facts we draw attention to a well-known feature in the Osireion at Abydos,[1] where, before the sarcophagus chamber, there is constructed in stone an island round which is a water channel. It is not impossible that this island, artificial though it appears, might have been regarded as representing the primaeval land which was believed to be the first to emerge from Nun, and on which the first sacred place was created.[2] This conception of a sacred place accords with the ideas disclosed by the Edfu tradition that the first sacred domain had strongly pronounced funerary associations. The same ideas seem to govern the organization of the cultus-place of Osiris at Philae, as has already been pointed out above.[3]

Very little has come down to us from the early temples. The relics of an early architecture do not enable us to reconstruct an absolutely coherent picture. We do consider that there are in many respects points of contact between the physical aspect of the mythical temples and the little that remains from the early sacred places of Egypt. At this point we must emphasize that the primitive temples of the Edfu texts, especially that of the Falcon, show a series of resemblances to the little that is known of the temples and the monumental architecture of Archaic Egypt. The connexions are all with protodynastic Egypt, perhaps also with the very end of predynastic period.

We incline to the opinion that the sacred book, the *Specification of the Sacred Mounds of the Early Primaeval Age*, records the successive phases of evolution of sacred places and temples in one

[1] Cf. Frankfort, *The Cenotaph of Seti I*, pp. 16–21, 29–31.

[2] Cf. p. 65.

[3] Cf. p. 43.

single region which can reasonably be regarded as the *homeland of the Egyptian temple*. Our study has furnished convincing evidence that this sacred book was based to a considerable extent, if not exclusively, on Memphite traditions and beliefs. It has every appearance of disclosing the history of sacred domains that were founded in the Memphite region during pre- and protodynastic times. The contribution of the Edfu texts is of high value and real interest, for from these records only can we learn what was the original Memphite type of sacred building and the organization of the real sacred enclosures at the dawn of history. For the Egyptians the Memphite sacred domains were apparently of a mythical nature; they were the work of the gods themselves and were regarded as the prototype of the normal Egyptian temple of historical times.

The theory that the Edfu Myth of Creation was taken over from the Memphite tradition may, perhaps, be supported by what the Edfu inscriptions tell us about the Nine Ancestor Gods of Edfu, who play an important part in the *Festival of the Sacred Marriage*.[1] The Ancestor Gods are not a part of the Memphite tradition, but they are of partly Middle Egyptian and partly Lower Egyptian origin (primarily of Heliopolitan–Memphite origin). The inscriptions tell us that these gods came from various places, and that they journeyed through the Two Lands and were buried at Edfu, thereby protecting and prospering Egypt:

> (they) travelled over the desert to Him-with-dappled-plumage and came to rest in the Necropolis in the South of Egypt; they gave birth to the inhabitants of Upper and Lower Egypt.[2]

Here, in a different context, we find unambiguous evidence that the temple took over gods who were believed to have been born elsewhere in order to strengthen the claims of Edfu to be the home of the Egyptian people.

Yet another valuable argument can be cited in favour of the theory that traditions could be taken over from one temple to another. The text referring to the cult of the Shebtiw at Edfu[3]

[1] For a preliminary study see Fairman, *BJRL*, XXXVII, 167 ff.

[2] E. I. 173,3–174,7; 382,4–15; II. 51,3–52,9; III. 301,8–16; 323,5–12; IV. 83,4–85,8; 102,17–103,13; 239,13–241,14; V. 61,17–63,16; 160,12–162,6; VII. 118,4–119,8; 279,16–281,2.

[3] Cf. *ZÄS*, LXXXVII, 41 ff.

makes it certain that this myth of the creation of sacred domains and temples was familiar at Heracleopolis. No shred of evidence is known from documents of Heracleopolitan provenance. But the Edfu text tells us that the Shebtiw created Heracleopolis by virtue of the magical rite of *sw-iḫt-tꜣ*. It refers to the *Mansion of the Ram*,[1] which might have been for Heracleopolis the first temple which was created and resulted from the sequence of creation of the Earth; it was founded by order of a defunct Earth-God on the *pāy*-land that emerged near the island of creation. We suppose that Heracleopolis might have used the Memphite tradition for the explanation of the origin of its temple or temples. This is, of course, a conjecture for which there are no textual data. But it is known that the Heracleopolitan religious system was strongly influenced by Memphite traditions. In our opinion, it does not seem unlikely that from Heracleopolis the Memphite traditions could have spread over to Upper Egypt and could, subsequently, have been taken over by the Edfu temple. Undoubtedly, and during Greek times in particular, the Edfu temple claimed to be the heir and the direct descendant of the original temple that came into existence in the Memphite region before the dawn of history.

It is, therefore, suggested that each cultus-centre in Egypt was influenced by the same Memphite traditions concerning the creation of the temple, but adapted them to suit its local needs. Thus at Edfu, the first *Mansion of the God* is said to be the temple of the Falcon. This, of course, is a tradition of a rather later date, if not only an Edfu tradition, to enhance the prestige of the cult of the Falcon Horus and Horus himself. Undoubtedly the traditions of other temples, if they had been preserved, would have shown that the first Mansions of the God were those of the local gods, and thus, from temple to temple, that other gods were the divine beings for whom the first Mansion was created at the beginning of the world. We have, for instance, already mentioned the *Mansion of the Ram* at Heracleopolis. We conclude with confidence that the Egyptian conception of the temple was Memphite in origin, just as the daily ritual service in the temple was of Heliopolitan origin.

At the end of this discussion we recall a very well-known belief

[1] E. IV. 359,2; this place seems to be regarded as a funerary place.

from historical times. Ptah is generally regarded as the founder and builder of the Egyptian temples.[1] In addition to the numerous instances which we find in the temple inscriptions of all periods, two quotations from the Edfu texts can be mentioned. In a scene portraying the foundation of the historical temple in which the gods are said to have acted, Ptah is described as supervising (*ḫrp*) the building of the historical temple at Edfu.[2] Another Edfu text tells us that Ptah was the god who was the first to create the temple in the dim past, and in accordance with his creation other temples were constructed over all the world.[3] But the main Edfu cosmogonical records do not refer once to Ptah. This seems to be an important historical fact. We venture to say that, in all probability, the Edfu texts disclose traditions of the Memphite region which were earlier than the constitution of the cults at Memphis during the Archaic Period. The historical Memphis might have adapted this myth, and, as a consequence, the chief god of the historical Memphis might have replaced the original creators. This hypothesis accords with what the Edfu evidence tells us of the sacred book which was believed to have descended from the sky to the north of Memphis.[4]

[1] Cf. Sandman, *The God Ptah*, pp. 32 ff.

[2] E. IV. 7,6.

[3] E. IV. 14,6.

[4] Cf. p. 262.

PART V

The Doctrine concerning the Origin of the Temple

CHAPTER 17

The Memphite Conception of the Nature of the Temple

The dominant thoughts behind the Edfu records, and especially the idea of the temple that emerges at the end of the Creation of the Earth, are, most likely, Memphite. The thread of Memphite and Lower Egyptian traditions is very strong and runs throughout all the mythological narratives. The Creators of the Earth would not be mentioned as the chief divine powers who created the temple not only in its material, physical form but also in its characteristics and its function, nor would the temple, as an entity, be thought to be the direct outcome of the Earth, if, in the background of the myth about its origin, there were not a single theory whose main concern was the creation of the *Substance* and its intimate derivatives. This central idea brings to mind the allusions to the *wisdom of the Sages*.[1] We know that they were believed to have foretold the existence of the world. But what they created was not animate beings, but *knowledge* and the *Earth*. It is, therefore, suggested that the *wisdom of the Sages* is precisely what lies at the heart of the Memphite doctrine of Creation.

In none of the Egyptian cosmogonical documents can we follow a connected and continued line of events from the very moment when the first terrestrial substance was brought into existence down to the time when its ultimate offspring, the *temple*, as an entity, had reached its final stage of development.

The Edfu records present a description of certain aspects of the creation of the world with special reference to the creation of the *primaeval island*. The characteristic feature of this theory is that each phase, each act of the creation, is interpreted as resulting in the origin of a sacred domain. Each new phase of creation brought new lands out of Nun, and in these lands there originated sacred places whose aspect varied and appeared more developed in each new phase of creation. The final stage of all the succeeding eras of

[1] Cf. p. 9.

creation which are described in our sources brought something new which influenced the formation of the sacred entity. The sacred domains of our creation story seem to be conceived to be the result of events specific to a particular period of the primaeval age. This appears to be intensified if we compare the final stage of events in the original island with the situation in the earlier *pāy*-lands. The same situation can be seen when we confront the circumstances in the original *pāy*-lands with those of the secondary ones which are described in the third and fourth record. Apparently they conceal views of a somewhat later and more advanced era. We are told that the gods left the original *pāy*-lands after life developed within the earliest type of sacred enclosures that were constructed there. They journeyed through the unoccupied lands of the primaeval age and founded other sacred domains.[1] There is a quite clear allusion to the tradition of a single centre in which the temple originated. From the point of view of the myth it looks as though the Egyptians believed that there was one land only in which all the orders of creation were effected and this was the land in which the Lord of All was the Earth-God and his immediate successor the *Winged One*.[2] All the other temples were a later creation. Their building was influenced by other streams of ideas different from those that can be discerned in the history of the temple in *Wetjeset-Neter*.

It also resulted from the study of the Edfu sources that the Egyptians believed in the existence of two sacred worlds. Strictly speaking, the first sacred world is represented by a primaeval island which, for reasons unknown, was destroyed and disappeared.[3] This island is described as being during the first period of its existence the *Homeland of the Primaeval Ones* and as the cultus-place of the Creator.[4] With the re-emergence of the island attention is concentrated on the creation of new lands, called *pāy*-lands, around and along the margins of the original island. These lands were the foundation grounds of the sacred domains, specifically of the domains of the successor of the Creator. The second era of the primaeval age, therefore, is of importance for the development of the domains that survived in historical times. The

[1] Cf. p. 190 ff, for other meanings of this mythological event.

[2] Cf. p. 169 ff. [3] Cf. p. 106 ff. [4] Cf. p. 75 ff.

text proceeds to tell us that on the edges of these *pāy*-lands there appeared yet another smaller plot of land which was the actual site of the first sacred enclosure of the god.[1] Thereafter other *pāy*-lands emerged on the margins of the already existing *pāy*-lands in which sacred enclosures were founded.[2] From these enclosures, which in their primary aspect were very little more than a mere fence, the *Mansion of the God* derived. The fact that the private realm of the Earth-God was the place in which all these events came to pass, and was also the birth-place of the temple, renders it possible to conclude that these trends of thought reflect and reproduce, in part at least, the contents of the Memphite doctrine of creation. Perhaps the Edfu accounts reveal in greater detail the theory of which a slight hint only has been preserved in the text of the Shabaka Stone. It is said that the Creator (Ptah) created the domains and placed the gods there.[3] It is to be remembered that, on the other hand, the Edfu sources furnish yet another valuable argument that behind this creation story are purely Memphite ideas. The phases of creation described are not interpreted as a physical and organic work. On the contrary, the idea inherent in this myth is that the main factor of the process was the *word* which caused the metamorphosis of the primary matter and gave it its final concrete shape. The creation of substances was conceived as a magical rite of creation in which the episode of uttering sacred spells (*ḏ3jsw*)[4] played an important part. In pronouncing spells the Creators effected the creation of the world of the gods which was the starting-point in the creation of the physical world of men. This magical manner of creation is, in particular, illustrated by the work of the Shebtiw,[5] who were believed, through the pronouncing of sacred spells, to have fulfilled the command of the *Earth-Maker*. The Edfu account reveals the belief that the sacred domain was created according to the *word of the Earth-Maker*.[6] He is never described as being physically present in the island or as having actually intervened in the process. The Egyptians seem to have believed that the commands of an intangible creative power were known, or were made known,

[1] Cf. p. 175 ff. [2] Cf. p. 207 ff.
[3] Shabaka Stone, 1, 58 ff. = Junker, *Götterlehre von Memphis*, p. 63 ff.
[4] Cf. p. 139. [5] Cf. p. 187. [6] E. vi. 17,13.

to other creating deities, the Sages and the Shebtiw in our creation story, who effected the actual work of the creation. This interpretation seems to be admissible if we remember that it is stated in the first Edfu cosmogonical record that the *God-of-the-Temple* actually gave the command for the creative action described as the *nḥp*, *fashioning*, and that he himself conferred it on the Shebtiw.[1]

Our Edfu sources allude to very many sacred domains and temples that were believed to have resulted from the creative work of the Sages and the Shebtiw. Of these the creation of two types of *temples* fashioned at different stages of the primaeval age in the *pāy*-lands is described in considerable detail. Each of them is pictured as the prototype of sacred domains that were founded in the original *pāy*-lands and in the secondary *pāy*-lands. The first and most primitive of these mythical temples is the temple in *Wetjeset-Neter* in which the primaeval Falcon was believed to have been adored. This temple developed around the Perch and is regarded as the final act in the long-drawn-out process of the Creation of the Earth. The second type of the original temples, which was created in the later *pāy*-lands, is that of the Sun-God. It is a much developed structure and was certainly not regarded as founded until after the creation of the world.

In describing the growth of the temple in *Wetjeset-Neter* much is naturally said about the creation of the Earth. A coherent picture is given of the development of the domain, the site of the temple, and, finally, of the house of the god itself. It is a series of consecutive phases of creation, each developing from its antecedent, each bringing a new aspect to what already was, but each new phase is the result of the activities of the same divine powers who were the offspring of the Earth-God.[2] We had in the primaeval island the *hìn-Homeland of the Primaeval Ones* and the resting-place of the Creator; then the Perch was planted, and was subsequently surrounded by a fence. A shelter was erected above it, and it was from this simple courtyard on the water's edges of the *pāy*-land that the *Mansion of the God* was born and was constructed at the command of the *Ka*. It has been noticed that the creation of the Earth proceeds side by side with the growth of the domain of the Falcon. The essential features of the first temple to be created

[1] Cf. p. 152. [2] Cf. *ZÄS*, LXXXVII, 45–6.

appear to have derived from the traditions attached to the site in which the Mansion was created; its existence as well as its characteristics were regarded as the continuation of what was in the site prior to its creation.

The close link with what had existed in the past is another striking feature of the history of the primaeval temple of the Falcon. *That which existed in the past and had died* is interpreted as the essential condition that determines the birth of the new sacred entity represented by the temple. The temple of the Falcon is described as having originated on land which had funerary associations and was of ancestral tradition. All that happened around the *sbḫt*-enclosure consecrated to the worship of the *Primaeval Ancestors* provides the rounded picture of a distinct phase. This *sbḫt*-enclosure presents the earliest stage of a constructed sacred place, and on such a ground the domain of the god of historical time took its origin. The temple of the Falcon, in the strict sense, appears as a renewal and revival of what existed in the past but had vanished. It develops in an unbroken line from the simplest form of the resting-place of a god who had died. The earliest form of the resting-place of the god is represented by the *ḏd*-pillar, which was replaced in the resurrected world by the *ḏbꜣ*-perch. And this Perch was the first and essential step in the creation of the temple.

In its earliest form the temple consisted of a court that surrounded a booth which screened and protected the Perch. For this reason the booth became the most sacred part of the temple in the final stage of its development.

We can thus see that the temple of the Falcon was in essence a natural event: it was the logical outcome, at the dawn of the world, of the need to provide protection for the god who is described as having a resting-place (the Perch) but no protection. It is from this simple fact that the temple developed. Since the temple of the Falcon appears to be the earliest temple, since its link with the past, the Ancestors and the funerary cults appears to be predominant, is it too much to suggest that the vital element in the constitution of the temple was the preservation of the close link with the Creator, the Ancestors and their cults?

It should be noted that the foundation of the temple of the

Falcon evolved from the bequest of the dead god, the *Ka*. This temple, having been constructed, was, in fact, a memorial of the dead ruler. Therefore, it had to be erected in the very same place in which his *ḏd*-pillar was, and in which, too, his blessed command (*wḏt nfr*) was enshrined.[1]

Behind the foundation of the temple in *Wetjeset-Neter* lies the tradition concerning the resting-place of a god which was imagined to be the *ḏd*-pillar. It can be stated with confidence that the connexion between the temple and the *ḏd*-pillar is a feature peculiar to the history of the temple in *Wetjeset-Neter*. No equivalent can be found in the documents referring to the history of the Solar Temples. The *ḏd*-pillar is a new fact in the history of a temple and certainly not without meaning with respect to the constitution of the temple. The *ḏd*-pillar in this myth is never described as a real object that would be found on the site in which the sacred domain was to be found; allusions are only made to its previous existence on the site. Its importance, however, can be illustrated by the statements by the Creator gods who were present in the *pāy*-land of *Djeba*.[2] They make it certain that there was a connexion between this symbol and the laying out of the foundation of the first enclosure sacred to the Falcon.[3] It looks as though the Edfu records reveal yet another, less known tradition attached to the *ḏd*-pillar. It has been noticed that the *ḏd*-pillar, as a resting-place of a defunct deity, is always mentioned before the start of a new phase of creation. The *ḏd*-pillar appears to determine the place in which the new sacred domain was to be created. Thus we have mentioned the *ḏd*-pillar in the primaeval island, then on the *pāy*-land; finally it was believed that the *ḏd*-pillar was included in the site of the temple. From all these circumstances a new sacred domain resulted, and each new sacred domain was in every instance the re-creation of a sacred place which once existed, but had vanished. The Edfu records proved that the tradition concerning the *ḏd*-pillar was implicit in the history of one sole temple. This is the temple which resulted from, and was the culminating act in, the process of the creation of the Earth; its construction was commanded by an Earth-God, and it was created to house the

[1] Cf. p. 202. [2] Cf. p. 203.
[3] Cf. pp. 145–9.

embodiment of the Soul of the Creator. This circumstance seems to hint at yet another belief. The presence of the *ḏd*-pillar *in situ* might have been one of the means which ensured the magical protection of the place, so that this particular place could be re-created after having vanished. It has been noticed how important was the act of resurrecting the vanished world before starting the creation of the sacred domains of the Falcon.[1] The essential element in the resurrection was then the presence of the *ḏd*-pillar, the erection of which had for its immediate consequence the re-vivification of the vanished world of gods. It brought out of the underworld the immaterial forms of the deities who formerly lived in that place; among them one is even described as the *protection of the ḏd-pillar*.[2] These circumstances do not appear to be incidental. We are of the opinion that the presence of the *ḏd*-pillar in the site may be explained as implying the idea of continuance in time, the idea of an indefinite existence, thus ensuring the sanctity of the place which was about to be revivified.

The event that happened at the dawn of the history of the temple in *Wetjeset-Neter*, therefore, would appear to be distinctive of this temple: this was the resurrection. The temple of *Wetjeset-Neter* is, in a sense, the resurrection of the *Home of the Ka*, the *Ka* who was an Earth-God.[3] It is true that the temples founded on the secondary *pāy*-lands were also the re-enactment of a former state. The idea of the resurrection, however, is not implicit in the tradition of their site and in the order of their creation. The account does not indicate that the resurrection of an earlier sacred domain would be an act preliminary to the foundation of the enclosure.

Not only the origin of the Temple of the Falcon but all the phases of its development appear to have been determined by what had existed in the past. The past is the main constructive element from the very moment when the first sacred domain was created in the island. The Falcon seems to have shared the first constructed enclosure in the island, the *sbḫt*-enclosure, with the ancestral deities. It would seem that it was believed that the place

[1] Cf. pp. 166–7; the idea of the *resurrection* in the history of the temple is specifically illustrated by the emergence of the soul of the deceased creator, cf. pp. 110–11.
[2] Cf. p. 134. [3] Cf. pp. 296–7.

of ancestral tradition, determined by the previous existence of the *ḏd*-pillar, was the only site in which the Falcon, as the embodiment of the Soul of the Creator, could find security. The fact that the ancestral element was in this creation story the means which ensured the god's security, may explain the presence of the Ancestor Gods in all the phases of creation of the sacred domains of the Falcon. It has been remarked that when the first sacred domain of the Falcon was created, the divine beings who formerly dwelt there appeared one by one on the scene. We suggest that they revealed themselves to protect the Falcon, since he had his resting-place but no protection. A closely similar situation can be found in the ultimate phase of the creation of the *pāy*-lands. The Ancestors, described as the *ḏdw*, *ghosts*, are present before the start of the creation of the lands. Moreover, the *Ḥeter-ḥer* is said to be present in the place where the Perch was to be set up; in another instance we find the Divine of Heart in the same position. Since the text does not mention any specific function which they exercised, we are tempted to conjecture that the part they played under these circumstances was precisely that of *protection*. This kind of protection completed by the Ancestors might have been believed to be implicit in the nature of the temple itself once this was being constructed. No allusion was made to these ancestral protectors when the first sacred enclosure was laid out. We do not find them either in connexion with the construction of the first temple nor later when other sacred buildings began to be constructed.

These ideas are foreign to the second myth about the origin of the temple. The temple founded in the secondary *pāy*-land is not a revival of the home of a defunct Earth-God. The origin of the Solar Temple appears to some extent artificial and arbitrary, and fundamental differences have been noticed in the main periods of its growth. The manner in which the site of the Solar Temple came to be regarded as sacred is entirely different. We have seen that the choice of the site of the temple of the Falcon was determined, and its sanctity was given to it, by what existed in the past; the sanctity of the Solar Temple was due to the victory of the god over his enemy and to the symbolic presence of the Earth-Maker. This second type of temple developed on a sacred plot of land in which the first construction to be made was an enclosure (*ỉnb*).[1] There is no reference to the *ḏd*-pillar or to the *Seat of the First Occasion*. In the secondary *pāy*-lands the existence of the temple began with the laying out of the foundation of the outer enclosure of the temple. Within this enclosure there was then erected the real temple, which consisted essentially of three rather complicated, juxtaposed units of rooms and halls around which was an ambulatory. In the interpretation of the origin of the second temple no allusion is made either to the past or to the creation, but certainly this temple was founded near to another and earlier divine settlement which, from all the evidence available, can only have been the *Temple of the Eldest One in Wetjeset-Neter*. There was thus a belief that the creation of another temple complex could primarily be effected only in the precinct of the area in which the Earth-God formerly dwelt. The link of the temple with the Earth-God who was the Ancestor (*Mȝ*), is apparent and is borne out by his symbolic presence on the site of the temple, then in the temple itself.[2] It confirms that the idea of the *Ancestor* closely associated with the Earth-God was also a vital element in the creation of the temple on the secondary *pāy*-land. This element, however, is here no longer genuine and implicit in the nature of the home of the god itself; it is only symbolized.

This second primaeval temple was made by the gods, who imitated the form of the protective abode of the successor of the Creator. They, therefore, imitated what had been naturally created in the past. And this imitation of what had represented the revival of the former domain of the Creator was, in fact, a victory memorial.

The second myth about the origin of the temple would seem to revert to the idea that the mansions (*ḥwt*) and the enclosures (*ỉnb*) could be multiplied all over the mythical world. It appears as though there was a belief that near a place in which the Earth-God was believed to dwell a company of divine beings settled down, but the place was unprotected, and, consequently, suffered an assault by the snake. The gods fought against the snake and defeated him. The area was cleansed, and after the symbol of the Earth-God had been brought to that place, a new divine settlement was founded exactly in the place where the enemy was killed.

[1] Cf. p. 239. [2] Cf. pp. 198–9, 257.

Subsequently, a fence or a wall of light material was erected around the place in which the divine company rested. This was the starting-point of the creation of the secondary mansion of the god. It may be suggested that the Egyptian idea was that it was repeated in this way from one place to another and thus it came about that so many mansions of gods could be founded in the mythical world. One of the essential prerequisites, obviously, for the foundation of these later temples was the symbolical presence of the Earth-God. It is abundantly clear from the account of the origin of the Solar Temple that a further requirement for the foundation was a fight, the successful outcome of which rendered it safe for the gods to settle down and order the temple to be built. The leading idea of the history of the temples which were believed to have been founded later in the primaeval age was the commemoration of the victory of the gods, and the principal function of the temple was to protect the god from his adversaries. And this appears, in all probability, the trends of thought which came to be the general tradition concerning the origin of the Egyptian temples. We already referred to this tradition in the first part of this study.[1] It seems to be of interest to add yet another document from the Edfu texts to stress its later general significance. There is preserved in the Edfu inscriptions the account of the origin of the *Temple of Mesen*,[2] which appears to be an early sacred domain of the Falcon in which the Falcon seems to have had his *Great Seat* (*st-wrt*). The account tells us that the sacred place of the Falcon was assailed by enemies, but Rēᶜ, Tanen as the *Ancestor*, and the Ogdoad came to the aid of the Falcon. It was only after the fight had ended victoriously that the gods settled down and ordered the building of the *ḥwt-nṯr*, the Mansion of the god. This record does not refer to any of the phases of creation bearing on the site of the temple; in contrast, it alludes to the presence of the Ogdoad,[3] who do not interfere in the process of the creation of the temple of the Falcon in *Wetjeset-Neter*. This account gives, undoubtedly, evidence of a derivative tradition. Since the Falcon had his original mansion in *Wetjeset-Neter* and many other sacred places in the original *pāy*-lands, it becomes

[1] Cf. pp. 51–2.

[2] E. VI. 174,15–175,5, and above, p. 41.

[3] Cf. p. 236, the Ogdoad is said to be present at the foundation of the Solar Temple.

clear that even the history of the Falcon's cult had two traditions concerning the origin of his sacred places. This view accords with the evidence found in the summaries of various traditions attached to the sacred place of Djeba which we find in the Edfu Building Texts, and to which we have already referred.[1] That from a definite moment the primaeval sacred place of any god was regarded as his *Great Seat* (*st-wrt*) *of the Primaeval Age* can be justified by what is said in two additional records concerning the foundation of the *Great-Seat-of-the-Primaeval-Time* of Rēᶜ and of Harakhte which were translated in our summaries.[2]

These three additional accounts seem to emphasize the originality of the myth about the *Temple in Wetjeset-Neter*. It appears that on the basis of the myth about the first temple of the Falcon new versions were made which, in all probability, originated in places of Egypt other than the Falcon's original cultus-place, and which were most probably influenced by the second theory concerning the fight as the prerequisite of the foundation of the sacred domains. In these derivative myths no allusion is made to a pre-existing sacred place *in situ*, but, on the contrary, the accounts refer to the journey or journeys which the gods were believed to have undertaken through the mythical world.

We cannot state dogmatically to what concrete sacred entity or entities the Mansions correspond which are described in the Edfu records as the prototypes of the Egyptian temples. It has been noticed in the principal sources of our study that when the command for the constructing of the place was pronounced,[3] the description of the temple is no longer accompanied by a connected set of mythological events in the same way as in the early stages of its history. The narratives refer only to the 'classical' type of deities who were believed to have acted in the building of the temples—Thoth, Seshat and the Builder Gods. This is, of course, a very common feature of Egyptian mythology. We may, eventually, think of an early cultus-place the memory of which survived in historical times, and to which all the beliefs and traditions known from the Edfu records were associated. Many of these traditions and mythological circumstances cannot yet be explained to our complete satisfaction. Nevertheless, it is clear

[1] Cf. p. 170. [2] Cf. pp. 41–2. [3] Cf. pp. 37–8.

that there the actual is combined with the symbolic and that this feature affects all the stages of development of the temple. The temple is treated as a physical entity which took origin on the edges on the primaeval island of creation in the same way as any existing being; the temple has its concrete shape and a physically real growth. But in its development it is conceived as being of a mythical nature. Its origin and development show close affinities with the material aspect of the creation. This relationship does not seem to have been limited to the *Substance* itself, but also shows a connexion with the divine power who created it. In its origin the temple seems to have departed from the place in which the Creator of the Earth revealed himself. It is known that the Earth-God is never referred to as being physically present in the island or on the *pāy*-lands. On the other hand, however, the text alludes to his 'likeness' that appeared in the island and assisted the procedures of creation. It is obvious that at this point the Edfu account follows two different streams of religious ideas. We are told that the nameless Creator revealed himself in his immaterial form which bears the name *Bꜣ ḥꜣtty*, the *Flying Ba.*[1] His revelation was followed by an episode which has every appearance of being the *consorting of the Soul of the Creator with the Falcon.*[2] Thereafter the Creator is said to have appeared in his material form. This is Tanen, who is described as performing another mystic act in which the sacred emblems of the Earth-Maker were handed over to the Falcon.[3] It has been seen that both of these episodes having been completed, there started the creation of the lands adjacent to the island, in which the Falcon became the supreme lord. From these events, therefore, developed a long period of creation which ended in the origin of the temple. It appears that the Falcon was believed to have been the only divine being fitted to consort with the Soul of the Creator. A further deduction that can be made from these episodes is that these two mystic events in the island of creation were the means that enabled the following phases of creation. When the vanished domain of the Creator was brought to a new life, and the sacred bird of the primaeval age assumed the characteristics of the Earth-God, there was a need to create an abode to house the embodiment of the Soul of the Earth-God.

[1] Cf. p. 16. [2] Cf. p. 133 ff. [3] Cf. p. 23.

This mystic union caused the origin of a new sacred entity which appears at the end of the Creation of the Earth. This final entity is the temple. In its origin the temple seems to have been connected with the belief in the embodiment of the Soul of the Earth-God. The two mystic episodes appear as having initiated the origin of the first house of the god and as having determined its creation and its primary function. The text intimates the view that these episodes happened only once in the primaeval age. The Egyptians seem to have believed that at the beginning of the world there was one sole temple which was born from the need to house the god who was elevated to the rank of the Creator, and who was the first divine being among the gods capable of uniting with the sky. His house was then given a name to commemorate the place in which this mystic union was believed to have happened: *Wetjeset-Neter*.

The myth about the origin of the temple of the Falcon is, therefore, the unique source to give us evidence of the history and characteristics of the earliest temple. It is, in fact, an unbroken history of a cult that originated in a world that had been revivified after having died, by the emergence of the Soul of the Creator, the *Flying Ba*. The emergence of the Soul from the Underworld marks the beginning of the life of a new sacred entity, the temple. If we remember once again the affinities of this temple with the creation of the Earth, there will be very little difficulty in concluding that this conception of the temple as an entity was Memphite in origin.

The Memphite theory was evidently that the first house of the god came into existence on a land that emerged from the primaeval waters close to the actual spot of earth on which the drama of the creation of this world commenced. All the other temples were a later creation and, in fact, an imitation of what was the actual re-enactment of the *ḥwt*-enclosure of the Earth-Maker. They were the imitation of the sacred structure in the original island in which the symbols of the first creating powers were kept, together with the emblems of the Earth-Maker.

CHAPTER 18

The Original Temple

The Temple in Wetjeset-Neter is described as a natural event. For this reason its history appears as the explanation of how the temple came into being. The interpretation of its origin furnishes us with an illustrative document of what was, from the Egyptian point of view, the essential condition of the Egyptian temple. Further arguments can be added to stress the theory concerning the original temple at the beginning of the world which was born from the need to provide protection for the successor of the Earth-God. In this connexion the deceased god, the *Ka*, is to be remembered. The situation in the *pāy*-land of *Wetjeset-Neter*[1] makes it inherently possible to conclude that the Egyptians believed that one temple only resulted from the command of the *Ka*. It is stated in the account of the origin of the *pāy*-land of *Wetjeset-Neter* that the place where the temple was to be constructed was ordered (*wḏ*) by the *Ka*.[2] In contrast, in the *pāy*-land of *Djeba* the site of the temple to be is described as a place in which the *Ka* ruled (*ḫrp*).[3] The temple, when constructed there, was merely the memorial of the *Ka*, but was most probably constructed according to the pattern of the temple in *Wetjeset-Neter*. Since the *Wetjeset-Neter* was earlier in origin than the other sacred places of the Falcon, it is tempting to suggest that in all the later *pāy*-lands the constructions were a mere imitation of what was commanded in the *Wetjeset-Neter*. This is, inevitably, a hypothesis for which there is no textual evidence. What appears quite certain is that the Egyptians believed that the temple in *Wetjeset-Neter* was the oldest among the mansions of the mythical age. The divine command of the *Ka* was issued only once and this happened in the *Wetjeset-Neter*.

It is apposite to recall that there are in the Edfu inscriptions a number of indications to show that a sacred place described as

[1] Cf. p. 160.
[2] Cf. pp. 219–20.
[3] Cf. p. 31.

Wetjeset-Neter was believed to have been earlier than other settlements of the gods. In the *Myth of Horus*[1] as well as in the *Legend about the fight of Horus against Seth*[2] a *Wetjeset-Neter* (eventually *Wetjeset-Hor*[3]) is described as the original domain of gods in which they apparently lived before they departed to fight against enemies. The *Wetjeset-Neter* existed before the foundation of many other sacred places which are said to have been established after the fight had ended. We cannot prove that the *Wetjeset-Neter* in the creation myth and that known from a mythological narrative already strongly affected by the Solar myth, were exactly the same sacred domain. What is, however, important is that both myths carry the same idea and allude to the tradition of an earlier settlement the name of which was similar to that of the first sacred place in our creation story.

The Edfu tradition also reveals that the temple in *Wetjeset-Neter* was believed to house a deity described as the *wr*, the *Eldest One*,[4] an unspecified deity who was older than the gods worshipped in the historical temples. This name is common in describing the original deity in the archaic cultus-places; in the main, however, it occurs as the subsidiary name of Ptah.[5] This brings to mind the allusions to the *inb-wr*, the *Enclosure of the Eldest*, in the Shabaka Stone.[6] We do not maintain the identity of the two sacred places, but we consider that both of them allude to the cult of the *wr*, the *Eldest one*, and that both have connexions with funerary services.

When we refer to the Edfu texts we find that this *wr*, the *Eldest One*, is, in fact, on a par with the *ndb*, the *Winged One*, who was in the tradition of a later date regarded as the *Sanctified God*

1 E. VI. 186,1–5; *JEA*, XXVIII, 82. For an earlier interpretation of the significance of this name see Sethe, *Urgeschichte*, p. 124. We do not claim that this primaeval *Wetjeset-Neter* is identical with the *Wetjeset-Neter* mentioned in the list of nomes in the Sanctuary of *Ne-wsr-Rēʿ*, cf. Kees, *Re-Heiligtum*, pp. 4–10 and *ASAE*, XVII, 134, 136; Mariette, *Abydos*, I, 28*d*, 44–5.

2 E. VI. 134,1 ff.

3 In these two later myths the transliteration *Wetjeset-Hor* is more likely than *Wetjeset-Neter* because we have there the Falcon Horus.

4 E. VI. 170,1 and above, p. 169.

5 Cf. Junker, *Die Götterlehre von Memphis*, pp. 25–37; Sethe, *ZÄS*, LV, 65; Kees, *Opfertanz*, p. 258, An. 98; *ZÄS*, LVII, 96, 116.

6 Shabaka Stone, I, 59 ff. = Junker, *Die Götterlehre von Memphis*, p.65 ff.

who came into being at the First Occasion.[1] Our Edfu sources probably allude to the cult of a nameless god, described only as a *wr*. This cult was celebrated in a place associated with the traditions of the *Temple in Wetjeset-Neter*.

The Edfu narrative equally explains the Egyptian idea of how it happened that this *Winged One* became the *Sanctified God.*[2] It presents an interesting account of the origin of the god who was the first to have a sacred domain and a temple; no parallel can be quoted in other religious texts.

The close affinities between the temple of the *wr*, *the Eldest One*, and the Earth are sufficiently clear from the Edfu accounts. Further evidence can be added to demonstrate this relationship. It has been noticed that the Earth-God, though he appears in various forms, is always present in the mythical scene. The start of each of the main phases of creation is interpreted as being anticipated by the revelation of an Earth-God whose names vary. In this series we had the *Ka*, who was, in fact, the first divine being to appear before the earliest phase of the creation of the sacred places commenced; then Tanen emerged and remained on the scene throughout the whole process; finally, the *Maker-of-the-substances* appeared in the capacity of the *Ancestor* in the later *pāy*-lands. It has also been noticed that the creation is not described as a manual and organic work, but on the contrary, it is interpreted as a magical rite of creation.[3] The construction of the temple shows much that is similar to the former process. The accounts refer to certain episodes of the foundation,[4] but they never describe how the temple was actually built, though mention is made of the Builder Gods. The temple appears suddenly as a whole, in the same way as the plots of lands on which the foundation was laid out. This brings to mind the manner in which the Shebtiw created the *pāy*-lands; only after they had recited sacred spells over certain *iḫt* did the lands emerge.[5] We have pointed out that the

[1] Cf. Junker, *Die Onurislegende*, p. 16 ff.; E. II. 36,11–13; III. 32,13; 11,2; 121,10–11; 123,13–14; 145,4; VI. 179,6; 181,3.10; *Urk.* VIII, 54, 13; C.D. II, 164,5.6; in E. III. 190,18; 181,1; IV. 37,15; 173,5; VI. 1,14 the god of *Wetjeset-Neter* is described as the *ntr ꜥ3*, the *great god*; in E. IV. 358,15–16; VI. 182,5, he bears the name *ntr ntri*, the *Sanctified God*.

[2] Cf. pp. 131–2, 170.

[3] Cf. pp. 186–7.

[4] Cf. p. 248 ff.

[5] Cf. pp. 137–8.

nature of these *iḫt* is never explicitly stated, but that they appear to be essential for the formation of sacred lands. The uttering of sacred spells over these *iḫt* seems to be a magical procedure whereby what was still uncreated was brought into existence and, moreover, what was already in existence was protected. It is of prime importance to recall that these *iḫt* have every appearance of being the most sacred objects of the *pāy*-lands; they are the sacred objects of the site of the temple, and a special guard was instituted in the *pāy*-land for their protection.[1] These *iḫt* might, indeed, have been regarded as the principal means which enabled the subsequent phase of creation; this then was the foundation of the temple. As we know from the account of the origin of the Solar Temple, some *iḫt* played an important part in the foundation. It may, very tentatively, be suggested that in both, the creation of the *pāy*-land and the foundation of the temple, we have the same substances.

The text acquaints us with a ceremony in which the Sages are said to have acted. What they performed was an episode described as *swr iḫt*,[2] which, certainly, took place before the construction of the enclosure started. There is a certain resemblance to the act performed by the Shebtiw in the creation of the *pāy*-lands; only the general mythological situation had changed. The magical procedure with the *iḫt* would seem to have been applied to the planning and laying out of the foundation ground of the temple. If this equation be correct, it would follow that these *iḫt* were also essential in preparing the sacred land for the creation of the temple. This episode would then show that the very beginnings of the creation of the temple included the same magical procedure as that which brought the Earth to its final aspect. This episode of *swr iḫt, magnifying the substances*, made it possible for the creation of the temple to be carried out. And this may, perhaps, explain why the *iḫt, substances*, were kept in the original *pāy*-land under a special guard. This circumstance may explain, too, why, when the temple had been constructed, there is no longer any allusion

[1] Cf. p. 180.

[2] E. VI. 175,1; in E. VI. 186,16 and 320,10 we read *ḏ3jsw wr iḫt*; we suspect that *wr* is to be taken as a causative *swr*; if this be correct, it would provide excellent evidence that this rite *swr iḫt* was believed to have been performed already in the *pāy*-lands after they emerged from Nun.

to them. They may have been diffused in the concrete appearance of the first temple unit.

On the other hand, however, considering the origin of the temple from the point of view of the *swr iḫt*-action, we may infer that the creation of the temple was conceived as an act which had for its effect the *swr*, the *magnifying* of the *substances* through which the surface of this world was created. Therefore, the temple in its origin and existence would increase and magnify the vital element that caused the Earth to be. In assuming this interpretation, the part played by the Earth-God in the creation of the temple is clear. We have seen in the account of the creation of the lands that when the Shebtiw performed the magical rite of *sw*, *endowing with power*, over the *iḫt*, the Earth-God, Tanen, was present in the site. He did not intervene in the process of the creation itself. He seems to have been present in the capacity of the 'protector'. In the interpretation of the creation of the temple we meet the same situation. Tanen attends the birth of the temple, though he stands outside its real and physical growth. The shape of the temple was the result of the activities of the Builder Gods,[1] another group of divine beings who were also called *Children of Tanen*.[2] They constructed on the ground which was created by the Shebtiw, and they were believed to complete the creative work of Tanen in this fashioning of the temple.[3] The chief function which Tanen seems to have exercised in the creation of the temple was, therefore, its *protection*. This would appear to be natural if we recall the capacity in which Tanen revealed himself in the field of reeds.[4] He is said to have emerged from Nun as the *sꜣ*-protection, and the first action which Tanen fulfilled in the field of *Wetjeset-Neter* was the creation of a magical protection of that sacred place. Additional evidence of this belief can be found in an interpretation of a later date, in which Tanen is said to have been in the primaeval water to protect (*ḥn*) the god.[5] The elementary form of the protection granted by an Earth-God is represented by two staffs in which some protective divine beings were believed

[1] Cf. p. 236.

[2] For the tradition concerning the *msw Tnì* cf. *ZÄS*, LXXXVII, 45, n. (*n*).

[3] E. III. 317,13, they are described as the *offspring of Tanen who completed* (*ir*) *his work* (*kꜣt*).

[4] Cf. p. 21.

[5] Cf. p. 140.

to have been embodied.[1] A closely similar situation seems to have occurred on the *pāy*-land of *Djeba* after the foundation ground of the temple was created. Tanen, again, proceeded to establish the protection around the god and conducted him in the most sacred place of the enclosure thereafter.[2] It appears that this manner in which the protection was constituted by the Earth-God may anticipate the main functions of the *Mansion of the God*, and, perhaps, through this procedure one of the characteristics of the temple was created: the permanent and eternal protection of the god upon the Earth. If this deduction be correct, it would mean that Tanen through symbolic actions initiated the creation of what was the concrete form of the protection of the god. He also contributed to completing the real nature of the temple by giving it its names.[3] In giving names to the temple Tanen consecrated it for its purpose: *to protect the god*. The temple, as an entity, was constituted on land which by its own nature was capable of protecting; it was a land of ancestral tradition. It does not appear that the land by itself could ensure absolute safety to the god. There was obviously a need to give material expression to what was natural in essence and implied in the land itself. This act, so far, was the duty of the Earth-God represented by Tanen. It follows that the divine power which was believed to reveal itself as the *protection* was believed to be the only authority capable of effecting this act. This circumstance bears out another argument to support the theory concerning the close link between the temple, the Earth-God and the Earth.

The history of the Solar Temple presents an analogous situation. Tanen is said to be present on the spot with his soldiers, who exercised the protection of the god before the elementary type of enclosure was constructed.[4] Tanen was also present on the site when the first enclosure was laid out. Although the text is rather obscure, it can be assumed that the episode of *Stretching of the Cord* was preceded by the performance of a magical rite which seems to have been performed again by Tanen.[5]

When the construction of the Solar Temple had been completed, Tanen is said to have come with Rēᶜ to see the house of

[1] Cf. p. 23. [2] Cf. p. 249. [3] Cf. p. 255.
[4] Cf. p. 34. [5] Cf. p. 36.

the god. The first act that was then to follow was the ceremony of *giving names*. We suggested that this ceremony has every appearance of *the bringing of the temple to life*.[1] It is quite certain that through this procedure only could the temple as an entity be believed to acquire its essential and final function: when given names the temple could exercise the protection of the god. We think that at this point there is an analogy with the manner of setting out the protection in the ancestral field; the staffs could not act unless they were given names. The final episode of this ceremony was again performed by the god-protector; Tanen conducted the lord of the temple to his sanctuary. As has been suggested, this act resembles the ceremony of the *handing over the temple to its lord* of the later historical temples.[2] The remarkable fact which seems to derive from all these allusions is that the ultimate phases in the process of the creation of the temple, by means of which it was brought to its real life, were completed by an Earth-God. The significance of this ceremony stresses, therefore, the link between the temple and the Earth-God, Tanen, and is another argument in favour of the theory that the temple was believed to be the direct outcome of the Earth. It is, therefore, natural that the Egyptians regarded Tanen, who existed before the first temple was created, as the *Ancestor* (*ḏfn*) of the temple.[3] We have pointed out in our discussion of the creation of the sacred domains of the Falcon how important was the element of ancestry in that creation.[4] In the final stage of all the phases that contributed to make the temple complex, there again the main part is played by an *Ancestor* who opened the temple to its life. A further fact to be recalled in this connexion is that in its elementary structure, the temple restored the *Enclosure* (*ḥwt*) in which the *Earth-Maker* was believed to dwell during the first phase of the existence of the island of creation.[5] In this fact lies the most important part of the theory concerning the creation of the temple. The *Earth-Maker* is said

[1] Cf. p. 248 ff. [2] Cf. p. 252 ff.

[3] Our records use two words in describing the *Ancestor*, *mꜣ* and *ḏfn*; for *Mꜣ* cf. above, p. 193, n. 3; *ḏfn* seems to be the name borne only by Tanen, cf. E. IV. 1,14; VI. 18,8; 174,11; 324,6; M. 81,8.9; *KO*, I, 240, no. 340; *Urk*. VIII, 141, 11; *ASAE*, III, 55; the meaning *ancestor* is clearly set out by the instances in E. IV. 278,1 and V. 62,17.

[4] Cf. pp. 166, 186. [5] Cf. p. 99 ff.

to have been the first divine being who had a *ḥwt*, *mansion*, as his resting-place. And this Earth-God seems to have been associated with this type of enclosure as far as its final stage of development. In the account of the *Festival of Entering the Temple* as it is known from the Myth about the origin of the Solar Temple,[1] the *Earth-Maker* is said to have been carried in before the legitimate lord of the temple took hold of it. This does not appear a mere ritual episode, but rather an act which derived from a doctrinal idea. The Earth-God was present in the temple at the time when this was definitely given to life. His symbolical presence in the temple might have been regarded as one of the means which ensured the continued existence of the temple.

The fact that the power of ensuring protection was conferred by the Earth-God on the temple after it was constructed, brings to mind yet another episode which was believed to have happened in the early stages of the existence of the primaeval island. The text of the first cosmogonical record explains that when the commands of the *Ka* had been made known to the Falcon resting on his Perch, the enemies appeared.[2] As a result the *Protector-god* revealed himself and was followed by another deity named *Ptḥ-nywt*, who also bears the name *The God-of-the-Temple*.[3] The God-of-the-Temple is known only from the Edfu account and none of the later Memphite documents alludes to him. This deity had apparently a cult which was celebrated at the Edfu temple. We find among the inscriptions decorating the outer walls of the Edfu Naos two ritual scenes[4] the texts of which supplement and accord with the allusions in the main cosmogonical records. We do not think that the belief in this *God-of-the-Temple* derives from a distinctly Edfu tradition. We incline to the opinion that the Edfu sources allude to a genuine belief. This *God-of-the-Temple* is said to have taken form in Tanen, the *First among the Ancestor Gods*. He was thus an Earth-God, who was born in Nun, from which he came to protect the successor of the Creator, the *Flying Ba*, from his enemies. The immediate result of his presence in the Island of Trampling was that the *sbḫt*-enclosure was created around the ancestral field of *Wetjeset-Neter*, and the Mansion (*ḥwt*) of the

[1] Cf. p. 39.
[2] Cf. pp. 19–20.
[3] Cf. p. 130.
[4] E. IV. 103, 9–13; 259,4–9.

Earth-Maker was restored. He summoned the two Shebtiw and gave them the order to create (*nḥp*). The result of this was that the *pāy*-lands were brought into existence. In the following narrative, however, there is no more reference to him. He is not mentioned at the time when the two last *pāy*-lands were created, which were ordered by the *Ka*, nor does he appear at the foundation of the temple in these original *pāy*-lands. It has also been noticed that in the account of the actual foundation and building of the temple of *Wetjeset-Neter* neither the Protector God nor the God-of-the-Temple is mentioned. They do not intervene in the foundation of the Solar Temple.

At first sight, in view of his previous activities, the absence of the *God-of-the-Temple* seems to be strange and unexpected. No explanation of his absence is ever given in the Edfu records; hence we are reduced to speculation. We suggest that the explanation may be found in the general Egyptian conception of the essential nature of the temple. It is well known that in historical times the temple was regarded as a living entity, that as a result of the performance of certain ceremonies the temple, its reliefs and its statues were thought to be animated and to be filled with latent life.[1] At this point we should stress the ceremony of *Opening of the Mouth*, the significance of which is known to us mainly from the Edfu evidence.[2] The account of the ritual of the *Consecration of the Temple* which was in use at the Edfu Temple refers to a rite of *wp-rȝ n Wṯst, the Opening of the Mouth in Wetjeset.*[3] The significance of this rite permits us to say that the rehallowing of the temple was, in fact, the reanimating of the temple. We may suggest that not only was the temple filled with life, but in a sense it was a living being. This, perhaps, may appear a new and original suggestion since it is never explicitly stated elsewhere. But surely, when one recalls that Tanen made the temple by conferring names on it, or that Rēᶜ-Harakhte adored the *Great Seat*, there will be a little doubt that the temple was regarded as a living being. Moreover, attention should be drawn to the *Morning Hymns*[4] in which the actual temple is awakened in precisely the same way as Horus

[1] Cf. Junker, *Stundenwachen*, p. 6; Blackman, *JEA*, v, 159; xxi, 6 ff.; Blackman and Fairman, *Misc. Greg.* p. 6; also *JEA*, xlviii, 84–7.

[2] Blackman and Fairman, *JEA*, xxxii, 75–91.

[3] E. iv. 313,13.

[4] Cf. p. 5.

the Behdetite and the co-templar deities. The temple itself and all its parts are addressed as an animate being who sleeps during the hours of darkness. When these facts are borne in mind, it is not unreasonable to conclude that the temple in fact was looked upon as a divine being. If this be so, it follows that the foundation and construction of the temple must have been the giving of concrete, material shape to a divine being who, originally, was conceived as a god. The *God-of-the-Temple* would not be mentioned at the foundation and the building of the temple because he *was* the Temple. Hitherto a definite personality but intangible, the temple, once built, gave him concrete, material form. Thus the temple as an entity would be the embodiment of the *God-of-the-Temple*, the *Son of Tanen*; hence, in its fundamental significance, the temple was the *Son of the Earth*. Consequently the ultimate outcome of the long-drawn-out process of the creation of the Earth was the concrete shape of the Son of the Earth, and this was the everlasting protection of the divine being who represented the embodiment of the Soul of the Earth-God.

We find in the interpretation of the abstract nature of the temple the ideas which are well known from the Egyptian conception of the connexion between a statue and a person. To illustrate the belief in the 'becoming immanent' reference should be made to the text of the Shabaka Stone in the first place. It is stated that Ptah

formed their body...Then the gods entered into their body (*ḏt*) of every kind of wood, every kind of stone, every kind of metal.[1]

The belief that the statues could become immanent is demonstrated by the rites of the Osiris cult.[2] One of the prominent ceremonies of this cult is that a model mummy of Osiris was used in the annual rite of the re-enactment of Osiris' embalmment. Through the ceremonial bandaging of a model mummy accompanied by the uttering of prescribed formulae the god was thought to become immanent in the figure.[3] This rite is interpreted in the *Ritual of the Khoiak Festival* in the following terms:

As for the fourth month, last day, the raising of the *ḏd*-pillar (takes place) in Busiris on this day of interring Osiris in the region (*iꜣt*) of

[1] Shabaka Stone, ll. 58–9.
[2] Cf. Junker, *Abaton*, p. 42.
[3] Cf Blackman, *JEA*, v, 159, n. 8.

Bāḥ in the vault under the *išdt*-tree, for it is on this day that the divine body (*ḥʿw*) of Osiris enters into him after the bandaging of Osiris.

This quotation from the *Ritual of the Khoiak Festival* is relevant to the mythical history of the temple in the first place through the allusion to the raising of the *ḏd*-pillar,[1] which is associated with the mystic act of the god's entering into his body. We discussed the funerary associations which the temple of the *wr, the Eldest One*, was believed to have had, and its connexion with the *ḏd*-pillar of the primaeval age. Here, it is to be observed that the temple, when constructed, was imagined as being the *ḏt*-embodiment, the physical shape into which the divine body, here the *God-of-the-Temple*, was believed to enter. These trends of thought may, perhaps, explain also the part played by the Earth-God at the *Festival of Entering the Temple.*[2] The Earth-God was believed to have entered into the image carried into the temple, and thus he was there present in his mysterious life.

The first function which the *God-of-the-Temple* completed in the primaeval island was the protection of the divine being who was the living image into which the Soul of the Creator entered. The *God-of-the-Temple* seems to symbolize and anticipate in his appearance what was the eternal protection of the god: *the temple.*

A further deduction that can be made from these allusions is that there seems to be a relationship between this *God-of-the-Temple* and the *Ka*. It is known that the temple as a physical entity was commanded by the *Ka*. Hence, the *Ka*, as a deceased deity, would appear as ordering the creation of the *ḏt, physical body*, into which the divine body represented by the Son of the Earth-God is to enter in order to form the protection of the living image of the Soul of the Earth-God. That this was the Egyptian belief is abundantly clear from the order of the creation of the domain of the Falcon. The *Ka* would not be mentioned as giving the instructions as to how to fashion the Perch, he would not be described as selecting the land which was the birth-place of the temple, if he were not related to the animate form of the temple, the *Son of the Earth*. It is, therefore, evident that the *Ka*, who is the first divine being from among the Ancestor Gods to appear at the beginning of this drama of creation, might have also been

[1] Cf. p. 123 ff. [2] Cf. p. 254 ff.

an Earth-God. His private realm was then the only place in which the intangible *God-of-the-Temple* could undergo the metamorphosis to receive his final and concrete form. This will be a decisive argument in favour of the theory that the temple as an entity was the direct outcome of the creation of the Earth. It is, therefore, natural to expect that, because the temple was regarded as an animate being it was believed that the temple had also its *Ka*. The *Ka* of the temple appears to be the deceased Earth-God of our myth. This hypothesis will accord with what another Edfu detail reveals, in which an allusion is made to the *Ka-of-the-Earth* in connexion with the temple. It is, therefore, appropriate to mention here once again the spell in which Rēʿ-Harakhte adored the *Great Seat* saying:

As long as the Ka-of-the-Earth lives for me, I made thee as (my) Per-khāʿw in the Mansion of the God.[1]

This spell seems to indicate the view that the Earth, indeed, was believed to have its *Ka*. And the existence of the *Ka*-of-the-Earth made it possible for the material shape of the Son of the Earth to be effected and multiplied thereafter. As the *Ka* was believed to be the founder of the temple, and here we read that the life of the *Ka*-of-the-Earth was the essential prerequisite for the creation of the temple, it follows that both the *Ka* as the dead god and this present *Ka* were most probably the same divine being. The dead ruler is the *Ka* of the Earth, and consequently he is the *Ka* of the temple. There is, therefore, supplementary evidence for the belief that the temple, after having been founded, was the memorial of the *Ka*. The concrete likeness of the Son of the Earth is the memorial of the Father.

A further deduction that can be made from this order of ideas is that the Earth, eventually represented by the Earth-God, was the *Ancestor* of the temple. The *Ancestor* (*ḏfn*)[2] of the temple is another new fact that has emerged from the analysis of the Edfu records. From the point of view of the conception of the temple as an animate being, this idea appears to be logical. This also explains why the Egyptians believed that the Earth-God is the

[1] Cf. pp. 233–4.

[2] This belief may throw some light on the association between the god and the *Ancestor* briefly mentioned in E. VI. 324,6, cf. above, p. 40

deity who had completed the creation of the temple. In giving the temple names the Earth-God, represented by Tanen, made an existing unit of the temple; he imparted to it the mysterious life of the Earth-God. Since the temple was in fact the Son of the Earth, the Earth-God in giving it names brought to life the physically real likeness of his son.

These beliefs exemplify the significance of the *reign of Tanen* and make it clear why the period in which the temples were created bears his name. Tanen was the chief divine personality who stood behind all the acts of creation. They are peculiar to the myth about the origin of the temple of the Falcon. No equivalents are found in the myth about the Solar Temples, which is more concerned with the presentation of a coherent picture of the growth of the temple itself. This myth refers to a later part of the history of the Egyptian temple. It is only the history of the temple in *Wetjeset-Neter* that reveals that the significance of the temple, all its characteristics and functions, were determined by the nature of the deity who entered into it and remained in his mysterious life in it as long as the temple existed on the Earth. Once the God-of-the-Temple entered into it and the temple gave him a concrete, material shape, it could be multiplied, and other temples could be created and founded over all the country, and thus the temples could everywhere claim to be the concrete shape of the *Son of the Earth*.

The major idea that underlies the creation theory implicit in the Edfu records is the metamorphosis of the unreal, the abstract and the symbolic to produce the concrete and the physically real. It was through the metamorphosis of the symbols that the lands of the sacred domains came into existence. The same process occurred in the origin of the temple itself. Its origin derived from the metamorphosis of the god who was believed to be the Son of the Earth.

To emphasize the link between the temple and the animate beings yet another tradition should be referred to. We know that the Builder Gods were believed to have constructed the temple, but very little is said of how they proceeded. It appears rather strange that the records mention the general line of their activities and refer to the fashioning of the outer enclosing wall and erecting of the sanctuaries. A tradition of a later date can be added, telling us that the Egyptians believed that the temple, described as the *Great Seat of Rēᶜ-Harakhte from the Primaeval Time*, was fashioned by the Builder Gods on their potter's wheel.[1] Since the Builder Gods are known as creators of animate beings in the first place and the temple is included in their creative work, there is another argument in favour of the theory that the temple was conceived to be a living being.

[1] E. IV. 343,10–13.

CHAPTER 19

The Temple Ancestor

The chapters from the 'history' of the mythical temples would not be engraved on the walls of the temple at Edfu if the Egyptians did not believe that their mythical lifetime had a direct bearing on the existence of the actual temple and that they were the starting-point in the existence of the latter. It is not improbable that the Edfu tradition claimed a relationship between the *Mythical Temple in Wetjeset-Neter*, the *Solar Temples* and the physically real *Temple of Horus the Behdetite* at Edfu. If this suggestion be admissible, the cosmogonical records will disclose the picture of what can reasonably be described as the *mythical past* of the temple at Edfu.[1] These texts would seem to yield the events and causes from which the Egyptians believed that the House of the god on the Earth derived, and which formed its characteristics.

The idea of a relationship between the historical temples and the sacred places of a mythical nature is, in fact, well known. Frequent are the instances in temple inscriptions in which the historical temple is equated with the *st n sp tpy*, the *Seat of the First Occasion*.[2] None of the texts known, however, explains the significance of this vague expression, the nature of this *Seat of the First Occasion*; nowhere is there any description of the origin and the development of the sacred entity on which the Egyptians looked as on the seat of the god in the primaeval age. Doubtless, the Edfu documentary sources are unique evidence to illustrate the Egyptian conception of the *Seat of the First Occasion*. They exemplify in great detail the idea of the mythical entity from which the actual temple took origin, and make it clear that the Egyptians believed that their temples developed from the abstract to the concrete.

The 'history' of the mythical temples recorded in the sacred book known as the *Specification of the Sacred Mounds of the Early Primaeval Age* seems to constitute the first phase in the life of the historical temple and is an integral part of its existence. The

[1] Cf. p. 4 ff. [2] Cf. p. 43 ff.

Egyptian idea seems to have been that the temple in its physical existence made concrete what had happened and what had existed before the dawn of history. In its foundation and building the temple revivifies the memorial built for the *Ka* in the mythical age; it imitates the house which was erected to protect the embodiment of the Soul of the Creator; the actual temple would seem to give a repeated continuity to the material form of the Son of the Earth. In brief, the cosmogonical records seem to allude in the first place to the belief in the continued rebirth of a sacred entity which after a certain period of life had disappeared, but was reborn in a new entity. This one bears the characteristics of its antecedent and reaches a further development. The mythical temple had its *Ancestor* in the Earth-God described as the *ḏfn*-Ancestor. He made from the outcome of the creation of the Earth the temple as the House of the god; in the same way the mythical temple as the work of the creator god seems to assume the function of the Temple-Ancestor of the real temple built as the House of the god of the Earth.

The close link of the Edfu temple with mythical cult-place is borne out by several sets of records which constitute a coherent series of documents. The Egyptians might regard them *as records of the mythical history of the temple*. A list of these accounts was already given in the introduction to this study.[1] Having analysed the cosmogonical texts, we must return to a number of these inscriptions which may be of special interest for the purpose of our study.

The best evidence of the belief in the *Temple-Ancestor* is furnished by the summaries of mythological narratives that were incorporated in the *Building Texts* which describe the history of the actual temple at Edfu. This temple is for the Falcon Horus the *Seat of the Primaeval Time* to which his statue was carried during the ceremonies of the *Handing over the House to its lord*.[2] The temple is the place where the god spends the day and sleeps during the night, and his dwelling-place is in its essential nature the *Blessed Place of the Soul which came into being at the Beginning*.[3] The foundation-ground of the actual temple is conceived as that deriving from the

[1] Cf. p. 7ff. [2] E. IV. 20,1–2.
[3] E. IV. 1,14.

primaeval time upon which the Builder Gods constructed the House of the God under the supervision of Ptah.[1]

It is appropriate to recall the ritual scene in which Thoth is depicted as offering a charter to Horus the Behdetite.[2] We suggested in the introduction that this scene implies that the cosmogonical records which follow have a direct bearing on the history of the actual temple at Edfu. Having discussed the contents of the cosmogonical records, we can hardly doubt that this divine charter meant the sacred book in which the history of the mythical temples was recorded. Evidently the Edfu temple claims for itself the honour that Thoth recorded the mythical past of this temple. The Egyptians might have believed that Thoth revealed to their chief god what his original house was, which his final house should resemble. But far more can be deduced from this simple ritual scene. There is brief but undeniable evidence of the belief in a direct continuity and relationship between a mythical temple which had once existed and had disappeared, and the historical temple. We know what was, according to the tradition, the culminating act of the mythical *reign of Tanen*: the creation of the Temple in *Wetjeset-Neter*. This temple was believed to have determined the origin of the temple of Horus at Edfu. This scene manifests the belief that the sacred entity which began its existence in the reign of Tanen continues to live in the actual temple. The mythical Temple in *Wetjeset-Neter*, is then revivified and is actually embodied in the existence of the temple of Horus the Behdetite at Edfu. The ritual scene which is added to the first cosmogonical record intimates the same belief.[3] It pictures a scene of adoration performed in *Wetjeset-Neter* which was believed to enshrine the Perch, the seat of the Falcon in the primaeval age. The god adored there was the *Sanctified God who came into being at the First Occasion*; this god, then, is in the Edfu tradition the living god, Horus the Behdetite.[4]

These two instances seem to reveal what was the essential feature of the organization of the actual temple. The god of the

[1] E. IV. 5,7. [2] Cf. p. 5.

[3] E. VI. 181,6–10 = XIV. Pl. DLXI.

[4] E. VI. 181,9–10; the king addresses Horus the Behdetite who is the Living One (*ʿnḫ*), who is, as the 'Sanctified God', adored in the Pronaos of the Edfu Temple.

historical temple was believed to be identical in his nature with the divine being who was sanctified *at the First Occasion*, the primaeval Falcon, the *Lord of the Djeba* (Perch).[1] Therefore, the place where the god was adored during historical times was conceived as being identical with the place where the Falcon was sanctified in the primaeval age of the gods,[2] and where he was acclaimed first as the god (*ntr*).[3]

This view is also illustrated by the *Building Text* of the Pronaos. The temple at Edfu is described as the *Great Seat* of Harakhte of which the true name is *Djeba since the gods of the Djeba (Perch) established it as the djeba (perch) of reeds.*[4]

Further evidence of this theory can be found in the scene of adoration of the *Gods of the Perch* (*ḏbꜣw*), who are the Shebtiw of our creation story.[5] The *Djeba* (Perch) is defined as the *Seat of the First Occasion* (*st n sp tpy*) of the Falcon, and the mythical event of the *Planting the Perch*[6] is projected into the situation of the actual temple at Edfu. This temple, so far as the Edfu tradition is concerned, includes and repeats the existence of the mythical domain on the edge of the primaeval island, the *Djeba in Wetjeset-Neter*, the creation of which was believed to have revivified and resurrected the existence of the vanished world of the Creator.[7]

The Edfu texts furnish further useful material which makes it possible to reconstruct the mythological situation with which the Egyptians surrounded the foundation of the historical temple. We have already referred to the lists of 'mythological names' which are incorporated in the main *Building Texts* of the Edfu temple.[8] We also suggested that they appear in many respects to be very brief summaries of various mythological narratives which described events which the Egyptians believed had a bearing on the history of their temple. Since these mythological names show a striking resemblance to what can be gleaned from the cosmogonical records, we suggest that these lists were written at Edfu with reference to the cosmogonical records. They had, most probably, the purpose of specifying what was believed to be

[1] E. VI. 182,9 and above, pp. 15–16.
[2] Cf. p. 307ff.
[3] E. VI. 182,10.
[4] E. IV. 328,5.
[5] Cf. *ZÄS*, LXXXVII, 52–4.
[6] E. IV. 358,3 and above, p. 14.
[7] Cf. p. 121.
[8] Cf. p. 5.

the mythical prototype of the historical temple of Horus and of describing briefly the characteristics of the ancestral temples which were believed to have determined the existence of the Edfu temple. The name-lists in the main Edfu *Building Texts* differ markedly from the shorter lists to be found in each cult-room or hall of the Edfu temple, and we do not doubt that they define the temple as a whole. It is worthy of note that in none of these lists is the Edfu temple referred to as the *Temple of Horus the Behdetite*. We read in them names of the sacred places of the Falcon in the primaeval age, the names of the mythical temples of the Sun-God, and finally names which summarize the events which were believed to have occurred in the far distant sacred domains and led to the foundation of the first temple of the Falcon and that of the Sun-God.

The list of names to be found in the *Building Texts* of the inner face of the Enclosure Wall presents us with a real summary of the *Myth about the origin of the domain and the Temple of the Falcon*. The temple of Horus at Edfu is interpreted as a place in which the god was believed to unite with his *sakhemu*, and a place of such a nature was believed to be the *First Province of the Falcon*. In the following series of names we find those already known from the first cosmogonical record, such as:

The Blessed Island of the Child; the Ancestral Territory of the Falcon; the Place of the Gods-of-the-*ḏd*-pillar since they were there from the primaeval time; the Mound of the Radiant; the Great Mound of the Ḥeter-ḥer; the Island of the Fury; the Place for Piercing; the Djeba of the God of Djeba; the Field of reed of the Soul; the Place of the Winged One; the Hill of the Soul; the Great Seat of Rēᶜ, the Eldest.[1]

This document seems to aim at proving that the actual temple could exist only in a place which by its nature was identical with the spot of the primaeval age in which the first resting-place of the god was created. Therefore, it appears that the names of the far distant, mythical cultus-places were regarded as the first means of proving the relationship and the continuity between what was and what exists. The Egyptian theory seems to have been that when the site of the actual temple was given names of the mythical

[1] E. VI. 11,1–9.

sacred places, it then acquired the nature of the former and could represent its continuation in the present days. The same idea is apparent from the names of the Edfu temple which we find in the *Building Text* of the Naos; the Edfu temple is said to be

the Throne-of-gods of the Deities of the Primaeval Age of gods, the Seat-of-the-Two-Gods, Rēᶜ and his ancestor Tanen, the Blessed Homeland (*hìn*) of their company of gods and the Mansion of *Ms-nḫt.*[1]

It is essential to mention here the name-list of the *Building Text* of the outer face of the Enclosure Wall, which is the most expanded document of this sort. This long list confirms that the sets of mythological names of the historical temple were not deliberately compiled, but were rather abbreviated copies of mythological records kept in the temple. We pointed out in the introduction to this study[2] that this list alludes to the *Sacred Book of the Temples* which was drawn up with reference to the historical temples according to a much earlier source; this then, it is highly probable, was the sacred book called the *Specification of the Sacred Mounds of the Early Primaeval Age.* The comparison of these two sacred books kept in one single temple shows that the word *gs-prw*, *temples*, replaces the expression *ỉ3wt n p3wtyw*, *the Sacred Mounds of the Early Primaeval Age.* The temples (*gs-prw*) of historical Egypt are here equated with the *ỉ3wt*, the *Sacred Mound.* If this equation be admissible, there is, therefore, an undeniable argument for the theory that the temples of historical times were regarded as descending from the genuine sacred places of the mythical age of the gods.

In the part of the *Sacred Book of the Temples* that survives on the wall of the Edfu temple names such as *Wetjeset-Neter*, the Great Seat, *Djeba*, Behdet, *Mesen* and the Mansion-of-the-god-of-the-Great-God are stressed. Explanations of their meaning are added and these explanations reflect the ideas contained in the main cosmogonical records, or summarize the events described in the principal sources. Several names included in this book appear to be artificial ones, formed with a view to summarizing various

[1] E. IV. 1,14 – 2,1.
[2] Cf. p. 6.

mythological events which were associated with the original cultus-places of the Falcon. The contents of this name-list make it clear that this record has every aspect of being a brief summary of the original sacred book of the *Specification of the Sacred Mounds*. It shows also that the myths and old traditions of the original cultus-places were used and re-used and applied to the sacred places of protohistoric and historic times; finally the same traditions were used to explain the origin of the last sacred place of the Falcon: the temple at Edfu.

The evidence of the name-lists recorded on the walls of the temple seems to show how important was the *mythical name* in the history of the actual temple. The names seem to be the principal means that carries the original nature of a particular sacred place to another. We have seen that the first sacred place that was created when the new period of the primaeval age dawned, was made like its prototype that had vanished. We have also seen how important was the part played by the 'name' in that process of creation. The first sacred enclosure created for the Falcon on the *pāy*-land bore the same name as the first sacred domain, and seems to have been regarded as the continuation of an earlier sacred domain. We have already pointed to the importance of the mythological names when applied to the site of the temple. We think that with regard to the temple itself we meet exactly the same situation. The mythological names, when used with special reference to the historical temple, seem to have every appearance of an outline explanation of what the temple was before it came to be a real and physical entity.

These mythological names are, in fact, an epitome of the mythical past of the temple. They specify the ancient sites from which the actual temple was believed to have descended, the nature of which is enshrined in the historical temple and thereby revivified. They determine what the 'Temple-Ancestor' was, the pre-existence of which ensured the creation of the historical temple. At this point we came to the same conclusion as that suggested by the Edfu preamble to the cosmogonical records. These lists of mythological names are also evidence of the continuity between what was and what exists. That which had once existed ensures the origin, the life and the prosperity of a new entity. There seem to be the same trends of thought as those already known from the mythological story. It is known that the mythical temple in *Wetjeset-Neter* resuscitated the existence of the *Home of the Ka*. Here the actual temple of Horus restores the mythical temple and with it the genuine cultus-place in which the Falcon was adored first.

Also relevant are the inscriptions engraved on the cornice of the Pronaos and the Naos of the Edfu temple.[1] This set of short inscriptions is of value and interest. They contain definitions of the abstract nature of the historical temple which show ideas closely related to those in the main Edfu cosmogonical records.

The historical temple of Edfu is described as the temple of Rēᶜ in his primaeval age bearing the name *Mansion of Ms-nḫt*,[2] a name which was given to it by Tanen. It is explained that the Creator (), who is the Earth-Maker,[3] settled there and protects the sacred domains (*nìwt*) in his great mysterious form of the Behdetite, and the Lord of the Wing (*ndm ndb*) safeguards his domain (*nìwt*).[4]

The major idea put forth in this short text is that the site of the Edfu temple was believed to be, in its symbolical nature, similar to the foundation ground of the mythical Solar Temple, the *Mansion of Ms-nḫt*, the origin of which is known from the Edfu cosmogonical records.[5]

This set of inscriptions proceeds to tell us that the Edfu site is the place of the Soul,[6] the Place (*st*) of the *Ancestor* (*Mꜣ*), the *Ancestor* of the gods who protects his children, the Great Place (*bw-wr*) of Rēᶜ,[7] the god's throne of the primaeval time in which *Ḥeter-ḥer* protects the Mansion-of-the-God.[8] It is also the Mound of the Horizon God,[9] the Resting-place of the *sjꜣ*-Falcon;[10] the Sanctified Ruler settled there while protecting the mansions of the gods within his Great Seat from the Primaeval Time; the *Pn*-God, the *ḏrty*-Falcon protects the sanctuary (*mꜣr*) of the god;[11] the Throne of the *ḏrty*-Falcon who protects the sanctuaries of the

[1] E. III. 199,10–206,9 = IV. 157,13–170,7 and 314,6–326,2.

[2] E. III. 199,11 = IV, 13.

[3] E. III. 199,12 = IV. which gives the full writing of *ìr-tꜣ*.

[4] E. III. 199,13–14.

[5] Cf. p. 245.

[6] E. III. 200,3.

[7] E. III. 201,5–6.

[8] E. III. 201,8.

[9] E. III. 201,14.

[10] E. III. 202,12.

[11] E. III. 202,14–15.

ḏrty-Falcons, and who uplifted himself over the gods,[1] and the *Ḥeter-ḥer* again is said to exercise the protection of his mansion.[2]

Very little needs to be added to demonstrate the resemblance between the ideas enshrined in these short descriptions and those known from the main cosmogonical records. Since the idea of the 'protection' in this connexion is repeated on several occasions, it is evident that the sacred place, which was equivalent in its nature to the god's seat of the primaeval time, was believed to be capable of ensuring the protection of the god in historical times.[3]

The texts bearing on the foundation and the building of the temple at Edfu offer many decisive arguments to support the theory concerning the 'relationship' as well as the idea of the *Temple-Ancestor* which was believed to have been revivified in the existence of the historical temple.

It is apposite to recall a passage from the *Building Text* of the Naos only briefly mentioned in the introduction.[4] As has been said, this text is evidence that the foundation and the building of the historical temple was considered as being on a par with the creation of the mythical temple in which the Creator gods acted themselves. The text of this record reads:

Stretching the cord in *Wetjeset-Neter*, laying out the foundation of the Great Seat of Harakhte. The King himself, his hands were on the pole while grasping the cord together with Seshat in order to set it up according to the words of the God-of-the-Throne on the blessed land of his domain, in order to lay out its four corners, to found its *wrmw* (?) and to construct its sanctuaries according to the norm.

He-who-is-south-of-his-Enclosure had done it in the past. He had erected the four corners upon its four sides. Seshat the Great loosed the cord over it (lit. its cord). Tekh directed the rites (lit. conducted that which should be done or performed). The Builder Gods set firmly its four sides (*ỉfdw*). The Ogdoad rejoiced while marching around them. The Sages sanctified its *ỉḫt* (sacred substances ?). He-who-is-in-Khenmu increased its renown (*swr mdw.s*, lit. made great its

[1] E. III. 204,14–15.

[2] E. III. 204,17.

[3] In this set of inscriptions there is expressed the idea that *the Great God is protected in his seat of the Primaeval Age*, E. III. 201,8.

[4] E. IV. 14,4–10, and above, pp. 4–5.

matters). It is the Ka who gives thanks for it for ever and ever... (?) the primaeval age. It is Tanen who established it while enshrining (*ẖr*) its lord.

In addition, a ritual scene bearing on the *Constructing of the Temple* which is to be found on the outer face of the Enclosure Wall,[1] reflects the same mythological situation. The ritual text reads:

Thy Temple is thine, having been constructed perfectly in the work of Ba-neb-hyt. Thy Majesty...to issue command in respect of it (?). Rēᶜ, the Eldest, having illumined the Two Lands, Tekh and Seshat the Great stretched the cord, the Builder Gods constructed the sanctuary(?) together. The Sages were together with them and made its foundation-ground greater than that in all the nomes.

Three other records can be mentioned which show obvious affinities with the idea that the origin of the actual temple was conceived as that of a mythical entity and consequently projected into the mythical age of the gods.

In a ritual episode of *Stretching of the Cord* engraved on the inner face of the Enclosure Wall, Thoth is represented as arriving at the foundation ground of the temple while reciting:

I came here in my true form upon the foundation ground of the Great Seat of Harakhte. I cause its long dimension to be good, its breadth to be exact, all its measurements to be according to the norm, all its sanctuaries to be in the place where they should be, and its halls to resemble the sky.[2]

Seshat is said to be there with Isden, while speeding the fashioning and the embellishment of the sanctuaries of the *Mansion of the Victory*.[3]

In a record incorporated in the cosmogonical texts the origin of the historical temple is described as being the foundation of the *Great Seat of Rēᶜ of the Primaeval Time*.[4] The *Builder Gods* are said to have come in haste

[1] E. VII. 49,4–9.

[2] E. VI. 168,10–169,3.

[3] For the *Mansion of Victory* cf. p. 35; here undoubtedly as a name of the mythical prototype of the temple.

[4] E. VI. 173,7–9.

to the Great Seat of Rēᶜ from the Primaeval Time, his eye expectant at their arrival. They constructed the Mesen in a blessed operation as the work of their skilful fingers upon the great foundation ground which *Sefekh-ᶜabwi* had made and Isden had drawn by his fingers at the command of Rēᶜ and Tanen, the company of the Early Primaeval Deities being in their train while praising Rēᶜ who created the Ka at the First Occasion, for ever and ever.

In closely related terms the foundation of the temple of Horus the Behdetite is described in another ritual episode of *Stretching the Cord over the temple.*[1] The temple is said to have been planned in *Wetjeset-Neter*. It was conceived as the laying out of the foundation ground of the Great Seat of Harakhte. Thoth is said to have specified the foundation ground of the Great Seat of Rēᶜ on the blessed territory of his domain, and to have given the dimensions of the temple and the Enclosure.[2] An additional record describing the *Builder Gods* tells us about the

Arriving at the Great Seat in the presence of their father Tanen and his grandson Horus, the son of their brethren. They issued command to their Majesties to construct the temple in order to alight therein. They placed the cubit of Tekh on their arms. Seshat, the Sages were together with them all.

Stretching the cord by Seshat. Rekh-sw was sanctifying. These Builder Gods established the four sides (*ỉfdw*) of their Enclosure (*ỉnb*), (even) the Enclosure of 300 by 400 cubits, 'Speedy of fashioning' men call its name. A sanctuary was therein, 'Great Seat' is its name. And all its sanctuaries are according to the norm.[3]

The link between the actual temple of Horus the Behdetite and the mythical temple of the Sun-God, the Great Seat, that can be deduced from the text of the ritual scenes at the Edfu temple, shows that the Edfu temple was regarded as the renewal, the restoration of the mythical *Great Seat of Rēᶜ from the Primaeval Times.*[4] This brings to mind the belief that Thoth recorded the ground plans of the *Great Seat* in the presence of Rēᶜ at the dictate of the Sages.[5] The Egyptians seem to have believed that the ground

[1] E. IV. 352,2. [2] E. IV. 352,12–14.

[3] E. IV. 353,4–8.

[4] This name occurs in the Edfu Texts in E. I. 70,16; 90,14; II. 33,10; 102,14; 107,14–15; IV. 353,10; 168,10; VI. 241,16; 173,7; VIII. 5,11.

[5] E. VI. 319,13–14.

plans of the historical temples were established according to what the Sages of the primaeval age revealed to Thoth. This belief recalls the episode of *swr iḫt, magnifying the substances,* which the Sages were believed to perform before the foundation of the mythical temples was laid out. The foundation and building of the temple, considered from this point of view, seems to repeat and renew the act in which the creation of this world culminated. The views and descriptions contained in the 'mythological records' of the historical temple are only an expanded version of what is very briefly indicated in the ritual scene which introduces us to the set of cosmogonical records to which we have referred on several occasions. The resemblance between these accounts and the cosmogonical records is striking. While using and adapting these records, the Edfu tradition evidently claims that the Edfu temple is the veritable descendant of the mythical temple that was created at the dawn of this world, that it is its true projection and reflexion, and that it preserves its genuine nature and all its characteristics. Consequently the Edfu temple was founded by the order of Tanen and Rēᶜ, and was founded on the land which by its nature was equal to the primaeval territory of the domain of the Sun-God. The foundation ground of the temple at Edfu was *the Blessed Territory of the God-of-the-Throne,*[1] *the Foundation ground of the Beginning,*[2] *the Blessed Territory from the time of the Primaeval ones,*[3] *the Field of the Wetjeset-Neter,*[4] *the Hinterland of the Primaeval Water* (*ḥbbt*).[5] Nevertheless, these texts present the idea that the site of the Edfu temple is equivalent to that of the Solar Temple. It is, therefore, reasonable to conclude that the *bw, foundation ground* of the historical temple at Edfu was conceived as being equivalent in its abstract meaning to the original *bw-tỉtỉ,* the *Place-for-Crushing*[6] of the mythical temple of the Sun-God. All these views find their conclusion in a statement frequently occurring in the main *Building Texts,* that the historical temple was founded in *the place* (*bw*) *in which it should be, even as the Ancestors first did in respect of it.*

On a foundation ground of such a nature and tradition was the building of the temple effected by the dictate of Ptah. Unlike the

[1] E. I. 23,7–8; III. 105,8–9; 114,10; IV. 4,8; VI. 6,4.
[2] E. VII. 44,14; 45,4.
[3] E. II. 30,9; III. 166,15; IV. 14,4; 73,12; 352,12–13.
[4] E. III. 166,16.
[5] E. III. 167,2.
[6] Cf. p. 36.

evidence of the main cosmogonical records Ptah is said to be the first divine power to create the first mansion of the god and to supervise the building of the temple complex. This shows that the Edfu tradition is not based on the original version of the myth about the temple in *Wetjeset-Neter* but refers to the tradition in which, under the influence of local beliefs, Ptah replaced the God-of-the-Temple.[1] It can, therefore, be assumed that the Edfu tradition renews the Memphite tradition of the myth about the origin of the first temple. If this be correct, there will be further corroborative evidence for the statements already expressed above.[2] The Edfu texts bearing on the abstract aspect of the foundation and building of the temple set out clearly that the early sacred buildings at Memphis were most probably made on the pattern of the prehistoric constructions in the region to the north of Memphis,[3] which the tradition looked upon as the starting-point in the history of the actual temples. Memphis would seem to have adopted not only the bare pattern of the construction, but also all the divine beings who were believed to be engaged in the creation of the temple, and with it also all the rites and traditions connected with the constructing of the primitive sacred buildings. But the chief god of the historical Memphis was superimposed on all the orders of creation. Although the mythical situation connected with the origin of the temple at Edfu shows a tradition strongly affected by the interpretation of a later date, it retains one of the essential thoughts of the original myth. The historical temple was believed to have been built as the *memorial for the Ka*, the *Ka-of-the-Earth*.[4] Another point of similarity to the mythical abode of the gods can be seen in the part played by the Earth-God in the building of the historical temple. Tanen is said to have conducted the lord of the temple in it at the festival of *Handing over the Temple to its Lord*.[5] This brings to mind the final episodes of the creation of the mythical temples.[6] Tanen, as the *Ancestor* of the temple, brought to life the mythical temple. He is, therefore, the *Ancestor* of any temple which derived its existence from the abode at the beginning of the world, and as *Ancestor*, he was believed to bring to life any historical temple. This mythological situation that was

[1] Cf. p. 293 ff. [2] Cf. p. 273 ff. [3] Cf. p. 262.
[4] Cf. pp. 309–10. [5] Cf. p. 309. [6] Cf. p. 256.

believed to have surrounded the origin of the historical temple can hardly be a local Edfu tradition. It may apply to almost any temple, and any temple in Egypt might have had in its possession such a set of records as are known from the Edfu temple, only adapted to suit local beliefs and traditions. The *Sacred Book of the Temples*[1] is a clear indication. It is, therefore, highly probable that in the Edfu records we have extensive evidence of a general theory applying to the essential condition of an Egyptian temple.

The Edfu temple was that of the Falcon Horus, who was regarded as the primaeval Falcon *sjꜣ*,[2] and as the *Sanctified God of the First Occasion*,[3] who succeeded the Earth-God. This temple was believed to have been founded in a place where the Earth-Maker dwelt. Moreover, the Edfu temple enshrines the tradition that this temple was founded in the same place as that of the secondary Mansions of the Falcon which became later on the first Solar Temple.

The temple was, in essence, the house of the successor of the Creator. It was also the home of all the divine powers who acted in the creation of the first temple. It is of interest to refer to the *Building Text* of the Pronaos of the Edfu temple[4] in which the divine inhabitants of the temple are listed. Side by side with the Falcon Horus and Tanen, the *Ancestor* of the temple dwelt at Edfu, and with him all the companies of deities who were engaged in the creation of the mythical temples: Isden and Seshat, the Sages, the Shebtiw, the Builder Gods, then the Sun-God with his Seven Souls and Fourteen Kas. It is, therefore, clear that the mythical *Temple of Ms-nḫt*, which was last to be created and was made to house all the creative deities,[5] found its renewal in the existence of the temple at Edfu. This belief offers decisive evidence to confirm the theory that the Egyptian temples were constructed on the basis of the old Memphite traditions.

The existence of the historical temple, therefore, was based on

[1] Cf. p. 6.

[2] In E. VI. 179,6 Horus the Behdetite is described as the *Sanctified god who came into existence at the beginning, the great sjꜣ-Falcon who came into being at the First Occasion*; for the primaeval *sjꜣ*-Falcon at Edfu, cf. E. VI. 183,7; 184,5; and III. 106,12; V. 44,10–11; 319,8; 319,12; 231,1.

[3] Cf. p. 16.

[4] E. III. 355,10–336,3.

[5] Cf. p. 245 ff.

the principle of the re-animating of a pre-existing entity, specifically on the restoration of the *Temple-Ancestor*. The Egyptians seem to have regarded the *Ancestor* pictured here as a mythical entity that bore the same name as the historical temple, and as the only means that provided the magical force that enabled the temple to come into existence. This magical force is defined as a kind of *protection*. We have seen this belief in the *protection* ensured by a power of ancestral nature from the very beginning of the history of the temple. It was believed to have started at the moment when the first sacred domain of the god was created on the edges of the primaeval island. From this very moment as far as the foundation and building we can follow in a direct line the belief that only the *Ancestor* or *Ancestors* provide the fitting circumstances for the creation of a new entity. This suggestion may, perhaps, add to the explanation of the significance of the relief in which Thoth is represented offering the sacred book to Horus the Behdetite, a scene which has already been recalled.[1] Thoth was believed to offer to the god the record of the past which was regarded as the essential element that ensured the life and the prosperity of the temple. A further deduction that can be made from this belief bears on the presence of the cosmogonical texts in the temple. Their presence in the temple, especially their being engraved on the walls, might have been regarded as one of the means that ensured the magical protection of the historical temple. This circumstance brings to mind the belief in the 'becoming immanent' to which we have already referred while discussing the abstract nature of the mythical temple.[2] If we recall the ceremony of the *Opening of the Mouth in Wetjeset*,[3] it appears that the conception which we meet with regard to the sculptures and statues on the walls of the temple, is projected in our myth into a mythological plane, and is here transferred into the life of the temple. When we project this episode, which was performed on behalf of the statue to imbue it with life, into the situation of the temple, the idea evidentally was that through the due performance of this rite the temple, as an entity and as an edifice, was enabled to become alive. In this manner the *Wetjeset* at the beginning of the world was re-animated in its existence. The ritual of the *Opening*

[1] Cf. pp. 5–6. [2] Cf. pp. 276 ff., 286 ff. [3] Cf. p. 294.

of the Mouth performed on behalf of the temple was the revivification of the magical power that resided in the abstract temple concept, the *Ancestor* of the temple, and thereby the mysterious life of the original House of the god was infused into the actual temple. The magic power that was believed to have resided in the texts bearing on the mythical past of the temple imparted to it the mysterious life of the original sacred entity.

CHAPTER 20

The Physical Appearance of the Temple at Edfu

We have seen that the Egyptians believed that the constitution of the historical temple was determined by a pre-existing entity of a mythical nature to which the historical temple was equivalent in its abstract significance. The temple is, in a strict sense, the concretizing of its Ancestor. It would be legitimate to enquire how far the belief in the symbolic relationship with the *Temple Ancestor* could have a bearing on the physical appearance of the historical temple.

The Edfu *Building Texts* disclose the tradition that the historical temple was constructed according to the words of the Creator[1] and that in its construction the temple was the work of the Ancestors.[2] On another occasion Horus the Behdetite is described as saying, *They found my house as the work of antiquity, and my sanctuary as the work of the Ancestors.*[3] The same document indicates that the original nucleus of the temple was *made like unto that which was made in its (temple) plans of the beginning.*[4] The adyton of the historical temple at Edfu was regarded as the god's *genuine Great Seat of the First Occasion.*[5] The Edfu texts tell us also of ancient books and writings which apparently were used for the constitution of the plans of the historical temple at Edfu. Much explicit information is given by the *Building Text* of the inner face of the Enclosure Wall; it is stated that the *Enclosing wall of the Throne of the Behdetite that surrounds the Great Seat in Upper Egypt is like unto the Enclosure of his Great Mansion in Lower Egypt.*[6] The same text also reveals that the King in constructing the Forecourt with the Pylon

made the protection around them in the form of this Enclosure at the four sides of all of them, even the four-sides building, according to that

[1] E. VII. 6,2.
[2] E. IV. 4,8; VI. 6,4.
[3] E. IV. 9,6.
[4] E. IV. 5,7.
[5] E. IV. 13,13.
[6] E. VI. 7,1.

which is (written) in the Book (*šfdw*) for Planning of the Temple which the Chief Lector priest Imhotep the Great, son of Ptah, had made.[1]

These quotations bring to mind the allusion to the ancient book which was believed to have descended from the sky to the north of Memphis.[2] It appears as though this book, which might have survived in the memory only, might have been incorporated in one of the drafts established according to the original version, and used as the starting-point in drawing the plans of the historical temples. This suggestion accords with what the two quotations from the Edfu *Building Texts* reveal; they point definitely to Lower Egypt as the place of the prototype constructions which were imitated at a later date in Upper Egypt. Moreover, they refer to yet another sacred book which is said to have contained drafts of ground plans of the temples. We cannot maintain the identity of these two sacred books. Since the second book, the *Book for Planning of the Temple*, is described as being from historical times and the authorship is attributed to Imhotep, it is possible that the second book was regarded as a later version of a sacred writing in which the description of the original sacred buildings was preserved. If we stress that the earlier, the mythical book, is described as having originated in a region to the north of Memphis, and the book of historical times was believed to have been established by Imhotep, it follows that the historical Memphis adopted and modified the pattern of the sacred buildings as they might have been constructed from reeds during prehistoric times in cultus-places belonging to the region which spread to the north from Memphis. Later, in the course of historical times, the ground plans of the early structures might have been elaborated to the stage which is known to us from the architecture of the Archaic Period and from the Old Kingdom.[3] The same plans then constituted the essential pattern of the building of the temples in historical times. The tradition looked upon them as on the work of Imhotep. The evidence from the Edfu texts propounds the view that the fundamental structure of the historical temple re-enacted the type of the early Memphite temples.[4] The Edfu textual evidence is not the only material of its kind. The inscriptions of the

[1] E. VI. 10,8–9. [2] Cf. p. 262. [3] Cf. pp. 263–6.

[4] Cf. Blackman, *JEA*, XXVIII, 87–8; Sethe, *Unters.* III, 130–1.

temple at Denderah, too, tell us that the temple was built according to an ancient book from the times of the 'Companions of Horus' which was also preserved at Memphis.[1] Hence, there is no doubt that the later constructions of Graeco-Roman times preserved and restored the original native type of sacred building.

Further illustration of the theory that the 'relationship' between the historical temple and its mythical *Ancestor* was not a mere tradition, but was based on real facts, can be found in general descriptions of the temple at Edfu. The organization of the actual temple reflects the physical appearance of its *Ancestor-Temple*. The overall dimensions of the historical temple were equal to those of its prototype, in other words, they were set up according to the ground plans of the ancient constructions of reeds. The overall dimensions of the Edfu temple were 90 by 110 cubits; its enclosure measured 300 by 400 cubits.[2] These measurements fit the descriptions of the first Solar Temple and also agree with the dimensions of the temple in *Wetjeset-Neter*.[3] It follows that the original nucleus of the Edfu temple built within the outer brick enclosure wall seems to reflect the physical appearance of the first unit of the Solar Temple,[4] and probably the original nucleus at Edfu imitates the aspect of the inner construction of the temple in *Wetjeset-Neter*.[5]

We know also from the cosmogonical records that the Solar Temple in the final stage of its development represented an entity of 240 by 90 cubits and that this complex was built within an outer enclosure of 300 by 400 cubits.[6] The Edfu enclosure (*inb*) was also 240 by 90 cubits.[7] At Edfu, of these 240 cubits, 110 cubits are occupied by the long side of the original nucleus, 90 cubits comprise the long side of the Forecourt, and 20 cubits represent the side dimension of the Pylon.[8] When this general division of the Edfu temple is compared to the overall aspect of the ground plan of the Solar Temple, we can here see definite points of contact. It looks as though the ground plan of the Edfu temple follows the pattern

[1] M.D. III, 78k, and Daumas, 'Le trône d'une statuette de Pépi Ier trouvé à Dendéra', *BIFAO*, LII, 165–70. The same tradition existed at Esna, cf. Sauneron, *Esna*, I, 65, n. 163.

[2] E. IV. 352,13–14.

[3] Cf. pp. 220, 240.

[4] Cf. p. 337.

[5] Cf. p. 333.

[6] Cf. p. 241.

[7] E. VI. 7,2–4; VII. 11,7.

[8] E. VII. 19,2–3.

of the early construction, but in an opposite direction. In the organization of the Solar Temple the first unit was a sanctuary of 90 by 20 cubits.[1] This would seem to correspond to the ground plan in which the Pylon was erected; the second unit, the courtyard (*ỉfdw*), would then correspond to the Forecourt at Edfu; the original nucleus would then re-enact the third unit of the mythical temple of the Sun-God. We know also that the Solar Temple was constructed in three successive phases.[2] The building of the Edfu temple, too, was effected in three phases.[3]

The *Building Texts* of the Edfu temple indicate that this temple as an entity consisted, in the main, of two units, the original nucleus or the Great Seat (*st-wrt*), which was framed within an enclosure forming thus a forecourt at its front, and an ambulatory around the main part of the temple.[4] The original nucleus was the principal residence of the Falcon. In the descriptions of this part of the temple the back central sanctuary is always named in the first place of the description. This circumstance and the position of the sanctuary within the temple reminds us of the importance which the back central sanctuary had in the development of the mythical temple in *Wetjeset-Neter*.[5] The position of the sanctuary accords with what we know about the most sacred part of the primitive sacred enclosures of the Archaic Period which we find represented on the seals of that period.[6] There is, at Edfu, a large court at the front of this back central sanctuary, which was filled with several cultus-rooms along the two side-walls, in the midst of which was placed the adyton. With the exception of all the subsidiary cultus-chambers, the general lay-out of this part of the temple resembles the ground plan of the temple in *Wetjeset-Neter*.[7] Moreover there are, at Edfu, at the south end of the court, two halls, just as there are in the organization of the mythical prototype. Although differences can be noticed in the detailed dimensions of the individual parts of the mythical temple in *Wetjeset-Neter* and those of the temple at Edfu, it seems possible that the set-up of the former might have been used as a starting-

[1] Cf. p. 334.
[2] Cf. pp. 245–7.
[3] Cf. Fairman, *BJRL*, XXXVII, 168 ff.
[4] E. VII. 12,6–7.
[5] Cf. pp. 223–4.
[6] Cf. p. 330.
[7] Cf. p. 332.

point for the ground plan of the original nucleus of the Edfu temple. In the history of the building of the Edfu temple the construction of this unit represented the first phase.[1]

In addition, during the second phase of the building of the Edfu temple, the Pronaos was erected at the front of the original nucleus.[2] The Pronaos at Edfu was the place where the Creator, Tanen, and all the deities engaged in the creation of the mythical temples, were believed to rest.[3] The date of its foundation and its function in the organization of the temple appear to re-enact the significance of the mythical temple of *Ms-nḫt*.[4]

At the end, during the third phase of the building, there were erected the Forecourt and the Enclosure (*ỉnb*), which formed an ambulatory around the original structure.[5] It is known from the Edfu texts that this part of the temple was used for the worship of the Sun-God.[6] We have already pointed out that this part of the historical temple has every appearance of re-enacting the main part of the mythical Solar Temple.

The analysis of the physical aspect of the temple at Edfu shows clearly that the organization of the temple was deliberately made, and was not an incidental one. Seeing the points of contact between the organization of the historical temple and that of some early constructions, made most probably of reeds and some other light material, we may assume that at Edfu we have a definite attempt to preserve the physical appearance of the original native constructions. It is tempting to think that, perhaps, in this way the tradition of the Edfu temple expressed the idea that this temple was not only a symbolical revivification of its mythical *Ancestor Temple* or temples; it was, in fact, a factual re-enactment of the ancestral temples.

The textual evidence of the *Building Texts* seems to indicate that the Edfu temple, as a physical entity, was believed to enshrine two distinct units which, primarily, were conceived as being of a mythical nature; each of these represented the natural outcome of various mythical events which were believed to have happened in a particular era of the mythical age of the gods. In the organiza-

[1] Cf. Fairman, *BJRL*, XXXVII, 167.
[2] E. III, 86,14–87,1.
[3] E. III. 355,10–356,3.
[4] Cf. pp. 243–4.
[5] E. VII; VI. 6,2–3.
[6] E. III. 355,7; V. 2,3; 3,3.

tion of the temple at Edfu we have, on the site of one single temple, the imitation of the earliest temple in which the Falcon was believed to have been adored first. In the actual temple the re-enactment of the early shrine and the enclosure of the Falcon assumed the function of the most sacred part of the temple; it was the principal place of worship of Horus in historical times. In the same temple there is a reflexion of the sacred enclosure which was believed to have acted as one of the early places of worship of the Sun-God. We can, therefore, see a close link between the principle that governed the organization of the temple at Edfu and the essential ideas enshrined in the cosmogonical records. It is evident that the set-up of the historical temple, which associates two originally separate units, was deliberate. The Edfu tradition seems to claim that the temple of Horus the Behdetite was not only a symbolical revivification of the temple in *Wetjeset-Neter*, but also its real likeness on the Earth; it was the concrete form of the house fashioned as the protection of the Falcon who consorted with the Soul of the Creator. In its own history the actual temple reflects the phases of the creation of the first house of the god.

The inscriptions engraved on the prominent architectural parts of the temple, especially those which are on the 'soubassement', constitute a valuable set of records which enable us to illustrate in great detail the history and organization, as well as the significance and functions, of the actual temple. A large book could be written on the basis of these documents. In our study we have sketched merely the barest outlines of the history of the actual temple. We do not enter into details of the organization of the historical temple since a proper study of the physical aspect and significance of the temple at Edfu is planned to be published later.

The records referring to the history of the actual temple at Edfu claim that the ideas that lie behind the constitution of the mythical temples are decisive moments in the history, the foundation and the building of the actual temple. We know from the myth that, when Horus settled in his primaeval domains together with Tanen, Rēᶜ joined them. After the enemy of the god was overthrown, then a settlement was made for Rēᶜ near an earlier mansion of the gods. These events appear to be decisive points in the history of the actual temple. They seem to underlie the principles of its organization. The main part of the Edfu temple represents the temple proper of the Falcon Horus. When this one was completed, near to it a cultus-place of the Sun-God was founded. This may explain why the Edfu temple as a whole represented two distinct sacred units. We find in the texts of the foundation ritual, recorded side by side, the name of *Wetjeset-Neter* and that of the *Great Seat of Rēᶜ*.[1] The historical temple, therefore, would concretize in its physical appearance that which had happened beyond the limits of historical times. It embodies in its existence the history of the sacred domains of the primaeval age. It re-enacts the aspect of the far distant mythical abodes of the gods; in this way the late temples of Graeco-Roman Egypt, in particular the Edfu temple, offer valuable evidence of the aspect and nature of the old native structures from predynastic times.

The traditions and beliefs attached to the early sacred places of Egypt constitute the *mythological history* of the actual historical temple. The Edfu temple was not only in its symbolical significance but also in its real appearance the original temple at the beginning of the world, the *Wetjeset-Neter* of the *Sanctified God*, the *Seat of the Eldest One of the Gods*.[2]

[1] E. IV. 14,4; 330,14; 331,4.9.14; 352,5.10.13.

[2] Cf. p. 236 ff.

APPENDIX

An Outline History of the Egyptian Temple[1]

The starting-point of this study has been a group of texts, most of them on the inner faces of the enclosure wall of the Ptolemaic Temple at Edfu, which on closer examination prove to be cosmogonical texts dealing with the creation of the Earth and the origin of sacred places. The information obtained from this group has been in part repeated and in part supplemented by a number of other inscriptions from other parts of the Edfu temple. As a whole, the texts are probably the most difficult and obscure in the whole field of Egyptology, and have never previously been studied. Many of the facts and ideas that they reveal have been hitherto unknown.

The Edfu records, as a whole, are a valuable source-book for the history of the Egyptian temple. They present us with a coherent account of the creation of the Earth in which is projected the history of the Egyptian Temple. It has been noticed that this theory of creation makes a distinct difference between the creation of the Earth and that of the rest of the world. The creation of the Earth, however, is interpreted as proceeding step by step with the development of sacred domains. The Egyptian theory evidently was that at the end of each of the succeeding phases of the creation of the Earth a sacred domain originated.

We have seen that this creation theory alludes to two distinct phases of the primaeval age, and that it was only in the second phase that the sacred domains that survived in historical times had originated.

The texts studied describe in the first instance how a primaeval island emerged from the primaeval waters. This island, in a way and for reasons unknown, disappeared. When it re-emerged and its life was renewed, new land began to form along its margins and it was on these lands, called *pāy*-lands, that the temple came into existence.

[1] Textual sources from which this study is derived, are found listed in chapter 1, see p. 7, n. 1, to p. 8, n. 5, for references.

The muddy island in the midst of Nun, therefore, was the original nucleus of the world of the gods. In it was the *Seat of the Creator* and the *Homeland of the Primaeval Ones*, the other creative powers; this is described as a definite, though primitive, cultus-place. As to the aspect of the Creator's resting-place, the Edfu records refer to four traditions: allusion is made to *the pool with the lotus* or *the field of reeds with the ḏd-pillar* or the elementary *ḥwt*-mansion, or finally the *place of the willow*.

This first sacred domain was destroyed, and darkness descended on the primaeval world of the Creators. It was revivified and as a land of ancestral tradition the original island assumed the function of a foundation ground for a new sacred domain from which the succeeding phases of the creation of the Earth emanated.

The second sacred domain in the original island had as its centre the *Perch*, a slip of reed in essence, which is said to be the principal instrument by which the sacred nature of the island was renewed. The creation of the sacred domain at the beginning of the second phase of the primaeval island started on the territory of the *Ancestors*. We are acquainted with three types of sacred places of the *Ancestors* in which, too, the cult of the new divine generation took origin. These are the *sbḫt*-enclosure around the Perch, the *ḥwt*-mansion, and the *sbty*-enclosure around the willow. The origin of these three enclosures, which could not be anything more than mere fences of light material enshrining a primitive resting-place of the god, is traced to the sacred places where the Falcon is said to be the first deity to be adored. The creation of these primitive sacred domains was, in fact, a resurrection and restoration of what had been in the past, but had vanished. And each of these three acts of re-creation of a former state resulted in a period of creation of new lands, the *pāy*-lands.

These *pāy*-lands, adjacent to the original island, were a vital element in the creation of the sacred domains of the Falcon in the primaeval age. They were primarily the realm of a dead deity, the *Ka*, and emerged after a magical rite of creation was performed on the edges of the island. The earliest part of their history is, in fact, a repetition and re-enactment of what was done in the ancestral domain: the erection of the seat of the god, which here, too, was the *Perch* and was set up on the marginal land of the *pāy*-land.

On the marginal land of the *pāy*-land once more the magical rite of creation was performed and bore out of Nun the surroundings of the *Perch*. This small area was of special significance. This was the *Home of the Ka* and this land became the foundation ground for the first enclosure of the Falcon, in which the temple evolved later on. Thus the *Perch* within a simple enclosure represents the elementary aspect of the first mansion of the Falcon.

Thereafter yet another phase of creation of lands followed and in these lands the *ḥwt*-enclosures were constructed as the earliest type of sacred building. In the same lands a new type of enclosure (*inb*) originated after a certain part of these *pāy*-lands containing the *First Place* was liberated from the enemy.

In the erection of these simple enclosures from reed around a primitive resting-place of the god a distinctive phase in the development of sacred domains was reached. It is demonstrated that each of the two rows of the *pāy*-lands had its own type of sacred enclosure.

Our sources speak of the origin of two types of temple: the temple of the Falcon and the temple of the Sun-God. Of these, the temple of the Falcon was the earlier, and was clearly regarded as the final and culminating act of the whole process of creation. This temple was a natural event. It originated in a primitive shelter of reed that was erected to protect the *Perch* on the water's edges on which the Falcon settled down; this shelter was the most sacred part of the elementary enclosure of the Falcon, and for this reason it was the first sanctuary of the primitive temple, which is described in detail and whose precise measurements are given.

This temple was oriented from north to south and was, in its elementary aspect, nothing more than a courtyard open to the sky and having one single sanctuary at its north rear wall. Then other cultus-rooms were added off the south wall of this enclosure, and finally this complex was surrounded by yet another greater enclosure. A temple of this aspect reflects a degree of development which was undoubtedly reached before the opening of historical times. A temple of this type was probably constructed in many places of predynastic Egypt.

The origin and growth of the temple of the Falcon constitutes the complete history of the first temple complex and illustrates the essential condition and nature of an Egyptian temple.

The starting-point in the creation of the second type of temple was the *inb*-enclosure surrounding the ground on which the temple evolved later on. This is the temple of the Sun-God, which was founded after creation had been completed. It was an artificial and somewhat arbitrary work, not showing points of contact with the natural growth of the temple of the Falcon, being rather of a more advanced and sophisticated type. It, too, is described in some detail and its dimensions are given.

This type of temple was, in its beginnings, a single rectangular sanctuary erected in the midst of a vast enclosure to the south of which a courtyard was made. Along the sides of this courtyard other chambers and halls were created, then yet another much bigger courtyard was made to the south of the already existing structure. Subsequently this complex was surrounded by a wall forming an ambulatory around these two courtyards.

Our documents seem to allude to yet another, much simpler, type of temple, said to be also that of the Sun-God. This consisted of a single enclosure enshrining one sanctuary only. At a somewhat later date a pronaos was erected at the south end of this enclosure.

These types of enclosures and primitive temples seem to reflect the development of sacred structures in a single region which, for this reason, may well be regarded as the *Homeland of the Temple*. The temples of this *Homeland* seem to represent the starting-point in the history of the actual temples in Egypt.

A very brief survey was made of our present knowledge of early temples in Egypt. There are no primitive temples known that preserve the precise form and dimensions of the mythical temples of the Edfu records, but it is demonstrated that there are numerous points of contact and resemblances and that, perhaps surprisingly, there appear to be definite links with the Archaic Cemetery at Sakkara.

The Edfu narrative acquaints us equally with the tradition according to which the site of the first temple was believed to have been chosen. The site of this temple was in a land which was sacred by its nature, and which was the gift of a defunct deity. In contrast, the site of the later temples was a battlefield.

The traditions and beliefs attached to the temple of the Falcon make it clear that it was believed that at the beginning of the world there was one sole temple. And this temple evolved from the necessity to protect the successor of the Creator. Its construction derived from the bequest of the defunct deity.

The principal consequences of these facts, beliefs and allusions are that, first, the historical temple in Egypt is regarded as the direct descendant of a primaeval temple that was erected on a low mound near the island in which the drama of creation commenced. There could, of course, have been only one such original place. Every cultus-place took this myth of creation and adapted it to local needs, and thus every temple in Egypt appears to have claimed to be the original place of the creation of the Earth.

Secondly, the temple was regarded as a living entity. We are already familiar with the ideas of the temple and its reliefs being animated, but it appears that there was more than mere animation. Reasons are cited for suggesting that the temple was conceived as the material embodiment of the *God-of-the-Temple* who attained concrete form in the temple, and who was the Son of the Earth.

Thirdly, and in some way most important, there can be no doubt that the traditions concerning the origin of the temple are basically Memphite in origin, adopted and adapted for each local temple; and probably they originated and were first formulated at the beginning of the Archaic Period. The history of the temple is presented as forming only a part of a much wider doctrine of the creation of the Earth. Therefore, the ideas that govern the form, origin, nature and significance of the normal cultus-place and the temple are Memphite, deriving from the Memphite cosmogonical doctrine, just as the formative ideas behind the daily temple ritual are Heliopolitan.

Figures

(a)

(b)

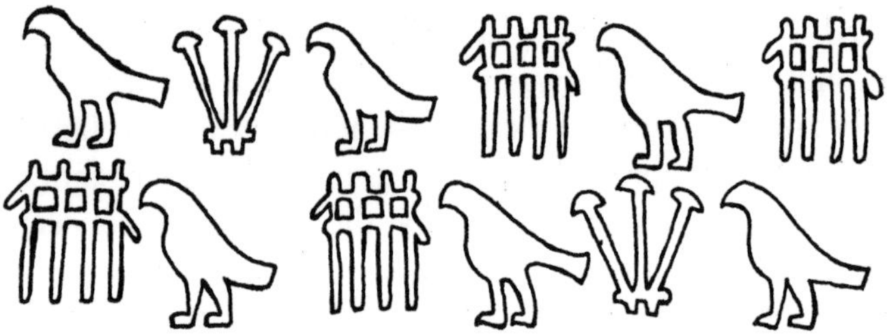

(c)

FIG. I

Primitive Resting-place of the Falcon

(a) Petrie, *R.T.* II, Pl. III, no. 4
(b) Emery, *Ḥor-Aḥa*, Pl. 32, fig. 35
(c) Emery, *Ḥor-Aḥa*, Pl. 31, fig. 31

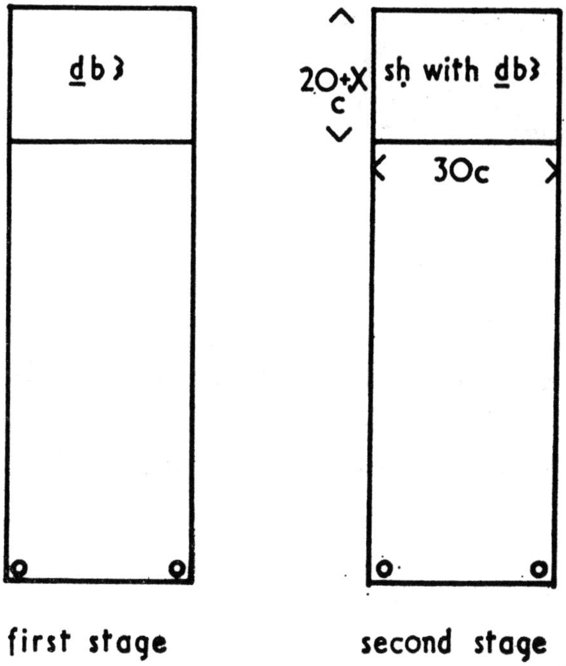

Fig. II
Primitive Enclosure of the Falcon

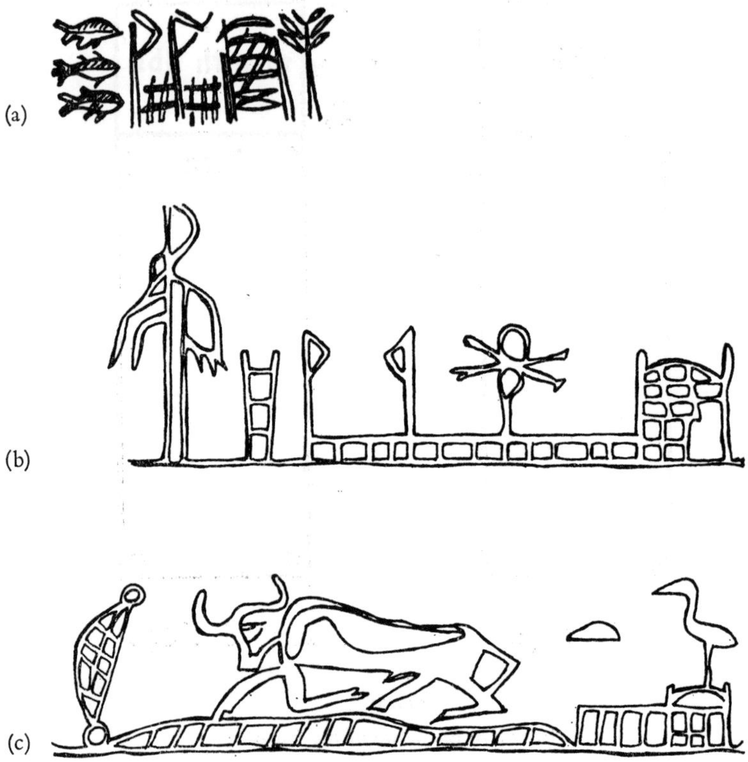

Fig. III

Primitive Enclosures

(a) *ZÄS*, xxxiv, 160

(b) and (c) Petrie, *RT*, ii, Pl. iii, A, 5=X, 2

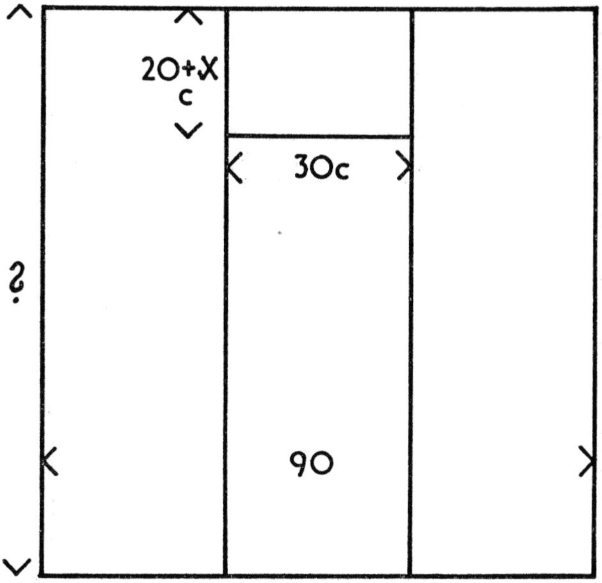

(a)

(b)

(c)

Fig. IV

(a) Primitive Enclosure of the Falcon (3rd stage)
(b) Petrie, *RT*, II, Pl. IV, 8
(c) Petrie, *RT*, II, Pl. IV, 9

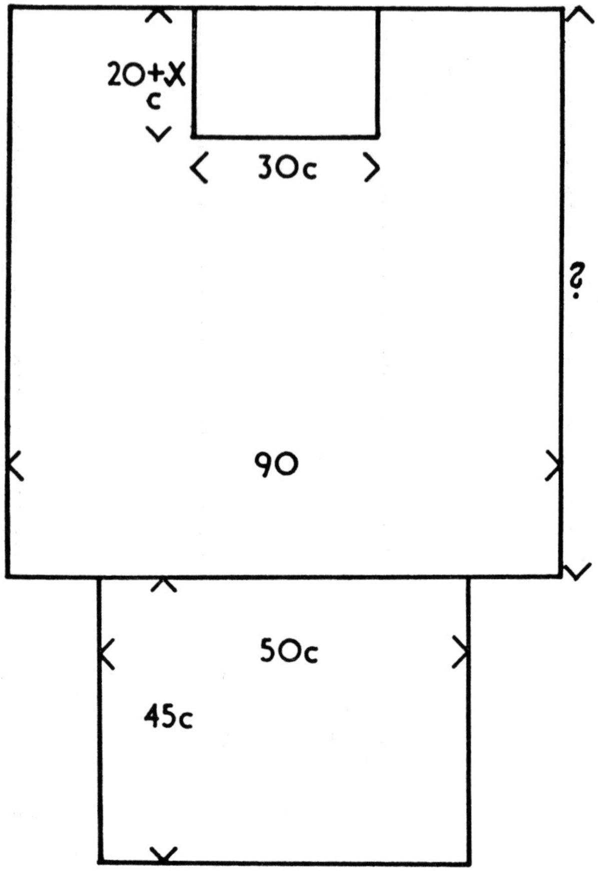

FIG. V
Primitive Temple of the Falcon (1st stage)

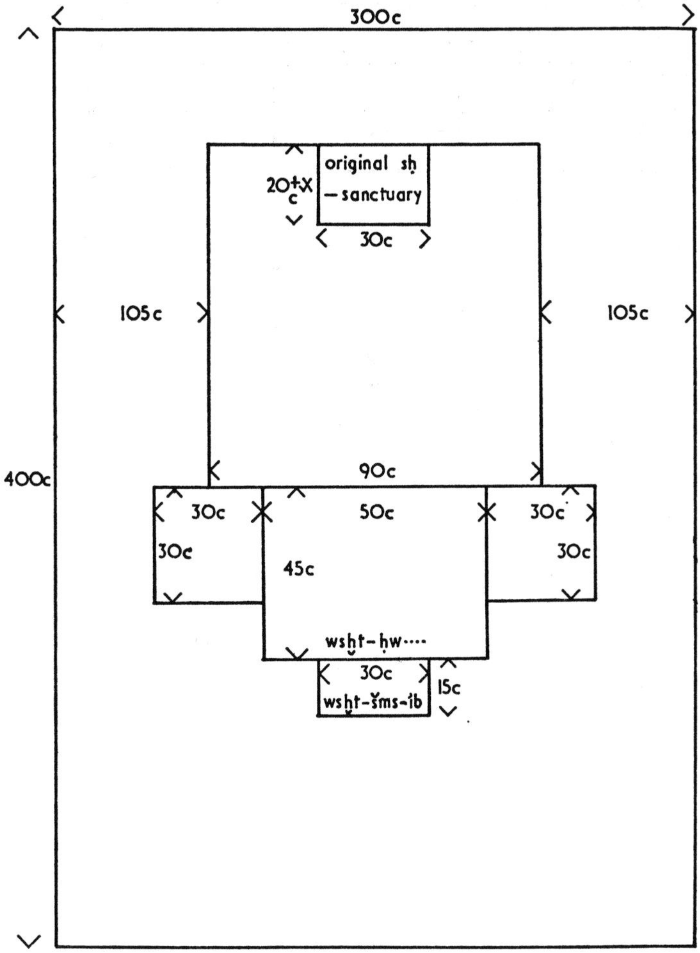

Fig. VI
Primitive Temple of the Falcon (final stage)

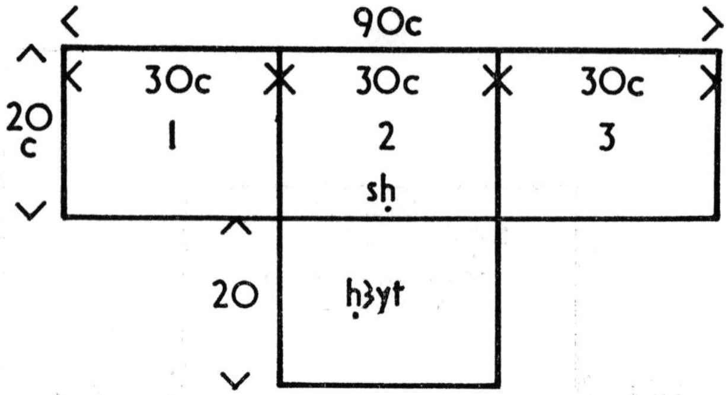

Fig. VII
Solar Temple (1st stage)

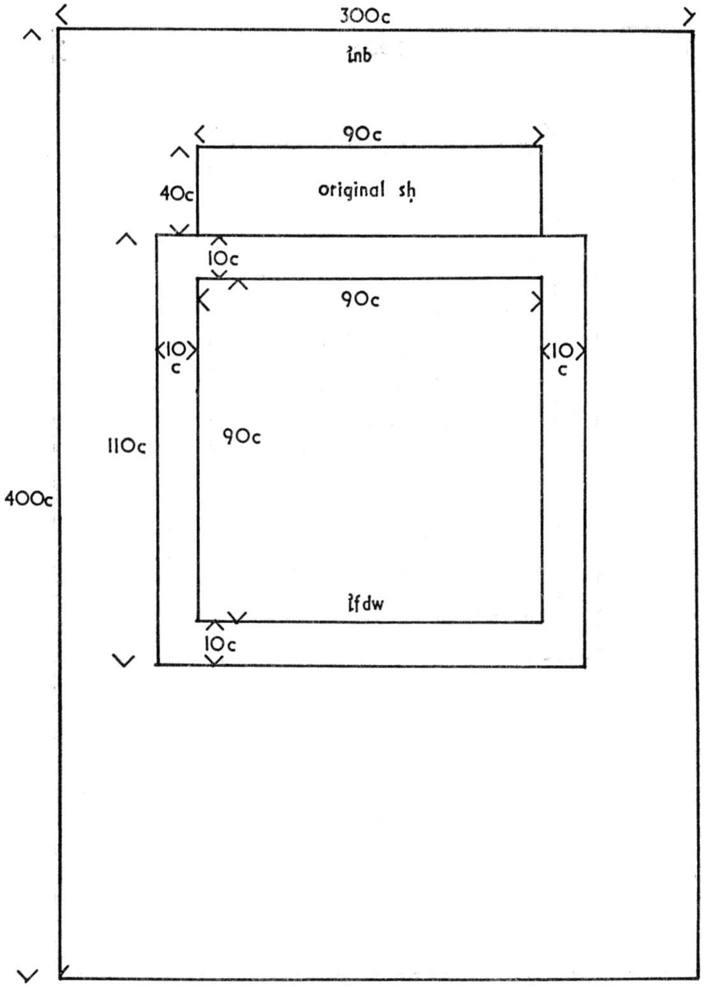

Fig. VIII

Solar Temple (2nd stage)

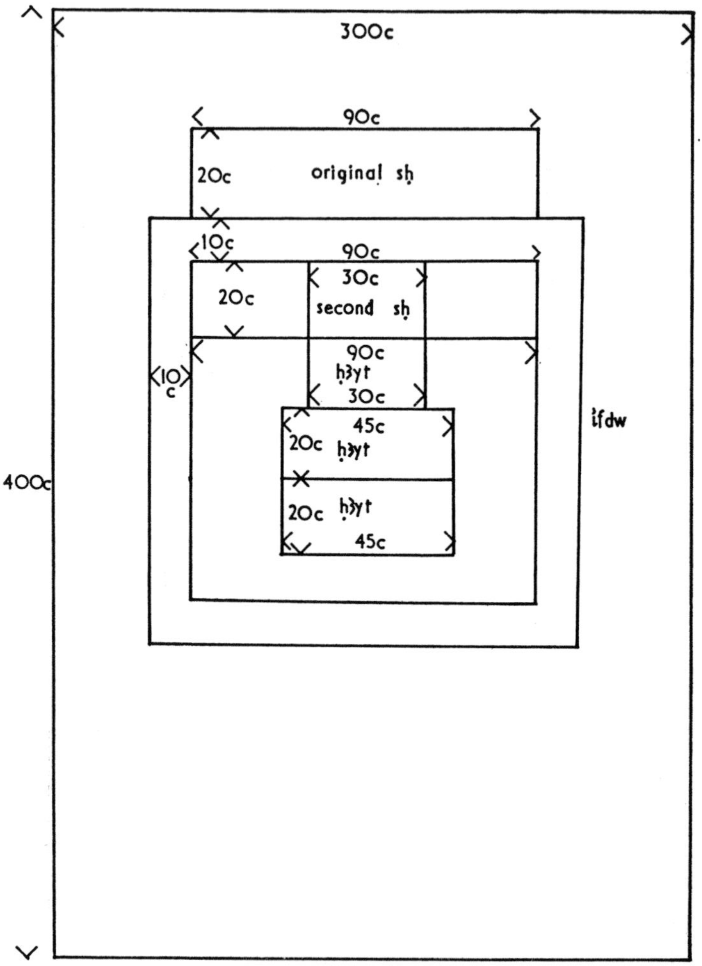

Fig. IX

Solar Temple (3rd stage)

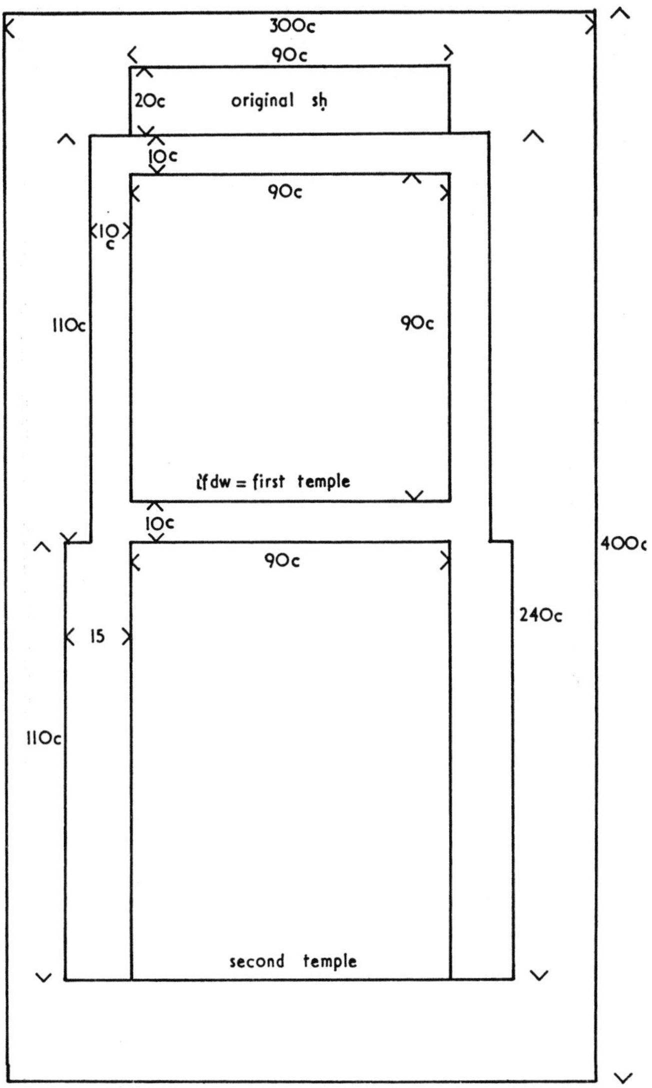

FIG. X
Solar Temple (4th stage)

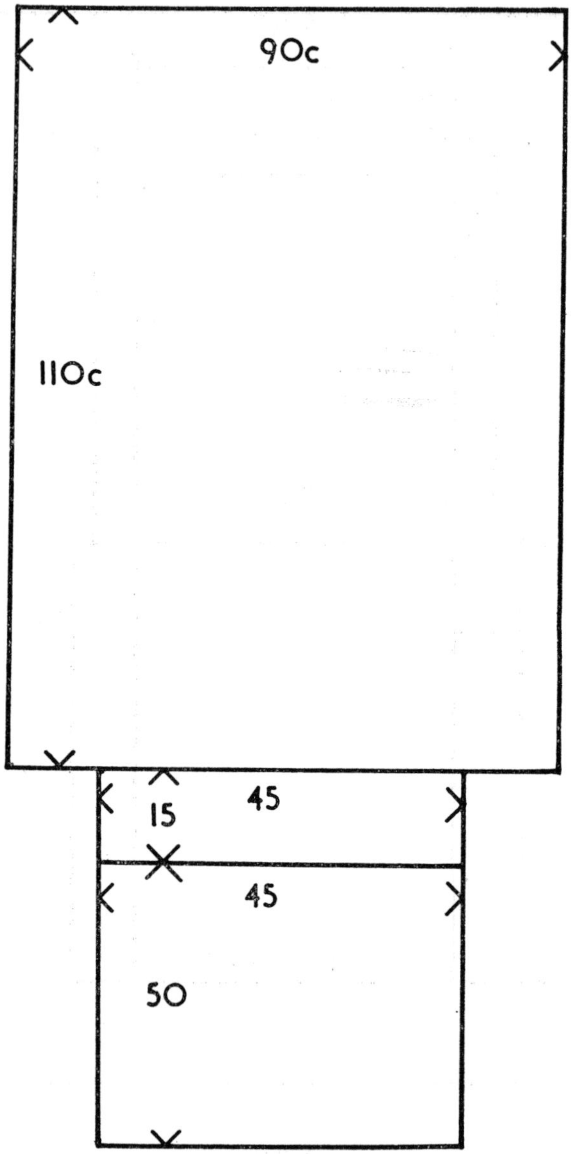

FIG. XI
Solar Temple (2nd type)

Bibliography

PRINCIPAL SOURCES

CHASSINAT-ROCHEMONTEIX, *Le temple d'Edfou*, vol. I. II, *MMAF*, X. XI (Paris, 1892. Cairo, 1918); vol. III–XIV, *MMAF*, XX–XXI (Cairo, 1923–34).

CHASSINAT, E., *Le Mammisi d'Edfou*, *MIFAO* (Cairo, 1939).

ANTHES, R., 'Atum, Nefertum und die Kosmogonien von Heliopolis', *ZÄS*, LXXXII (1957), 1–8.

BADAWI, A., 'La première architecture en Égypte', *ASAE*, LI (1951), 1–28.

—— 'Philological Evidence about Methods of Construction in Ancient Egypt', *ASAE*, LIV (1957), 51–74.

BLACKMAN, A. M., 'Sacramental Ideas and Usages in Ancient Egypt', *RT*, XXXIX (1921), 44–78.

BLACKMAN, A. M. and FAIRMAN, H. W., 'The Myth of Horus at Edfu' (II), *JEA*, XXVIII (1942), 32–8; XXIX (1943), 2–36; XXX (1944), 5–22.

—— 'A Group of Texts inscribed on the Façade of the Sanctuary in the Temple of Horus at Edfu', *Miscellanea Gregoriana* (1941), pp. 397–428.

—— 'The Consecration of an Egyptian Temple according to the Use of Edfu', *JEA*, XXXII (1946), 75–91.

BORCHARDT, L., 'Der ägyptische Tempel mit Umgang', *Beiträge zur ägyptischen Bauforschung und Altertumskunde*, Heft 2 (Cairo, 1938).

BOTTI, G., *La Glorificazione di Sobek*, *Analecta Aegyptiaca*, VIII (Copenhagen, 1959).

BOYLAN, P., *Thoth, the Hermes of Egypt* (1922).

BRUGSCH, H., *Thesaurus Inscriptionum Aegypticarum* (Leipzig, 1883–91).

—— *Dictionnaire Géographique*, vols. I, II (Leipzig, 1879).

—— 'Bau und Masse des Tempels von Edfu', *ZÄS*, VIII, 153–61; *ZÄS*, IX, 32–45, 137–44; *ZÄS*, X, 1–15.

—— 'Eine neue Bauurkunde des Tempels von Edfu', *ZÄS*, XIII, 113–23.

DE BUCK, A., *De Egyptische Voorstellingen betreffende den Oerheuvel* (Leiden, 1922).

CHASSINAT, E., *Le temple de Dendara*, *MIFAO*, I–V (Cairo, 1934–52).

—— 'Le temple d'Horus Behouditi à Dendérah', *Rev. de l'Égypte ancienne*, I (1925), 298–308.

Daressy, G., 'Hymne à Khnoum du Temple d'Esneh', *RT*, xxvii (1905), 82–93, 187–93.
Daumas, F., *Les moyens d'expression du grec et de l'égyptien, ASAE*, Cahier 16 (Cairo, 1952).
—— *Les mammisis des temples égyptiens, Annales de l'Université de Lyon*, xxxii (Paris, 1958).
—— 'La structure du mammisi de Nectanébo à Dendara', *BIFAO*, l (1952), 133–55.
—— 'Le trône d'une statuette de Pépi Ier trouvé à Dendara', *BIFAO*, lii (1953), 163–72.
—— 'Sur trois représentations de Nout à Dendara', *ASAE*, li (1951), 373–400.
Drioton, E. 'Le texte dramatique d'Edfou', *ASAE*, cahier 11 (Cairo, 1948).
—— 'Les dédicaces de Ptolémée Évergète II sur le deuxième pylône de Karnak', *ASAE*, xliv (1944), 111–62.
Dümichen, J., *Bauurkunden der Tempelanlagen von Dendera* (Leipzig, 1865).
—— *Baugeschichte des Denderatempels* (Strasbourg, 1877).
Emery, H. B., *Great Tombs of the First Dynasty*, iii (London, 1958).
Erichsen, W., and Schott, S., 'Fragmente memphitischer Theologie in demotischer Schrift', AWLB (1954), 303–94.
Erman, A., *Die Religion der Ägypter* (Leipzig, 1934).
Fairman, H. W., 'The Myth of Horus at Edfu (i)', *JEA*, xxi (1935), 26–36.
—— 'Notes on the Alphabetic Signs employed in the Hieroglyphic Inscriptions of the Temple of Edfu', *ASAE*, xliii (1943), 191–310.
—— 'Ptolemaic Notes', *ASAE*, xliv (1944), 263–77.
—— 'An Introduction to the Study of Ptolemaic Signs and their Values', *BIFAO*, xliii (1945), 51–138.
—— 'Worship and Festivals in an Egyptian Temple', *BJRL*, xxxvii (1954), 165–203.
—— 'A Scene of the Offering of Truth in the Temple of Edfu', *MDIK*, xvi (1958), 86–92.
Firchow, O., *Thebanische Tempelinschriften aus griechisch-römischer Zeit, Urk.* viii (Berlin, 1957).
Frankfort, H. *The Cenotaph of Seti I at Abydos* (London, 1933).
Gardiner, A. H., *Ancient Egyptian Onomastica* (London, 1947).
—— 'Horus the Behdetite', *JEA*, xxx (1944), 23–60.
Grapow, H., 'Die Welt der Schöpfung', *ZÄS*, lxvii (1931), 34–8.
Greven, L., 'Der Ka', *Ägypt. Forschungen*, xvii (1952).

JACOBSOHN, H., 'Die dogmatische Stellung des Königs in der Theologie der Alten Ägypter', *Ägypt. Forschungen*, VIII (1939).

JÉQUIER, G., 'Les temples primitifs et la représentation des types archaïques', *BIFAO*, VI, 25–41.

JUNKER, H., *Grammatik der Denderatexte* (Leipzig, 1906).

—— 'Die Götterlehre von Memphis', *APAW* (1939).

—— 'Das Götterdekret über das Abaton', DAWW, LVI (Vienna, 1913).

—— 'Die politische Lehre von Memphis', *APAW* (1941).

—— 'Die Onurislegende', DAWW, LIX (Vienna, 1917).

—— *Der grosse Pylon des Tempels der Isis in Philae*, DAWW (1958).

KEES, H., *Die Götterglaube im alten Ägypten* (Leipzig, 1941).

—— 'Eine Liste Memphitischer Götter im Tempel von Abydos', *RT*, XXXVII (1925), 57–76.

—— *Untersuchungen zu den Reliefs aus dem Re-Heiligtum des Rathures.*

LACAU, P., 'Notes sur les plans des temples d'Edfou et de Kom Ombo', *ASAE*, LII (1954), 215–28.

LAUER, J.-P., 'Etudes complémentaires sur les monuments du roi Zoser à Saqqara', *ASAE*, Cahier 9 (Cairo, 1948).

—— 'Evolution de la tombe royale égyptienne jusqu'à la Pyramide à degrés', *MDIK*, XV (1957), 148–65.

LEFEBVRE, G., *Le tombeau de Pétosiris* (Cairo, 1924).

MARIETTE, A., *Dendérah*, I–IV (Paris, 1870–3).

MOND, R. and MYERS, O. H., *Temples of Armant* (London, 1940).

MORENZ, S., *Die ägyptische Religion* (Leipzig, 1961).

—— *Der Gott auf der Blume* (Leipzig, 1954).

DE MORGAN, J., *Kom Ombo*, vols. I–II (Vienna, 1895).

La naissance du monde. Sources orientales, vol. I (Paris, 1957); section 'Ancient Egypt', pp. 19–91.

PETRIE, W. M. F., *The Royal Tombs of the Earliest Dynasties*, part II, (London, 1901).

—— *Heliopolis, Kafr Ammar and Shurafa* (British School of Archaeology in Egypt, XVIII (1912)).

PORTER–MOSS, *Topographical Bibliography*, VI (Oxford, 1939).

QUIBELL, J. E., *Hierakonpolis*, Egyptian Research Account, IV (1900).

RICKE, H. *Bemerkungen zur ägyptischen Baukunst des Alten Reiches*, I (Zürich, 1944).

—— 'Der "Hohe Sand in Heliopolis"', *ZÄS*, LXXI (1935), 107–11.

—— 'Eine Inventartafel aus Heliopolis im Turiner Museum', *ZÄS*, LXXI (1935), 111–33.

Robichon, C. and Varille, A., 'Description sommaire du temple primitif de Médamoud', *Recherches d'Archéologie*, xi (Cairo, 1940).

Roeder, G., *Hermopolis 1929–39* (1959).

—— 'Zwei hieroglyphische Inschriften aus Hermopolis', *ASAE*, lii (1954), 315–442.

Sandman-Holmberg, M., *The God Ptah* (Copenhagen, 1946).

Sauneron, S., *Quatre Campagnes à Esna* (Publications de l'Institut Français d'Archéologie Orientale, Le Caire, 1959).

Schott, S., 'Mythe und Mythenbildung im alten Ägypten', *Untersuchungen*, xv (1945).

Schweitzer, U., 'Das Wesen des Ka', *Ägypt. Forschungen*, xix (1956).

Sethe, K., *Urgeschichte und älteste Religion der Ägypter* (Leipzig, 1930).

—— *Das Denkmal memphitischer Theologie*, *Untersuchungen*, x, 1–80.

—— *Amun und die Acht Urgoetter von Hermopolis*, *APAW* (1929).

Vandier, J., *Manuel d'archéologie égyptienne*, ii (2) (Paris, 1955).

van de Walle, B., 'Le temple égyptien d'après Strabon, xvii, 1, 28', *Latomus*, xxviii (1957), 480 ff.

de Wit, C., *Les inscriptions du temple d'Opet à Karnak*, *Bibliotheca Aegyptiaca*, xi (Brussels, 1958).

Wolf, W., 'Der Berliner Ptah-Hymnus', *ZÄS*, lxiv (1929), 17–44.

Index

1. NAMES OF GODS

22-2

2. NAMES OF SACRED PLACES

HISTORICAL

MYTHOLOGICAL

Place-of-the-Well, 181, 200
Province-of-the-Beginning, 65, 66, 68, 72, 86 n. 3

Seat of the Eldest One of the Gods, 322
Seat of the First Occasion, 14, 37, 43, 133, 135, 158, 281, 300, 303
Seat of Harakhte, 310
Seat of Rēʿ of the Primaeval Time, 301, 309, 310
Seat of the Sun-God, 106, 122
Seat of the Two Gods, 33, 40, 192, 253
Shore of the Western River, 227

Tanen-ḥotep, 33
Tep-tôwi, 18
Territory of the Ancestors, 18, 117, 125

Throne-of-the-Gods, 305
Throne of the *ḏrty*-Falcon, 307

Underworld of the Soul, 15, 16, 110, 111, 114, 116, 118, 127, 133, 183

Wetjeset-Neter, 7, 14, 17, 19, 20, 21, 22, 23, 31, 32, 89, 123, 124, 126, 131, 134, 135, 136, 137, 138, 140, 143, 144, 145, 147, 149, 151, 153, 156, 157, 163, 165, 170, 174, 178, 182, 189, 195, 196, 209, 213, 219, 220, 224, 231, 232, 236, 237, 242, 249, 255, 263, 274, 276, 278, 281, 282, 285, 286, 287, 288, 290, 293, 294, 298, 305, 308, 310, 311, 312, 314, 318, 319, 321, 322

3. EGYPTIAN WORDS

ȝw-ib (likeness of), name of a protective symbol, 31
ȝm, fumigate, 205, 249 n. 4
ȝt, hour, 200 n. 1

iȝt, primaeval mound, 8, 9, 9 n. 4, 50, 77, 154, 157, 167, 209, 210
  iȝt n pȝwt tpt, mound of the early primaeval time, 146
  iȝwt n pȝwtyw, mounds of the Primaeval Ones, 305
  iȝwt n tȝw, mounds of the lands, 90
iȝw, adoration, 249
iw, island, 12, 55, 65, 66, 72, 75, 86, 87, 90, 172
iw ʿḥȝ, Island of Combat, 13
iw Mšd, Island of Meshed, 155
iw nšni, Island of Fury, 189, 192
iw ḥtp, Island of Peace, 13
iw swḥt, Island of the Egg, 87, 72
iw titi, Island of Trampling, 13, 87
ifdw, four sides, enclosure, 35, 36, 37, 42, 239, 240, 242, 245, 308, 310, 319
in rn⟨.w⟩, to utter the names, 138
inb, enclosure, 29, 36, 41, 207, 220, 221, 222, 239, 242 n. 2, 243, 245, 246, 260, 281, 310
inb-wr, great enclosure, 287
inb rwt, outer enclosure, 240
ir, to construct, 221
ir iḫt, to present offerings, 249
Ir-tȝ, the Earth-Maker, 60, 62, 62 n. 1, 63, 65, 97, 99, 104
iḥw, fields, 17, 138, 173, 183
iḫt, relic, 14, 16, 27, 28, 30, 111
  iḫt n pʿy, 180, 181
iḫt, substances, 24, 30, 31, 132, 149, 152, 153, 154, 158, 162, 172, 193, 200, 217, 249, 254, 288, 289, 290, 308, 311
ist, crew, 180
išd-tree, 132, 296

ʿnḫ, the Living One, 302 n. 4
ʿnḫ, bouquet, 132
ʿḥʿ-snake, 60
ʿḏ-mr, 231

wʿrt, 33, 108, 109, 111, 188
  wʿrt ḫnty, 188
ww, territory, 29
wbȝ iwʿw, 63
wp rȝ n Wṯst, 294
wr, the Eldest One, 236, 259, 259 n. 1, 287, 288, 296
  wr n Wṯst-nṯr, 36
  wrw n wrw, 76, 78

4. GENERAL

5. SACRED BOOKS OF THE EDFU TEMPLE

6. EDFU TEXTS TRANSLATED IN THE PRESENT STUDY